AF748580

Perfect Fundamental Values and the Development of Africa

Erik ESSOUSSE

Perfect Fundamental Values and the Development of Africa

From African Renaissance to Illumination

Foreword by Simon Bolivar Njami-Nwandi

Postscript by Prof Jacques Fame Ndongo

L'Harmattan
Cameroun

From the same author

La liberté de la presse écrite au Cameroun. Ombres et lumières, L'Harmattan, November 2008, 366 pages, ISBN: 978-2-296-06562-8

Valeurs fondamentales parfaites et développement de l'Afrique. De la Renaissance aux Lumières africaines, L'Harmattan, 27 juillet 2018, 470 pages, ISBN : 978-2-343-15298-1

With contributions from CERCUDE and OVAFOPAC

5-7, rue de l'Ecole-Polytechnique, 75005 Paris

http://www.editions-harmattan.fr

ISBN : 978-2-343-19570-4
EAN : 9782343195704

Dedication

I dedicate this book to God, the Creator of heaven and earth. I give him all the glory that belongs to him. He is the maker and true source of inspiration thanks to his perfection based system, the supreme stage of creative thinking and action that charts a course for the world and human life.

Foreword

African literature has just been enriched with the publication of a new book born from the fertile mind of Dr ESSOUSSE Erik, an epic with a revealing title, *Perfect Fundamental Values and the Development of Africa. From renaissance to illumination.*

The author's ambitious goal is an inclusive development of Africa. This goal can be reached using a succession of perfect fundamental values as reference system. The goal is as lofty as it is established at the supreme stage of divine perfection. The kind of development advocated by ESSOUSSE Erik for his continent, Africa, is a super-creation. However, God is the supreme Creator. The new African, created in the image of God must rise towards his creator with all the virtues he embodies, to take full control[1] of his destiny.

The editorial comment of the book is downright theocentric. That is why, it is dedicated directly to God, the Creator of heaven and earth, who constitutes its true source of inspiration. Had Africa, the cradle of humanity, not set the example, in bygone days, of an outstanding rise through the incredible civilisation of Negro-Pharaohnic Egypt, mistress of Greece and the Romans? From this glorious ancient history, the author retraces the evolution of the planet's inhabitants, sustained by great evolution of minds, the best of which are of religious order like Judaism, Christianity and Islam, not excluding Asians with their age-old divinities. ESSOUSSE Erik affirms that the strength of spiritual reflection is the same for all religions, including animism, mysticism and magic!

Nevertheless, as a Christian and son of a pastor, he gives more importance to Christianity whose teachings built the shield of a Western world, which is now the almighty and undisputed master of the entire world. As a matter of fact, ESSOUSSE Erik's father is Pastor TJECK Amos, a well-read man and staunch believer of the 20th century. He

---

[1]"You made us for yourself, O Lord, and our heart is without rest as long as it isn't in you", The Confessions, I.

attended the French Protestant Mission Teachers' Training School of (MPF)) of Ndoungué, a twin institution to the American Protestant Mission Teacher's Training School (MPA) in Foulassi. It is here that the rallying cry, now Cameroon's national anthem, was composed in 1928. It must be noted however that Amos TJECK was an excellent teacher. The students trained with diligence usually scored 100% at official examinations in the colonial era. It is but normal therefore that his son, Erik, christened, "Child of Light" by my wife, is today a master of excellence by the grace of God, thanks to his moral uprightness and effective intellectual and professional abilities.

Serious ailments call for serious measures! Under-development is a serious ailment. But this ailment is not incurable. Our author believes it can be eradicated, provided we follow the salutary path of opening our minds to Teachings that plumb the depths of ignorance, mediocrity and misery. In this regard, the author prescribes the renaissance of African teachings. This is a far-reaching programme that requires resources of divine essence from which must emerge a superman, equipped with perfect values described by the author as perfect fundamental values. This expression is an ontology of creativity drawn from an apodictic knowledge. Knowledge acquired from training, education, culture and fundamental research.

Human evolution has nowadays attained the utmost level of growth that constitutes an inexhaustible mine of resources from which Africa must draw to rise again. ESSOUSSE Erik borrows constructive elements thereof, which he uses with remarkable dexterity to posit the magnificent fabric Africa needs to achieve a sense of wellbeing and happiness. This is dubbed, 'Renaissance of African Illumination' by the author. A wide-ranging project that needs highly-skilled actors, alluding to the thought-provoking sources of perfect fundamental values.

To get a good grasp of his broad research scope, the author takes his readers on a marvellous cultural jaunt whose historic overview is nearly encyclopaedic. The substance of his book is derived from a cross-spectrum of scientific fields such as theology, philosophy, history, geography, ethics and aesthetics, mysticism, magic, just to name a few. Such intellect is no pointless grandiloquence. It rather reflects the prowess of genius, which snatches the soul from mediocrity to commit it to perfect fundamental values. From this emerges the pyramid of invention and innovation that constitutes the reference system worth consulting before any attempt at development. This influences the author to state that development is not only an economic issue bound to uncontrolled growth in view of sensual pleasure and luxury. The moral input borne by the decency of Africa's Social Education must humanise the frantic quest for wealth just for the sake wealth.

The ensuing renaissance is a passageway to systematic, judicious and rational growth. It must be purged of all the flaws of inertia, nonchalance and indolence. It's a vigorous action that demands a craftsmanship capable of producing tangible results, source of progress and prosperity. It relies on community solidarity for a collective production, the fruit of each and every one of us. Ultimately, we'll end up great and proud for having participated in the natural creation of wealth meant for equitable distribution. The renaissance of teachings is intended to restore homogeneity in the African society, the bedrock of equality and fraternity.

According to ancestral wisdom every fall must be analysed from the spot where we tripped. Mindful of this, ESSOUSSE Erik takes a step back to find out what caused the fall of Africa, in order to overcome the hurdles ahead, through an instant awakening of everyone, and cautious strive for a better future. The lecture given in this comprehensive book enjoins Africa to wake up from slumber and embark a challenging but exalting future. Resourcing through perfect fundamental values elevates us to God the creator and provider of a noble life void of all flaws, through superior knowledge, a source of excellence.

Yaounde, 20th October 2017

Simon Bolivar NJAMI-NWANDI

Pastor and African patriarch

Preface

The Centre for Applied Research and Outlook on Culture, Democracy and Development (CERCUDE) that I created in 1997 and the Cameroon Order for Perfect Fundamental Values (OVAFOPAC) put in place in April 2014, for research on development issues and perfection values respectively, were of great assistance in the writing of this book, in terms of facts on Africa's development. They prioritise fundamental, systemic, applied and reference research on the tricky issues of development in Africa.

This book is titled *Perfect Fundamental Values, Reference System and Development of Africa: From African Renaissance to Illumination.* It lays particular emphasis on development basics, some of which are permanent and everlasting, and mostly derived from the divine system and from humans, and that revolve around the constant perfection of humans, to lift them to the level of perfection and excellence. It is only upon attaining this supreme level of knowledge and effective practice, that humans can achieve development, for they must have mastered true, perfect and everlasting knowledge. At this stage, they must have discovered thc promethean fire of the gods of knowledge and the Holy Grail of purity of the Mind that opens the door to the perfect teachings of perfect knowledge. This pinnacle enables humans to comprehend and appropriate tried and tested knowledge that allow for the development of human societies. These perfect skills constitute the reference system always adopted to steer the development of States. The Western Christian world was the first part of the world to have better systematised the perfect values experiment, by harnessing the wealth of excellent skills developed by early ancient civilisations (Egyptian, Greek and Roman) and the advent of the Bible which finely standardised these sublime values. High values that progressively forged new humans, in the West and wherever they were meticulously applied like in nowadays Asia, who are perfect and creators of development. This *homo faber* and *economicus*, well-drilled in perfect and multifarious skills that became initiators of modern day development.

Such is the progressive appropriation of perfect knowledge values that must be emulated by Africa, to engender this new *homo faber*, *Homo Deus*, which is perfect and creative. This is the founding axis of life and development of human societies. This trailblazer is designed to obtain the study of the fundamentals of knowledge that trigger true and sustainable development. The said fundamentals are known and tested nowadays. They were soon followed by the Western Christian, Judaic Israelite, and Asian Buddhist, who experimented it with success. The Hindus Indian and Muslim Indonesian are still lagging. Africa is lying in ambush and patiently burnishing her weapons to optimise the assimilation and implementation of the perfect and fundamental values of development. But, to succeed, the continent must draw from its millennial community culture, enriched by the contribution of Christianity, Islam and the high Western scientific standard. Thus, Africa's efforts towards genuine development must require this complete blend.

In a nutshell, in the course of writing this book, the author had to contend with some hurdles, given that he was compelled to refer to the past in order to understand how the West achieved the optimal development acclaimed by all, and later emulated by emerging countries. And from this double experience that illustrates a similar logic in the appropriation of perfect skills, as vector of development, helping Africa to equally follow that example, in order to break out of extended stagnation from which it's emerging with much difficulty. Reference to the history of development in human societies through the ages, as well as reference to systems of divine order, esoteric, philosophical, mystical, magical, alchemic, cultural, scientific, political, economic, technological and industrial-inspired systems helped in the identification of a consistent set of timeless perfect values. These values most certainly favour human cultural, social, political, economic development as well as human bliss and happiness on this blessed earth.

I will not conclude without extending my heartfelt thanks to those who lend me invaluable support: first all, my wife, Caliste ESSOUSSE and my children with whom I read, re-read and discussed certain aspects of this book. Then my friends and disciples of the Order of Perfect Fundamental Values among whom I postulated these themes time and again and garnered their multiple remarks and constructive criticisms. Special thanks to Dr MBEBI Raymond, who proofread the book, made valuable suggestions as well assisted in the search for certain additional information. Finally, Dr Olivier MANDJECK, renowned researcher and excellent analyst on development issues, who also reviewed the book and made highly valuable proposals. Not forgetting my secretary who helped in typing the manuscript, and who at the end enjoyed her initiation into perfect fundamental values, which she says have given her insight to the fabulous world of perfect knowledge.

I extend my final gratitude to Reverend Dr Simon Bolivar NJAMI-NWANDI, top Church official and committed politician as well as Prof Jacques FAME NDONGO, eminent man of letters and committed politician who accepted to read my manuscript. Both of them made valuable suggestions and respectively wrote the preface and post face of this book after acclaiming its great quality.

Contents

Introduction

Africa in search of common sense or the ideal approach for its development

Here is one more book about Africa, a continent renowned for its fascinating history and its glorious culture, its diversified population composed mostly of youth and its abundant natural agricultural and mineral resources. But this exceptionally colourful Africa, so naturally blessed with soil and sub-soil resources is in the headlines worldwide because of its level of under-development fraught with a good number of ills: under-development, poor governance, poverty, mass youth unemployment, diverse conflicts (political and armed), health, educational and economic challenges. It is a vast continent composed of 54 States with a surface area of 30 310 000 km^2 and a current population of more than one billion inhabitants that is expected to double in thirty years. In terms of surface area, the continent ranks 3rd after Asia and America and 2nd in population, after Asia. More than 60% of this population is predominantly young. Africa has enormous potentials for development. In this regard, the continent faces a monumental challenge at multiple levels: demographic, geostrategic, geopolitical, ecological, economic and diplomatic. These multiple challenges leave no one indifferent, beginning with Africans, the hardest hit, then foreigners, that is, the major world powers in particular and many other entities. Looking at this grim picture of Africa, attempts to find development solutions and models that can rescue the continent from her under-development have all proved unsatisfactory. Africa is thus at the crossroads, in quest for common sense or the ideal strategy that can secure its optimal development, hence a planned, integrated, homogeneous and prosperous society. This book therefore constitutes a fundamental, systemic, applied and reference research on the nagging challenge of Africa's development.

The originality of this study is to prove that global development as witnessed nowadays, ardently sought by Africa and any other form of State development, and is a painstaking process that requires an understanding of multifarious perfect skills and values. Tried and tested, they have proven their effectiveness over time and space. All these perfect values are common knowledge nowadays. Others may be experimented with time. Africa through Ancient Egypt was the first continent to set the pace by implementing these values through the construction of pyramids that, up to date, are among the wonders of the world. The western world, through its incredible results obtained in development, have built-in these values in all domains and have made them a reference. Emerging countries are now emulating and replicating this approach especially the scientific, technological and industrial facet. It behoves Africa to find its way back to this inevitable course to which she was first to chart early in the history of man on earth. This will be done mostly by emulating, or even replicating and outclassing the West as well as emerging countries that went even further in the cultivation and promotion of perfect values in every sector of society. In this regard, Africa must rely on her own intellect and sensibility, to promote a model African who is exceptionally well-trained and capable of taking development in Africa to the pinnacle, a development that must revolve around the mastery of perfect fundamental values.

As a matter of fact, inspiration for this study arises from an unpleasant realisation that Africa is slow in finding glimmers of hope. This book is also a result of my readings, meditations, findings throughout my secondary and university education, as well as my professional career. I cannot forget that it is the ultimate result of my life as a Church child. My father served as Pastor of the congregations of the Union of Baptist Churches Cameroon (UEBC) for 50 years, alongside my mother, who remained a steady rock in his life for more than 60 years of marital life. Then this trajectory and example which left an indelible mark on my entire life. I was thus steeped in the Gospel that conveys the perfect fundamental values of life. I spent this solid Christian childhood at Ndikinimeki, now Mbam Division, in Yabassi and Yingui, my native region, and lastly in major cosmopolitan cities like Douala, Yaounde in Cameroon and Paris in France.

Ndikinimeki to Yabassi and Yingui is covered by the full luxuriance of the equatorial forest. In my early years, I was enraptured by the sparkling nature of this region, charms of a thousand flavours and sounds, to a point that even to this age, I still find enormous pleasure crossing kilometres of the forest to Yabassi and Yingui. These kilometres of forest form a veritable green gallery that offers a spellbinding and unique view, with its grass, trees and assorted plant species which are invaluable to the people's cuisine, pharmacopeia and other edifying uses. This life, spiced by profound spirituality, led me to quickly understand that fundamental and sacred values govern and shape the life of humans on this blessed earth. And by the time I read the Bible, Koran, Buddhism, Taoism, Hinduism, animism and write-ups of some great thinkers that transcend time, I better understood the meaning of life and the perfect fundamental values that definitely enlighten gloriously guide it. This solid Christian education, enriched by other schools of thought, gave me a strong clear foundation for cultural reflection, thereby giving me a perfect insight to life and its challenges. My stay in the Western world also enabled me to understand why this part of the world, despite its excess materialism, succeeded in standardising a set of perfect values that helped it to attain an outstanding level of development. Their positive fallouts are invaluable to humanity as a whole. They have also become the pacesetter for life in other parts of the world as is the case for Africa, the cradle of humanity and first glimmer of light to illuminate humanity.

Moreover, my thorough study of diverse spiritual, intellectual, philosophical, metaphysical, mystical, magical, cultural, social, political, economic systems, applied to social reality prompted me to understand that perfect and multifarious knowledge is now the true catalyst of every genuine development. This perfect knowledge embodies a set of values derived from God and humankind. These divine values appropriated by humans, equally illuminate the development trajectory of nations. That is why we posit that God himself is the first perfect value and man the end result. They collaborate in a dynamic symbiosis. When man attains perfection, he attains an almost divine status, he becomes Man-God (Homo Deus), which makes him a creator. For it is with God, gods and superior men that one acquires a superior and creative spirit. Our premise is that the Bible which spreads Judaism and Christianity and the Koran which spreads Islamism, are first of all books of knowledge before becoming books of religions. The same is true for Buddhism, Taoism, Hinduism and animism. The perfect values advocated by these different religions, many of which intersect, generally focus on perfection or perfecting man, and rendering him a supreme stage capable of understanding and of acting in the shining light of true and perfect knowledge. These different channels of knowledge show that life is, first and foremost, centred on the mind, which is the invisible, immaterial and immortal energy. The Mind is the active power and force that illuminates effective thinking and action. Societies and men who dominate the world are those led mostly by the Mind and not by matter alone. For the Mind is motion, while matter is static and immobile. It is the Mind that transforms matter and not the reverse. It is the Mind that triggers reason, thinking and meditation which improve intelligence and wisdom, values which are sure and have been tested over time. The Mind is therefore an accurate gateway to the understanding and acquisition of perfect, durable and everlasting knowledge. When one attains this supreme state of true knowledge, he is developed in terms of his mind, skills and actions. It is clear that true development originates from man himself, who is the primary resource par excellence among many other resources. Any development scheme that fails to place these realities at the centre of its concerns and to devote fitting resources for it may not be effective. It is such solid training of human resources that elevated the Western world and emerging countries. That is why their development is escalating as we can witness with our own eyes. In this light, higher education in Cameroon and in Africa as a whole, remains the source of fundamental and practical knowledge that provide access to the development of the economic know-how of the world, through the production of wealth. Universities and training institutions are essential vectors of growth. They should mould highly-skilled Africans, making them new, perfect beings, who are creators of development. This means development is basically a construction of humans as illustrated in this book.

In this book, we demonstrate that perfect and eternal knowledge enables man to unravel the hidden mysteries of life that offer extraordinary avenues for science, action, technique, technology and industry. It is unfortunate that in Africa, people still often stick to the appearance of things, when real things are beneath appearance. Plato's myth of the cave of shadows and lights best illustrates this reality of appearance and hidden realities, and in the Book of the Hebrews in the Bible, it is most expediently stated that what is visible stems from the invisible. The Bible is the book that best unravels the mystery of hidden things in a logical manner. The Western Christian was first to achieve its outstanding development, because the Bible was the first book published by Gutenberg printing press in the 15th century. The teachings of the Bible, added to knowledge acquired from Ancient Egypt on the one hand and Ancient Greece and Rome, on the other hand, enabled Europe to clearly understand and implement the fundamental and sacred laws of life which include supremacy of the Mind, faith, intelligence, wisdom, discursive thinking, discernment of good and evil, truth, freedom, justice, honesty, hard work and the culture of saving, goodness, family, love, peace, not leaving out the culture of aesthetics, beauty, exactness, excellence, bliss, etc. In a nutshell, supreme divine and humanitarian values (which constitute an illumination), shape thinking and logical approaches, as is the case with great thinkers (Descartes, Kant, Leibniz, John Locke, among others). These essential values serve as eternal reference frames often used to resolve multiple problems in life and the development of human societies as mentioned earlier. These perfect values enable man, as he discovers and practices them, to evolve from his spiritual, intellectual and moral inferiority to maturity and superiority. This perfection is wont to raise man towards the pinnacle of knowledge, as it is at the heart of creativity. Countries that are founded on perfect knowledge, such as the Christian Western world and the emerging countries of Asia and America, have taken great strides towards development. By so doing, we demonstrate that the knowledge that leads to development is a long process and a chain that has subsisted and transcended time and space, that is, from the origin of human life on earth. This perfect knowledge is invaluable to all and in every era, it has no colour, it is merely spiritual, atemporal and immutable. This long process must be well understood by Africans in order to lead them steadfastly into the evolution of savoir-faire, intelligence, training and true knowledge that supports development. Above all, we cannot stop at moulding an African who is a development creator and innovator. As a matter of fact, development sprouts from a creative mind, that is, from thought it gradually spreads to matter as Romans of the Antiquity said.

We intend to demonstrate that this process started on earth with the first human civilisation, which was of black origin, and whose cradle is Africa where man emerged. This civilisation started in the Palaeolithic and Neolithic Age and spread to Nubia (now Sudan), ancient Ethiopia and Egypt. It soared under the authority of the pharaohs, who are demigods and possess great mystical powers. Some of the pharaohs were Blacks. This outstanding negro-inspired Egyptian civilisation passed on to humanity multifarious knowledge: astronomy, mathematics (algebra and geometry), philosophy (Platonism, borrowed from Egyptianism), Pharaohnic esotericism, theology, architecture. The art of building pyramids and temples remains an enigma still studied nowadays to discover their mystical and technical science. This perfect knowledge which originated from Africa, was replicated by ancient Greece. Théophile Obenga, cited by Mbog Bassong (*La pensée africaine*, Editions KiyiKaat, 2012, P 90), recalls that the abovementioned Egyptian sciences were thought to Greek students (Orpheus, Homer, Solon, Thales of Miletus and Pythagoras, Œnophilus, Eudoxus of Cnidus). The ancient Egypt era in Africa lasted for more than 3000 years B.C.

The ancient Greek took over, under Alexander the Great, and fostered a remarkable civilisation in the Mediterranean basin, which lasted for more than two centuries (331 to 148 B.C.). His influence even expanded to Africa where he created the city of Alexandria in Egypt. This city is still famous today. The famous Alexandria library which was destroyed by fire is still fresh in our memories as it resulted to the loss of very important documents. This civilisation is noted for its philosophers, scholars, and mostly for the love for knowledge, wisdom, interest in whatever is beautiful, elevation of the mind, as well as for its political organisation that gave birth to democracy. This outstanding civilisation fascinated the prosperous progression of ancient Rome for over six centuries (146 B.C. to 476 A.C.). The innovation extended to Asia. Constantine, a Roman emperor, succeeded in building the city of Constantinople in modern Turkey, now called Istanbul. This masterly accomplishment of ancient Greece and Rome (heirs of ancient Egypt), the dominant designer of great civilisations, made the cradle of Western and even human civilisation. The said Western civilisation has dominated the world since the 19th century, thanks to evolution of skills and the industrial revolution. This evolution of skills paves the way for the advent of the new European who is perfect, creative and ingenious in spiritual, intellectual, moral, ethical, mental, scientific, technical, technological and industrial aspects. This period of profound evolution in ontology, mysticism, metaphysics, magic and strategy in Europe, corresponds to the European Age of Renaissance and illumination that lasted from the 16th to 19th century.

Such spiritual and qualitative transformation and regeneration helped the European to attain the pinnacles of knowledge and perfection and to gain full access into the realms of true and eternal knowledge.

This phenomenon accounts for the spectacular development of Europe and the Western world in general, as witnessed nowadays. This domineering European culture that spread to North America (United States of America, Canada), was cultivated on the hallmark of true, consummate and perfect knowledge and a Judaeo-Christian and scientific essence. Japan, of Buddhist tradition, also achieved its spectacular development, by proceeding to its renaissance and an evolution of skills while walking in the footprints set by the Western world in science and technology. Asia, which today, is on the verge of achieving its development, has copied and is almost overtaking the West and Japan in the domains of science, technology and industries, by delving, most certainly, into its Buddhist and Hindu culture and ancestral traditions based on: love for education and knowledge, affection for family, order and discipline, hard work, the culture of building nest eggs and the unwavering willpower to succeed.

In fact, a recap of the trajectory to the development of human societies, as earlier explained, is a useful exercise which helps us recognise that development depends, in essence, on the perfect command of sound and true know-how that is founded on a firm way of life and that is useful in every era, because it concerns problems related to humans, whether European, American, Asian or African. It stands that we cannot discuss the development of Africa as if its origin is unknown. For development, as a matter of fact, is a protracted process that goes through phases as is the case of the western world explained by W.W. Rostow. He has a point, for irrespective of the variant and different experiences, development usually evolves from a primary through a higher to a refined level, as is witnessed in the life evolution of man from childhood to old age through adulthood. At this point, to understand development and make it a success is an end-result of the mastery of perfect knowledge and values by man himself.

This is the pivotal and foundation pillar that man must resolutely build on. These skills are multifarious and permanent, or even eternal, to best understand their depth and power. They are grounded on a set of values: spiritual, intellectual, ethics, moral, aesthetics and sacred, values intrinsic to education, training, research, creativity and culture, civic and citizen, social and health, political, scientific, technical, technological and industrial, economic and managerial values, and values that procure satisfaction and bliss. This far-reaching skills form the reference system that must be adopted by any country evolving on the route to development. Thus, development today is no longer a matter of chance or trial and error. Some of these perfect values, notably the sacred values of God, religion, wisdom, family, solidarity, communitarism, honesty, discipline, love, hard work, etc. were already deep-rooted in ancient Africa: Egypt, Ethiopia, Nubia and even the Great African Empires (Ghana, Mali, Benin, Congo, etc.). Unfortunately, the ruthless intrusion of Europe into the course of this satisfactory evolution of Africa, in the 15th century, halted development in the continent for five centuries because of the extreme trauma caused by slavery, colonisation, ruthless domination and imperialism. Subsequently, the debased, broken, disorientated, abhorred, humiliated black man plunged into an extended and profound period of decadence. It is only when Africa won back its independence from 1960 that the continent resumed the painful rebuilding of its life and development. Such salutary and creative rebuilding can only regain all its substance and steam if driven by the black man's aspiration for perfection, a level that opens the gateway to the realms of knowledge. These topmost values of thinking and action embodied in perfection would enable the African to restore his dignity, honour and greatness. Through these perfect values, he can rediscover the powerful illuminations of knowledge that form the bedrock and creative basis of life and development.

These perfect values, if acquired, experimented and practised as it should be, will bring the African back to his culture of altruism, communitarianism and an appendage of the soul in the face of the draining materialism of a capitalist and technocratic economy. Thus, fully-regenerated by these strong values, the African would, with much pain, rediscover the long lost creative paths to development that carry the Rebirth and illumination of knowledge which give him a place in the modern world. This is the newfound, perfect and creative African, equipped with this new luminous, creative, humanist, scientific, technological and industrial approach that Africa needs today. This was the case with the perfect and creative New Man, born of the European Renaissance and Enlightenment in the 16th and 18th centuries, the Renaissance of Japan in the 19th century and of Asia in the 20th century up to the beginning of the 21st century. This great step towards the realms of knowledge, will bring about a veritable Promethean, spiritual and mental revolution of Black Man. The Black Man needs to develop his divine, superior and luminous nature, by getting even closer to God, gods and superior beings who incarnate this great and powerful light.

Through this new altruist humanism of modern times, Africa provides a lesson and a fresh impetus to the development of mankind in general, and to societies of the 21st century and future centuries, thereby paving the way for an era of millennial, or even eternal prosperity for itself and humanity. In this way, Africa appropriates the power of the Mind, which is the vector of life, knowledge, action and development. Consequently, Africa will, like the West of yesteryears and Asia today, offer to humanity a humane and sublime approach, full of freshness and delights, towards greater development. In this regard, Prof Ebénézer Njoh Mouellé talks about an Africa in a constant evolutionary frenzy in his book, *De la médiocrité à l'excellence*, as opposed to the essentially materialistic and technocratic development of the Western world. Freed from all these debasing and downgrading complexes, Africa, in turn, is once more gradually becoming a continent that paves the way for today's humanity, even though confronted by multiple scourges. In this way, we posit that Africa is slowly and steadily reaching the crossroads, thanks to its gradual grasp and appropriation of absolute skills and their values. It must therefore produce this complete Man, capable of creating the highly sought development. The path is tedious, but Africa has begun discovering and mastering it. Mankind is the key equation of development and he must be equipped with a solid and multidimensional training. African educational systems must systematically adopt this approach. Béchir Ben Yahmed stated that only the most resolute African countries shall join the virtuous circle of developed countries. The next book, according to him, will explain how Africa is meticulously putting into practice these perfect fundamental values, in the domains of education, health, politics, economics, technology and industries. They are yet to be fully mastered, so for now, they can only achieve limited development. They often place Africa on the clear-cut path en route for development.

This book is subdivided into four parts:

Part I: Perfect fundamental values, Africa's reference system and development: a tentative definition and explanation of these notions within the purview of a successful orientation of Africa's development.

Part II: The successful development of the Western Christian through an implementation of perfect fundamental values: an example to consider, or even copy by Africa so as to make the most of it.

Part III: The correlation between the practice of perfect fundamental values and development: case of emerging Asian countries, another example to be considered, or even emulated by Africa.

Part IV: The cultural Revolution of Africa and African Renaissance for the advent of a new, perfect and creative African, capable of developing the African continent.

This shaping of our thoughts provides an insight to how Africa must metamorphose, through its own cultural and mental revolution, in order to best master the paradigm of fundamental values of development. The pertinent explanation of the notions of development and under-development will enlighten the reader on the challenges of Africa. This is because a well-understood and mastered development leads not only to economic growth in terms GDP and GNP, but also to contentment of citizens, thanks to effective governance from the supervisory State.

The rebirth of Africa requires that the continent must first of all be industrialised. This path is inevitable in the course of attaining economic development, with a view of addressing the tricky issues of unemployment and above all, youth employment. The realisation of the industrialisation Africa is being debated. Some posit that Africa can accomplish the technological leap that allows the continent to land in the post-industrial stage, by leap-frogging the industrial phase per se. This stance is a gross imagination, given that the conception and application gap is so wide that Africa would find it difficult to bridge the post-industrial era. Others may rather be entrusted with a broad range of activities, with Africa kept in a persistent state of dependence. Given the numerous problems confronting Africa (education, food, lack of infrastructure, youth unemployment...), industrialisation must be considered as an inevitable solution. Moreover, integration of African States is uncompromisingly important so as to enable them constitute major groups for a more effective integration into globalisation.

In a nutshell, this book constitutes an arduous task to demonstrate how Africa must appropriate the founding and central axis of true knowledge base on fundamental values of perfection and excellence to achieve its development. This is the path taken by all countries that have accomplished their development. In other words, the African must attain the fundamental knowledge that would transform him into a creator and expose him to all opportunities for a genuine and authentic development. This book stresses on the fact that Africa and African States must take all necessary measures to produce high quality human resources, as it's the real catalyst of any development. The enormous funds mobilised by Africa over the years to stimulate this development have had limited impact given that the multitudes expected to jump-start and construct the continent are far below standards.

Part I

Perfect Fundamental Values,
A Reference System for Development

An attempt to define and explain these concepts in the framework of the successful orientation of optimal development of Africa

This part focuses on definitions and explanations of concepts that are related to perfect fundamental values, development, and even underdevelopment. For it is established that development starts with man who is the end result and the centre of any social project. Man is developed in the first place, through the mastery of global and multidimensional knowledge, and brought towards the zone and environment that needs transformation. This knowledge is of divine and human essence; that is, it borrows the knowledge that comes from God and that which passes through man. Therefore, this development borrows from the course of education, knowledge and also from authentic and multifaceted training. This solid education must lead to light, perfection and creativity. Creativity, in itself, is the possibility of imagining and inventing something new and original. It is at this supreme, complete and absolute level, that we find all the enlightening lights of the mind and true knowledge, while envisaging an efficient action, for sure and concrete results. A thorough study of the various spiritual and religious orders like Judaism, Christianity, Islam, animism, Taoism, Hinduism, Zoroastrianism (Mazdeism) was necessary to achieve this. The same is true for philosophical, metaphysical, literary, cultural, scientific, political, economic, technical and industrial systems. The in-depth study of all these divine and human systems makes it possible to interpret and decipher the mysteries and hidden, obscure and unknown realities, so as to move towards development with certainty.

Successively, the first chapter explains the concept of perfect fundamental values for the development of man in general while the second chapter elucidates the themes and concepts related to perfect fundamental values of the divine sphere, in view of the development of man in general and of the African in particular. In the third chapter, we project the other forms of divine wisdom conducive to perfect knowledge. We present the perfect fundamental values of human and terrestrial life for the development of Man in general and the African in particular in the fourth. The next chapter is about the fundamental values as a reference system and a science and in chapter six, we give details to the concepts of development and underdevelopment.

Chapter I

Definition and explanation of the concept of perfect fundamental values for the development of man in general

In this chapter, we will define the concept of perfect fundamental values for the development of Man in general and the African in particular. As mentioned earlier, man can only develop if he is himself developed in his thought, mind, spirit, and his action, and driven by the enlightenment of true knowledge of what is good and just. The constant improvement of man plays a preponderant and an unavoidable role in this. Man has always sought this perfection and will seek it throughout all ages, through systems of thought and paths of knowledge that help him expand his often limited horizons. He seeks them especially in these two most explored tracks namely, the divine inspiration path and the human path. To consider divine discourse as something for places of worship, that is, monasteries or mosques, without involving it in the education of man (simply a citizen), greatly shrinks the field of human knowledge. South Koreans, who are nevertheless of Buddhist tradition, have taken an interest in the knowledge of the Gospel in order to grasp its quintessence, in order to broaden their spectrum of knowledge. We see in their success the result of this salutary curiosity. Man's perfection is the centre for the global, spiritual, intellectual, circular, scientific, technological and practical understanding of development, as it opens unparalleled perspectives in the rich and inexhaustible world of true knowledge. It is this true knowledge, this sure and tested knowledge that Africa needs for its development. For we demonstrate that development is first and foremost a question of perfect knowledge whose practical extension is a logical consequence.

I- Definition and explanation of the concept of perfect fundamental values

The concept of perfect fundamental values is at the heart of the issues of life and development, since they carry great power with diverse positive values in terms of knowledge and action. This is especially true for the value "perfection" which is often the subject of controversy. Let us emphasise that it raises man by allowing him to become completely and perfectly enlightened, able to understand the complex stakes of life and development. To dissect the concept of perfect fundamental values, we shall dwell on the following definitions:

"**Value**", according to the French dictionary *Le Petit Larousse illustré* 2000 edition, means, among others, that which is posited as true, beautiful, good, important and produces the desired effect, which has the required qualities and serves as a reference in the moral, intellectual, physical or even practical levels.

This term refers to essential and perfect subjects such as: truth, good-looking, beauty, good, perfection, excellence, justice, ethics, intelligence and wisdom. It refers to what is very good, virtuous, classy, distinguished, satisfying and leads to the approval of all.

According to the same dictionary, the term "**fundamental**," is an adjective which refers to what is at the base of something, which relates to the essential. Note that in the plural form, it is "**fundamentals**". It refers to principles, to ideas constituting the foundation and essence of a science, a doctrine and an art. What is fundamental refers to important notions such as the essence of things which is the intimate and permanent nature of things. It is similar to the notion of centrality and seems unavoidable.

Perfection, according to the same French dictionary, *Le Petit Larousse* edition 2000, emphasises that perfection is the quality of what is perfect, which meets all the required qualities, which presents no defects and is complete. Perfection refers to the wholeness, the totality, the absolute and to that which gives complete satisfaction. And this reality of satisfaction is not a utopia because it exists well in the world of humans and in the beautiful nature that is offered to us and in multiform achievements that are unanimous in their relevance. Perfection leads to positive thinking which is, to always think and take good actions.

Perfecting means the action of making perfect, perfect oneself, becoming the best and excellent in one's field. Perfectionism is the excessive search for perfection in everything.

Moreover, the *Macmillan Essential Dictionary for Learners of English* also notes that: "**Perfection**" is a state in which someone or something is perfect. **Perfect** (adjective) means as good, as accurate or complete as possible, with no faults, completely suitable or right.

Perfect (verb): means to make something completely free, from faults or to make it as good as it can be". In German, this term is "gut" or "perfeckt". In some Cameroonian languages, it exists as bellow

- In the Tunen language: "buese".
- In the duala language: "bwam"
- In the bassa language: "lam, longe"
- In the beti language: "emben"
- In bulu language: "aben"

In French and English and in several languages, this word exists and refers to what is very good, complete, excellent, best, and full and gives total satisfaction. Perfection is a capacity and quality that pushes man into constant self-improvement for his permanent perfection, in order to become the best, excellent and complete because he has reached the lights of true and eternal knowledge.

The French Bible dictionary, *Nouveau Dictionnaire biblique* (*New Bible Dictionary*) reinforces this understanding. According to this dictionary, improvement denotes what is complete, united and perfect; it also signifies putting in order and making ready for service. One could add here, a very good service (*Le Nouveau Dictionnaire biblique révisé, éditions Emmaüs 2004 pages 1008* [The New Revised Bible Dictionary, Emmaüs Publishers 2004, page 1008]). There are also terms of holiness and purity which are synonyms.

Perfection is the stage of knowledge that makes it possible to master theory and practice in order to achieve a concrete and satisfying result. It refers to obligated results in everything that one undertakes.

The Bible further clarifies that perfection is the holiness and purity of God which is also attributed to man whom He created in His image and likeness. Rev. Dr. Bouba Mbima Timothée, Rector of the Protestant University of Central Africa says that the holiness of God comprises an unavoidable imperative of moral behaviour. God says to men: "You must be holy, because I, the Lord your God, am holy." Reverend Bouba observes that this statement of God is loaded with consequences and admirably describes the vocation of each man and woman. He says that God is perfect and invites every man into perfection. Thus, perfection resides in God and it is only from Him that it can be communicated to the human being. He adds that we are all created in the image and likeness of God, and the perfection of God. His absolute uniqueness, has left His mark in each and every one of us. He therefore believes that human beings remain the, and or become the vehicles, instruments and multipliers of God's perfection for the world. According to him, the reading from the book of Leviticus in the Bible on the holiness and purity of God conferred on man (Leviticus 19: 2) shows that God is the Holy One and the creator of all human life, and the human being is both blessed and bound by the perfect holiness of God. That is why all human life is perfect, sacred and inviolable (preaching of Sunday 1st November 2015, in Église Espérance Yaoundé (Yaounde Church of Hope) of the Union of Congregations of Baptist Churches Cameroon, on the occasion of the worship service dedicated for peace in Cameroon, in solidarity with our compatriots from the Far North who are facing Boko Haram attacks).

According to *Le Nouveau Dictionnaire biblique* (The New Bible Dictionary), holiness is a fundamental quality of God and His Spirit. It is an indispensable virtue for every true believer. The Hebrew word Kadesh means physically, ritually, morally and spiritually pure. Holiness consists of being set apart, entrenched, consecrated, and separated from all defilement as much as possible. To be holy is to be pure, without blemish, which is to be cleansed of all defilement of the flesh and the spirit. Holiness refers to what is always more moral and more spiritual. The holiness of man is closely related to that of God. The holiness of God, on which our own depends, is indeed the combination of righteousness or absolute purity and infinite love (*Le Nouveau Dictionnaire biblique*, p. 1157). The *Petit Larousse illustré,* édition 2000, emphasises that the word holy (adjective) presents God as sovereignly pure and perfect. The word saint is also used to describe someone who, according to the gospel, led an exemplary life, practised the evangelical virtues and was canonised. It also refers to one who leads an exemplary moral or religious life, with a venerable and pious character. Perfection, holiness and purity are qualities and virtues that go together. They are the expression of a moral and virtuous exemplary life. That is, life that is conducive to acquiring true and authentic intelligence, wisdom and knowledge, -an attitude that conforms to the spirit of progress and development.

Purity is synonymous with holiness. Purity has a moral and spiritual meaning, that is, moral purity. Perfection in itself refers to what is innocent, honest, and upright. This is said of Jesus Christ and Christians. The servant of God has pure intentions. Wisdom is pure. A heart dedicated to God is pure. It is like limpid water or gold free from its impurities such as infidelity, conflicts of interest, mixed feelings, hypocrisy and insecurity.

An impure heart that disagrees with the nature and character of God cannot have the knowledge of God. Purity is obedience that submits all thoughts, feelings, and actions to the authority of Jesus Christ. Purity is first and foremost internal and extends to all areas of human life. It sanctifies and controls all movements of the body and mind (Bible Dictionary, op.cit.,).

According to the preface of the French version of the Quran, the preface writer (la présidence générale des Directions des Recherches scientifiques islamiques de l'IFTA de la prédication de l'orientation religieuse [the general coordinator of the Directorates of Islamic Scientific Research of IFTA preaching on religious orientation]), emphasises that the Quran is recognised by its characteristics of universality and perfection. He adds that the Holy Quran has been an unaltered book and a book revealed by the All-wise, the Most-worthy of praise. Its strict and integral application procures dignity and happiness for its faithfuls in this world and beyond. The verses of the Quran are perfect and are from a Sage, a perfect expert.

Ebenezer Njoh Mouelle, in his essay *De la médiocrité à l'excellence. Essai de signification humaine du développement (*From mediocrity to excellence. An essay on human significance of development), demonstrates the evolution of man from minor to major, from his incomplete state to his complete state through the phenomenon of positive metamorphosis.

To popularise this important value, we have created the Order of Perfect Fundamental Values (OVAFOPAC) for the appropriation, education and training of the African man for his complete perfection in the spiritual, physical, intellectual, philosophical, metaphysical, magical, civic, material, and the financial domains up to his happiness and fullness.

II- Controversy surrounding the "perfection" value

The term perfection often raises controversial debates in Africa and elsewhere in that, some say that perfection is not of this world. This approach is dangerous because it understates the significance of this important value that lies at the heart of life and development issues. If perfection is not within human reach, how then can one claim to achieve things of quality and excellence, as some among us, around us, and in the world often do? If the term exists and is commonly used in all languages, how can one deny the evidence, even if this value requires a sustained effort to acquire and practise it? Therefore, reducing the meaning of the word perfection in one's understanding, strength, and practice, diminishes the possibilities of achieving levels required to achieve sure and satisfying results. In the meantime, we currently use and practise some terms that are synonymous with perfection. These are words like excellence, interesting, fabulous, etc. By using these synonyms, we mean the same thing. It is thus established that, those who understand and practise these superior values, in all their fullness, are developed in their minds, intelligence and actions. They realise things that win the assent of all. They have attained spiritual, intellectual, moral and ethical maturity and superiority and also actions that lead, with certainty, to development. Development is, in the first place, a question of knowledge and the practice of perfect knowledge. It is matter of ideals and necessary values to assimilate which lead to it with certainty.

In reality, perfection raises controversy because it is also at the heart of divine and human life. This is because man is created in the image of God and he is, himself, a god if he practices divine and Christian virtues. Jesus Christ, in His teachings, says to those who follow and listen to Him: "Be perfect as your heavenly Father is perfect" (Matthew 5: 48). Jesus speaks with authority to men and it is practically an order that He gives them to be perfect because they also have the nature of God. They should not fool themselves about it. God has conferred on man His own nature. Man must not, by ignorance, underestimate such a wonderful gift that brings him closer to God in the same way as we are also close to our earthly parents. Since man has a divine nature, he also has the fundamental qualities of his creator, which include perfection, purity, holiness, intelligence, wisdom, honesty, integrity, justice, kindness majesty, magnificence, glory, strength, power, abundant life, fullness, eternity by the Spirit, etc. Let's not be afraid of words, it is this perfect nature that must be appropriated by the human being to build exemplary societies and to achieve development, as experienced by many human communities around the world.

Reverend Bouba Mbima Timothée, in his preaching, quoted above, says that God cannot ask us to do what is beyond our ability. He asks us to be perfect. This means we can be perfect. He asserts that baptism leads us into the perfection of God by means of insertion into Christ and his Spirit. It would be a misinterpretation that with this new perfect life, one is satisfied with a mediocre life lived under the sign of a minimalist ethic and a superficial religiosity. Every Christian must recognise that he carries within himself the elements of the perfection of God. He is called to put them at the service of others. He must express his perfection to all. Finally, every human has perfection in him but there is a problem at the levels of the freedom to live it or not and to externalise it or not. Reverend Bouba adds that the call of man to perfection by Jesus Christ is above all a portrait of Himself. He is the merciful one who is tilted towards physical and moral miseries. He comforts and seeks to appease them. He is the architect of peace. He invites us to forgive unceasingly. His attitude is a lesson that shows us the path to perfection. We only have to let him model us so that we can finally draw His portrait in the world. Like a stained glass window, we reflect its light so that all men are enlightened, freed, and enjoy life in abundance and have an evangelical appetite. Reverend Pastor Njami Nwandi Simon Bolivar adds in one of his powerful sermons that Jesus Christ is the model par excellence of the accomplishment of God's will. Reverend Bouba emphasises that, quite often, man's problem is to speak badly of perfection. Man puts forward a false conception of it. When one speaks of perfect men in the Bible and the Quran or any other holy book, one imagines distant and extraordinary human beings, with exceptional renunciations and sacrifices. Yet perfection does not exclude the limits of human nature. On the contrary, it implies that man recognises his Christian identity and mission in the world, and finally, give up himself to the dynamism passionate love of God, with all his qualities which include his faults and his passions. To achieve this, man must get rid of all that is cumbersome, such as his pride and claims. If we give God priority in our lives, we will find perfection. Only God can fully satisfy us. When we say that perfection is not of this world, we mean that it is not a stationary state. It is dynamic. It is a path, a process that is a priority for man. This perfection, which Jesus Christ talks of, is not for the future, it is for here and now. Perfection is a disposition of the heart. It completely transforms man into a new and fully blessed being.

Following Pastor Bouba, we add that it is only at the level of perfection, holiness and purity, that one clearly apprehends the wonders that the Creator has reserved for man for a blessed life. In perfection, holiness and purity, life is simply outstanding. An outstanding life ranges from what is highest in moral, intellectual, artistic and creative issues, to feelings and conduct that reach great elevation.

Purity, holiness and perfection are very important values and are the heart of development. Purity has produced puritans. The latter were members of a community of Presbyterians who were hostile to the Anglican Church in England and strictly attached to the letter of the Holy Scriptures. The Stuarts (kings of England of Scottish origin from 1603 to 1714) persecuted them in the seventeenth century, causing many to immigrate to America. They are the first builders of the United States of America, through their rigour and attachment to the evangelical principles of life which are faith and hope for a better destiny. Today, they still constitute the stump of the spiritual and moral base of America, certain European monarchies and even some Muslim and Buddhist societies. This moral rigour forms the spiritual, intellectual, ethical and moral framework of the American society and the Protestant monarchies of Northern Europe and Europe as a whole. So much importance is attached to the fundamental values of freedom equality, truth, integrity, justice, success and happiness since they are the essential foundations of American and European societies. These let to their well-known success, and which brought them to the top of the world.

It is at the level of perfection, purity, holiness, excellence, intelligence, wisdom and discernment of things that one appropriates the lights of the Spirit and of knowledge that illuminate the paths of development. Perfection is therefore the supreme stage of knowledge and action at the level where things are done with the idea of perfection. This is the development which is the successful and constant fulfilment of what we achieve and it is also what brings total satisfaction and leads to happiness.

It occurs that perfect fundamental values are essential, central and basic, and they lead to a life of excellence, intelligence, wisdom, justice, good, in short, to a full and happy life. They refer to feelings and very high conduct. They appeal to an exemplary moral rectitude. It is at this level that one becomes creative and gets the spirit of creativity and inventiveness. The divine way, via the perfect knowledge that it confers, is the proper way to become a creator. Whoever imitates God, the first creator, also becomes a creator.

These perfect fundamental values are of divine and human essence, this is what we will be explaining in the following chapters.

Chapter II

Themes related to perfect fundamental values of the divine sphere, with a view to the development of Man in general and of the African in particular

In the preceding chapter, we explained the notions of perfection, holiness, purity, and related terms and their synonyms. To better understand the importance of themes and concepts related to perfect fundamental values, we are inspired by systemic doctrines from the Bible (Judaism, Christianity), the Quran (Islam), Buddhism, Hinduism, Taoism, Zoroastrianism and Animism. These doctrines allow us to define the perfect values of the divine sphere which concern God and man. These values and themes positively and powerfully structure the thought of man and organise the development of human societies. We mainly rely on the Bible which is first of all a book of perfect knowledge. It is the guiding, fundamental and reference book, at the service of a creative, full and successful life. It retraces divine sphere values that are very useful to man.

I- The Bible, a guiding, fundamental, central and reference book for life, for perfect knowledge and the development of Man. The Bible, source of supernatural, natural knowledge and primacy of the Spirit

Africa has put up with and accepted the gospel of God and of Jesus Christ contained in the Bible. The knowledge contained in this book has been a determining factor in the development and progress of the Western world that spread it to Africa. Africans must not exploit this book superficially. Like the West, they must exploit it thoroughly and draw the substantive marrow for their awakening and progress, and not just as a book reserved for Church life. The Bible tells us about the supernatural life that belongs to God alone, His kingdom, all the spirits that revolve around it, and His values. The Bible is a book that gives primacy to life in the Spirit because God is Spirit, the invisible and eternal energy that descends on the man who believes in God, and who knows and practices His wonderful word. The Bible also teaches about the natural life, that is, the life of man and all the physical environment that surrounds him. It shows that man is created in the image and likeness of God and that he has the divine nature if he practices divine and Christian virtues. In this way, he is the privileged partner of God for the development of the universe. Primacy is given to the spirit and not to the flesh and matter because the human societies that control the world are those that are guided by the energy of the mind and not by that of matter. The societies that give priority to the Spirit to lead their actions dominate the world. This is thanks to the immortal and infinite power of creativity, innovation and invention of the Spirit. A Buddhist Chinese ambassador to Cameroon in the 2000s, on the occasion of the Communist Party Congress of his country, said China will strengthen the spiritual for success in the businesses of this great country.

Father Placide Tempels affirms this reality for Africa, when he declares that "the Primitive originally had faith and worship of the Supreme Being and the Creative Spirit" (Placide Tempels, *La philosophie bantoue*. Présence africaine. 4th edition 2013, Pg. 21). When one sees the artistic and architectural achievements as well as the knowledge conveyed by the first brilliant human civilisation of Negro origin of ancient Egypt, one realises the relevance of the declaration of Tempels (Cheikh Anta Diop. *Nations nègres et culture* Présence africaine. Réédidé en 2015)

The Bible tells us that God is the first perfect value and man created in His image and in His likeness, is the second perfect value. The Bible informs us about the logic that inevitably leads to perfect life, as long as we agree to follow its enlightening and edifying teachings. These writings are lessons of great relevance and power. They are a great light for man. They are the measure of authentic knowledge. When one attains it, one clearly grasps the omnipotence of knowledge, the true meaning of words, concepts, laws, ordinances, precepts, commandments, teachings and themes that organise an orderly, structured, disciplined, harmonised and successful life.

The meeting of the African Biblical Leadership Initiative (ABLI), organised in Yaounde on 20th September 2017, recommended the practice of biblical truths and values by Africans, for a more dignified and prosperous Africa. The subject is "Leadership in Africa, a commitment to Excellence". ABLI wants to bring the Bible back to the decision table in order to ensure that biblical values are shared at all levels so that Africa's resources are better managed and Africans can benefit from all the fruits and blessings God has given them.

Cameroon and Africans are enrolled in emergence. They must absolutely embrace this promising and saving school of perfect fundamental values which are the central and creative values of life and action which is reflected in the African culture. The Bible has a central role in this understanding and presents an inestimable comparative advantage. It gives a precise insight into these values which are the sure way to achieve perfection and creativity, which is, the ultimate stage to understand the paths of development. It gives man sufficient knowledge to brighten his path and make him a creator, because he is the image of God. In this way it is a book of knowledge and above all, the book of true knowledge.

The Bible has proven itself through the ages. In the course of exploiting it, one takes all power and measures of these values. One must exploit it regularly as it is with the basic school books (primary, secondary and higher). It is the precise, complete and exhaustive understanding of the Holy Scriptures and other writings worthy of the name that confer a powerful culture for clear reading and the success in life. The Western world which still dominates the world today experienced this from the 15th century and managed to establish its strong cultural base. Some Western countries such as United States of America, United Kingdom, and the monarchies of Northern Europe, Sweden, Denmark and Norway still maintain this spiritual rigour. Other countries that also practice this spiritual rigour include Japan, China, South Korea, Malaysia, Singapore of Buddhist background. To add, there is Saudi Arabia, the oil monarchies from the Middle East and Indonesia of Muslim background. Only countries that perfectly apply this intellectual and moral rectitude constitute the axis which dominates the world. The Bible, if well studied and understood, enlightens every man in his own environment to help him appropriate the values of his own culture and elevate him to perfection and creativity. That's why the Bible is the guiding, central and fundamental book of life and development. It is a scholarly book that demands that it be studied in a very committed way, in order to get the best out of it in all areas and aspects of divine and human life.

In fact, one might want to question the place of divinity in these concerns which are related to the development and progress of people. To understand this necessity, it is worthy to note that the divine sphere, like the human sphere, is first and foremost a space of life and knowledge. Divine knowledge claims the first place in the world of knowledge, since it is the source of all true knowledge. It presents itself as the code of life that clearly explains all divine and human realities. The Bible is thus a guiding, fundamental and reference book on the vital issues of divine and human life. All evidences are in agreement with this. Anyone who complies with these fundamental teachings raises his knowledge to the highest degree and sets it at its peak. He then has the capacity to become a creator and a superior being and accesses the asymptotic level and the crest line of true knowledge. Moreover, the Bible is the first book that was published for the first time in several copies by the Gutenberg printing press in 1455. It is the best-selling book in the world, with more than six billion copies sold. God therefore imposes His supremacy in the galaxy of knowledge by occupying the first place through His holy book. In this respect, the Bible and the Quran, which convey monotheism, are mines of information for the training and development of man in the sense of perfection, holiness and purity. Even if this double revelation was conceived around the Mediterranean basin where the white population is in dominance, it is useful to all humanity. For, they convey central values for human life. It is important to note that they are first of all books that distil supernatural and divine, even natural and human knowledge before being considered as books in the service of religions that make it an object of infinite controversy. On the other hand, he who seeks reliable information and rejects complicated dogmatic discussions is sure to be well served and to be edified in many aspects of spiritual, supernatural and natural life, and to also find the enlightenment that illuminates intelligence and confers wisdom. In real terms, the Bible raises man to a very high level of knowledge, creativity and inventiveness; it causes man to completely change the network and the level of knowledge. It conveys man to adjust spiritually, intellectually mentally, morally, scientifically, to fullness. Other religions and routes of knowledge such as Buddhism, Hinduism, Confucianism, Taoism, just to name a few, evolve in this direction. Animism which is the traditional African religion has this capacity, if only Africans return and deepen the research on its essence as Father Placide Tempels did. The pantheons of the Egyptian, Greek and Roman gods also express this mysticism of wisdom, thanks to the qualities and values embodied in these gods. Man wants to lift the veil of mysteries that surround him at all times. Human knowledge does not always succeed. If man identifies himself with God and His holy and perfect nature, enters into His logic and takes His Holy Spirit, then he becomes a new man, a divine creature who acquires the divine power which opens the knowledge of all mysteries to him. He thus possesses the life of light and codes enabling him to understand everything, to acquire the true knowledge of God and the gods, which opens the boulevard and logic of true and fruitful development. He becomes a new creature and a creator by this radical transformation of his intelligence. It is really at the divine level that one discovers and understands the ways of true creativity. God is the creator so, the one who follows and imitates Him also becomes a creator and an inventor. The Western world has extraordinarily lived and demonstrated it.

Those who constructed the Western world received this grace from God. His word gradually showed them the mystery of life as well as hidden and physical things. Africans and all human beings who follow this perfect training also gain access to this creative and inventor spirit. The blacks of ancient Egypt had this creative capacity. This is seen in the brilliant civilisation that they established in the Mediterranean basin which was imitated by all the peoples around, especially the Greeks and the Romans. They even acknowledged to have received all the elements of civilisation from the Negroes of ancient Egypt.

In addition, the preface to the Quran in the French language also emphasises that this book is a supreme constitution that organises both spiritual and temporal life. This book covers a wide range of issues, including dogma, law (sharia), morality, preaching of Islam, the use of good advice, constructive criticism, warning, arguments and testimonies, historical reports and references to the cosmic signs of Allah. It is a book of discernment so as to distinguish good from evil, error from the truth, righteousness from unrighteousness and light from darkness. This book does not only contain a very rich and fertile spiritual teaching, but also a very rich moral which is supported by a corpus Juris with precise and detailed legal rules making it a very elaborate scientific discipline. It is a miraculous and inimitable book whose conveyed word is revealed to Allah alone (God).

In the five pillars of the Muslim religion, fasting strengthens faith and prepares one for the difficult trials of life, Al-Haj (the pilgrimage to Mecca) includes specific rites and conditions to be obeyed. Such conditions include purity of faith and virtue which helps to strengthen cohesion between thought and action. Knowledge, belief and conviction condition a firm faith in God and His word.

The Bible and the Quran and even all religious systems worthy of the name, Buddhism, Animism, Hinduism, Taoism, are related to each other through the values of knowledge, perfection, purity and virtue that confer a pure consciousness, for a healthy, holy and active life.

II- Themes and values of the divine and supernatural sphere, conducive to perfect knowledge

We have already developed some of these values in the previous section, especially the values of perfection, holiness, and purity. To examine this question, we observe that these themes are as relevant in the supernatural and divine sphere as in the natural and human sphere, because the main actors of the Bible are God and man.

God, the first perfect value

The Bible tells us that God is the first perfect value. It is very important to understand who God is in essence and what He brings to humanity created in His image and in His likeness. He is perfection, purity, holiness, and the creator par excellence, as we have presented before. All religions declare it unequivocally. These are the virtues He has generously given to man who is made in His image and likeness. All put together, they express His ineffable purity, His glory and Majesty, His elevation and supreme grandeur, His horror of evil and His hatred for sin (*Dictionnaire biblique révisé et augmenté éditions Emmaüs, 2004 P346-352* [Revised and upgraded Bible Dictionary Emmaus Editions, 2004 pg 346-352]). God is thus the first perfect fundamental value, with His kingdom and all the values that are developed there. To rely only on the Holy Bible, which contains the books of the Old Testament, the base of Judaism and the New Testament, the foundation of Christianity, we consider it a mine of knowledge in all fields apart from any doctrinal and dogmatic controversy. The nature of God is clearly revealed in it. God is the source of all true knowledge, life and authority. God exists above and outside everything. The whole universe is subject to Him. He is King forever and ever (Ps. 10: 16). He invites man who is His main partner in developing the earth to follow Him and imitate His holy and perfect nature. He is the creator of heaven, earth and man.

He is eternal (Yahweh), who is at the origin and the end of all existence. He is a unique God, incomparable and the moral affirmation of divine fidelity. He is the God who wants to unite with man and give him His life. The root Yahweh is at the same time Being, Life and Immortality. Truth and fidelity are united in Yahweh Elohim who comes into contact with man, warns him, judges him and promises him salvation. Other expressions composed with the same name complete this revelation of providence and divine salvation. They include: Yahweh Jireh, the Lord who provides; Yahweh Rapha, the Lord who heals; Yahweh Shalom, the Lord my peace; Yahweh Raah, the Lord my shepherd; Yahweh Tsidkenu, the Lord our righteousness. Truly the Saving God answers all the needs of our being. To know Yahweh is to recognise His nature, His character, His sovereignty, His work of judgement and salvation. God is Adonaï, Lord and Master. He expresses the sovereignty and so expresses the feeling of dependence of man on the service of his creator to whom he belongs and owes obedience. Therefore, through the name of God, one can see that Biblical revelation has remained the same, from its origin and that through the various forms of His name, the character, identity, will and acts of God are expressed. He is holy, pure, love, perfect, just, right, intelligent and wise. He is merciful, compassionate and slow to anger. He is omniscient, omnipresent and omnipotent. Apart from His name Yahweh, He is also called EL, an appellation of Semitic origin, in the Canaanite and Chaldean languages, hence Elohim (power of God), one of the oldest appellations of God. Thus in the Semitic origin and in the descendants of Abraham, God has names which underline a virtue: El-Shaddai (Almighty God (Gen. 17. 1), El- Elion (God Most High Gen.14: 18), El-Olam (God of Eternity Gen. 21: 33), El.Ganna (Jealous God Ex.20: 5), El- Hai (living God, Joshua 3: 10). God is also light (1 Jn1: 15) and the Father of lights (James 1: 17). He is forever the light of His people (Isa 60: 19-20). The word of God is compared to light (Ps 119: 5) which, with its power of illumination, communicates to men the commandments and judgements of God (Pv 6: 23). Light is often used to describe the action of the word of God under the guidance of the Holy Spirit. So it illuminates the soul (2 Cor. 4: 6), it communicates the direction of God (Ps 112: 4), it makes prosperous and fills with joy (Ps 27: 1). Finally, light is an image of Christians in general (Matt. 5: 44). God is also His word; this is the power of God himself and is sharper than any double-edged sword and penetrates even to the dividing of soul and spirit, joints and marrow (Heb. 4: 12). By this power, the word is creative and produces many miracles. God is thus clothed in glory and magnificence and in majesty, qualities which He has also generously given to man (Ps 21: 4-7). The glory of God expresses the radiance that emanates from His person because of all His perfections.

God is thus a unique God, creator of the universe and all that is in it. He is a father for all men, since He provides all their needs. He is the perfect expression of knowledge, intelligence, wisdom and perfection. He made Himself fully known in Jesus Christ, His son, who came in the flesh to save this world and to show the perfect image of God, so that man would no longer doubt who God really is. Everything that comes from God is sacred. It imposes itself by its high value and we owe it absolute respect. Any society that enters this central understanding knows how to identify and discern what is sacred and very important. It can thus lay hold on the paths of moral perfection and rectitude. So, to enter into knowledge without having this original reading of things constitutes a major handicap for those who want to discover the world in its depths. In the first place, the basic elements of life and knowledge are lacking in human comprehension, yet there are those who wish to ignore or underestimate God and who say that He has only to stay where He is, and that He has nothing to do with the issue of development and man. Some even think that He is the God of certain people and not others. Some see in development only the economic, financial and material aspects, forgetting that the underpinnings of development and life are primarily spiritual and cultural. However, perfection, excellence and sublime values are found in all cultures. The Bible has really expressed them well. Life resides in the Spirit and this leads to true knowledge. This word is the logos that ancient Greece has developed. In the Old Testament, the Hebrew term "dahar", translated by logos in the Septuagint, affirms that God is a God who speaks, reveals Himself and communicates about Himself. Consequently, creation is realised by means of the word of God, which establishes an equivalence between the spoken word and the material fact. The idea of logos is close to the term wisdom. Personified wisdom is the first creative act of God (Pv 8:22), which is then associated with the rest of creation.

God is Spirit, power, strength and glory

The Holy Spirit

God is Spirit. This spirit is an immaterial power that comes from God and descends on the believing Christian. It infinitely multiplies its abilities and makes a creator. He has no material and carnal substance that is why He is eternal, omniscient, omnipotent and omnipresent. His glory is manifested in His perfections. Those who trust in Him and study His word understand the primacy of the Spirit in all actions of life. They capture the central knowledge that leads to development in a better way. God is the laboratory and the crucible of all the spiritual energy that governs the universe. To drink from God fortifies the human spirit and multiplies its possibilities to infinity.

The Holy Spirit which is the nature of God is symbolised by breath or wind (spirit means breath), dove, oil, living water, the seal and a deposit. He is called the Spirit of God, the Spirit of the Lord, the Spirit of the Father, the Spirit of Jesus according to the New Bible Dictionary. The Holy Spirit is power that comes from God. He has a distinct personality, as is the case for God the Father and the Son, and is divine energy in man and in creation (Acts 1: 8). The Holy Spirit is at work in creation. He quickens man. He inspires sacred authors and all who receive Him, to lead their lives in clarity, perfection and light. Having the deposit of the Spirit believers are filled by Him with all the fullness of God (Ephesians 3: 16-21). Thus, God becomes truly all in all. That is why He is God of gods and Spirit of spirits. So a man regenerated by the Holy Spirit is a child of God and becomes a new creature. In the Old and New Testaments, He qualifies some for a special task, for example Moses, Aaron, Joshua, the prophets, the Judges, the Kings, Jesus Christ, the Apostles, etc. God still inspires men and women today for His work and that of humanity. The Holy Spirit is at work in Jesus Christ. The Holy Spirit aided Jesus Christ throughout His entire career and He can help anyone chosen by God. By the Spirit, Jesus Christ was conceived, anointed, sealed, filled, clothed with power, led, offered as a sacrifice and resurrected. This Spirit is also indispensable for man today to conduct his actions and development with discernment and in the light of God. The baptism of the Holy Spirit gives regeneration through new birth and spiritual resurrection that takes place in the heart of man when he puts his faith in God and Jesus Christ. The Spirit enlivens and gives a new existence to become one with Jesus Christ and the other members of the body of Christ. This fullness is obtained by faith in God and in Jesus Christ. One obtains the anointing and the gift of the Spirit (or spiritual gift). A spiritual gift is the supernatural qualification given to every believer for service in the body of Christ and in the world of men. The Apostle Paul enumerates a number of gifts of the Holy Spirit. They include wisdom, knowledge, faith, healing, miracles, prophecy, discernment of spirits, tongues and interpretation of tongues, gifts of being an apostle, of teaching, of helping, of governing, of being an evangelist, of a pastor and of exercising liberality.

The Holy Spirit produces only good feelings: love, faith, joy, peace, goodness, faithfulness, kindness, self-control, patience, fullness, hope and fulfilment. That is why God is strength and power for all who put their faith in Him, and drink from this strength, power, and benefit from it. This experience of man with God is mysticism. All those who live this intimate relationship discover life in its true explanation and dimension.

To conclude, a society led by the Holy Spirit is completely regenerated. It evolves in the great light of perfect knowledge that comes from God for its development. Europe succeeded to realise the spiritual and Cultural Revolution that leads to the perfect knowledge for its development from the 16th century.

The Europeans, quickened by this Spirit, carried out the same revolution in the new continent in America, to build the United States of America, the first world power from the 20th century to present. The daily reference of this great country is of divine order.

Africa cannot do otherwise for its development. It must allow itself to be transformed by that powerful immaterial energy that comes from the Creator and is at work in one way or the other in all developing societies. It is also a question of perfect knowledge.

Should we deny such compelling realities that carry so much power for action? First of all, should the Bible that carries so much power be written by Africans so that they believe in truths so obvious for knowledge-hungry consciences, since the South Koreans have questioned European missionaries about the realities of God and His Spirit?

In fact, we cannot speak of God without mentioning the person of Jesus Christ who is the incarnation of this perfection that has manifested itself in the world of men, so that they are inspired by Him. Such is the case for the prophets and apostles who are also the messengers of God and who led an exemplary spiritual life that can serve as a model for men. Imitating Jesus Christ also leads to perfection. He is the sublime incarnation of this high value in the world of men. This is what is required of every man, to lead an exemplary life, to behold and concretely live the wonders that God reserves for man to make him a god. When we lead this exemplary life, we carry the mark of God in our carnal lives.

God, source of life and creator of all things

In God we have these, the source of life and the origin of all things. This understanding is crucial to compel man to turn first to God to seek the light that illuminates his dark and ignorant life.

To fully associate God with the discovery and knowledge of this world is a process of wisdom that leads man to fullness. Without life we do not exist and we are nothing, that's why life is sacred and inviolable. In order of priorities, life comes first and it comes only from God. In this sense, Genesis 1:27 corroborates this truth "God created man in His image. He created him in the image of God.

To define life, we prefer the definition and explanation given by *Le Nouveau Dictionnaire Biblique* (New Bible dictionary) which is complete to that contained in *Le Petit Larousse illustré* 2002 (Larousse illustrated dictionary of 2002). So the notion of life is complex and it can mean, the vital principle, the breath of life from God who makes man a living being (Genesis 1: 2, 7), the period or duration of the existence of a man, life as a direct gift of God, which for its duration, absolutely depends on Him or the sum total of relations and activities of a man which together constitute his life. Life is synonymous with the means of life support, synonymous with happiness or well-being (Psalm 1: 1-3), a precious gift in a vital relationship with God. Life is also man in his immaterial self. The immaterial self is the seat of affections and desires, the fullness of his activities and relations in the material and spiritual field. A full life is one that enables man to attain the divine nature. This is the level of the true and accomplished man, the stage of all beatitudes and all spiritual, material and financial happiness.

In fact, the spiritual is the central theme of the New Testament: the life from above that is communicated to believers through the mediation of Jesus Christ. As logos (verb, word), Jesus is the source and sustenance of all life in the world, whatever the form. The Logos is the light of men (John 1.4). Jesus came into the world to give life. He gives eternal life in communion with God. The definition of eternal life that Jesus Himself gives us is that we should know God and Jesus Christ, whom He sent, and have a personal relationship and communion with Him. This life is both a present possession and a wonderful hope for the future.

By faith, the believer already enters into a vital relationship with God, receives new power and carries out new activities. In the book of Revelation, the apostle John recalls the crown of life promised to those who are faithful until death, the living water offered to the thirsty (21: 1), and the tree of life that gives life (22: 14). He even mentions that the victory of the believer enables him to sit on the throne with Jesus. Man is even co-heir with Jesus. These are celestial and divine realities. This is a true feast of life (New Biblical Dictionary, op.cit., 1320).

This explanation of life is complete because it takes into consideration the material and spiritual dimensions of life. The material dimension constitutes that part of man that dies and the spiritual dimension the one that does not die and is eternal. It is this spiritual dimension that conceals all the creative powers and permanent innovation. The French language dictionary *Le Petit Larousse* gives a less dense definition since it says that life is the set of phenomena (nutrition, growth, reproduction common to organised beings which constitute their own mode of activity from birth to death).

With this comprehensive understanding, man also proclaims the importance of life. The Universal Declaration of Human Rights states in Article 3 that everyone has the right to life, liberty and security. This right is repeated in the African Charter on Human and Peoples' Rights. The 18th January 1996 Constitution of Cameroon also states, in its preamble, that: "Every person has a right to life, to physical and moral integrity and to humane treatment in all circumstances. Under no circumstances shall any person be subjected to torture, to cruel, inhumane or degrading treatment".

President Barack Obama highlights this truth in his excellent book: *The Audacity of Hope: Thoughts on Reclaiming the American Dream,* pg. 72. He declares: "We hold these truths to be self-evident, that all men are created equal, that they are endowed by their Creator with certain unalienable rights, among which is the right to life, liberty and the quest for happiness". He adds that these simple words constitute the foundation and substance of the belief of the American people's government.

The exaltation of knowledge, science, intelligence, and wisdom in biblical teachings and the word of God.

True knowledge and the Logos

God is the expression of true knowledge that does not deceive and leads inexorably to the truth. This is in conformity with the reality of things, but especially with the word which leads to the salvation of man. The Logos is the expression of the true word of God that does not deceive and leads to the truth and salvation of man. Greek philosophy has made it an important theme. Stoics, convinced of the rationality of the universe, see in the Logos the unifying principle or force that is at the origin of the universe and controls it.

The New Biblical Dictionary states that knowledge, according to the Old Testament, means lucidity, perception, or consciousness. It means knowing, learning, understanding and experiencing. In the New Testament, it means almost the same thing. On the other hand, God has given man the intelligence and the desire to know. The knowledge of God which comes from God is true knowledge that frees man from ignorance. God has perfect knowledge and has given man perfect knowledge also, since He has given him His own nature and fullness (Ephesians 3 vs. 19).

The knowledge and practice of the word of God makes it possible to see beyond appearances, since they come from the supernatural which is above the natural. This was the case of the prophets who seemed to have had an additional eye to see beyond realities perceptible by the five senses. Jesus Christ had this gift perfectly. Thus, there exist the eyes of the flesh and also the eyes of the spirit which search and see the hidden things that belong to the divine realm. The Holy Spirit who is the Spirit of God is the One that gives, to those who believe in God, this supernatural ability to search hidden things. He searches everything, even God Himself, and teaches all things. The knowledge of the word of God is the perfect light that enlightens man. So the knowledge of God, to man, is the best source for science and technology. It opens to him all the perspectives of supernatural and natural knowledge. There are several renowned men of science who testified and still testify on the relationship between science and the knowledge of God as we will further develop.

The New Biblical Dictionary adds that true knowledge produces in us the fruits of life; it frees us through the communication of truth; it is eternal life; it makes us grow spiritually; it preserves us from idleness and sterility.

It establishes true unity. It must increase and deepen in us. It can do everything to infinity because it takes roots from God and Jesus Christ in us. It allows a full entrance into the kingdom of God (2 Pet. 2:11). It is therefore the knowledge of the perfect word of God that gives true and authentic knowledge. It is very useful as it frees man from all obstacles, opens him unlimited horizons and gives him the best opportunities for life. It renders man concrete through sciences, arts, technology, technique and the production of wealth of all kinds for his well-being. The word of God is effective and must be fulfilled. It is truth, trustworthy and just in its affirmation. The word of God is the same whether in the past, the present or the future. The word is also all powerful and creative. The word of God immerses man in His kingdom, which is a space of all possibilities and successes. It floods the man with a real light so that he sees clearly, very clearly for the discernment of all truths. This is how the Gospel which is the word of God announces the good news of His kingdom and all the inherent promises. The one who is curious to learn and believe in this wonderful word edifies himself and fully understands the complex realities of divine and human life. All mysteries become clear before him. The reality of the development of human societies becomes understandable and its realisation possible. This is why God identified Himself in His word which is the logos that the Greek philosophers like Heraclitus of Ephesus, Plato and Philo have magnified.

In what way would this beautiful presentation of divine knowledge hinder the paths leading to development? Since most of the words used in the Bible are used in the language and activity of humans.

Science

Godly science structures the mind of man, leading him into the paths of true knowledge, intelligence, wisdom, logic and sustained reflection. It gives a deep discernment which opens broad perspectives that lead to the sciences of man, technique, creativity, technology, industry and the production of multifarious immaterial and material wealth.

Intelligence and wisdom

The impact of intelligence, wisdom and sublime life

The Bible shows wisdom in all its grace, beauty, and high spiritual dimension. It also indicates that the divine word leads to wisdom, love, instruction, intelligence, justice, equity, righteousness, knowledge, reflection, skill, understanding riddles and the science of discernment. It also leads to knowledge and common sense. The initiator of logic and discursive reason is God. It obviously precedes the great masters like Plato, Aristotle, Descartes, Kant, etc. by whom the scientific spirit has taken shape in the course of history. The Bible also explains that wisdom is an ornament on the neck, the apple of the eyes which must be written in the heart. We see that it's in relation to the essential parts of the human body, that we better highlight the importance of wisdom. Furthermore, in the eyes of God, following the order of riches, life, knowledge and intelligence, wisdom surpasses gold, silver, pearls, all objects of worth. In the divine order, intelligence, wisdom and knowledge give long life, health, material and financial wealth, happiness and peace. It is not by chance that the Americans have written on the dollar, their national currency, "In God we trust". This expression has even become a national slogan. It is not by chance that they became rich and even today are the richest in the world, and they consider themselves a hyper power. This is because they have total trust in God that He is the main inspiration of their life, despite their well-established secularism.

This beautiful definition of intelligence and wisdom goes well beyond the human definition. It is complete and clearly shows all the benefits that come from knowledge, intelligence and wisdom. We did not find a definition as complete and clear as that on knowledge, intelligence and wisdom. And King Solomon amplifies this understanding.

King Solomon himself asked God nothing but intelligence to judge His people and discern good from evil. God gave him even more. He gave him a wise and an intelligent heart, so that there was none before him like him and no one will ever be like him. In addition, He gave him riches and glory.

We will end with this eulogy of wisdom done by King Solomon himself in *The Jerusalem Bible*: "In wisdom is, a spirit that is intelligent, decent, unique, multiple, subtle, mobile, penetrating, undefiled, clear, impassable, friend of good, prompt, irresistible, beneficent, friend of men, firm, sure, carefree, able to do everything, watch everything, penetrate through all minds, all intelligence, the most pure and subtle. For above all movements, wisdom is mobile; it crosses and penetrates all because of its purity. It is a fragrance of the power of God, a pure emanation of the glory of the Almighty. Nothing unclean can penetrate it because it is a reflection of eternal light. A stainless mirror of the activity of God, an image of His goodness. On the other hand, in isolation, it is capable of doing everything and in itself, it renews the universe. From age to age passing through holy souls, it makes them friends of God and prophets, for God loves only those who dwell with wisdom. It is more beautiful than the sun. It surpasses all the constellations. Compared to the light, it prevails, because it gives way to the night. But, evil does not triumph over wisdom. It stretches from one end of the world to the other and it governs the universe with kindness. Wisdom has cherished and sought after the universe from its youth. He sought to take her for a wife and he fell in love with her beauty. She burst her noble origin by living intimately with God, for the master of all had loved her. It is actually initiator of the science of God and it decides what he does. If in life wealth is a desirable good, what can be richer than wisdom which operates everything. And if it is intelligence that operates, who is more than intelligence, the worker of what is? Do we love justice? Its labourers are its virtues, it teaches temperance and prudence, justice and strength, there is nothing more useful in life for men. Do we still want a rich experience? It knows the past and conjectures the future. It knows the art of handling maxims and solving enigmas, signs, wonders; it knows them in advance, as well as the succession of eras and seasons.

Therefore to frequent it or live in its intimacy, does not cause bitterness or pain, but pleasure and joy". Is it not right to say that with this perfect knowledge, life is simply sublime?

This eulogy to wisdom by a great king recognised at all times for being a wise man is eloquent. All civilisations preceding ours have always praised wisdom and knowledge. They are Egyptian, Babylonian, Persian, Median, Greek, Roman and African civilisations. It is therefore this appropriation of wisdom that leads to perfection, to be immersed in the light of the Spirit as was the case with the prophet Daniel. King Nebuchadnezzar saw him as having the spirit of the gods, the lights of intelligence and extraordinary wisdom (Daniel chapter 5 verse 14). Wisdom and intelligence are the prerogatives of the saints, those who claim them and even every community that develops them and places them at the heart of their system of organisation. This wisdom of God is observed and amplified in its purity, perfection and holiness.

Other characters of God

Apart from knowledge, wisdom and intelligence, the Bible exalts other divine fundamental values like love, goodness, good, truth, justice, peace, light, freedom, salvation, virtue, the kingdom of God, fullness, miracles, mysticism and happiness which are the marks of God which He has generously given to man.

Love is the link of perfection and fulfilment of the law. God is love. According to biblical teachings the supreme virtue is love. It is a virtue that generates only good and makes it possible to treat one's neighbour as oneself. Love qualifies the man who practices it perfectly and who loves God to be His friend as was the case of Abraham, the prophets, the apostles and the saints. The practice of love is always good, very good. Love is the very nature of God. That is why He has lavished the human being with so many benefits, to the point of giving him His own nature. Consequently, the human being is also love and must demonstrate it in all their daily actions. This would create a better and sublime world. Love never perishes. It is full of virtues: it is patient, it is not envious, it is not proud, it does not do anything dishonest, it is not irritating, it does not suspect evil, it does not rejoice in unrighteousness, it rejoices instead in the truth, it forgives everything, it believes everything and it has hope in everything. It is eternal. Love transforms all social relationships from within: in a couple, between parents and children, employers and employees etc. Love settles in the heart of man through the Spirit of God that he receives. In turn, he loves God and his neighbour.

Goodness, good and joy

Firstly, goodness and joy come from the divine nature. The New Bible Dictionary notes that in the Bible, goodness is essentially associated to God. God is good because He is a morally perfect and generous being. Goodness is not an abstract or ideal notion, it expresses the grace of God, what He does, creates, orders, gives and approves in man. His blessings translate into material blessings. In addition, God lavishes spiritual graces. He always promises to give man what he needs.

Obedience to God is good, pleasant, beautiful and useful to man. Obedience is seen in good works which are the adornment of the Christian. That's why we must not be tired of doing good. Doing good is a divine privilege that He gives to the one who imitates Him. Good works are the fruit of the word; they glorify God and lead to salvation. He who practices the commandments of God is a good person. Goodness gives a good conscience. It gives grace and a good reason before God and men.

Joy is also a state of having a good conscience. God is the source of true joy and gladness. Joy is naturally derived from the believer's relationship with God. Joy is also linked to the announcement of the good news of the Kingdom. The word demands that Christians should always be happy. Goodness and joy are marks of those who love God and practice His commandments of love, peace and justice. Goodness and joy render us optimistic, and everything is for the best in the world.

Truth

God wants to produce this truth in man (Ephesians 4 vs. 15). It is the solid foundation of all human relationships. Christ is the truth and He proclaimed the truth with definitive authority in order to suite human understanding. Truth is the revelation of God for the salvation of man. It is synonymous with faith, faithfulness, loyalty, security, honesty and integrity.

Righteousness

It comes from God because He is just, equitable, impartial in His judgement of all peoples (Isaiah 30:18). The New Bible Dictionary adds that righteousness is the quality of what is right, exact, and consistent and which respects the law and social rules. It is also fairness, accuracy and probity. To justify someone is to recognise or declare them righteous. Thus, man was justified by Jesus Christ, he is declared righteous and made whiter than snow (Isaiah 1: 18). There is no condemnation for him any longer (Romans 8: 1), for God sees him in Christ, clothed with the perfect righteousness of His divine son. Justification makes man to conform to the divine nature.

The peace of God surpasses all understanding (Philippians 4:7). God is a God of peace. In God's peace, man knows joy and happiness. He lies down and sleeps in peace, and the ways of wisdom are peaceful.

And God gives us peace in anyway and at all time. Peace gives rest to the heart and the spirit so that they can prosper in good works.

Light

God created the lights, that is, the sun to light the day, the moon and the stars to light up the night. Light is necessary for life, growth, the necessities of existence, for comfort and joy. The idea of light is often associated with God Himself. God is light (1 John 1:5). In essence He is three times holy, pure, unblemished and glorious. In His action, He reveals, attracts, quickens, purifies, enlightens, preserves and rejoices. He is named the Father of Lights (James 1:7). He is the light of His people (Isaiah 60: 19-20). Likewise, Jesus Christ is the true light that enlightens men by bringing them salvation. The word is light on the path of man, so that he can see clearly and walk with certainty.

The word of God is compared to light which, with its power of illumination, communicates to men the commandments and divine judgements. Light is often evoked to describe the action of the word of God under the guidance of the Holy Spirit. It lights up the soul. It communicates God's direction. It makes you prosperous and joyful. Finally, light is an image of Christians. When believers become sons of light, they see in them an irreproachable behaviour, they themselves assume the duty to radiate this light around them. The light of God that He Himself is, goes far beyond the light of day, that of the sun, the moon and powerful stars because He is the creator.

This report shows the degree of intensity of the divine light that enlightens everything and exposes even what is hidden. Was this expression the "century of European Enlightenment" not borrowed from the Holy Scriptures and from God and used with a few nuances? Today, Africa itself is also addressing this era of Enlightenment for its rebirth. Who else but God and His powerful teachings can best illuminate Africa and Africans?

Freedom

Freedom is fundamental in Bible teachings. The idea of freedom is always opposed to that of slavery or imprisonment. Thus freedom is by definition is the happy condition of one who is freed from slavery and has the opportunity to live a happiness previously impossible. In the epistles of Paul, the enemies of freedom are sin, law and death. The ministry of Jesus Christ is to grant freedom. He sets the believer free from sin and the law. He also releases from the power of darkness, superstitions and the fear of death. Even today Jesus Christ frees from alcohol, drugs and despair. For man to acquire freedom, he must serve God and Jesus Christ. By doing so, he puts himself under the law of Christ, the law of freedom, the law of love and peace. He thus has the freedom to serve God and men instead of serving only himself. Freedom is nowadays a central value that has given birth to liberalism that dominates the political, economic, social and cultural sectors.

Virtue

The Bible dictionary notes that virtue translates what causes admiration, that is, greatness, sovereignty and goodness. Thus, this term used for God expresses the virtues of God, in other words, His magnificent works and His great deeds. The apostle Peter says that God has called us by His glory and by His virtue, for the manifestation of His divine power, to participate in His own glory and goodness, and His active force and His power. Virtue also refers to moral excellence. It is an essential quality for life in the faith. It is also good conduct, moral energy and firmness of character.

The French dictionary *Le Petit Larousse illustré, 2002*, describes virtue as the constant disposition to do good and to avoid evil. At the human level, it is the attitude of a good moral conduct that is borrowed from God.

Salvation

It is a very important foundation of the divine and Christian life in that man is saved by God and His son Jesus Christ from his state of sin, so that he can inherit eternal life. Thus, the Judeo-Christian religion is for salvation, that is, it is entirely based on the fact that man, who is totally bound by the fall to death and eternal perdition, needs to be redeemed and saved by the intervention of a divine saviour. This salvation religion goes beyond simple religious morality that gives man good behavioural advice and advocates the improvement of his condition by his own efforts.

In the religion of salvation, God is the saviour and redeemer of peoples and nations. What saves is His person, His presence and His victorious intervention. This is why the psalmist continues to magnify the salvation of God. This salvation includes all spiritual and earthly deliverances. This salvation that was initially given to the people of

Israel, was extended to all people through His son Jesus Christ (Yahweh saves). For salvation is found in no other name (Acts 4:12). Jesus Christ is the prince of our salvation, the author of eternal salvation (Hebrews 5: 9). He came to find the lost. The Gospel is thus the word of salvation preached in all places. He is the power of God for the salvation of everyone who believes (Romans 1:16). The grace of God is the source of salvation which is in Jesus (2 Timothy 2:10). Salvation is a basic value, because whoever is convinced of being saved lives a new life full of self-assurance and faith in himself and in the future. He does not fear anything because he lives a life consistent with perfect values.

Kingdom of God, of fullness, of miracles, of wonders, of mysticism, covenant of God and Man

One cannot speak of God without mentioning His kingdom just as one cannot speak of man, without mentioning the earth where he lives. The kingdom of God is the sphere where God reigns, where His will is respected and fulfilled. His will is thus fulfilled in heaven and on earth. This notion of heaven shows the elevation of God and the effort that man must make to reach God in His perfection and height. The reign of God on earth is manifested in Jesus Christ who came to announce the Good News of the Kingdom of God. The kingdom of God therefore looks like a perfect place where there are only wonders. It is likened to a treasure, a pearl of great price, yeast that rises the dough, good seed, the source of life and things, the sovereignty and power of God, the spiritual world or spirits, to the rock on which one builds one's life.

Generally, only good news, blessings in abundance, graces, gifts, virtues, various charisma, miracles and wonders come from the kingdom of God. Knowing the kingdom of God gives knowledge of perfect values and especially the victory that they confer, as expressed in the book of Revelation in the dedication to the seven churches. This is to a point where Jesus Christ fully elevates the Christian who is attached to Him, to sit with Him on His throne. What grace and elevation for the man who believes in God and obtains such great favour and honour!

The kingdom of God opens up fabulous opportunities for man to widen his horizon towards the infinite, that is, from poverty to enrichment, from despair to hope. One could say that it is the realm of fairy tales, tales of a thousand and one nights. It is the kingdom of dreams, of faithfulness, of infinite opportunities that are fulfilled. For,

God is faithful to accomplish what He promises. It is the kingdom of perfect bliss and of covenant between God and man.

The Covenant of God and man

The human being is the only creature with whom God has made a covenant. A covenant is an agreement between two or more people. Human covenants often lack a permanent value. It is quite different when God deigns to be one of the contracting parties. God gives man a generous promise that will only be accomplished if man fulfils certain conditions. God promises man eternal life and protection provided he obeys Him. There is the first covenant between God and Israel. He promised that He would be their God and make them a great nation if they observe the 10 commandments. He also entered another covenant with Abraham and his descendants, to give them the land of Canaan as an inheritance. The covenant with Noah was that he will not perish with the Old World and that there should no longer be any flood. With David, He promised a perpetual throne to his posterity.

Then there is the new covenant in Jesus Christ, more spiritual than the first and the Holy Spirit is the dispenser. Founded on faith, it is addressed to all nations and Christ is the mediator. It brings to man salvation and abundant life. When one enters into this covenant, one obtains the life of the beatitudes which is a blessed life in great happiness.

In reality, the covenant with God brings us into the universe par excellence which by the power of its laws, precepts, teachings and codes, confers the divine and magical capacity. This capacity is that of miracles and wonders, it allows the man to surpass himself, because he can rise and identify himself with God.

Signs and wonders

Signs and wonders are generally from God and those who walk in His intimacy. The Bible Dictionary emphasises this, pointing out that a miracle is a supernatural intervention in the outer world, bringing a revelation of the presence and power of God. It adds that for those who believe in a personal God, the possibility of a miracle is not at all doubtful. It also notes that one could compare the miraculous intervention of the Lord in this physical world to that of the will and muscular strength of man, who controls and neutralises the laws of nature. The New Testament define miracles by the terms "dunameis" powers, "terata" wonders, amazing acts. A miracle is a powerful act and whoever believes in the power of God in his life experiences miracles.

The French dictionary Le *Petit Larousse illustré* defines a miracle as a phenomenon interpreted as a divine intervention. It is the same as magical or supernatural wonders. All believers who have experienced the truth of the gospel in their hearts and the regenerative action of the Holy Spirit, personally know something of the power of God and the reality of His revelations. He is a new creature in God and in Jesus Christ and understands these things well, and because he understands the true things, he can obtain them. For the new birth in the divine life is certainly a miracle and opens one to this wonderful and blessed life, full of benefits.

Inventions made by men through the power of intelligence are miracles of science (printing by Gutenberg, electric energy, automobile, aircraft, ship, submarine, rocket, phone, internet, different vaccines to keep away diseases, etc.). Understanding the mystery of the kingdom of God confers power for a miraculous, wonderful and full life.

Fullness

It is in God and with God that we measure what fullness represents. This ability is not common in the common man. But with God, it becomes palpable and communicative. It defines what satisfies. It designates the Greek word "pleroma", which signifies the state of what is completed, that is to say, in its highest degree of development or intensity. It also designates totality. It is the fullness of God which is also the "pleroma of good, which is, as good is the pleroma of God, and evil is the pleroma of the world which opposes God." For the Greek Philosopher Philo, God fills everything, penetrates everything and contains all things. To him, logos or wisdom are the pleroma of God. God gives this pleroma to man since God wants us to have all His fullness (Ephesians 3: 19). Does man really experience all the extraordinary grace that can give him the divine nature and understanding of all things? The Bible says that anyone who is close to God and His wonderful word understands everything, can do anything and is happy.

Happiness

Happiness is God's. Whoever believes in God and practices His wonderful word, which is full of promises, is normally happy. The

Bible is a true compendium of lessons that lead to perfect happiness. The Bible demonstrates that happiness lies in the knowledge and practice of the word (Pr 3: 13-19). The blessed is the one whom God fills with good things. Therefore, happy is man who is righteous, the one who is immersed in the divine ways (Psalm 1: 1-2), puts their trust in the Lord (Psalm 40: 5), fears Him (Psalm 112: 1), walks according to His law (Psalm 119: 1), finds His wisdom (Prov. 3: 13) and listens to Him (Prov. 8:34). That person is rich in God-given gifts for a fruitful life, forgiveness, divine protection and a privileged relationship with the Lord (Psalm 33:12). Happiness, the fruit of God's blessing, is also realised on a second axis in the fullness of this life. The signs here include wealth, success, prosperity, family and beauty. This fullness is fulfilled in the beatitudes which lead to bliss and rapture.

For the beatitudes lead to the benevolence of God. The believer who puts this complete trust in God lives and dies happy in the Lord (Rev 14: 13). This fullness leads to mysticism (read *Spiritualité et libération en Afrique* [Spirituality and Liberation in Africa] under the supervision of Engelberg Mveng, Harmattan, 1987).

Mysticism

In fact, mysticism is the religious or philosophical attitude which affirms the possibility of a perfect union between man and God or the absolute in contemplation or in ecstasy. The Middle Aged Christian of the Western world has greatly developed this dimension of contemplation and ecstasy as we will further develop. Hence the multitude of orders born at that time and even today. Catholics have greatly developed this dimension, which is observed in the various orders and charitable works. However, this term is often misunderstood and misinterpreted in every way. Some even think that it is a mysterious way which is opened only to the initiated; others equate it with more or less sordid practices. On analysis, it appears that it is the ignorance about the word of God that leads to this incomprehension.

By immersing oneself deeply in the perfect word of God, we reach this mystical dimension that allows us to understand the true meaning of divine and human realities. We converse with God and we are His intimate friends. This is the essence of mysticism.

How does this knowledge of the kingdom of God, which expands the horizon of perfect perception of things, hinder the understanding of the world and development issues? The kingdom of God, apart from what is already said above, is nothing other than the reign of perfect and sublime values which we have already developed above.

To receive this wonderful life, full of grace and enriching blessings, man must have a close communion with God, in order to live a true covenant with him. This was the case of illustrious people in the word of God such as Abraham, Isaac, Jacob, Moses, Noah, Jesus Christ and many others. Man must live an intimate life with God Himself, His son Jesus Christ, His Holy Spirit and His wonderful word. This intimate communion of man with God comes from fullness and mysticism.

It is this intimacy with God through faith that makes miracles and wonders possible in the life of the believer.

Symbolism in divine knowledge is edifying

Biblical teachings of the New and Old Testaments edify us on the different symbolisms that increase human intelligence and wisdom, much like the stories, myths, and narratives that African, Greek, Roman and other cultures convey. The tabernacle Moses built under the command of God is an image and a shadow of heavenly things. Zion, the holy mountain represents the elevation of God and whoever wants to access it must be pure and perfect. The Law of Moses represents the covenant between God and the people of Israel. Each one can make this covenant with God to serve God and men. Through this covenant, God chooses men to whom He entrusts a mission. For example, He chooses Moses and Joshua to bring Israel out of Egypt and lead them to the Promised Land, Canaan. The land of milk and honey, symbols of the wealth and abundance bestowed on Israel in the Promised Land. They can also represent wealth and abundance for any convinced believer. Also, Noah through whom God forbids Himself from ever destroying the world by a flood and by whom He reiterates the blessing to man. Abraham too becomes the father of a multitude of people and believers. Manna represents bread from heaven and abundance. Paradise symbolises happiness and a place of happiness for man. Gold and most precious stones represent wealth, glory and majesty. Animals like the lion, eagle, crocodile and hippopotamus represent strength. Others represent cunning and prudence like the serpent, simplicity like the dove, wisdom and foresight like the ant, wisdom and a proud look like the horse and youth like the eagle.

In the New Testament, Jesus Christ, the lion of the tribe of Judah is the expression of the perfect power of Jesus Christ, for the salvation of humanity. The Holy Spirit is symbolised by the wind or breath (spirit means breath). The cross symbolises the supreme sacrifice of Jesus Christ for the salvation of humanity. The New Testament is the message of God for the salvation of man. The tree of life represents God, life and knowledge. The branches of the tree of life represent man attached to God and who produces many fruits. Manna here represents Jesus, the true bread of life. The kingdom of God is compared to leaven that raises the dough, to the seed that sprouts, grows, multiplies and produces many fruits, to talents that express different gifts, to the hidden treasure that is eagerly sought, to the rare pearl and the net filled with fish, an expression of abundance. The kingdom of God expresses love, peace, justice and fullness. New Jerusalem is the perfect city. White represents purity, holiness and perfection. Fine linen and pure gold represent inner purity. The crown represents glory. The numbers two, three and seven represent assurance and perfection. The seven burning lamps and the seven eyes symbolise the seven spirits of God. The crown is the emblem of authority, dignity and royalty. The golden cups filled with perfumes symbolise the prayers of the saints. The saints symbolise the divine family.

This supernatural knowledge and many others give man an unheard-of knowledge that gives him intelligence, wisdom, the key to understanding everything. For example, he understands the natural and human and the supernatural and divine realities. When we take ownership of all these perfect values, we have the code of reference and proper conduct, Ariadne's thread, the sure way to go towards integral development of man and human societies. These perfect values are the framework that guides and plans life and development activities. That is why the communities that have appropriated this ideal setting, the guiding and fundamental framework of perfect life and knowledge, have gradually been able to invent their emancipation and their progress. For the divine teachings have trained them to understand how life is organised by intelligence and wisdom. The divine way is really a sure route that does not deceive. This intelligent journey is against all dogmatism and is only aligned with the truth. In this sense, the Bible is considered a book of knowledge par excellence. Such was the case with the founding fathers of the United States of America and many other people who derive the greatest benefit from their perfection and development from it, away from controversial interpretations of various religious backgrounds.

When one possesses this global vision of the perfect nature of God which He has conferred on man, one comes out edified with all the dynamic potentials. By all these values, God reserves a real royal feast for life, for the man who understands His ways.

Divine values as opposed to values of darkness and obscurantism

These perfect values of God are totally opposed to the values of darkness and obscurantism, which are, according to the Bible sin, arrogance, forgery, insolence, hatred, wickedness, foolishness laziness, infidelity, lies, hypocrisy, murder, lust, perversity, dissolution, deviance, impurity, immodesty, divisions, quarrels, corruption of morals, ignorance, misery, poverty, disorder, indiscipline, selfishness, ingratitude, iniquity, violence, greed, traps, impiety, theft, rape, unrestrained love for money and pleasures of the flesh, disobedience, intemperance, cruelty, rebellion to parents and authorities, treachery, cynicism, anger, excesses of all kinds, permissiveness, etc. All these negative behaviours obstruct the ability of the mind to move easily in the direction of creativity, innovation and invention. They block good inspiration, help to destroy man and constrain development.

Many of these flaws are still observed today in human societies. They block the paths that lead to the development and happiness of man. The Bible also exposes natural knowledge in which man is the central actor.

III- Themes and values of the natural sphere for perfect knowledge in the Bible

Man is the main partner of God. The Bible demonstrates it masterfully. The Bible tells us that man is the second perfect value after God. The Bible also tells us about other aspects of natural life. That to lead a successful life, man must himself apply the perfect values of God mentioned above, because he is in the image of God. As he does so, he discovers himself as God planned and programmed him. God and man therefore progress in an intimate and fruitful partnership, especially the believer in God. Through this intimacy, God also makes him a creator.

Man, the second perfect value after God and the object of divine blessing as well as miraculous and wonderful promises

The Perfect Man, a Man god (Homo deus) and a creator

The human being has received an immense privilege of being created in the image of God and His likeness. This confers upon him the undisputed status of the second perfect value after God and also a creator on the earthly level. We practically receive a divine status since it is said that practising Christian virtues confers on us the divine nature (as we flee the corruption that exists in the world 2 Peter 1: 4). The psalmist solemnly affirms that God created man a little lower than Himself and crowned him with glory and magnificence. He gave him dominion over the works of His hands and put everything under his feet (Ps 8: 6-7). Teachings on the training of man give the detailed ways that lead to his thorough fulfilment, success and happiness. This rises to the point that, as an extraordinary fact, God has blessed man and given him His own fullness, His divine nature, thereby making him His child and finally a god. He confers on him the divine nature if he (man) embraces it and the values which are proper to it. These values include, the Holy Spirit in the first place then, supernatural life, love, holiness, purity, perfection, knowledge, intelligence, wisdom, strength, power, patience, peace, truth, righteousness, freedom, kindness, joy, beauty, brilliance, magnificence, splendour, greatness, dignity, honour, glory, faith, tolerance, moderation in all things, temperance, humility, sobriety, simplicity, prudence, sincerity, virtue, integrity, loyalty, faithfulness, courage, forgiveness, hospitality, compassion, sense of family and self-control. In reality, we are repeatedly saying that, all these perfect qualities show that man is a god if he accepts to live these perfect values in their power. All these values are blessings that God gives to man. They allow man to fully access the kingdom of God, so as to better understand the paths of creativity.

In doing so, blessing is grace granted by God to man. He satisfies the faithful with material and spiritual goods, which include long life, offspring, peace and prosperity. He blesses the work of his hands and all his endeavours. He blesses nations that become sources of blessing for others. The gospel which is the good news of God is a great blessing to man.

This good news culminates with the beatitudes, the point where man is proclaimed blessed, because he is the object of God's benevolence.

Thus, in sapiential literature (on wisdom) it is said that happy is the man who is immersed in divine ways, puts his trust in God, fears Him, walks according to God's law, finds wisdom and listens to Him (Proverbs 3: 13). He is rich in gifts made by God: - a fruitful life, forgiveness, divine protection and a privileged relationship with God. In this privileged relationship between God and man, the latter reaches the fullness of God and the omega point where he grasps the supernatural and natural as well as heavenly and earthly realities. God clearly states that He is the God of gods and Spirit of spirits. Who are these gods and spirits, if they don't share and live these divine values? We have explained how Buddha by his moral and spiritual life became a god. We are likewise gods, if we give ourselves this moral and spiritual rigour. Believers are thus the reflection, the imprint and the concrete expression of the living God. That is why He exhorts us to an exemplary life so that those who live this life of exceptional quality glorify Him in heaven and on earth.

In a word, the Bible is a science book that trains the spiritual, intellectual, rational, logical, methodical, moral, scientific, technical, and technological framework which remains a foundation for human life. This book trains man to become aware of all talents he is endowed with and how to use them to become a creator in the image of God. And finally, man has succeeded through all his scientific, technical, technological and industrial prowess. The Bible teaches him to understand the ways of intelligence, wisdom, knowledge, discernment of good and evil, right and wrong, truth and error, fair and unfair as well as light and darkness. It trains man for meditation, reflection and logical reasoning. When man puts in such an effort to attain divine knowledge which is perfect, they are sure to be on the path to development.

He possesses the code of life which leads him into the truth and the light of knowledge. He has therefore understood the alpha and the omega of knowledge. In reality, alpha is the beginning of true knowledge and omega is its peak. That is to say, the point of inflection which makes it possible to understand the functioning mechanisms of thought, which is the engine of creation, creativity, science, technology which lead to development. This bright knowledge structures the thought of man in a coherent, solid, harmonious and effective way. He has a code of life and an infallible conduct. Hence the infallibility of the saints and all those who devote themselves to this rigorously exemplary life.

The canonisation of Popes John XXIII and John Paul II at the Vatican on 27th April 2014 testifies their holy lives which confer on them the nature of God. They have reached the fullness of the Spirit that gives them perfect knowledge. These basic values constitute the values that man has taken back to acquire a pure conscience, which are also the foundation for a solid, successful, victorious and blessed life. It is an unstoppable way to come out of his minor towards his major as well as his spiritual and practical superiority, as seen by philosophers Kant and Njoh Mouelle. When one is armed with all these spiritual and practical weapons, one is already developed in one's head, mind, spirit and action. It is only necessary to refer all these to nature and the material to be transformed by science and technology.

Other aspects of natural knowledge in the Bible

The Bible, a book of supernatural knowledge, also provides information on the natural life. It does not only provide information about man but also all areas of life like animals and fish of all species, vegetation of all species, water, precious stones buried in the ground including gold, diamond, jasper, sapphire, emerald, sardonyx, topaz, chrysolite, onyx, etc., luminaries (sun, moon and stars), precious materials (fabrics, carpets, precious woods, perfumes, precious plants), agriculture, breeding, architecture, the art of building with precise measurements, the technique of making perfumes, working the precious stones and wood, to make all kinds of works, the art of invention, to make fabrics, to sew, to decorate, the art of writing, the art of colours (blue, crimson, purple) , the art of war, creating wealth, being rich, governing, leading the family, sanitation cautions, law, geology, morality, the art of managing the dead, the sharing and transmission of inheritance, town planning, surveys with all indications given on the division of the land. God laid down in the Old Testament the fundamentals of moral and practical life and in the New Testament the basics of spiritual life and salvation for the complete regeneration of man.

Ultimately, the foundations for human success rest on knowledge, intelligence, wisdom and many other well-defined values of God. With this high training received from God, man can embark on the human adventure, to become a creator in the image of God.

Chapter III

Other forms of divine wisdom
Other cultures develop this theme of wisdom that predominates in divine logic

I- Asian wisdom

In this light, we will look at the ancient divinities of Asia: Buddhism, Taoism and Confucianism, Hinduism, Zoroastrianism (Mazdeism).

Buddhism

Buddhism is a religion from its founder Buddha. Buddha means the awakened, in the sense of the awakening of the Spirit. His real name is Sidharta Kautama. He is of Indian origin. He did not receive the awakening of the Spirit through fellowship with God, but through personal concentration for a certain time, which allowed him to be awaken to the Spirit to understand human suffering and seek solutions for him. We reach this state of suffering through nirvana. Nirvana is the personal liberation of suffering and its causes, characterised by dissatisfaction and suffering. One attains nirvana through discipline, ethics, meditation, discernment and wisdom (Reference Point May-June 2016 pg. 28). Buddhism is thus the search for enlightenment without God. It teaches the means of cultivating perfect goodness and wisdom without the help of God, the acquiring of supreme knowledge without revelation, on being redeemed without any mercy and on having salvation in which everyone is his own future. The book *L'humanité à la recherche de Dieu* (Mankind's search for God) states that Buddha who never claimed to be God became a god in the full sense of the word because he embodied the highest values of God's own wisdom. Buddhism is widespread in most Asian countries where its ideas of purity, moderation, wisdom, order, discipline, effort at work, family, respect for authority, serve as a basis for the culture of development. Buddhism, though divided into several standards and schools, has become a religion shared by hundreds of millions of believers in Asia and the world.

Taoism and Confucianism

Taoism and Confucianism, peculiar to China and advocated by two sages Lao-tzu and Confucius, came to reinforce in this country the edifice of wisdom, intelligence and moderation peculiar to Asian religions. Taoism leads to the path of perfect wholeness. The spiritual preparation in it is intense.

Hinduism

It is the dominant religious and philosophical system in the Indian subcontinent. Hinduism develops Veda which is knowledge or science in Sanskrit. Veda is linked by four sacred texts: Rigveda, Samaveda, Yajurveda and Artharveda which are said to contain all divine wisdom. One just needs to believe in their divine and sacred origin to be Hindu.

Zoroastrianism (Mazdaism) of ancient Iran (Persia)

Zoroastrianism is the religion of ancient Iran (Persia). It's led by its prophet Zarathustra who believes in an abstract entity (God) that he called Ahura Mazda (the being that possesses wisdom). During a ten year solitary stay in the mountains, in the depths of his thought, thoughts beyond his limits, Zarathustra recognised this entity and commended it with poetic mantras "Words that awaken thought". This Ahura Mazda entity (which gives Mazdism or Zoroastrianism of ancient Iran), is endowed with six attributes: Justness, Right Thought, Self-control, Serenity, Evolution and Perfection as well as Immortality. "Mazda, the moment I recognised You in my thoughts, I understood that You are at the beginning and the end of all that is and that You are the source of Right Thought. And when I saw You with my inner vision, I knew that You are the true creator of justice and the judge of all actions "(in the newspaper *Le Point*, Thursday, 21st and 28th December 2017 no. 2364 -2365 pg. 102). The psalmist in the Bible also affirms that God is the source of all things. Moreover all these themes have also been abundantly developed in the Bible. The Mazdeism dualism recognises the world as the theatre of struggle where the principle of Evil is opposed to the principle of Good, but the final triumph is won by the latter. The sacred book of Mazdaism is the Avesta.

II- African wisdom and animism

Traditional Africa, where traditions exist, has always been called wise because the practice of traditions and customs was strict and also the fact that this grace of wisdom is granted to all people without discrimination. Traditions and customs took the place of values and laws. They punctuated the real life experiences of tribal, ethnic and national communities. They were dynamic with the virtues they conveyed and which were subjected to strict observance. They included values of honesty, dignity, discipline, family and the respect for chiefs, patriarchs, parents, elders. The values of solidarity and communalism, hospitality, human warmth, hygiene, cleanliness, respect of initiation rites for the passage from one age class to another or for entry into a caste (hunter, blacksmith, craftsman, etc.) or for marriage. Society had a schedule that flowed from the order of things. There was no written law, but the nature of these things was self-evident, as was dictated by the existence of men and their gathering. The oral culture did not seem to be equivocal, since the traditions and customs were handed down from generation to generation exactly as they are done in Judaic culture according to the written prescriptions of God transmitted to Moses. This impeccable way of living gave birth to African wisdom, as was the case with European, Asian or other wisdom. Moreover, textbooks have dedicated this expression of African wisdom. This wisdom is traced by Placide Tempels in Chapter 3 of the book "*la sagesse et la critériologie des bantous*" (Wisdom and Criterology of the Bantus"). He asserts that the wisdom of the Bantu is the penetrating view of nature, beings and forces. True wisdom is ontological knowledge (of being). The ancestors and elders are the depositories of this wisdom which comes from God, (*La philosophie bantoue* [Bantu philosophy], op.cit., Pg.50).

This African wisdom is conveyed by tales, proverbs, legends and myths. Ancient Greeks are not the only ones to have a mythology. They may have preserved it better than Africa. The Malian Hampâté Bâ, the great writer of African orality, has demonstrated this African wisdom in his poem Kaidara. The narrative that emerges from this poem is initiatory, because the narrated story leads to the price of a quest punctuated by hardships, to a knowledge hidden from the eyes of the common, and revealed to the one who shows his capacity to receive wisdom. Kaidara is a character known in the Mandingo epic, the founder of the Mali Empire, Sundiata Keita. Kaidara is the genius of knowledge to whom three characters, guided by a mysterious path (throughout an underground journey), are led. He is the one who uses his fortune to obtain knowledge that wins and gets what he wants. One recognises in him an ocean of wisdom and science and he is filled with joy. This initiating approach to knowledge shows that pursuit of science and wisdom is a privilege of all peoples and all cultures. When Europe came to meet Africa from the 15th century, it is this wise Africa that she found in front of her, gunpowder and its own specific inventions. European explorers recognised it themselves (Cheikh Anta Diop, op.cit.).

Wisdom is really an attribute of people. The divine wisdom granted to the people of Israel, which bestowed on Jesus Christ, the Asiatic wisdom and the African wisdom are the tangible proof. Human, moral and religious values are the prerogative of all peoples, with simply different densities, which certainly create different abilities in intelligence, wisdom and action.

Tonye Bakot in his book *Les proverbes bassa, pour une approche culturelle Mbene* (Bassa proverbs, for a Mbene cultural approach) (Édition du Schabel, 199 p), highlights all the themes of human and social life that emanate from these proverbs. He says they are found in all human societies and include friendship, assistance, fraternity, money, wealth, poverty, kindness, blessing, courage, effort, endurance, strength, consciousness, wisdom, intelligence, hate, spitefulness, caution, animals, hunting, food, teaching, education, commitment, determination, hope, fidelity, family, children, sex, weakness, danger, failure, generosity, gratuity, sharing, egoism, cunning, youth, old age, time, day, night, season, victory, strategy, peace, joy, happiness, solidarity, tolerance, health, disease, culture, tradition, society, customs, knowledge, technique, work, life, death, pain, suffering, truth and trust.

Victor Tonye Bakot stresses that proverbs belong to the heritage of humanity. They are found in most human groups with written or oral civilisation; it is a collective imagination made from wisdom that goes back to the dawn of time and which constitutes wisdom specific to each people. He gives some examples: in French and here translated to English (Victory without risk is triumph without glory or again, the heart has its reasons which reason knows nothing of, in Latin (simitis simili gandet: birds of a feather flock together), in Beti language (Nso ngon, ngul ai manyam: unity is strength), in bassa (Woo wada u nkan be jomb: a single hand does not tie a bundle). He recalls that these proverbs originate from two written civilisation languages and two other oral civilisation languages. They make it possible to search for the permanent quest for knowledge (op.cit., Pg.11-12).

Animism, which is the African religion, conveys this orderly philosophy of community life. This community life is exalted by president Paul Biya in his famous book *Pour le liberalisme communautaire* (Communal Liberalism), Éditions Marcel Favre, 1987,158 p. Animism exalts the spirit that is in action in natural phenomena and animal objects. This spirits include, the spirit of the forest, the spirit of water and the spirit of ancestors.

Animism comes from the Latin word animus, meaning "the Spirit". This religion is founded on the belief that nature is governed by spirits and that everything is governed by a spiritual entity (Le Point references May-June 2013, 96, op.cit.). This reference to the Spirit or to spirits is no stranger to Africa as concerns her relationship with God, as Placide Tempels also acknowledges in his book *La philosophie bantoue* (The Bantu Philosophy).

Animism is therefore a form of dynamic belief since it recognises the action of the spirit in the social life of man and in natural elements. That is why Cardinal Tumi opportunely recognises that the Gospel has brought a better light to the understanding and practice of our traditions and customs which also convey the notions of spirit, love, peace, justice, truth and wisdom. African wisdom has always made sense, in that, the respect for traditions and customs was not a fantasy. Offenders incurred or were subject to penalties proportionate to their errors. The reality of knowledge commands that it's vital for Africa to find this fundamental value of wisdom which is the expression of enlightened societies. That Africa should develop its animist religion which contains all the ferments of spiritual dynamism. Buddhism has become a religion because of the pure spiritual life of Buddha. Every belief that one raises towards pure and perfect dimension necessarily agrees with divinity. Christianity and Islam should not extinguish the African animist religion. All these sacred ways pursue the same goal, the fulfilment and happiness of man. They complement each other. Judaism, Christianity, Islam, Buddhism, Hinduism, Taoism, Animism are different ways of expressing divinity. All these voices complement each other and man, in the course of learning, finds a way of expression. That is why human beings of these different backgrounds are grouped in the United Nations and other universal bodies that use the same language: the discourse on humanisation processes.

In the light of the Holy Scriptures, Buddhist, Taoist, Hindu and Animist teachings, it can rightly be concluded that nothing solid can be done without the mastery of wisdom, intelligence and perfection which are the trademarks of God given generously to man and to every man without exception. What differentiates men and peoples lies in the various ways of appropriating these values. Those who take full ownership of them and make them their reference system do better, advance quickly and develop easily.

Chapter IV

Perfect fundamental values of human and terrestrial life for the development of Man in general and the African in particular. Man on earth, master of his destiny

Man has evolved little by little from ignorance and being in minority, to the illumination of knowledge. This is true, without any exception, for every man: European, Asian, African, American, and Arab. Perfect knowledge derived from God, as we have explained above, has been instrumental in man's education. This has been clearly demonstrated in the Western world and other continents including Africa.

This being the case, what themes must man take into account in order to achieve development within his living environment. Curiously enough, bearing in mind man's behaviour, he simply adds his own themes to those derived from the divine realm. Since man, is created in the image God, he has a divine task to develop the world, especially the earth on which he lives. In this way, man himself is a creator. To achieve this man is in needs, among others, knowledge, intelligence, wisdom, science, perfection, essential qualities bestowed by God. The characteristics man takes on from God are mostly designed to confer a pure conscience for awakening his mind, which is the energy that mobilises thought and cognitive forces as well as action. This energy of the Mind is a sort of fire that sustains and inspires all human actions. By going back up to God, man takes the measure of true and authentic knowledge as we have explained above. Thus, by associating divine knowledge founded on perfect truth to human knowledge that targets the same goal, we can acquire solid, comprehensive, circular and practical knowledge, bearing myriad fruits and efficiency. These two forms of knowledge are not paradoxical, they, on the contrary, complement each other in a beautiful synchronisation that thrusts man right into the realm of knowledge that enables the development of man. This human knowledge inspired by God and by man himself is centred on a wealth values. They include spiritual, intellectual, moral, ethics, aesthetics and sacred values. Values of education, training, research, secularism, creativity, invention, inventiveness and innovation. In another light there are cultural, civic and individual values, social and health values, political values, scientific values, technical and technological values, economic, managerial, material and financial values and finally values of success, satisfaction, life of abundance, happiness and bliss.

I- Spiritual, intellectual, ethical, moral, aesthetic and sacred values

These values instil in man a pure conscience thanks to their sacred and divine qualities. They are derived directly from the creator. In this way, man takes a true measure of knowledge from the creator of life to become a creator as well. These values transform man into the image of God and his likeness, to acquire divine nature. This includes: life, the mind, knowledge, intelligence, wisdom, love, holiness, perfection, purity, perfect capacity, good, goodness, honesty, integrity, devotion, justice and equality, virtue, faith, fidelity, truth and rigour, temperance, moderation, tolerance, peace, patience, humility, simplicity, nobility, peace and harmony, dignity, honour, beauty, aesthetic, inspiring, glory, magnificence, generosity, uplifting of the soul, majesty, happiness, perseverance, firmness, recklessness, courage, solidity, permanence, stability, positive thinking, maximum capacity, force, strength, dream, vision, self-control and many other related values. The fruits and powers of the mind confer a clear and crystalline conscience. Societies that grasp this truth make them their highly-valued sacred moral charter. This gives them a healthy and methodical reasoning ability, given that they are illuminated by divine light. This is the deep spiritual wealth of knowledge that enlightens the human mind, in other to fit it into the logic of intelligence, true wisdom and creative invention, and confer to the mind all its power, in terms of methodology, rational and scientific approach for achieving political, economic, social and cultural development. These values are a true light that illuminates man to render him creative, inventive, imaginative and prospective, for man has wide horizons and can see very far. He is not sterile, inactive, apathetic or immobile. He is fully proactive.

1- Primacy of life, the Mind, knowledge, intelligence, wisdom in human life and development

Knowledge, intelligence and wisdom are the cornerstones of life and development. In the section on the divine world, we have expounded on their source and importance, that they stem from God and His perfection. This extends to a point where God has bestowed on man an infinite creative knowledge because God has equally made man a god in his image and likeness. In this regard, the Mind is the engine of man's life and thought. It's this mind that mobilises thought, leads to knowledge, intelligence and wisdom. Nothing can be achieved in development and the human set up without this triptych.

As we have explained above, God gave a full definition of knowledge to man to the extent that man made good use of it. The definition given by man only complements it without overriding it. We could even confine ourselves to the definition of knowledge by God. A form of knowledge that inexorably leads to truth, intelligence and wisdom. It is the application of perfect values in life for success in a blessed life.

Thus, human wisdom added to that of God affords man an unmatched understanding of the realities of life. The explanations of knowledge, intelligence and wisdom developed in the divine realm shed full light on these original values. They definitely clarify the approach that can be adopted thereof in life. Knowledge, intelligence and wisdom are therefore at the centre of development issues. This implies that structures tasked with transmitting these perfect values must be solid: family, religious, school, academic, vocational and social structures. They must convey strong values embraced by all. It is worth recalling that the two forms of knowledge are complementary: natural human knowledge and supernatural as well as divine knowledge. These two forms constitute a full and global knowledge. They offer full understanding of the natural and terrestrial, and the celestial and divine realities. These two forms of knowledge are indispensable and inseparable for an exhaustive and perfect perception of life. This life must pave the way to development and comfort. The human mind as a result plays an instrumental role in the acquisition and mobilisation of knowledge.

The human spirit, driving force behind subjugating knowledge, intelligence, wisdom and mainstreaming thinking

The human spirit (the mind) stems from the Spirit of God. And we have proven all its might. It is the driving force and principle of life. There is no life, without the spirit. The body is nothing but matter that is mortal. It is only a recipient and host of the Mind.

Le Pétit Larousse defines the Mind as a vital immaterial principle, an incorporeal substance. It is the principle of thought, of intellectual activity and intelligence. In fact, it is an energy, an internal force that mobilises man's thoughts so that he can conceive all what he thinks. It is the breath of life breathed into man by God to make of him a living being (Genesis 2.7). This breath is the spirit and this spirit is consubstantial with the nature of man, it is the engine of life. Even in the Bible, the spirit is symbolised by breath. Thus, man is also flesh and spirit, which confers on him duality. This reasoning enables man to understand the universe in which he lives, to comprehend the universe in its diversity, in order to best subjugate it. This immaterial power is opposed to matter, it is not visible to the naked eye, contrary to matter. Even though the two main components of man, life and the universe are the spirit and matter. This key comprehension guides all knowledge regarding all the options of man for his harmonious advancement. When this energy, the spirit, is under the control of God, the human being acquires the divine spirit called the Holy Spirit, which is a superior force that multiplies human capacities borne by their paroxysm, the omega. The regenerated human being becomes a new creature, a new man endowed with superior powers. This superior Mind regenerates the corrupt and soiled nature of man and grants him better clarification on human and divine realities, so that he can acquire the supreme knowledge that leads to artistic, technical, scientific and technological creation. For, all said and done, it is this new superior and creative man who develops science and technology, which is equally spiritual knowledge to analyse matter and transform it. This powerful energy mobilises human strength in thorough thinking about ideal solutions for any difficult situation, and complex development issues in particular. This new man who possesses the divine spirit therefore has all the assets to spearhead development. Njoh Mouelle believes so too, as he affirms that development must be concerned with promoting the advent of a particular type of man: the creator[2].

The spirit (Mind) is therefore at the heart of any dynamic system of creativity and progress. It is essentially in motion, it is contrary to immobilisation and inertia. It does everything, capable of everything, influences everything and probes everything. It is really the right way to successfully acquire knowledge, intelligence and wisdom, the

[2] Ebénézer Njoh Mouelle, *De la Médiocrité à l'excellence. Essai sur la signification humaine du développement*, CLE, 1988, pg.8.

principal avenues towards development. That is why Plato posits that the true universe is that of the intelligible which gives primacy to ideas on the tangible world. Platonism actually prunes soul/body dualism, that is, the spirit/matter. This primacy of spirit/matter is as old as the world. Understanding it clearly and perfectly, so as to use it as clue in the appropriation of skills, constitutes a giant step towards comprehension of the truth and logic of thinking. It is the fire of the spirit that transforms matter, so we can imagine all the energy needed by the spirit to become a lever that elevates and transforms matter. This is actually a revolution in the thought for true knowledge which is the vector of development. Those who study and develop the spirit capacity know that, for the spirit to attain its maximum capacity to dominate matter, it must generate a power ratio in the spirit to the tune of 70, or even 80% in order to perfectly transform matter. In this ratio, matter in all its mass only represents 20 to 30% power. In other words, knowledge must have a power that far surpasses matter to be able to transform it with the abovementioned ratios. That is why we talk of 80:20 or 70:30 ratios. The human body itself is the matter hosting the spirit (mind). Any human society that fails to discern this difference or spirit/matter complementarity with the strong dominance of the spirit, would find it really difficult to cultivate a logic of perfect knowledge and consequently development. French writer, Saint Exupéry most suitably stated that it is the breath of the spirit on matter that transforms it. The mind has an eternal capacity, it opens up infinitely, it is not as static as matter, that is why its capacity to act is maximal and it can act permanently on matter. God, the Creator of everything, determined the dimension and global knowledge that concerns all terrestrial and celestial knowledge in this famous formula whereby, He is the Alpha and the Omega. Only the mind has this immortal and infinite elasticity. This omega point opens the door to infinite knowledge and creativity. That is why great philosophers of all times developed the thinking dialectic and placed it at the centre of human activity. The mind, which is a permanent movement of thought and action, is at the heart of dynamic and successful societies. It constantly mobilises more energies in a movement that is ever ascending and creative. When President Jacques Chirac declared, during the France-Africa Summit of Yaounde in 2004, that Africa consumes more than it produces, or when President Paul Biya, condemned immobility and inertia in the Cameroonian society, this, as a matter of fact, referred to the same reality: the mind is yet to realise its full potential in African societies. The primacy of the mind over matter is yet to be total and even well understood. So long as this situation persists, spiritual, intellectual and creative mobility will remain poor. Immobility and inertia will continue to dominate, alongside poor and low creativity and innovation. God, the creator of everything, is a mere Spirit. That is why he is eternal, immortal and almighty. It is equally a revealed mystery. The human spirit of man is also a creator because it can elevate itself to the divine dimension. It for this reason that, when we imitate God by conducting an in-depth study of his gospel, we understand this fundamental truth, which releases and mobilises all positive and even hyper positive energies. The mind has an incredible and a simply unthinkable power. It is a great mystery that has stayed hidden for long or even unknown to men, but today, it has been unravelled. It therefore allows man to better appraise the reality of the Spirit, such as to develop it as an instrumental vector of life and development of human societies.

The mind thus allows understanding of superior and sublime, natural and celestial truisms. It absorbs everything, especially fundamental truisms, the vector of any true knowledge. These fundamental truisms set man free from ignorance, obscurantism, fatality and from all limitations that obstruct valuable changes. Such is the spirit of renaissance in Europe and European enlightenment of the 18th century that accounted for the continent's boom and the outstanding development that has succeeded right up to this 21st century. Thought always precedes action, the verb, that is, thought is at the origin of any creative process. As we can read in the Bible: in the beginning was the Word, the Word was God, without Him nothing was made that was made (Jean 1: 13). Greeks of the Antiquity, known for their wisdom, appropriated the famous and symbolic term "Logos". This Greek term is nowadays used in reference to the quest for rationality. In Greek, depending on the context, it may mean: speech, language, dialect, words, reason, intelligence, foundation, principle, motive, proportion, calculation, report, relation, story, thesis, reasoning, argument, explanation, statement, proposition, phrase, definition, etc.[3] African orality in African societies was a form of logos, since it served in every communication and conservation of customs and traditions. Orality is also word or logos.

---

[3]*Le Point Références*, July – August 2011, op.cit., pg. 100.

The mind streamlines thought in a coherent, logical, precise and organised logic such as to generate ideas and fine-tune themes. In philosophy, structure is an ordered and autonomous abstract set of independent elements, whose relations are governed by laws, serving as intelligibility model of the objects studied in diverse sciences. Logic stems from logos, it is the science of reasoning per se, of coherence and common sense.

Other spiritual systems have, with more or less exactitude, developed this spirit/matter duality: Islam with Mohamed, Buddhism with Buddha, Hinduism and animism. This superior and spiritual knowledge can elevates the human being to the realms of mysticism, which is nothing but a communion with God and the absolute. It gives the understanding of the mysteries of life and mitigates vagaries and chance to the maximum, to set man on the path of certainties. These spiritual systems constitute fundamental realities, without which nothing substantial can be achieved. They explain the meaning of life as Shimon Peres, former Israeli president, opportunely stated. Philosophers of the Antiquity excelled in this approach. Because of the effective results it produces, this spiritual power has magical impact. Magic is considered here as the desire to undertake positive actions and practice superior and sublime values.

In this intellectual and spiritual approach, ancient Greece set the pace with great minds and philosophers of all times: Plato, Aristotle, Socrates, Aristophanes, Zenon of Elea, Herodotus, Epicurus, Zenon of Kiton, Hippocrates, Pythagoras, Solon, Thales of Miletus, Demosthenes and many others. From Ancient Rome we have Ciceron, Tacitus, Virgiles, Horatius, Ovid, Tite-Live. Nowadays, African thinkers are equally following this laudable path. From Cameroon, Ebénézer Njoh Mouellé, Marcien Towa, Abwa Daniel, Engelbert Mveng, Mongo Beti, Jacques Fame Ndongo, Achille Bembe, Christian Tumi, Bakot, Njami Nwandi Simon Bolivar, Jean Marc Ela, Eboussi Boulaga, Calixte Beyala and many other. From Senegal, Léopold Sédar Senghor and Cheikh Anta Diop. From Nigeria, Wole Soyinka, Chinua Achebe and from Burkina Faso, historian Joseph Ki-Zerbo. From Ivory Coast- Cheikh Hamidou Kane, Bernard Dadié, etc. Great minds are also found in all other areas of human activity. In politics there are great political monuments like Kwame Nkrumah, Nelson Mandela, in industries there is Dangote. In music we remember Manu Dibango, Youssou Ndour and in sports, the Cameroonian footballer, Roger Milla.

Senegalese film-director Sembene Ousmane and his compatriot, sculptor Ousmane Sow. There exist some great industrial captains and African artists who enrich this gallery of great minds.

This spiritual bee-hive enabled Europe to become a cultural, artistic, scientific and technological centre. Rendered discoveries possible from the 15th to the 21st century. The survival of Africa depends on the capturing of this spiritual dimension that would help the continent to kick-start its renaissance, for it would adopt the driving force, which is the mind. This power of the mind would enable the continent to successfully garner the dormant energies of its people, such that primacy of the mind should finally set in, as is the case in the West and increasingly in Asia. Deng Xiaoping, successor of Mao Tse Tung, was wont to saying that Mao was 70% good and only 30% evil. In other words, Mao was a great mind who mastered the perfect values. He is the architect of modern China.

When the mind is weak, control of matter is also weak. That is why the inertia that still characterises minds and actions in Africa are deplored. Africa has to undertake its spiritual revolution, that of thinking, Promethean and Copernician, to appropriate the powerful and valuable fire of the mind. Such revolution would lead to a spiritual adjustment in the educational, scientific, technological, civic, cultural, economic, political and social systems. This will lead towards enlightened pinnacles and realms of knowledge and practice. To achieve this, Africa needs well-trained human resources, capable of meeting all challenges of development, because their knowledge is perfect, certain and complete. This is the path of man the creator, the Homo Deus, man-god. In this regard, some strong values set man on the track of this spiritual evolution that we intend to describe below, such values include love, purity, perfection, integrity, justice, truth, dignity, bliss, etc.

2- Love

God gave a perfect definition of love. Love is the link of perfection and the fundamental value in all His teachings. Man has also made it a fundamental value. How beautiful it is to utter this word, how sweet is it and it is evocative of so many delights. That is why it is also a value at the centre of life and development-oriented issues. It is the link of perfection between the divine and man as well as between man and man.

Love is thus a deep feeling that pushes one person towards another or towards a divinity, or inversely a divinity towards man. It is the supreme virtue, that virtue in which the human being finds fulfilment in a perfect and total manner, which is expressed in his full social life, in this case, we would talk of bliss, which is the asymptotic line, the crest line, the pinnacle of such fulfilment. As a powerful and overbearing feeling, love stimulates man, his spiritual, intellectual, moral, physical and civic qualities. Love makes of the citizen, a noble being, a patriot committed to the good social cause, we can then talk of patriotism, which is love for the fatherland. Love makes man to excel, for man recognises in the other a being identical to himself, towards whom he must express affection, compassion and comprehension. It is a major value at the service of his neighbour and for development.

Love rejects conflicts, enmities, quarrels, jealousy, divisions, useless and sterile complexes. Such love, whether it's according to the Greek expression philia (feeling of friendship), agape (love of God for man) or Latin (caritas, charity), frees man from fatality, withdrawal, egoism, wickedness, arrogance, pride, hatred, which are mind-numbing and anaesthetic feelings. These feelings block any impulse of generosity and service towards fellowman. This is detrimental to developmental issues and offer no possibility for full development. Such love for the good of the other, altruism, brings us closer to the evangelical and spiritual definition in all its glory. It is really the greatest virtue. The love highly sought by man however remains a permanent quest for him who finds it difficult to appropriate this fundamental value. Love is a catalyst for the human mind, which is corrupted and often drained by narrow-minded wickedness and egoism. These ills, contrary to love, provoke deviant behaviours. Such deviance is the source of so many ills that plague man: injustice, favouritism, hardening of the heart, effortlessness, dishonesty, theft, cheating, shortcuts and all sorts of permissiveness. The absence of love has disastrous consequences on the evolution of human beings; it drains the heart which is the seat of the noblest feelings; it strips them of any fertile humanity that would have elevated them right up to the divine, to plunge them into the abyss of animality, ignorance and indignity. This love, philia or agape, is opposed to Eros which is solely a carnal desire.

Considered in its dynamic meaning, love elevates man and transports him progressively towards the realms of truth, knowledge and total fulfilment. By practising love for divine and the love for fellowman, we can really place ourselves at the service of one another and humanity with great zeal. That is why some people create charity organisations at the service of others, and even those who create lucrative ventures, make judicious use of human resources and perform useful work, conducive to development. This is the case of certain wealthy people who channel part of their fortune into charity: Rockfeller, Bill Gates, Fotso Victor and many others. This includes multiple undertakings by charity associations.

By practising this love with joy and relaxation, we can reach the realms of bliss, we can tackle life in its ascending, descending and cross-sectional dimensions, understand the height, depth, length and width of things. In this elated state, development can really find a fertile ground. Such spiritual, intellectual and moral elevation leads the human being to fundamental issues of life and development, and affords him eternal inspiration. Philosophers have brainstormed at length on this theme, be it: Plato, Jean Jacques Rousseau, Spinoza, Descartes, Hegel, Jean Paul Sartre, Kant, Pascal, and Martin Luther King (in his book, *I have a dream*).[4] The same applies to us in our Order of Perfect Fundamental Values, (OVAFOPAC) - its French acronym. It equally obtains in religions that constitute a central theme: Judaism, Christianity, Buddhism, Islam, Hinduism, and Animism.[5]

Love must therefore be understood in its practical and concrete dimension in view of a vibrant, powerful and constantly renewed action to bring out the best in man. If this praxis of love inspires thought and daily actions, the possibilities for progress in human societies in general and Africans in particular, would be immense. In this exalting and galvanising posture, there is always a solution to problems encountered. We must therefore get into the ideal position and be guided by the powerful catalyst that love incarnates. It is a binder, oil that lubricates

---

[4] Plato, *Le banquet*, in Revue le Point philosophie, testez-vous 500 questions pour tester vos connaissances pg. 86.

- Émile Rousseau : *Discours sur les fondements de l'origine des inégalités parmi les hommes, confessions.*
- René Descartes, *Le traité des passions de l'âme*, published in 1649.
- Saint Thomas d'Aquin, *Somme théologique*, Ibid., pg. 87.
- Jean Paul Sartre, *L'existentialisme est un humanisme ; L'être et le néant.*
- Emmanuel Kant, *Fondements de la métaphysique des mœurs*; *L'anthropologie d'un point de vue pratique*, Ibid., pg. 87-88.

[5] *Le monde des religions*, March-April, 2012, « L'amour au cœur du christianisme et du bouddhisme », pg. 81.

feelings, ennobles feelings, and lifts feelings to render those who take hold of it, active, available and constantly listening to others. That is why the gospel describes these theological virtues as perfect binders, the fulfilment of the whole divine law and the most important. We can therefore conclude that it should also be at the heart of the development of human societies and not the reverse. Love and forgiveness have enabled Africa and Africans to overcome the bitterness caused by the trauma of slavery, colonialism and exploitation. The African Church, full of the gospel message played a prime role therein.

3- Purity, perfection, holiness, honesty, integrity, piety, freedom, virtue

We have said it earlier that, people tend to believe that these qualities are unique only to God or gods. Those who believe so are horribly wrong because these qualities are also attributable to humans, for they inspire them to live a moral and practical life, devoid of blemishes, corruption, aberrations, permissiveness, impurities, imperfections that alter the beautiful human nature. This spiritual, intellectual and moral rigidity is ideal to better capture creative inspirations, a nature bereft of default. It also contributes to perfection and excellence of man who is made in the image of God and who must search for these virtues to attain the perfect stature of God. But in reality, these virtues are preserved for all those aspiring to excel in their activities and lives. These qualities compel man to distinguish himself through a straightforward, honest and perfect social behaviour, by conforming to the moral rules of probity, loyalty and fidelity. Perfection, purity and virtue are qualities that humans and Africans in particular, must seek to cultivate in their effort towards development. These virtues can lift man to the realms of illumination of the mind and knowledge. During the European classical era, preference was for an honest man, that is an accomplished man, a cultured mind and who was ideal in that era. This reality should still be valuable nowadays. Puritans were behind the birth of the United States at the beginning of the 17th century. They sailed across the Atlantic Ocean to live in the new continent, driven by their strong convictions based on fundamental values of purity, holiness, piety, integrity and hard work. The early settlers were theocratic like at the beginning of the biblical period when man was guided by God. Driven by these convictions, they dreamt of creating a new world as John Winthrop proclaimed in a famous sermon, "model of Christian charity", better known under the name, "city upon a hill". It is this mystical and mythic vision that inspired the American dream that has driven the different generations of this great country. These puritans dreamt of building a paradise on earth. This dream was later transformed into an ambition to construct the greatest, the most powerful, the most admirable country in the world, where people would be stronger, more beautiful, in better health than elsewhere and where those who give in their effort can succeed. This dream became a reality in less than two centuries.[6] Protestant countries of Northern Europe (Denmark, Sweden, Norway, and Finland) practice the same virtues and have flattering classifications in the index of development and corruption, for they occupy the first positions as the least corrupt countries in the world. They feature among the most industrialised countries and have a very effective social safety network. In these puritan societies forged by rigorous religious and moral values, deceit is a defect that is severely cracked down on. If well understood and assimilated, these values breed men of solid moral and spiritual virtues and obviously healthy societies.

The canonisation of Mother Teresa (born Agnes Gonxha Bojaxhiu) founder of the congregation of Missionaries of the Charity by Pope Francis, 4 September 2016, is testimony of her holy, pure and perfect life. Back in 2003 during her benediction, Pope John Paul II extolled her as an indefatigable benefactress of humanity. In her fight for the underprivileged, she aimed at procuring love for individuals in agony (Cameroon Tribune No. 11173 of 6 September 2016, pg. 48).

4- Justice and equity

God says His throne is founded on justice and equity. The true measure of these values is given. Justice is the maximum capacity to respect the rights of every citizen. It is a moral principle that acts in view of equity, which virtue consists in being fair and respecting the rights of others. It is equally a sovereign State duty to define substantive laws and to resolve disputes between citizens liable to the law. It is action by which an authority, a judiciary power recognises the right of every one. It is a system, an administration striving for the respect of established rights. Justice is as a result a principal axis designed to regulate the smooth function of human communities, be they relations between individuals, between individuals and diverse public or private

[6] Le Journal *Le Point* hors-série. « Faits et mythes »: March – April 2012 pg. 84.

institutions or even between the latter. Justice protects the weakest against the strongest, it restores the rights of every citizen answerable to law. In this light, it plays an important role in restoring the truth. Its contribution to political, economic, social, legal and cultural development is indisputable. A good judicial system helps to resolve disputes between liable economic citizens, for a smooth functioning of free competition and rules of the game. It is a defence against all forms of disorder and escalation detrimental to the equilibrium and firmness of the society. To accuse someone who is right and acknowledge as right someone who is wrong, is an extremely bad justice, as certain African States often do where the notion of a judicial power, independent from the executive power, is only still creeping in progressively. Justice that is worthy of its name can only be effective if we succeed to institute a balance of powers as Montesquieu recommended in the 18th century, that is, between executive, legislative and judicial powers because once one of the powers wields excessive authority over the other two, risks of abuse become inevitable. Nowadays, all political systems tend, more or less, to follow this path of separation of powers. Africa is equally joining the bandwagon. The advent of the International Court of Justice (ICJ) with its avatars of a double standard justice decried by African countries, all the same, reflects a desire not to condone the impunity covering large-scale crimes, as had been the case unfortunately. Courage requires that we constantly strive towards greater balance of powers, in order to achieve a justice bereft of any archaism, in view of greater freedom and total fulfilment of man. In Africa, this Rule of Law is gradually being put in place. This Rule of Law protects the rights and freedoms of individuals.

In sum, justice helps to combat a situation where only the strongest prevail. This has been explored by authors like John Locke, Thomas Hobbes, and Jean Jacques Rousseau, who proposed alternatives in the form of hypotheses on the forging of a political society.[7] Whereas, the modern State takes us further away from it every day. An effectively implemented justice leads to peace and the harmonious development of a society.

---

[7] Thomas Hobbes, *The Leviathan,* 1651.
John Locke, *Essay on civil government,* 1690.
Jean Jacques Rousseau, *Du contrat social,* 1762.

5- Truth, rigour, fidelity

Truth is often distorted by man. It cannot, however, be ignored and it must be told with all its force, to produce the desired effect. God is the truth: why is man seeking to distort the truth?

Truth is what conforms to reality, to the certainty that we have about a given situation. It is knowledge that conforms to reality, which obtains general consent. Living in truth is a cardinal virtue in the life of human societies that are well-organised and forged on spiritual and moral values, less influenced by corruption and perversion. This enviable situation allows for real strides towards development, for we go straight to the point and the essential. This situation allows for things to be done exactly the way they should be done, and not otherwise. Truth is a stimulant to intelligence and wisdom and even their product. It seeks for accuracy, precision, reliability, certainty, rigour, a great intellectual exigency, which all enlighten a clear vision of development options. Truth contributes to perfect execution of projects. Not seeking the truth or an attempt to ignore it or skirt it, and to create unfavourable situations are attitudes that produce poor results. It must be said that truth is at the heart of development, for truth is a well-constructed road, hydro-power dam, building, it is the act of conforming to the prior specifications defined and established for proper execution of the project, such that all experienced observers should ascertain that the project is well executed, according to principles of good practice, solidity, durability, stability, aesthetics and harmony. Thus, this virtue is essential to the execution of projects, essential to the welfare of populations, as is often witnessed in Africa or elsewhere. This absence of truth creates confusion and twists results in the execution of social projects.

In reality, poor execution or substandard execution, does not lead to the truth known, expected and desired. Truth is the perfect norm, the reference sought. It is thus obvious that each time we abide by the truth, we stay on the right direction, that which is fair, ideal, enlightening and obtains the approval of all for the good of all. To practise the truth constitutes a high sense of honesty, integrity, dignity and honour, it is the hallmark of great societies and great men, who have understood the meaning of things and of true life. The view therefore that all these perfect fundamental values are a mere evangelical preaching is completely flawed and stems from ignorance. Rigour is also akin to intellectual exigency and great accuracy. It paves the way for fidelity, which is a disposition and a resolution to seek the truth and accuracy.

6- Dignity, honour, greatness, nobility, sublimity, glory, magnificence, majesty, bliss

It could be assumed that these values are known, but are they acquired, Possessed or are they well assimilated and internalised? Nothing can be taken for granted. Nothing serious, durable, solid can be done without them, they are the practice of a form of ascetism that keeps away the narrow-minded feelings of egoism, withdrawal, cupidity, corruption, wickedness, ignorance, as well as all feelings that debase and downgrade. They broaden the horizon of vision and constitute strong motivations, they enrich man's mind, affording him energy that is constantly renewed. We know of no strong Nations, staunch men and women, winners without these galvanising capacities. Their daily practice render them creative, imaginative, inventive. They strive to have a permanent panoramic vision, bearer of solutions. They render one generous, affable, courteous, well-groomed, respectful, polite and confer elegant manners and the capacity to always fine-tune actions. All what is undertaken with this spirit generates good deeds. These values culminate into sublimity derived from the sublime. The sublime is what stems from a high moral, intellectual and artistic value, which is kind of perfect, marvellous, the highest state in feelings and style.

Contrary to common believe, nobility, dignity, honour, glory, influence, majesty are not the preserve of certain persons, certain people, continents, or even a skin colour. These are spiritual virtues to forge, cultivate, perfect, in view of enlightening attitudes and behaviours. Every African stands to benefit from imbibing these enriching values to depart from the beaten tracks of the approximate, pseudo-values and of all the disorders noted in our countries. It is only in greatness that great things are achieved. Let us not be afraid of seeking for greatness. This superior life can only lead to happiness, which is a state of satisfaction and bliss. Happiness really exists contrary to what some people claim. It is dynamic and maybe that is why some do not see it. There is a point "P" from which when the spiritual and material conditions are gathered, one claims to be happy. It is not perception of the mind, some people have clearly experimented it and do bear testimony. When one is in such realm, one is on the brink of bliss. Note that bliss is the state of a fulfilled person. This is the state we desire for African citizens, for whom we are conducting this study.

We are convinced that this is the only way possible to forge man the creator and developer.

The jubilee of Queen Elisabeth, celebrating her sixtieth year of rule in 2014, flaunted before the eyes of the world, the splendour and glory of a monarch and a country, Great Britain, which has developed in their history, values of greatness, nobility, majesty, honour, dignity, wisdom and perspicacity. The flaunting of the splendour observed is a reflection and an image of a people who have successfully developed these high values. Seeking and practising these values enhances man and his society. These values glorify man and constantly push him to excel. They confer respect, consideration and admiration.

7- Beauty and aesthetic

Beauty and aesthetic are values not well-developed in Africa nowadays, compared to certain continents where they play a very important role. The ugliness of our towns, our neighbourhoods, and sometimes of our homes says a lot on the little consideration granted to these values. To understand these values and cherish them, a high spiritual dimension must be developed, for beauty and aesthetic are, above all, of spiritual essence. A beautiful landscape, a beautiful painting is first admired by the mind. Anything beautiful attracts and inspires admiration. Beauty incarnates what is noble, fine and sublime, which is remarkable in terms of its importance, which conforms to propriety. Beauty is the trait of what is intellectually and morally worthy of admiration and interest, which procures total satisfaction. Any beautiful thing speaks for itself, one has to know how to admire it so as to know how to conserve it as such, or even improve it. The fact that the dimension of what is beautiful and good is not always perceived objectively in our countries poses problems of creativity in our societies that are running out of fertile imagination. In our construction plans for diverse infrastructures, beauty is apparently not sufficiently taken into account, for beauty is founded on respect of norms: light, forms, colours, lines, finishing, harmony, aeration, solidity, judicious choice of material. The culture of beauty stems from training and a resolve to impose it. When a work of art respects universally recognised canons, it can only be beautiful. The beautiful African masks and statues found in our museums and in great African and Europeans museums, have nothing to envy from paintings of Picasso, Michelangelo or Leonardo da Vinci. If well mastered and well expressed, beauty culminates into the sublime. Plato extolled beautiful souls, beautiful thoughts, beautiful actions, and beautiful bodies in an ancient Greece that sought and practised perfection. Beauty must be perceived in our constructions and other realisations, to render our towns and our villages attractive, for our comfort and to the delight of our minds. It is merely an expression of spiritual elevation.

8- Faith and self-confidence

Faith is the firm assurance in what we search and wish to accomplish, it is the true and clear knowledge of the path trodden. The best successes are those founded on solid faith, forged on convictions and unshakable knowledge. Faith relies on the discernment of things, it follows the path of common sense, sense that is good and must lead to good solutions and good results. Under no circumstance, can ignorance or ignorance of the obvious realities of life lead us there. Africa must therefore avail itself of this clear vision of things founded on mastery of fundamental values, which are obvious highways to positive results. Uncertainty is proscribed when we aspire for better days. Good assumptions and hypotheses are the right way. Faith enlightened by true, tried and tested knowledge leads to victory, to satisfaction of the best thought intentions. A healthy faith allows one to be able to count on self and others. Africa cannot minimise this beautiful capacity that is the reservation of those who have solid and established convictions. Such faith leads to happiness, to best choices and decisions. Faith draws inspiration from proven ways, systems of thought and organisation that are the weakest in the world, be they philosophical, religious, cultural, political and economic, or European, African, Asian or others. These movements provide a positive orientation in the efforts of human beings towards innovative and revolutionary values, those that have as end-result the preservation of the human species and not its destruction. Africans need these certainties, they must by themselves also contribute to the development of these dynamic and powerful values, which alone is capable of setting and bringing them towards the pinnacles of thought, knowledge and achievements, whose credibility, reliability and pertinence are recognised by all. This faith and unshakable self-confidence can place Africans at the centre of world challenges and not on its periphery, as is apparently still the case nowadays. It's faith founded on the illuminations of knowledge, which leads to true and lasting development. The divine and philosophical systems that set enlightening norms are of great help in this quest.

9- Peace and harmony

All politicians or Statesmen or even any other credible person will agree on the fact that nothing solid, serious and durable can be achieved without peace. Peace is a state of calm, serenity and harmony between individuals, communities or States. It is also the absence of hostility, war and trouble. Peace implies that the different actors in a society and different institutions are working in real complementarity and harmony, since each element effectively keeps to the role agree upon by the different parties. It is the desire to dominate that creates conflict situations, which disrupt peace. The culture of peace and respect for others must be cultivated among members of the society. Cameroon is today known to be a country of peace within an environment often beleaguered by unrest. This situation must persist to enable efforts made towards development produce concrete results. That is the price to pay for the development of our African societies. Peace can prosper with a progression of knowledge and positive action of all, at national, regional and international levels. Africa has gone through a lot of trouble to resolve the multiple conflicts that afflicted the continent: the Congolese crisis in 1960, the Biafra war in Nigeria in 1970, the Erythrea war in Ethiopia that led to the birth of two States, Ethiopia and Erythrea, the war in Sudan that also ended with the birth of two States, South Sudan and Sudan. Great efforts are being made in Congo-Kinshasa, today, to restore peace in that country, just like in Somalia, in the Central African Republic, Mali, etc. International and regional organisations are sparing no efforts in sanctioning belligerents who obstruct the peace process. Whereas peace or its maintenance, wherever it is disrupted can be restored through dialogue between the protagonists, which requires listening to one another. President Paul Biya, when receiving Mrs Irina BOKOVA, Director General of UNESCO in Cameroon, on 16th September 2014, extolled peace and dialogue in these eloquent terms: "Lasting peace cannot be imposed, it is built and lived daily by mutual acceptance and tolerance which lead to and promote dialogue. Since wars begin in the minds of men, it is in the minds of men that the defences of peace must be constructed". Peace promotes harmony which creates reconciliation, understanding, conciliation of feelings, ideas between several persons and societies.

10- Humility, moderation, temperance, tolerance

A wise man once declared that humility comes before glory. It enables humans to have a true measure of each other, to accept one's own qualities and flaws, to get the correct measure of challenges, bereft of any arrogance and subtlety. It also enables humans to best assess the situations they face, to be able to find befitting solutions thereof. Contrary to what is commonly believed, humility elevates, rather than demeans man. At no time, should one be overwhelmed by a misleading exhalation, even in the face of success, for success means new challenges to go even further. The pride, arrogance that precedes a downfall are the exact opposite of humility. Pride, arrogance lays one open to a wrong analysis that culminates into poor hypotheses and conclusions.

Likewise, moderation, temperance and tolerance are the corollary of humility, given that they keep any excessive attitude at bay, they lead to discernment of the positions to be adopted. In general, wisdom calls for moderation and tolerance in every situation. Moderation allows for an objective analysis of challenges, it encourages realism, compromise, acceptance of others. Wisdom is essentially marked by moderation, temperance, comprehension and conciliation.

11- Patience, perseverance, firmness, audacity, courage, voluntarism

Development cannot put up with favouritism, laxity, tinkering, lack of seriousness, discipline and courage. It demands working on the duration, medium and long term. In other words, development requires patience, the capacity to find a way to achieve results; perseverance and commitment which are constancies in sustained and relentless action; audacity, which is the courage to face the most complex and unexpected situations; courage that is the strength of character, steadfastness in the face of any difficult, or even extreme situation. Time is a factor linked to development, when not properly taken into account, there is risk of precipitation and getting entrapped in unpleasant situations. That is why there is a saying that to conquer with no risk, is to triumph without glory or even that he who goes slowly goes steadily (*qui va piano va sano*).

12- Solidity, permanence, stability and the rock

Building on something solid, stable, on what lasts always procures genuine satisfaction. There is a stock-phrase whereby you should build on rock and not on sand, a way of seeking all these values of truth, peace, love, honesty, seriousness, justice, dignity, intelligence, wisdom, which necessarily lead to putting in place things that last, which can resist bad weather, shocks, the ups and downs of life. Whenever we follow that path, whatever we undertake is founded on an immovable and an unalterable rock. Whatever follows contrary paths, of permissiveness, chance, approximation, negligence, corruption, confusion, cannot result in anything durable, permanent, solid or stable. Structures, constructions, spiritual and material edifices that resist vagaries are those that opt for these positive highways and that testify the pertinence of their choice and their usage. Things in Africa do not always follow these highways, it is not surprising therefore to find roads with gaping holes, newly erected structures ridden with cracks, plans drawn and immediately discarded. One cannot lay it on with a trowel, Africa must develop a culture of solid and eternal fundamental values, anything artificial, temporary, ephemeral is essentially fragile and ridiculous.

13- Good, positive thinking

Good is good as a common saying goes, and always doing good generates good things. The culture and practice of doing good confers onto whoever does it and the beneficiary a constant feeling of comfort, satisfaction and happiness. The Bible stresses on the act of always doing good and never getting tired of doing good. Good thus conforms to the idea that one has about what is excellent, perfect and satisfactory. Good expresses the idea of strong moral qualities. This virtue is at the heart of any system that functions properly, that respects the rigid norms of action, in view of enriching results. In doing good, all wheels of the society function wonderfully, they intermingle consistently and in a well-deserved synergy. In such ambiance of cohesion in a well-oriented action, a community has chances of magnifying its results in an exponential manner. Doing good automatically has as corollary, wellbeing. Anyone who takes up this action affords himself the opportunity of a happy life. In such logical life perspective, success is guaranteed. Optimism, the tendency to believe that all is well in life, strengthens this attitude of doing good. This dynamic attitude culminates into positive thinking. It embodies all what is beautiful, exalting, and sublime for a salutary action. It embodies kindness, generosity, altruism, justice, truth which are virtues of great men and people. This positive thinking transforms whoever practises it, into influential agents of development, away from the cautious attitudes marked by egoism, withdrawal, refusal to serve or offering poor service to others.

Positive thinking institutes a completely new paradigm that prompts genuine change in mentality in order to cast aside defeatism, fatality and all forms of blockages. Positive thinking generates solutions and abounds with dynamic formulas.

14- Maximum capacity, perfect capacity, strength

Maximum capacity is the ability to carry an effort to the end, an arduous effort, the path followed to obtain the result expected, since one gives the best of oneself. Such effort is first spiritual, intellectual, moral, ethical and physical to generate beautiful thoughts, beautiful knowledge, beautiful souls and beautiful actions. In short, this is spiritual, intellectual and action performance taken to its height. It reflects the mastery of religious, spiritual, moral, intellectual and action values, that resolutely lead to success. Maximum capacity embodies best solutions to avoid failure. It's the ideal path to success, to obtain what was targeted. It relies on effective grasp of stakes and challenges encountered. Maximum capacity is at the heart of the practice of perfect fundamental values. It is a visible sign that man has absorbed these values and thanks to them, he can henceforth achieve everything. It is equally the maximum in praxis.

Perfect capacity, is to stride effectively towards the highest degree one aspires to attain, it is the asymptotic and exponential level that uplifts one to the final stage, where one understands how to do better and better. Once a people acquires or conquers this aptitude, their ascension to progress becomes inevitable and their evolution gathers speed. This implies much work in all areas (education, training, research, action). This is the final dimension that is attained and that is possessed by all countries that have achieved development, and are sustaining it and are taking it further. This is the stage that helps one to reach the level of superior beings, of a superman or simply of gods (Homo Deus). The ambivalent nature of the human being enables him to be man by way of his earthly nature and god through his spiritual nature. This spiritual nature lifts him to the level of God, and permits him to become a creator and to carry on the creative work began by God. In other words, the human is the upholder of the creative work began by God, which is why Jesus Christ most opportunely told his disciples that if you imitate me, you would do greater things than I. Today, man creates cars, planes, ships, spatial vehicles, vaccines, etc., things that were not existing in the era of Jesus Christ. These human creations are also synonymous to miracles in the era of Jesus Christ, even if they are of a different nature. But, this phenomenon is miraculous, for miracle means a phenomenon interpreted as a divine intervention, as well as a stunning, extraordinary, wonderful, exceptional act or result. All inventions by man that are useful to man are a miracle, as we just stated. To achieve this miracle, one must accede to perfect capacity and knowledge. When Gutenberg created the printing press in the 15th century to produce writings in a large-scale, that revolution was considered as a divine miracle. Perfect capacity is a strength, an energy, a power of true knowledge that enables one to achieve everything.

15- Dream, vision

A dream, as in the word to dream, falls under fiction, what one imagines, what one desires to obtain and achieve and that is not yet considered as real. In this regard, one may dream of all what one wishes to obtain to achieve beauty, good, truth, perfect, what is prestigious, sublime, in short, all what may permit one to project oneself into the future, eternity. A dream today is the reality of tomorrow, as is often said. Ambitious persons or societies are those that dream. Dreaming is at the heart of thought and the spirit, it is immaterial, but has to be transformed into something material and concrete, for it is through dream that one prepares and builds great structures. The world as it is today is the product of those who have dreamt of making it a beautiful achievement.

The greatest political, economic, social and cultural achievements generally stem from the craziest of dreams. Can a people who do not dream achieve major things? Can they develop great and gigantic projects? Can they participate in a positive transformation of the world? We do not think so. Martin Luther King dreamt of an America stripped of racial discrimination, this dream has almost become a reality. The same applies for Nelson Mandela about South Africa, two monuments in human history and, moreover blacks. How is it possible that Africa lacks imagination and a dream? Childhood is the ideal period to dream, for one is bold, vigorous, ambitious, or more so, it is the period to make one's dreams come true but pervading and excess materialism has stifled this quest, to the advantage of the quest for easy and immediate profit. The country that has best grasped this truth is the United States of America where each generation enriches the dream for its country. This is a dream for better opportunities, for a society of prosperity, abundance, success and happiness. A dream allows one to consider all projects that one wishes to explore. Let us not kill dreams, let us fan them, to develop a strong and prosperous Africa. The US President, Barack Obama, a black, dreamt, he dared and he became the first black president of the number one world power (Barack Obama: *The Audacity of Hope*. Presses de la cité. 2007). He dedicates this book to his maternal grandmother who was a rock of stability throughout his life, and to his mother whose courage and love continue to inspire him. In a nutshell, he grew up steeped in perfect fundamental values that opened broad horizons and perspectives. God also talks to men through dreams that announce beautiful opportunities or warnings of imminent dangers. Former Israeli President Shimon Peres extolled dream by admitting that so long as your dreams are great you remain young.

16- Mastering of destiny

Destiny leads whoever chases it towards hundreds of goals he hopes are good, pleasant and satisfactory. Mastery of destiny requires one to know what is needed to move resolutely forward. The fundamental bases of a successful and balanced life lead well-organised men and societies towards mastered destinies. They compel one to steer towards a positive direction and to keep a firm grip on the wheel. Mastery of destiny requires that one should know what he desires, how to get it and what means to employ. This ability channels efforts in a coordinated manner, for the best results. This vision must be made popular in every society so that everyone should strive, at all times, towards the right direction. This would avoid walking in different directions, in view of effective collective action. African people and rulers must have a thorough understanding of truth and resolutely pursue it. A mastered vision of one's destiny helps in pooling the energies of every one for happy ends. It is an enriching vector that leads to rapid development. This is because today, more than ever before, developing countries need a clear vision of their future to strive towards better days, so as to spend less time in developing the areas that certain people took centuries to develop because they had no model to emulate, if not the existing divine model in the Holy Scriptures. African countries like the emerging countries must move faster and further by appropriating proper human values. In this globalised universe, science and technology are at the disposal of those who wish to appropriate them, for a promising future.

A constant practice of their values requires rigour, clarity, coherence, objectivity, truth, rationality, precision, research and constant innovation. At this point we quote Ebénézer Njoh Mouellé in his essay of 10 July 2015 at the Cameroon Cultural Centre in Yaounde, during the launch of activities of the Order of Perfect Fundamental Values, an Order he created, for promotion of the said values. When man appropriates these high values, they lift him to the spiritual realm that shapes his mind and thoughts in a positive manner in view of a logic, knowledge, intelligence and wisdom to live successful and blessed life.

When man is therefore organised in his mind for these original and divine high values, he becomes a creator and he finds direction for life and the values to adopt, to orientate development.

II- Values of education, training, secularism, research, creativity, innovation, invention and modernism

Education, training, research, creativity, invention cannot be ignored in any acquisition of quality human resources. When French President François Mitterrand came to power in 1981, this logic was a cornerstone of his programme, which France had to work on to catch up with countries like the United States of America and Japan. Education of the human being is at the heart of development issues. It is a fundamental State mission for production, organisation and dissemination of cultural, scientific, technological, professional and ethical knowledge, for the development of a nation and the progress of humanity.[8] Education thereby tends to teach, train, instruct man to enable him grasp the stakes of development. National education from a broad perspective contributes to that end, it is the wealth of services tasked with the organisation, direction and management of all public and private

[8] Law No.005 of 16 April 2001 of the Republic of Cameroon to guide Higher Education, Article 2. Also read *les grands dossiers des sciences humaines. Les grands penseurs de l'Éducation* No.45 Dec.-Fev. 2017.

learning establishments. In order to generate a high performance education much desired by all, it must target the following objectives:

- quest for excellence and perfection in all areas of knowledge
- support development activities at scientific, technical, technological and industrial level
- train and fine-tune the skills of senior staff
- improve the culture of ethics and national conscience
- promote democracy and advancement in democracy
- encourage bilingualism in a country like Cameroon that has English and French as official languages
- promote national languages

  In this regard, education:
- cultivates intelligence, logical thinking, a critical mind, discursive reasoning, conception of simple to complex ideas and themes,
- encourages innovation, individual and collective creation,
- participates in forging the Rule of Law,
- contributes to thematic debates, advancement of research,
- participates in the intermingling of populations and in national integration,
- fosters the emergence of a democratic culture, the culture of peace, development and tolerance.[9]

Myriad great thinkers have brainstormed on education during the European era of Renaissance and Enlightenment: Montaigne believes that it must help to elevate moral sense, practical sense and the sense of criticism. The ultimate goal is a happy, free and virtuous life. Jan Komenoky, a Czech, protestant theologian and great educationalist posits that education can be defined as a product of its end-result, man must be forged in the image of God. Man must renew this image that was disconcerted by the collapse. Education consists in attempting to bridge the chasm and rebuild man in the image of God, by cultivating knowledge, action, moral wisdom and freedom. Education, according to John Locke, must afford one control over his passions and use reason as guide. John Locke has a utilitarian and pragmatic vision of an education that conforms to the Anglo-Saxon culture.

[9] Article 2 of the Law to guide Higher Education in Cameroon.

Emmanuel Kant upholds education through reason to attain perfection. Education consists in taking the child from an irrational state to a rational moral state such as to render him autonomous and free. Freedom is to abide by the law that one has set for himself, a rational law, applicable to humanity as a whole. Ensure that your maxim is universal.

Jean Jacques Rousseau places the child at the centre of the educational process. Edgar Morin states that education should teach the complexity and contradictions in knowledge, enabling a better understanding of others. He even wonders how one can restore the ancient ideal that is equally the Illumination ideal of a global approach to knowledge where temperance, courage, wisdom and justice reign. Condorcet credits education with a liberating role that enables the cultivation of perfectibility. Gaston Bachelard considers that learning involves a proper identification of one's errors to better mitigate them. He considers that cultivating the scientific mind is not synonymous to gathering skills, rather it pertains to a fundamental transformation that encourages the pupil to break from the past and to assume a new way of thinking. He considers that what is true in the scientific approach equally applies to the teaching of science, whereby the notion of epistemological obstacle refers to that of pedagogic obstacle. To Bachelard, overcoming the pedagogic obstacles must be at the heart of the teaching of science. He believes that one cannot learn without committing errors. One has to commit errors before overcoming them. Obstacle is thus a phase of knowledge, a mandatory passage[10].

Indeed, education must seek to forge a healthy man in a healthy body and mind, a man who is complete, creative, intellectually, morally well-trained. Education must stress more on the creative, inventive and innovative mind of man.

Education therefore plays a role in the general empowerment of the individual at spiritual, intellectual, physical, moral, civic, political, economic, social and cultural levels through the perfect acquisition of scientific, technological, cultural and professional skills. Education must be concerned mostly with affording learners, a strong spiritual and moral platform. As Rabelais affirms, science without conscience can only ruin the soul. Countries that develop faster are those whose enrolment rate at all levels of learning are higher and of quality, like the emerging

---

[10] Review, "*Les grands dossiers des sciences humaines*", pg. 12-38

countries: South Korea, Brazil, Malaysia, India, Mexico, Taiwan, Singapore, South Africa, Mauritius, Botswana, etc. In Africa, certain countries have already boldly raised the percentage of annual State budget appropriated to education to 20% or even more. For investing heavily in education in an intelligent and methodical manner, can improve the knowledge and know-how of populations and promote development. South Korea witnessed a giant leap forward in its development due to its passion for knowledge, it is a cultural sponge with an enormous thirst for knowledge, and its labour force is the best trained in the world. This manner of conceiving education is founded on the rage to succeed, promotion of individual initiative and refusal of withdrawal. Any country where children are well-educated produces good results in terms of public policies. Education whose results are obvious must consider the needs of professional set-ups. It must correspond to these set-ups, hence the famous slogan "training/job adequacy" became a priority for business executives and increasingly for universities. Professionalisation of teachings thus remains the *credo* of education and training. Something that poses problems today in Africa, is that, to a large extent, school and university learning is still theoretical and is not often adapted to the needs of the job market. Many jurists, arts students are still trained and inadequate efforts are consented in the scientific and technological fields that rather generate so many jobs. Efforts in secondary and higher education must focus on this scientific and technological fields. Africans are still capable of launching vast highly-specialised research programmes in the domains of agriculture, livestock, pisciculture, mines that form part of their natural environment, to turn them into veritable poles of labour-intensive production, and equally tackle food self-sufficiency problems. Similarly, nothing stops African countries from embarking on high- level research designed to manufacture cars, planes and ships. Expeditions to the moon are not the preserve of certain races. Africa just needs to be capable of focussing energies in providing the best training to intermediate and senior staff. It is also a matter of ambition, vision and dream. Africa must therefore dream of a medium or long term execution of major agricultural, piscicultural, mining, industrial projects. Other countries beyond Africa have done so before, Japan yesterday, China today and other Asian countries. Africa's turn would most certainly be today and tomorrow. Education is an essential means of achieving it, but then, Africans need a very solid education, tried and tested by concrete and high standard results. All critics are now of the opinion that Africa is the new destination and new frontier for economic development, provided the challenge of education and research is met.

Africa cannot ignore learning the technique of manufacturing tyres. Making an inroad into industries requires mastery of this technique and production of electricity. Appropriating this technique of tyres constitutes an initiation into technology. We tend to lose sight of this reality in Africa. Chinese wise men understood this very well and started by large-scale manufacturing of bicycles. This mastery of the technique of tyres ushered China into the dynamics of the technology. It is obvious today that China has practically caught up with the industrialised countries in terms of technological and industrial progress. It is even expediting devices into space, proof of its technological mastery. China is also manufacturing heavy transport aircrafts. Education of young Africans on mastery of fundamental values relating to the divine, can contribute to mastery of ways leading to intelligence, wisdom and discernment of abstract and practical realities. This ways seem to be increasingly neglected for solutions that are essentially natural and human. By so doing, the global vision of things is obscured.

We have already extensively affirmed and explained that, man is a creator, for he was created in the image of God who is the creator of everything. That is why any man who maximises the development of his divine nature can only become a creator, for he would accede to the illumination of knowledge, intelligence and wisdom. To become a creator is not a feat of chance, it is authentic knowledge that can lead us there. That is why any educational system must develop strong spiritual values to lift its human resources to the realm of creativity, inventiveness and innovation. We must have open and powerful horizons of knowledge to possess such creative capacity. Poor and approximate education is not enough. No useful path should be neglected in providing quality education.

Consequently, we cannot mention these themes without linking them to research. The research, creativity, invention, innovation quartet is at the heart of development issues in modern economies. And that is the cardinal weakness of African educational systems and economies. An optimal practice of these capacities would sustainably boost all sectors of the economy. Developed countries are granting absolute priority to that.

Creativity, invention and innovation, proceeds of the realm of knowledge and thought, they are at the heart of science, technology, industry and all are bold social transformations. They stem from the superior dimension of knowledge. They lead man to the omega point, which is the culminating point in the mastery of knowledge. This ultimate dimension enables man to perceive the illuminating lights of the mind that lead to all discoveries and creative inventions of new artistic, cultural, material and financial realities.

The invention, creativity, innovation and modernism advocated by research constitute giant strides for societies that invest substantial means therein. All sectors of society need this form of commitment to propel the economy towards pinnacles of competitiveness and creation of wealth. Modernism is a trait of whatever is modern. Modern times are, in general, considered as the period opened by the industrial revolution. Modernism refers to what belongs to the particular time when a relatively recent period is marked by constant scientific, technological, artistic and industrial progress. The modern is in contrast to the old, former, outdated, classical, and traditional.

Nowadays in Africa, many socio-economic sub-sectors are lagging behind, due to poor creativity. Its added value in African economies is poor. That is why African economies remain marginal economies, in contrast to developed economies that constantly monopolise top positions. Thanks to their creativity, they always have the possibility of emerging from bad spells. In modern contemporary societies, intelligence, which resolves every problem, must back research, innovation, creativity and invention. Economies that develop at a sustainable pace are those that develop the mastermind of intelligence, thought, the spirit of innovation and creativity. Israel and many other developed and emerging countries follow this path. Africa must, each year, invest no less than 1% of its GDP in research for development. Conversely, a solid culture is a powerful factor of development. Israel used science and technology, to circumvent the mishaps of its natural environment in order to achieve the success that we know. To have a global vision of development, the culture of development must play a leading role.

Is secularism an obstacle to inspiration from divine values in educating and training the consciences of African consciences?

Why make mention of secularism in this discourse? It is exactly to show that it does not constitute a watertight wall between the Church and the State or God and men, so as to avoid isolating God from men and getting adrift of the enriching inspiration procured by its proximity. For it is more and more noted that a brutal application of secularism without any discernment that makes believe that the State is a space that cannot practise the sublime and uplifting values, developed in the Gospel. Note that when these values are mastered by the State in the public arena, their real value is toned down. And as we mentioned earlier, the Bible is, above all, a book of knowledge before being a religious book. The United States of America developed with success a dynamic secularism that still tied them to the source of divine inspiration, since their slogan is: "In God we trust". Many enriching gateways exist between the Church and the State and between God and men. This fruitful harmony is useful to the social development of people, religions, which remain free in their interpretation of the Holy Scriptures. The United States of America is a secular State, but the foundation of their ethics is of divine essence, far from religious posturing, to the point where they adopted as main motto, "In God we trust", for their currency, the dollar. That is a way of indicating that secularism is not an obstacle to the development of divine values in education, teaching, creativity and practical life. Only excess secularism of the society deprives people of education, culture and creativity, the enriching values of love, truth, justice and good, and drains the hearts of African and even of world citizens. An intelligent and enriching secularism must be practised and not the reverse. The 2016 Francophonie Day retained as theme for meditation and action: sharing and love, evangelical values par excellence.

Secularism is the independent trait of religious or partisan conceptions, of a system that excludes churches from the exercise of political and administrative power, especially from public teaching. In general, this involves preserving the State space from any inference from religions, as if to say like Jesus Christ in his famous teaching: "Give to Caesar what belongs to Caesar and to God what belongs to God". This will to separate the State from the Church and religions is highly commendable, for it, most certainly, precludes any confusion harmful to the impartial exercise of civil power, as is the case in most modern States, excluding certain States where religion is the State religion and where religious codes influence State institutions.

Nevertheless, this separation of the State from religion must not give the impression that the State is an amoral or an immoral space where everything is allowed. The State cannot constitute an obstacle to essential values. Note that the consciences of citizens and all those working within the State are formed and influenced, beforehand, by religious and social values. These servants of the State or other social entities, live within these spaces, armed with this spirit of love, service, solidarity, virtue, effort, objectivity, impartiality, propriety, general interest, discipline, obedience, fidelity, humility embodied by divine, religious values and churches, and equally borrowed by public service ethics. Man must always keep in mind the divine origin of man and most of these values, such as to bear in mind their true measure and real level. Values that underlie the State sector are not necessarily antinomic to those of the Church, it all lies in the interpretation given by each and every one. It has been illustrated in the pages above that religious values are generally secularised and brought down to the level of man. Man is even the product of the State and Church. It can only be a fruitful synthesis of these two influences for the pleasure of these two institutions as we have explained earlier. It is therefore important to understand these divine and religious values brought down to the level of man. All said and done, we believe, on the contrary, that the State and Church must pool their efforts so that the citizen, beneficiary of their services, should receive the best guidance. While the Church forges the conscience of the individual, making him a good citizen, the State does its utmost best to afford him all the rights he is entitled to. And citizens forged by these humanitarian and religious values are the best agents in the society.

Moreover, it is of common knowledge that secularism was instituted in France in 1906, when the spiritual, mental and moral foundation of citizens was already forged by the religious institution that, for years, served as the chief authority in the Western society. When secularism was instituted, the honesty of man, a product of the church's training came into existence.

In conclusion therefore, the Church and the State do not oppose each other, they are rather complementary, and the collaboration of the sabre and word is illustrated perfectly by the Pope who wields temporal and spiritual power with much pleasure. Victor Tonye Bakot, the then

Archbishop of Yaounde, emphasised this enriching collaboration between the Church and the State in these terms: “But permit us to mention some stock-phrases that in a significant manner, describe the role of the church on the Cameroonian public scene”. On the eve of the independence of Cameroon under French administration, on 31st December 1959, Jean Marie Maury, the then Apostolic Delegate for French-speaking Africa, celebrated a thanks- giving mass at the Cathedral of Yaounde, thereby manifesting the solidarity of the Holy See with the State and the Cameroonian people. This tradition, instituted by the representative of Pope John XXIII at such an important and crucial event in political life, was respected for twenty years. Indeed, the feast of January 1st, and then that of May 20th, long included an official programme whereby the first act of the day usually consisted the celebrating of a religious service in places of worship in Cameroon: Catholics, Protestants, Muslims, which recorded the attendance of a representative of the State (District Head, Sud-Divisional Officer, Federal Inspector and later the Governor).

In Cameroon and other countries, the national anthem and flag constitute sacred symbols. That the national anthem is sang within the frame of an official celebration in the church should not be a source of polemics. This is not exclusive to Cameroon, for *la Marseillaise* is often sung in cathedrals in Paris, awakening in the conscience of every believer, patriotic fervour in the presence of God, because love for God does not exclude love for the fatherland and because the nation of men is the nation created by God. In the presence of God, love for the fatherland is transfigured and glows under a serene face that gives direction to the commitment of believers to the nation and church. For any patriotism and nationalism without spiritual guidance may easily slide into chauvinism and xenophobia.

In the United States for instance, newly elected presidents take oath of office on the Bible. Some pundits cite the principle of State secularism to illustrate that there is a clear-cut separation between the two institutions. By so doing, they forget that what we refer to in the constitution as “gaudium spes” (GS) affirms that true secularism is open and the two institutions (Church and State) must maintain a healthy collaboration. They talk of liberty of all.

We could add to this assertion the oath taken by judicial assessors during their installation and absorption into the magistracy profession: “I swear before God and men, to honestly serve the people of the

Republic of Cameroon in my capacity as magistrate, to render justice in accordance with the laws, regulations and customs of the Cameroonian people, without fear, favour or malice, to keep the secret of the deliberations and to conduct myself everywhere and always as a worthy and loyal magistrate". I consider this double allegiance to God and to men as a complete and wise attitude.[11] Bakot adds in the following terms: "To the Pharisees who set him a trap about the payment of taxes. Jesus replies: Give to Caesar what belongs to Caesar and to God what is God's" (Mark 12, verse 17). General opinion could find in this answer given by Jesus, the real foundation for a separation between spiritual and temporal power, as well as the source of the principle of secularisation in modern societies. It is obvious that at no time did Jesus intend to casually express doubts about political power, but this does not mean that Caesar, or rather the Emperor, is not spiritually and morally accountable for his political actions before God. Jesus respects political power, even though he does not approve any excesses and abuse of this power.

Church/State relations are founded in long-standing historic tradition. It would be painstaking to provide an exhaustive list of events and treaties that have marked such relations. A few examples show that Africa inherited this age-old tradition, and is striving to uphold it by adapting it to its environment in the light of a contextualised teaching of the church. Throughout the era of Antiquity, Emperor Constantine, the one who understood that the State needs the Church for prosperity and social peace in the Roman Empire, enacted the Milan Edict in 313. He put an end to the persecution suffered by Christianity right from its birth. Emperor Theodosius the Great, gave up his title of "Pontifex Maximus", in 380, and conferred it to the pope. This is the emperor who transformed the church into a State institution, thereby laying the groundwork for medieval theocracy. Crowning of the king by the pope is a criterion of political legitimisation and constitutes a spiritual shield against drifts towards blind totalitarianism. Such is the case with the crowning of Charlemagne in the year 800 by Pope Leo III. Theocracy breeds utopia: bringing the reign of God down on earth and unity of the two powers (spiritual and political) at the service of this reign. In theory, this utopia is seductive, but in practice, it has proven complex and

---

[11]*Cameroon Tribune* No.10120/6321 of Friday, 22 June 2012.
Read Richard Laurent Omgba, *Culture et émergence d'une nation, pour une approche humaniste du développement*, l'Harmattan, 2016.

difficult. It could not survive the rivalries between the two powers with the advent of democracy, which, far from keeping God away from the city, grants him the place he deserves in the heart of man, under the guidance of the Church.

Note that democracy broadens the scope of public freedoms in the name of secularism, but it does not cast doubt on the ecclesial institution, nor on its evangelising mission, or even on its role in the social life of the States. In the face of the siege of Vienna in 1529, and then in 1683 by Turks, in Austria, it was the Church that spurred the population to resist, thereby avoiding an annexation of the territory. Ignaz Seipel, prelate and chancellor (1922-1924/1926-1929), on his part, courageously resisted Nazi hegemony, though Austria was finally absorbed by Germany in 1938. This role of the Church in the history of Austria makes this prelate a leading figure in the Lander Austria. The Church and the State therefore have a long-standing history fraught with diverse fortunes, but which shows that the State and religion have need for one another for the good of the citizens. A politically organised society is a place of hope. Drawing lessons from this reality, the Second Vatican Council, after clear admission of the responsibility, dignity and importance of the role of those who govern, strongly affirmed that "the State being a political community and the church are not be mixed up". Therefore, stressing that there must be a distinction between the Church and the State. The Second Vatican Council prescribed a harmonious collaboration between these two institutions for the common good of all[12].

Secularism in its concrete and dynamic form shows that the State and religion, far from opposing each other, are complementary for the common good of the people. We have already demonstrated that the kingdom of God is a very useful realm of knowledge that can enable man to broaden his horizons and prowess. Strong, balanced and stable societies are those that maintain a fruitful relationship between the Church and the State, between God and men. Societies that depart from the ways of God, cut themselves off his benefactress and fruitful source, with all the underlying risks and perils. The protestant and puritan democracies of North Europe are a perfect example of this prosperous relationship between the Church and the State and between God and men.

---

[12] Cameroon Tribune of Thursday 2nd January 2012 in the forum of ideas .p.10.

III- Cultural values

Culture is the foundation of development, as President Léopold Sédar Senghor was wont to say. Because it raises the education and training of man to its pinnacle thanks to the high spiritual, ethical and aesthetic values it embodies. It gives room for the understanding and the raising to higher heights the set of habits, customs, religious, spiritual, intellectual, artistic, material and economic manifestations and social expressions that define and distinguish a group, a society. For this purpose, we must have a measure of this supreme understanding of the strong and eternal values. We have shown that this true measure comes from God, who is the source of authentic and eternal knowledge. God draws man towards the pinnacle, to better clarify him through his system founded on perfection. Culture is also a set of convictions, shared values, and ways of seeing and acting, behaving, that guide the behaviour of an individual or a group.

That said, culture is an element that characterises a society, it colours it, affords it a distinct identity. Culture assumes all its measure when it is elevated to perfection, to excellence and to the sublime. Where it is clear in its benchmarks, well assimilated and understood by beneficiaries, it confers a strong identity on a people. Culture gives people a clear view of the stakes in life and development. Such identity is expected to rid itself of all complexions, so as to enrich all external dynamic contributions, while constituting a source of inspiration for every people in order to participate in the universal civilisation cherished by President/poet, Léopold Sédar Senghor. Culture is not static, it is dynamic and must evolve. It must evolve with the society itself from the primary stage to a planned, sophisticated and perfect stage. Perfection is the culmination of a culture that evolves. Africa therefore has no inferiority or superiority complex to overcome, the continent has only to dig into its rich cultural heritage, which it must continue to improve and which is envied by other cultures: its languages, its history, its music, its dances, its traditional folklore, its sculptures, its culinary, dressing and architectural arts. Africa must step up its development of science, technology as well as perfect and rational knowledge without neglecting to continue developing its values of communitarianism, solidarity, sharing, family, hospitality, warmth, enthusiasm and overflowing soul that characterise the continent.

African culture must emerge progressively from lethargy to regenerate, reinvent itself and become the showcase and gateway to the continent. It must become the element that structures the development and emergence of Africa. Africa must transform its heritage of cultural, mining, agricultural, forestry, pastoral, silvicultural, touristic and other resources into myriad scientific, industrial, commercial, financial opportunities, but equally enriching, dignity and ennoblement opportunities for its people suffering under the yoke of poverty. That is why Africa must truly appropriate the scientific and technological culture to give added value to these primary riches. Africa must, more than ever before, focus seriously on the valorisation of its riches, I order to become job creative, so as to fight against poverty and prepare the prosperity and abundance that everyone is fervently hoping for. And as Engelbert Mveng clearly affirms about Africa: "it is through the virtues afforded him by the relationship to transcendence that the African succeeds to overcome his resentment and to transform the aggressiveness of history he has suffered into dialogue, into a fight for love and fraternity with others[13]". To go an extra mile, all perfect cultural values must be upheld as a way of life, behaviour in view of an optimal development.

Africa must channel these cultural values into perfect fundamental values for African and national identity, in view of its successful integration into globalisation, which is a give-and-take appointment. We cannot join globalisation on the cheap with only raw material and culture. They must undergo optimal transformation that render them consumable by all. African cultures must catch up with the pantheon of modern cultures that dominate the leading bunch of domineering societies.

In sum, the African must have a culture of fundamental values that serve as a springboard for the emergence desired in view of reviving our economies. This is because these values embody all aspects related to the development of people, in general, and Africans in particular. Let us not delude ourselves, development has never been a spontaneous generation, it relies on solid, clear and authentic benchmarks constituted by perfect fundamental values. Africa must therefore commit to this beneficial culture of perfect values to lift its culture very high, for these values lead to the sublime, which is the essence of the most brilliant achievements. Africa can do this by respecting and

---

[13] Engelbert Mveng, *L'Art d'Afrique noire, liturgique cosmique et langage religieux*, of 1974, quoted by the newspaper *Mutations*, No.0397 of Thursday, 12 July 2012, pg. 7.

seeking to achieve in all what it undertakes: beauty, the sublime, the solid, good, very good, and the perfect that must definitely become part of African culture. The culture of perfection and excellence must become the paradigm of African culture. For a well thought out and lived culture constitutes a solid reference benchmark for comprehending life and the direction it must take.

Africa must further develop our positive customs and traditions and embrace all fruitful values that would thrust the continent into the arena of international competition, such as to seek to rival the most influential cultures. Africa must even seek to do better in order to become a brilliant culture, a continent that sets the pace for humanity, for humanity still expects that, especially in this era of triumphant materialism with prospects that cast doubts on fundamental values. CHEIKH ANTA DIOP most opportunely affirmed that history and African languages are the solid foundation on which a brilliant culture can be forged for Africa. African culture must assimilate and conquer science, technology and industry to create modern economies, creators of jobs for the young African. This elevation in science and technology can only be done through a pure and perfect culture.

Civic and individual values can consolidate Africans in this dynamic and modern culture.

IV- Civic and individual values

An education, a training and a solid and a healthy culture can awaken the conscience of people and confer them strong and profound civic and individual values. For this purpose, they must be assimilated, understood and practised for all in a beautiful harmony and cohesion.

Civic values are at the centre of the life of the citizen in the society, and at the heart of his obligations towards the society. Such values include the love for education and training, respect of State institutions, the republican form of the State, authority, family, parents, elders, in couples, respect of the property of the community and an impeccable patriotic attitude. A good citizen is one who practises these values with the greatest rigour, which demands politeness, discipline, hard work, courtesy, service, availability and who does not balk at rendering service. He is allergic to reprehensible behaviours, he is forever committed to the harmonious future of the society through a vigilant assumption of his role as social agent. He is cited as model in the family, in professional, political, religious, associative life. A solid society must develop these individual values to the highest level, to breed reference citizens and patriots, intrepid development agents of their country, of humanity and of universal society. They are soldiers, always ready to serve, they are apostles of an ordered society, mobilised for major causes that elevate to good and wellbeing. They must be cantors of ascetism, effort and rigid ethics. We could thus dwell on some civic values: a profound change in mentalities, patriotism and general interest, respect of State authority, institutions, ethics and morals, love for the family, politeness, courtesy, affability, hard work and effort, discipline, seriousness, individual and collective ambition.

Profound change of mentalities

Obscurantism, ignorance, laziness, placidness, corruption, confusion and all forms of disorder cannot lead to genuine development. These practices of another time constitute a crippling break to the progress of Africans, they develop the logic of under development, poverty and misery. It is clear that the logic of development relies on the universally positive values listed, known and practised. It is thus clear that one cannot develop through acts contrary to this effect. A change of mentalities and behaviours is indispensable. We must turn our backs to these outdated and dark attitudes, to embrace positive practices, bearers of lights for the mind and true and liberating knowledge. The great and famous French publicity agent, Jacques Seguela, most opportunely affirmed that money has no ideas, but ideas make money. For the generation of wealth or riches per se is a process originating from ideas, thought and knowledge. That is why rich or richer countries are those that best master this processes. Keeping to bad practices is a sure bed of poverty and destitution. Irrespective of what is said or believed, it is one of the reasons for Africa's backwardness and poverty. Change of mentalities helps to change the angle of perception, to evolve from the realms of darkness and ignorance, to those of illumination, knowledge and positive action. It helps to adjust one's mind to the highest values of knowledge for them to lead Africans towards the strata of integral development.

Patriotism and general interest, respect of authority, institutions, ethics and morals

Patriotism is love for the fatherland, it is the interest, commitment shown to the fatherland. Such patriotism expressed at its extreme can involve self-sacrifice for one's fatherland. It is this feeling of great commitment that pushes any patriot to pledge their life for their country, with the aim of carrying the country to the highest peak of its development and splendour. Such patriotic fibre is justified by the fact that the fatherland groups a political community of individuals living on the same soil and tied by a feeling of belonging to one same cultural, linguistic community. This community shares the same cultural, or even spiritual values, which brings its members closer. Such patriotism often leads to a nationalism that affirms the primacy of the nation's interest over interests of the groups, classes and individuals that constitute it. Patriotism, fatherland, nationalism, nation, civic responsibility are strong terms that refer to exalting feelings, feelings that determine the maximalist commitment attitudes for one's country, for respect of authority, institutions and its republican form. Lack of patriotic or lukewarm commitment tend to limit and retard the actions and motivations of citizens of a country. Their best expression is a powerful catalyst that increases the ardour of the people to work relentlessly in view of a better future for their community. Countries driven by fervent patriotism and nationalism progress more rapidly towards their economic, social and cultural development. They grant top priority to the civic education of their children and citizens, in order to instil in them civic education and high values. This civic education affords the spirit of general interests, respect of public and private property. Such civic education strengthens respect of authority and institutions espoused by citizens. The fatherland requires from these citizens a very high moral sense founded on values and rules of action that obtain as norms of action in the society and bind everybody.

Love for family

Family is considered as the basic unit of the human society. Its origin is of divine essence to take all its size and importance, it comprises the father, children and all other dependent members, to the point that in Africa, we talk of extended family or community. It is an inevitable reality of life in society, it abides by particular rules, among others: love, fidelity, solidarity, respect, protection, security, understanding and harmony. Children must respect and obey their parents, who in turn display love, protection and guidance. Parents are expected to bring up their children by instilling in them strong social values and virtues, ensuring their education and training in the strictest manner possible. This attitude of protection and benevolence pushes children to obey and love their parents. Such affectionate and tender relationship creates a peaceful, warm and cordial atmosphere within the family. In this practice, the African culture does not deter from what the Holy Scriptures, particularly the gospels preach.

For this purpose, parents are expected to develop in their own life irreproachable spiritual and moral values, so as to serve as models in the eyes of other members of the family. The father, head of the family must lead members of the family with firm authority, but without wickedness and acrimony to avoid frustration. He must, in this regard, be impartial, friendly and tender. The mother, procreator, must show proof of qualities of fidelity, tenderness, softness and love, in order to offer the man and other members of the family, warm guidance, suitable to harmony in the couple. She must be forever tender and firm, at the same time, towards her children, such as to preclude any form of laxity. Such a healthy, holy and pure atmosphere can only posit good understanding among members of the family who would feel reassured and safe. Any family organised in this manner can only constitute a haven of peace for each of the members, who would find in the family an ideal forum for emancipation and optimal development. That is why it is commonly said that, when the family runs well in a country, that country tends to evolve harmoniously, since the aggregation of families that are organised, solid and structured around fruitful values, can only be enabling to rapid development in a country. Such families can be developed with purety of heart and perfection.

Due to all these assets, society in its components, citizens, families, schools, churches, government... can only be dynamic and a source of happiness and success for its members that stem from balanced families. There is need therefore to spare no effort such that the family, tribe and its members should be fed with all these positive values. The family, a reflection of an organised society, must be the crucible of strong spiritual, intellectual, moral and republican values. It must be an expression of beauty of the mind. It is this form of healthy mind, bereft of any permissiveness, which should be cultivated. These positive values must be handed down from generation to generation for permanence of the society.

Unfortunately, nowadays, permissiveness has engendered diverse forms of perverted behaviours within African families: decline in parental authority, excess individualism, pride, disobedience, ingratitude, lack of respect, solidarity and love, embezzlement, crime, organised crime, trickery, duplicity, drug abuse, alcohol abuse, all forms of excesses, cupidity, robbery, theft, rape, cult of placidness, etc. This unfortunate situation has severely undermined the family in its foundations. This is not what Cameroon and Africa needs. Africa rather needs a healthy society with a solid spiritual and moral platform to take on with chances of success, the development of the continent. Africa must truly forge healthy families that take the pain to seek the perfect fundamental values that constitute and continue to constitute the strength of human societies. In this regard, African communitarianism must rely on a solid foundation and reform of the family and African cultures. It must cease to be a term bereft of its meaning as days go by.

Politeness, courtesy, affability, hard work and effort, discipline, seriousness, merit, sense of responsibility and serviceabilty

Any society that has a solid and established culture naturally develops these values of politeness, courtesy, affability in human relationships: the said humans then forge ties marked by harmony, conviviality, understanding, dignity, mutual respect and consideration. Such high civic culture paves the way for an appeased community.

As a fundamental value par excellence, work is at the centre of human activity, in that it is applied to the quest for knowledge, creativity, innovation, production, transformation of nature in its multiple facets, in view of procuring the basics needed by every human being in life. Work is therefore effort consented to perform a given task and to achieve a result. Work is measured in the amount of time and energy devoted to perform a task. This amount of energy and time must be effective for the result obtained to be satisfactory. That is why all social systems posit and exalt this value. Note that people who achieve rapid development are those whose practice of this virtue is optimal or even perfect. Why it is commonly said that the world belongs to whoever gets up early? It is generally because they have the capacity to devote more time to finding solutions for the diverse problems afflicting man's existence. Can certain under-developed countries claim today to respect the same standardised work schedule set at eight hours of work? Should we not work for longer periods in Africa, especially with set objectives like aspiring to become an emerging country or attaining the Millennium Development Goals (MDGs) or the Sustainable Development Goals (SDGs)? To achieve these, Africa needs another work approach. In Europe, the most competitive countries like Germany and England are those that maintain the highest work schedule capacity and time at work. German economic leadership in Europe is not usurped, it is the product of sustained effort in work effort. Countries like China, Japan, and the Asian dragons form part of this club of countries that have raised work into a national value. Can African countries continue therefore with a work approach that does not yield satisfactory results? Given that growth rates hardly rise above 5%, and knowing in general that only double digit growth rates enable economies to be competitive, in order to release enough income for investment, designed to create jobs and roll back poverty.

Work as a human activity which favours creativity and production, must be well thought out and organised in Africa. And yet, difficulties related to development exclude from the work and production circuit entire portions of young generations, thereby keeping away hardworking hands from the economic circuit. Work and effort require discipline, order, seriousness, rigour, selflessness, a sense of responsibility. Work and effort also require ambition and resolve, and meritorious workers must be upheld as models for the others. Africans stand to gain by investing their energy in sectors within their reach and that may procure them hard currencies and substantial financial means: agriculture, livestock, forestry, craft, and arts.

Individual and collective ambition

Ambition is an extraordinary booster in the vast field of development. It is an ardent desire to succeed. Being ambitious in this way is an exciting viaticum for whoever follows that path. This capacity must be sought relentlessly by Africans, whether individually or collectively. Ambition shows the way, the right way to follow. It is exalting and exciting. It mobilises energies in a positive manner. This virtue should drive every human being and Africans the more, who still have much work to do for the wellbeing of their continent. Ambition leads to emulation, to try to copy those who have made it and even to better it, enables one to excel. For once the capacity to fight and to nurse innovative ideas is acquired, this impetus propels the human to the top.

V- Political and republican values

The political and republican values we are developing concern: the republic, human rights, democracy, freedom, the Rule of Law, the nation, governance or good governance.

Apart from the monarchies of Morocco and Lesotho, Africa as a whole has opted for the republic as form of State organisation. That is a cardinal political choice. The republic is the political regime whereby power is a public thing (*res publica*), which implies that those who hold power wield it not by virtue of a personal right (divine, hereditary right), but by virtue of a mandate conferred by the society generally through periodic elections. Thus defined, the republic is in contrast to monarchy or royalty, but should not be confused with democracy. A monarchy can be democratic (Great Britain). Actually, the words republic and democracy are often used differently (*lexique des termes juridiques 3e édition*).

Africa must protect its republican form of the State through the fundamental elements that characterise it: human rights, democracy, freedom, Rule of Law, nation, governance, administration.

Human rights

Civilised humanity set out inalienable human rights, specific to the wellbeing and comfort of man, to shield man from traumas caused by wars, and preserve his dignity and honour. The French Revolution in 1789 started to enact these rights and the universal declaration of human rights of 1948 solemnly enshrined them, in the aftermath of World War II, in order to combat the barbaric acts that had appalled the conscience of humanity, for advent of a world where human beings will be free to talk and believe and be set free from terror and misery. In this regard, the advent of a better world is considered as the highest aspiration of man. These different rights were equally set out in United Nations Charter, the charters of regional organisations like the African Union and the different constitutions of African States and elsewhere. Africa effectively adopted the African Charter on Human and People's Rights, which takes into account the virtues of these historic traditions and their values of African civilisation. The African Charter on Human Rights sets out the rights and obligations of the people.

a) The rights concern:

- Every individual is equal before the law
- Every individual is entitled to equal protection of the law
- Human beings are inviolable
- Every human is entitled to respect for his life and integrity, liberty and security of his person
- Freedom of conscience, profession and free practice of religion is guaranteed,
- Every human has the right to receive information

- Every human has the right to association, meeting, movement
- Every human has the right to freely participate in the government of his country
- Every human has the right to property
- Every human has the right to work under equitable and satisfactory conditions
- Every human has the right to health, education, participate in the cultural life of the community
- Every human has the right to promotion and protection of morals and traditional values recognised by the community
- Protection of the family, a natural element and basis of the society is guaranteed by government
- Protection of persons with disabilities is guaranteed by government
- Every human has the right to existence, self-determination
- Every human has the right to free disposal of their wealth and natural resources
- Every human has the right to their economic, social and cultural development.

b) Obligations on their part centre on:

- Duties of the individual towards the family and society, the State and other legally recognised communities
- Respect and consider his fellow beings
- Preserve the harmonious development of the family
- Respect for parents, take care of them in case of need
- Serve his national community by placing his physical and intellectual abilities at its service
- Preserve and strengthen national independence and the territorial integrity
- Preserve the fundamental interests of society
- Preserve and strengthen positive African cultural values, in the spirit of tolerance, dialogue, consultation and, in general, contribute to the promotion of the moral wellbeing of society
- Contribute to the best of his abilities, to the promotion and achievement of African Unity.

These rights and duties take up fundamentals related to the full emancipation of the African man for his genuine happiness. They affect: life, education, health, peace, security, freedom, property, family, dignity, economy, national independence, social and cultural development.

The review of these values that are well taken up in the different declarations and conventions show ample proof that humanity has taken clear and true cognizance of all aspects inherent to the wellbeing of man. It now suffices that they be applied resolutely. Africa must cease from contenting itself with evocation of these values and apply them strictly. People who practise them perfectly are those who develop at a fast pace. These are the values put into practice by all great countries and which afford man a cordial environment for his salutary and fruitful action.

Democracy, freedom, Rule of Law, nation

Human societies, from time immemorial, have imagined and created systems of government: theocracies, monarchies, oligarchies, aristocracies, dictatorships, democracies. Ultimately, the democratic system has finally found its way into a majority of States, according priority to freedom. In this evolution, political and economic liberalism has gained grounds and has become a reference in politics and economics. Thus, democracy, which is synonymous to republic is the government of the people, by the people and for the people. It is the political regime that promotes the participation of a majority of the population in government business. Democracy allows for great freedom of action in political, social, economic and cultural activities. It encourages the spirit of creativity, it offers everyone his opportunity in society, it is a system that dishes out opportunities, universal values, founded on cognizance of the inalienable nature of dignity and equal value of all humans. It promotes freedom of press, freedom of association, freedom of meeting, multiparty politics, free, fair and transparent elections, Rule of Law, full respect of human rights, an appropriated democratic culture. Democracy, is equally marked by separation of powers, transparency and justice in the management of public business, governance, economic and social development through an even distribution of natural resources, for equal access to education, training, health and separation of powers, dialogue at all levels, among citizens as well as between the State and civil society. Democracy implies participation of citizens in political life and enables them to exercise their right of control. Democracy must correspond to the historical, cultural and social realities and specificities of every people, while respecting universal principles.

Democracy is also a political forum for the Rule of Law and protection of human rights, it promotes long term stability and legal as well as judicial security. Thanks to the freedom atmosphere it forges, democracy equally creates conditions for a mobilisation freely accepted by the population for development. It is for that reason that democracy and development are inseparable. They are factors of durable peace.

On the other hand, democracy is measured by the yardstick of scrupulous respect and full accordance of all civil, political, economic, social and cultural rights to all, accompanied by guaranteed mechanisms. These are conditions essential to their acceptance of institutions and to their motivation to become integral actors of political life.

In a nutshell, for the promotion of a democratic culture and respect of human rights, it is advisable to cultivate the spirit of tolerance and promote the democratic culture in all its forms. This is done by raising awareness through education and training of public officials, all actors of political life and all citizens, about the ethical exigencies of democracy and human rights, while strengthening national, consultative institutions and not only promotion of human rights.[14] This global framework for the democratic system, adopted by African countries highlights its primacy in modern African societies.

Different liberal laws have been voted, since 1990, on the constitution, multiparty, freedom of press, freedom of meeting, freedom of association, the judicial power, economic deregulation, and free and transparent elections. In that regard, Cameroon has taken a great leap forward in terms of democratic freedom and Rule of Law. The constitution has been amended by reaffirming the republican form of the State and of its sovereignty, instituting a bicameral parliament, National Assembly and Senate, independent of the magistracy by putting in place a judicial power. The Constitutional Council has been put in place, as well as an audit bench, an independent body for

---

[14] - Bamako Declaration of the International Organisation for the Francophonie on Democracy, Human Rights and Freedoms within the Fancophonie of 3rd November 2000.

- African Charter on Democracy, Elections and Governance. Ethiopia (Addis-Ababa), 30th January 2007.

organisation and management of the different polls. A new electoral code, gathering in a single document all electoral laws, a new decentralisation policy with the creation of regions and transfer of powers and financial resources to councils. A governance programme has also been put in place, a national commission for human rights and freedoms, and a criminal procedure code.

Thus, the mechanism of a liberal democratic system is in place and evolving in a non-reversible and methodical manner, according to an expression cherished by President Paul Biya.

In reality, freedom is a very important value due to its impact on the life of man. It is part of the natural rights of man like life, equality and the quest for happiness. The United States of America has made it the central value of their social organisation system.

Rule of Law, nation, administration

To consolidate the Rule of Law, it's necessary to assure the independence of the magistracy, freedom of the bar association and promotion of an effective and accessible justice, for this is the guarantor of the Rule of Law and an effective administration for application of laws and guidance of the people. The capacities of the Rule of Law must be developed in view of enabling them to enjoy all the independence necessary to performance of their mission. That is why the State must stay strong to promote a strong democracy. The Rule of Law must then remain "a powerful organisation of political power and the most politically organised human community, the most refined in terms of its authority machinery: highly advanced division of labour among the ruling authorities, a complete system of norms and sanctions defining the roles and social statuses, concentration of the material strength of the most important constraint whatsoever (military, police, prisons), in view of ensuring order within and along the borders".[15] Speaking of the Rule of Law, Narcisse Mouelle Kombi rightly affirms that: "the ideal Rule of Law presupposes that existing law in all segments of social life, irrigates all arteries and articulations of the State entity and its activities. It refers to a pandemic and endemic Rule of Law where the Rule of law is promoted or law reigns. This implies the cumulative presence of at least two criteria: deference of the Rule of Law to law and hierarchical structuring of law". In this light, the author lays emphasis on the role of

[15] Paul Biya, *Communal Liberalism*, Editions Pierre Marcel Favre, 1987, France, pg. 30.

the State. In his view, "the State, a political society par excellence, organises the law as long as it is the one that does the organisation. It is built on the law as much as it is structured by law. As product of this society, the law is basically a factor of social organisation of the State and within the State. Institutionalisation of this organisation, its foundation on the framework of law is a sign of legal-political modernism. The Rule of Law is a modern State deployed within the frame of a legal order".[16]

Joseph Owona supports this view by indicating that the State is the supreme, omnipresent, almighty territorial authority.[17] This evolution in the organisation of modern States is different from the state of nature developed in its time by Thomas Hobbes, John Locke and Jean Jacques Rousseau. This state of nature was the situation of man prior to the organised society. Thomas Hobbes pointed out that under the state of nature, men are at war against all. The social contract alone enables the advent of a sovereign state tasked with ensuring the group's survival.

The State, through the administration that performs its action, thereby seems as an accomplished form of the organisation of men in society. It must be the subject of all attention, such that its action should be effective and at the service of all. It is the impartial regulator of all initiatives that converge towards the wellbeing of all citizens. Countries that have succeeded the most are those that have developed solid States. In Africa, the State, through its often centralised organisation, is the crucible that leads to the nation, with the latter considered as a racial, historical and cultural, linguistic and economic community. It brings together people wishing to form a cultural group, owing to their tribal, ethnic, linguistic and religious distinctive identity. In this regard, there is a problem of unifying national languages. That is why Africans have chosen the languages of colonial masters, French, English, German, Portuguese, and Spanish as national languages. However, sustained efforts are being made to integrate local languages in the national frame. Cheikh Anta Diop affirms that African languages are a capital element of African culture.

---

[16] Narcisse Mouelle Kombi. *La démocratie dans la réalité camerounaise, Libertés, légitimité et modernité politique sous Paul Biya*, Éditions Dianoïa, Paris, 2014, pg. 127.

[17] Joseph Owona: *Droits constitutionnels et institutions Politiques du monde contemporain*. L'Harmattan, Paris, 2010, pg. 1770.

In reality, the State is criticised in Africa for its inability to promote development. Some critics think that it is ill-adapted to the form bequeathed by the colonial masters. That is why the reforms underway are trying to grant more powers to the people through decentralisation to resolve local problems. In Africa more than elsewhere, the Rule of Law must stay strong to create befitting conditions for development and offer the people a wealth of basic social services. Francis FUKUYAMA even believes that the weakness of the State in Africa retards development. In this reflection on the place of the State in development and governance, Eugène Nyambal suggests that the State should be reinvented. He reveals that the State can, either promote the wellbeing of society, or become a source of economic and social stagnation. He points out that the industrial revolution in Europe and the boom in South-East Asia show at what point an effective State can constitute a factor of development. He therefore proposes for Africa, a State capable of spurring development. This State must be a Strategist State, capable of assuming, not only its republican functions, but equally the functions of provider of public goods, facilitator and strategist. The State/facilitator must accomplish the passage from State/manager to State/catalyst. For that purpose, two challenges must be met: the first consists in conducting modernisation of the State with success by appropriating a meritocratic public function, which is less stuffed, better trained and counselled, better remunerated, capable of producing rules, controlling their application, evaluating and correcting results. The second challenge consists in strengthening the efficiency of monopoly regulatory bodies that have been transferred to the private sector, notably in the water, electricity, telecommunications sectors (for example in Cameroon, Camwater, ARSEL, ART). He adds that the State/strategic coordinator must play a long-term role, in order to prepare major strategic options, ensure their coordination and monitoring, in conjunction with representatives of civil society and the private sector. He also considered that this strategic function becomes so important that, for the first time in the history of humanity, due to globalisation, every nation must improve its economic rank as compared to other nations. Every nation must also create a comparative advantage, to attract investments, produce and sell more than others. In such an environment, government must help the community to maximise its wealth creation potentials. In Africa, this means that government should bypass the structural adjustment programmes, centred on an ambitious vision for a future in partnership with the private sector, and equip itself with means to mobilise individuals, for the purpose of reaching the objectives targeted over a long period.[18] To strengthen the strategic capacities of State in Africa, he proposes the creation, among others, of a National Agency for Science and Technology.

Ultimately, he advocates a pragmatic conception of the State corresponding to the challenges faced by societies. For historically speaking, the supremacy of the West relied on the putting in place of strong States, with a spirit of conquest inside and outside the country. This notion of strong State to be put in place in Africa is taken up by American Francis Fukuyama, in his essay on the history of States. He considers that donors and Western States go too far in terms of disengagement of the State in the economic sector in Africa, to give way to market forces alone. He finds that incompatible with the level of under-development in Africa.

Governance or good governance

To stick to the reality of these past decades, governance or good governance refers to sound management of State business. It mostly fits into the neo-liberal vision of the Bretton Woods financial institutions, after the fiasco of the structural adjustment policies. It implies State disengagement from the productive sector, designed to turn the private sector into a catalyst of growth, in view of wealth production. In this way, Hugues François ONANA stresses, in his essay, that: "By prescribing State streamlining or at a minimum, resizing of its role, the multilateral financial institutions postulate that the latter should adopt a paunchy profile and that its centralisation should reach a significant threshold. In the place of the tough State set up after independence, governance is intended to institute a flexible and regulatory State that hardly intervenes in the economy[19]".

All in all, governance institutionalises the theory of "less States" in the place of "better State"[20]. The vast political and economic reforms initiated in Cameroon and in Africa since 1990 are in that regard: they affect public administration, justice, decentralisation, economic and

---

[18] Eugène Nyambal : *Créer la prospérité en Afrique, dix clés pour sortir de la pauvreté.* L'Harmattan, 2006, Chapitre 3 : réinventer l'État, pg. 63-83.

[19] Hugues François Onana : *Pratique de la gouvernance au Cameroun : Entre désétatisation et démocratisation.* L'Harmattan. 2011. pg. 77.

[20] Same. For more information, read the second part of the author's book: l'État dans l'optique de la Bonne Gouvernance. pg 77-176

financial management. Cameroon launched the governance programme in 1995. Governance is concerned with the need to put the chill at all times on approximate management of the State and society, and involve a maximum number of citizens in this management that must satisfy the principles of performance and competitiveness. In reality, the State must stay strong while leaving private initiatives and the private sector to play their role of creating wealth. Even in the West to date, the State remains the last rampart in the face of all challenges. This was again obvious during the different economic and monetary crises of these past years.

VI- Social and health values: health, cleanliness, hygiene, salubrity, employment

Importance is often accorded to health, as a series of actions and prescriptions implemented by administration and related to protection of the health of citizens, by specifying the fact that these actions and prescriptions must prioritise hygiene, cleanliness and salubrity. Whereas, this triptych is top priority in the health system, the latter is the state of somebody whose body is in good condition and spared by diseases, by adding mental health to ensure balance of personality and command of one's intellectual faculties. Hence, this results to a physically healthy citizen in a healthy mind. That said, health, as well as hygiene, cleanliness, salubrity, associated to the individual, must be priority values, they form part of the identity of a people. In that light, Africa has a long way to go to render the citizens responsible for the implementation of these fundamental values. Looking at the dirtiness of our towns and villages, our homes, our hospitals, makes us come to terms with the long road to becoming references in terms of public health, worthy to be cited as models. The definitions of these terms illustrate their importance. Hygiene is the part in medicine that studies individual or collective means, principles, practices aimed to preserve or promote health. Cleanliness is the quality of what is unsoiled, that is well cared for, cleaned, done with care, tidy. Salubrity, close to hygiene is all measures prescribed by administration for the hygiene of individuals, animals and things. In this regard, it is part of public salubrity that concerns all. Proper practice of hygiene, cleanliness and salubrity contributes to sound health. These reflect a good working health system.

In reality, any well-educated person of good health is an effective agent, who is ready to chip in his contribution to the development of his society. Health for all remains the greatest challenge for Africa. For now, it remains a slogan, for much still has to be done, in the face of these pandemics still plaguing Africa: malaria, AIDS, Ebola, hepatitis, cerebrovascular accidents (stroke), diabetes, etc.

Conversely, job creation is at the centre of development concerns. Like health and education, it is also a right claimed by citizens of any country. All African governments are making great efforts to address the job conundrum. To effectively resolve this problem, audacious development policies are sought by these States through industrialisation of the economy, which would provide a substantial added value to wealth production, a source of multiplication of decent job opportunities.

VII- Scientific, technical, technological and industrial values

In order to exert greater impact on destiny, man developed science, techniques, technology at the service of industry, driven by logic of perfect values that arrange things in the right direction.

The revolution in science promoted techniques, technology and industry conducive to development and transformation of material. Africa must undertake this revolution through scientific, technical and industrial prowess.

Science is meant to analyse natural facts and realities through tried and tested methods in view of development. Technique is the set of science applications in the domain of production. Technology, on its part, is the study of tools and machines used in industry. It is also the series of economic activities that produce material goods through transformation and implementation of materials. Industry provides additional value to wealth production.

Following the logic of knowledge, man developed science, technique and technology, which are perfect fundamental values, for the transformation of matter. Matter itself is a perfect value. Thus, matter and the mind are the two perfect values that constitute the cosmos. People who understand and master this truism have made their development a success. The results of science, technology and industry have propelled modern civilisation to unparalleled levels of development, affording man powerful and multifaceted resources that are tantamount to a miracle and feat. This is raised to the point that certain authors like Japanese-born American Francis Fukuyama believe that the West is standard-bearer of this remarkable human evolution attained at the end history (*La fin de l'homme. Les conséquences de la révolution biotechnique*, 2003). Thanks to science, technology and industry, man organised his practical life on earth by promoting: education, training, the State and State institutions, human rights and humanitarian rights, economy for the production of goods and services, industry for the optimal transformation of material for production of goods, medicine and health for sustaining and prolonging life, agriculture and livestock, information and communication technologies, aeronautics, space conquest. Through scientific and technological prowess, man was able to subjugate the forces of nature and put them at his service as well as wellbeing.

These multifaceted skills, scientific and technological progress enabled the Western world to launch the industrialisation of Europe in the 19th century and to carry on through consumer society in the 20th century, then to globalisation and global knowledge society in the 21st century. Mastery of know-how is the most spectacular evolution undergone by man to reach the summits in human development. Thus, the logic of knowledge considered clearly through the divine strata is concretised and magnified in the human realm, to become the sole dynamic that leads to development. Divine science, natural science and technology have converged to instil in man an extraordinary ability to command his destiny.

The power of science, technology and industry

Marc Fonte-Cave, chemist and holder of a Chemistry chair on biological processes, underlines that the power of Chemistry is ever on the rise. Synthetic biology has witnessed significant progress thanks to knowledge of living Chemistry. It is now possible to use cell factory to produce useful things. There is better understanding of the mechanisms of brain plasticity throughout its development and new windows may be opened for adults. Research works on brain-machine interfaces have as goal to develop electronic pro-theses. There is increasing mention of enhancing the human. Man is a technical animal that, at each generation, takes up from where the previous stopped. The computer extends the brain as the tool prolongs the hand.

Attempt to enhance man (Homo Deus) or the quest for transhumance through artificial intelligence

Science has pushed its prowess until it is now making attempts to invent the immortal man. There is talk of enhancing man. In regenerative medicine, there is talk of bio-artificial organs. The boom in cell therapy, with discoveries of stem cells and their reprogramming has seriously changed the game. Biomaterial can now be associated to those that serve skeletons of human cells. The latter proliferate and colonise these matrices enabling recreation of pieces of branch and trachea, blood vessels, veins, arteries, bladders. That is the future that seems to beckon to tissue engineering and regenerative medicine, for they eliminate any risks of rejection inevitable in classical transplants.

Artificial intelligence (AI)

After that, the next step would consist in a genetic modification of vital organs to enable them live for long and perform better. The most convinced Transhumanists have no doubt that, one day, this will be possible. But their ground-breaking development at the moment, is artificial intelligence. Bill Gates, founder of Microsoft, confided that a quarter of research work done by his corporation is devoted to artificial intelligence. His dream is to replicate cognitive processes in a computer. Many laboratories worldwide, in Japan, the USA or Switzerland, are trying to model the brain. One word, very much en vogue in Silicon Valley, in the USA, is "disrupt", which is the ability to shake up the established order and the certainty that man would improve the machine as much as the machine would improve man. Better still, another word, "singularity", a concept invented by mathematician Vermor Vinge in 1993, points out the time when the machine would be capable of surpassing man, reprogramming itself to increase its capabilities to the infinite, or even acquiring a conscience via a computing power that is currently beyond imagination. In his book, *La chute de l'Empire humain*, Grasset, 22nd March 2017, Roland Bouée, Executive Director of *Cabinet-Conseil Roland Berger* analyses the prowess of artificial intelligence (AI) in the weekly journal, *Le Point* No. 2323 of Thursday, 16th March 2017. pg 57 and said: "the intelligence of the machine lies in its capacity to take up a substantial volume of information, extract from it what is meaningful to a question posed, to provide rapid pertinent answers, but also enrich skills as it processes the problems keyed-in in a relatively specific reference domain". Thus, "there is no need to be divine to grasp the interest of this type of artificial intelligence for enterprises that must process and extract meaning from a great volume of data: internet giants, new American or Chinese champions, health, insurance, banking, financial services, legal consultancy sectors, as well as all enterprises operating in a totally unreal world". Given that human action is only the fruit of intelligence, "it is no surprise that a number of major investment funds and banks are snapping up, at premium price, the best artificial intelligence experts working with IBM, Google or elsewhere… We are on the threshold of a new world, that of machine reinforced decision, to which could be attached the acronym, MDRP, for Machine Reinforced decision process".

Life expectancy may be unlimited

Whoever will live for 1000 years is already born. This is a conviction of Silicon Valley, notably among Google executives (a rival of Microsoft). Note that in the era of Adam and Noah, people were already living a very long life: Adam 930 years, his son Seth 912 years, Enoch son of Seth 905 years, Kenan son of Enosh, 905 years, Methuselah descendant of Seth, 969 years. Noah himself 930 years (the Book of Genesis, Chapters 5 to 6). This longevity declined with corruption of the human gender. Is science hoping to reinvent this epoch and surpass God? Google is in the vanguard of the Transhumanist ideology that aims to euthanise death. Google created calico, a biotechnology enterprise tasked with meeting the challenges of ageing and related diseases for the purpose of extending human life. For all practical purposes, the biotechnological revolution may accelerate the nibbling of death. Life expectancy has more than tripled already. It has evolved in France from 25 years in 1750 to more than 80 years and increases by three months per annum "(*Le Monde Hors-série. L'histoire des inventions. Jusqu'où irons-nous ?* 2015, pg 173 et s.)." To succeed in extending life in a spectacular manner, heavy technologies must be considered by making use of the power of NBIC (nanotechnologies, biotechnologies, computer and cognitive science). Life engineering with genetic therapies, stem cells, and artificial organs would shake up the health system. A radical modification of our biologic functioning and our genome will be necessary. Brain would then constitute the greatest obstacle. Why live long with a sclerosed brain? Preserving the plastic brain presupposes heavy engineering. Living long may become a reality, but at the price of a complete redefinition of humanity.

In this scientific euphoria, Yuval Noah Harari, author of the bestseller "Homo Deus" or man god, is convinced that: "based on the principle that humans have almost resolved the three major problems — famine, epidemics and wars — they would focus on a new agenda: accession to divinity. This upgrade of our specie, thanks to genetic manipulations and artificial intelligence, is alleged to have commenced. The new religion is dataism, which explains to us that the whole universe is only a flux of data, flux of information and not physical forces and molecules"[21].

According to Transhumanists, disease and ageing are not a fatality. The future man would resemble a website. Meaning a prototype-organism bound to continually improve thanks to NBIC. To what extend could we modify our biological nature, our DNA, to roll back death? Biotechnologies are more and more spectacular and in the course of time, without being conscious of the impacts of science on us, we are becoming Transhumans, which is technologically modified men and women. Laurent Alexandre notes that most of us accept the bio-revolution so as to age less, suffer less, die less (*Le Monde Hors-série*, op.cit.,). This researcher fears that medical and ethical power should fall into the hands of leaders of the digital economy like Gafa (Google, Apple, Facebook, and Amazon) as well as IBM and Microsoft, who would be masters of such medicine. Laurent Alexandre considers that manipulating the living to kill death requires intellectual capacities beyond the reach of our biological brain. He believes that only an artificial intelligence (AI) can render one immortal. According to Ray Kurzweil, chief engineer at Google, an artificial intelligence will be one thousand million times more powerful than a constellation of all human brains by the year 2045. He is convinced that our memory and our conscience can soon be transferred into microprocessors, which will enable our mind to survive our biological dead. The objective in this conception of existence is therefore no longer to repair the body, but to enhance the body as well, by rendering it eternal by merging the body with the machine to give birth to a cyborg. Life would then be a matter of maintenance, where parts of our organism would be replaced just like parts of a car are changed, the latter endowed with an unlimited mileage (*Le Monde Hors-Série*, pg 176). Science has gone as far as inventing an artificial heart. This, born from collaboration between surgeon Alain Carpentier and the *société Matra*. The said heart weighs 900g against

[21] The weekly information journal *Le Point* No.2347 of 31st August 2017, pg. 46-43.

500g for the human heart. It was implanted for the first time on 18th December 2013, at *Hôpital George Pompidou* in Paris, in a man aged 76, who died 74 days later. A second implantation took place at *CHU de Nantes*, on 5th August 2014. The patient, a man of 69 years, lived for 9 months with his cardiac prothesis. He died on 2nd May 2015 (*Le Monde Hors-Série*, op.cit.). Prof Ebénézer Njoh Mouellé developed this theory of Transhumanism in a conference at the University of Yaounde, on Thursday, 16th July 2015.

In reality, this conception of existence is frightening to more than one person. Philosopher Roger-Pol Droit considers that it is pure fantasy of self-creation. He believes that every man is brother to Prometheus, inclined to place himself at the side of God. He feels ashamed for not having been born or well-conceived and reliable as machines. And he is tired of being a mere product of chance and genetics. British physicist Stephen Hawking, on BBC at the end of 2004, impressed public opinion, when he declared that the development of artificial intelligence could spell the end of the human species. In January 2015, certain scientists and business executives even published an open letter, calling for limitation of risks incurred by humanity due to the development of machines, on the website of the Future of Life Institute, an American organisation. The philosopher, Roger Pol Droit, recalls the agitation caused in 1996 by the birth of the cloned ewe, Dolly. Everybody was convinced that men would soon be cloned. That turned out not to be the case, thanks to international agreements and the refusal, for ethical reasons, to manipulate the human genome. To him, the future of human adventure must not be left in the hands of scientists alone, but depend on absolute transparency in civil and civic responsibility (*Le Monde* Hors-Série op.cit.,).

Against this backdrop of scientific and technological turmoil, the industry plays a pivotal role. It has contributed to a lot of progress in development through the phenomenon of economic growth. Industry propagates technology in all sectors of national economy and technology increases productivity in economic sectors. The industry thereby asserts itself as catalyst of economic growth. Industrialisation produces the following positive effects: it augments the general economic productivity of national economies, it modernises priority sectors through an adequate input of intermediary products and capital goods, and it improves living standards through the provision of durable and current consumer goods at low prices, through a multiplication of well-remunerated jobs. Without industrialisation, economic growth cannot be triggered in Africa. African States must develop the capacity of implementing strategies of operating industries that require State intervention measures just like Asian countries steered a dynamic industrialisation policy. The agribusiness and mining sectors based on abundant agricultural and mining resources offer far-reaching opportunities[22].

Science and faith

Divine science, science and technology have converged to instil in man an extraordinary ability to command his destiny. This complementarity between God, man and science is brilliantly expatiated in the famous and solid review, '*Le Monde des Religions'*, No. 39 of January – February 2010. This review points out that: "On condition that they develop in a clearly independent manner, religious faith and scientific approach are both indispensable to any doubts about our origins, and to construction of our common humanity", and adds that spiritualties talk of intention, finality, sense, science of rationally and experimentally testable causality relations. This review goes on to affirm that the positivism of scholars has finally established a compromise with religion in the terms used by Auguste Comte, a sociologist: science would desist from dwelling on the whys of phenomena, to henceforth focus on the hows. In seeking to establish laws instituting normal relations between facts observed, it would refrain from speculating about the causes of phenomena on religion.[23] Another great mind, Stephen Jay Gould, speaking of the relation between science and religion, proposes a co-evolution between faith and scientific approach that may be complementary and not antagonistic.[24]

Two American Nobel prize winners agree with and even go beyond that opinion. They are Charles TOWNES, Nobel Prize winner in Physics in 1964, inventor of the laser, lecturer at the University of Berkeley, and William Phillips, Nobel Prize winner in Physics in 1997, researcher at the National Institute of Standards and Technology of

---

[22] Louis Sangare, *Industrialisation et développement économique accélérés en Afrique*, l'Harmattan, 2015, pg. 11 et s

[23] Le monde des Religions: No. 39 January-Februray 2010 pg. 46 – 48.

[24]Ibid., pg. 48-49.

Washington. They express their views on interactions between spirituality and scientific progress.

To Charles Townes, science and faith are universal and even similar. To clear up things, he adopts a relatively extreme position, affirming that the differences between them are superficial, and that on observing their real nature, one discovers that characteristics of the two domains are almost identical. He considers that faith, which is essential in religion, is equally so in science. To him, the scientist needs faith when he gets down to work and an even greater faith to conduct his most difficult works with success.[25]

To William Phillips, being an ordinary scientist as well as an ordinary Christian seems natural. It also seems natural to many scientists he knows who are genuine believers. He considers that nothing can prevent him from believing in God. He affirms that his scientific knowledge underscores his faith. Even if faith is non-scientific (not anti-scientific), it is nonetheless rational. Upon observing the order, comprehension and beauty of the universe, we can conclude that what he sees was deliberately created by a superior intelligence. His scientific appraisal of the coherence and wonderful simplicity of nature strengthens his believe in God.[26]

Other men of science find a complementarity between science and God. Jean d'Ormesson, of the French Academy, points out that God is at the origin of everything, the final purpose and explanation. To Albert Einstein, science without religion is lame, religion without science is blind.

Trinh Xuan Thuan, astrophysicist and Buddhist, lecturer at the University of Virginia in the United States, reveals that the universe is governed by perfect laws, these laws, in his view, have properties that are usually attributed to God. They are universal, they are absolute, for they depend neither on whoever is studying them nor on the State of the system observed. They are eternal, timeless. He states that the properties of distant galaxies seen in their space, may be explained with the same physical laws, than nearby galaxies seen in their maturity. They are omnipotent, for nothing in the universe from the smallest atom to the biggest galaxies can avoid their influence. He believes that if Newton and Einstein had never existed, the theories of universal

---

[25]Ibid.,pg. 36.
[26]Ibid.,pg. 38.

gravitation and relativity of time and space would still have been discovered sooner or later by other researchers.[27]

These explanations are enough proof that mastery of divine, celestial, human and terrestrial knowledge, paves the perfect way to respond to the problem of development, as is the case in the West and Asia. Divine, supernatural human and natural knowledge are complementary. Whoever fully appropriates these two knowledge can consider that he has found the truth about things or the way to that truth. The case of the West that followed that path is proof enough. This is exactly the two-fold knowledge that we have sought and expatiated in this book, to understand why some people achieved development and not others. They covered a long and rough trajectory that leads man from darkness to illumination of the Mind, from ignorance to knowledge, from minority to superiority and to power for a successful action. Likewise, we have illustrated that secularism cannot constitute an obstacle to fruitful relations between the State and the Church, or between God and man, since all aspire for the wellbeing of man. In the light of past developments and testimonies of great men of science and faith, we can state that Africans must not neglect any source of knowledge, be it divine or human, for it is this global knowledge that affords a global and perfect vision of knowledge. In reality, authentic development stems from mysticism and magic, in terms of mastery of perfect natural and supernatural laws and their successful application, for a large part of the unknown that is revealed by the divine Mind and that sheds light on several mysteries.

Africa and the need for scientific, technologic and industrial research

This emphasis on scientific, technological and industrial prowess merely tends to illustrate to African that research for development is unavoidable. In one word, the practice of intelligence remains at the centre of development. It enables man to multiply his abilities and activities at infinitum, for job creation. Hence we must continue to offer solid training to the African elite. For the future of humanity can be conquered in mastery of knowledge. Africa can only meet the challenge of its development with this form of ascetism and this culture of knowledge. The fierce rivalry raging among the great powers in the

---

[27] Journal Le Point N° 2049-2050 of Thursday 22 and 29 December 2011: Questions sur l'existence de Dieu pg. 87, 108, 116.

domain of knowledge is proof of the unavoidable development of all forms of knowledge. In this atmosphere of surge in knowledge, Africa must absolutely produce its scholars in all sectors of science and technology. It must encourage the young to be self-reliant and to build their potentials by creating jobs. It must strive for transfer of high-performance and innovative technologies, welcome the input of a more and more organised Diaspora that is not sufficiently made use of. Profitable participation of women in nation building. Develop the vast domain of agriculture and livestock with multiple potentialities that are not yet sufficiently exploited and explored. Creation and generation of communication infrastructures for free movement of individuals and goods in an Africa united by a prosperous common market. The execution and multiplication of different sources of energy essential to industrialisation and the stimulation of the vast informal sector. Development of scientific research to its pinnacle. Revamping and growth of the tourism industry and promotion of our millenary culture and revival of our sports industries to help the young to better flourish in high-level professional sports, which would enable young African professionals to earn astronomic salaries worldwide.

We observe therefore that man, a perfect creation, has acquired the perfect knowledge that leads to progress, like the Western developed countries and now emerging countries like China, by relying on great wise men and visioneers like Georges Washington, Abraham Lincoln, Charles de Gaulle, Buddha, Confucius, Tao, Martin Luther King, Mao Tse Tung, Chu en Laï, Deng Xiaoping, Mandela. Thanks also go to a critical mass of talents in all socio-economic domains. Africa must also, at all cost, maintain and develop the tradition of intelligence, wisdom and knowledge.

At a time when Africa is embarking on the arduous path to development, it must revisit the trajectory of countries that had preceded the continent on such path, find out how they mastered every knowledge leading to development. This will enable the continent to best grasp the fire of the Mind so as to ensure its own development, and make use of its own genius, by bringing to the community of nations, the freshness of its mind driven by altruism, enthusiasm, solidarity and communitarianism. Africa can bring to science and technology a new humanism that will open other avenues or these domains for the wellbeing and progress of humanity. For knowledge is an unlimited and infinite field, where one can draw as much as one desires, it is really the true space of liberty. Africa has its place, provided it understands that it is the right path to follow and commits firmly to it, for in reality, and is not yet the case. None can prevent another from seeking knowledge. That is why nations that dominate the world are also those that possess global knowledge, which embraces all aspects of human life. It is such knowledge that leads inexorably to scientific, technological, financial, material, military and diplomatic power. This culture of knowledge is well taken up by former Israeli president Shimon Peres who most opportunely affirms that world currency will be knowledge. He specified that an electronic currency based on knowledge will replace all currencies of the globe. This will require significant changes in the banking system, but it will constitute an important adaptation to the new age. He adds that we must begin to measure growth by the scientific potential in research laboratories.[28] He however considers that Israel, despite its small size and lack of natural resources, is an economic success thanks to the wings of science, for it really matters, that is the scientific potential, education, know-how, knowledge of languages potential are all perfect forms of knowledge. He points out that Israel has transformed the lack of natural resources into an advantage by maximising the human potential of the people, for the Jewish people are driven by a constant feeling of dissatisfaction, they are never satisfied with the existing situation, and they shun the idea that something can be impossible. As pioneer in nanotechnologies, Israel has benefitted from an investment return in this domain, multiplied by 50. Israel is now laying emphasis on neuroscience and comprehension of the human brain.[29]

VIII- Economic, managerial, material and financial values

Free-market economy and promotion of the private sector

We have already explained that freedom has become the paradigm of this activity in modern societies.

Nowadays, free-market economy is at the centre of development issues. Economy is thus all activities engaged by the human community

[28] Le Nouvel Observateur No.2569 of 30 January 2014. pg. 38.

[29] Nanotechnology is a technology that applies microelectronics to the manufactuing of devices for structures at a nanometre scale, nanometre is a unit of measurement for length, equivalent to a thousand millionth metre.

Neuroscience is the set of scientific domains that study the nervous system related to the production, distribution and consumption of wealth. It equally extends to the new economy tied to the development of new information and communication technologies. Economic science is bound to a continuous expansion, because the study and knowledge of economic mechanisms and phenomena, which bring about a sense of method, observation, analysis that culminates into concrete solutions for the production of wealth. It requires science, technology and industry.

Economy has as finality the material, cultural and financial wellbeing of man. It is a very important activity in well planned, organised and structured human societies. It procures all material, financial and social goods needed by the human (food, housing, dress, healthcare, education, training, culture, etc.). Thus, in this respect, schools of thought are competing to find the best formulas to resolve these problems: free-market economy is the economic system founded on market forces, on the principle of free trade, free play of demand and supply and that limits State interference; socialism favours the redistribution of the fruits of growth; planned or managed economy is founded on State planning; social democracy associates the advantages of market economy and social justice; concerted economy is that where the State and economic partners concert.

Generally speaking, market economy now dominates the world and Africa, it encourages, private initiative and market forces. To put in place a solid economy, the available wealth and goods production, distribution and consumption must be well-organised. For that purpose, values of management, professionalism, obligation of result, leadership must be developed.

Africa's major problem is that the continent still finds it difficult to effectively structure its economy for an optimal production of goods.

Management

In modern economies, management has taken a big dimension, for it demands optimal management of the enterprise and society such as to produce satisfactory and excellent results. Management therefore refers to administration, running of an organisation. Such management must obey good practice, beginning with quality human resources that lead to production and distribution for an optimal and measured consumption. In this regard, the objectives to attain must specify the multifaceted and adequate means (financial, human, and environmental). The obligation of result must become a religion. Within every country, the managerial approach is even more complex and implies a global vision of the organisation to be put in place, through the different powers, sectors and within each power and structure.

Professionalism to be the best and emulate the best

Professionalism is the ability to be competent and possess the spiritual, intellectual, moral, scientific, technological and managerial qualities required in activities engaged. In other words, it means excelling in whatever one is doing for effective and indisputable results. This attitude is necessary in African societies to steer their development to a success. African elites must absolutely appropriate such attitude, as the people of developed countries had done and those of emerging countries are increasingly doing. That's precisely the superior level of competence lacking in Africans, to the point where they constantly resort to a foreign expertise that is so costly to our States. Africans must get rid of such complexes, by promoting true quality human resources that square with those of developed countries. To achieve that, African States must invest in training for its human resources on a permanent basis. Such was the case with Japan, Israel or South Korea, whose soil and sub-soil are poor in resources, but which opted for solid training for their senior staff and succeeded in topping the chart of industrialised powers. That is what emerging countries like China, India and many others did. To that end, Africans must aspire to be the best, and emulate the best. To be best means attaining the highest level of quality in one's domain to the point of making a lasting difference, as compared to mediocrity and approximation. Africa must commit to the powerful universal norms that procure satisfaction without upsetting the concerned. Intelligence is not a matter of race. Intelligence grants access to globalisation and global economic integration, to enjoy the inherent opportunities, rather than raising their spectre. Ambition and courage are required to stand firm in the face of inevitable pitfalls one is bound to encounter. These norms are accepted by our countries within most regional and international organisations they belong to: the International Monetary Fund (IMF, the World Bank, the World Trade Organisation (WTO), the United Nations Organisation system, the African Development Bank (AfDB), the International Federation of Football Associations (FIFA) and many others.

There is no shame in emulating or even copying countries that have excelled in the domains of scientific, technological, industrial and commercial know-how, others have done so before Africa, we should follow suit, to better innovate and lend our spiritual freshness to this realm of development. Africa has to get down to work, as we have stressed above.

Such is the high level of expertise that has enabled the Europeans, the United States, to develop and stay at this level for close to two centuries. This means that whenever one is best, professional, excellent, perfect, concrete and fruitful results are inevitable. That is why emulating the best would enable us to catch up with them, or even to be better, provided we spare no efforts. Japan imitated the European countries in its industrialisation, to the point of doing better in certain state-of-the-art technologies (computer, car manufacturing). The emerging countries in Asia and elsewhere are on the same track. Thus, there has emerged in economy the notion of catch-up of under-developed economies that are expected to attain the level of developed countries, especially in the scientific, education, training and industrialisation domains, with all its positive consequences and spill over effects.

In Africa, on the contrary, professionalism is not yet an established culture, several sectors still suffer severely from amateurism and approximation. The World Football Cup tournament that took place in Brazil from June to July 2014 best illustrates this in the case of African teams. Less prepared than other teams, they failed to produce good results. This means that at the level of world competition, there is no approximation or compassion, what matters is performance that produces results. The gap to be bridged by Africa is enormous. Africa must get down to serious and relentless work. That is the price to pay to meet the challenges of globalisation.

Leadership

Hampaté Ba, an African wise man was wont to state that a leader must always know where he's going and where he wants to lead others to. This attitude clearly shows that the leader, whoever holds the domineering position, the top rank must be a visioneer, a person versed with experience in the professional, social, or even family domains. The leader knows what he wants for the community under his care. This position requires of the leader exceptional qualities of intelligence, wisdom, discernment, courage, decision, moderation and many others. The leader must be able to set their specific and strategic objectives that can stir up and advance societies. That is why leadership is always tied to a name and to a given period. That was the case with Charles de Gaulle, who led the resistance to victory over the German occupation of France in 1945. Mao Tse Tung who acceded to power in China, in 1949, after the long march, and led the country to political emancipation. One of his successors, Deng Xiaoping, led China to economic development and emergence as from the 1980s. François Mitterrand, the cantor of French socialism, shook up the Gaullist right hegemony, bringing the socialists to power in France in 1981, introducing change in power. Moustapha Kemal, after a series of victories over the Armenians, Kurds and Greeks, formed the Secular Republic of Turkey. The Great Zulu Leader, Tchaka, succeeded to challenge English dominion in South Africa. King Behanzin provided a staunch resistance to the occupation of his country, Dahomey (now Benin), by the French. Even more recently, Nelson Mandela led the Republic of South Africa to reconciliation between the white and black communities, following decades of fierce racial discrimination against blacks. Several business executives, eminent craftsmen and dignitaries of liberal professions have shown proof of influential leadership in different sectors of social activity.

Assuming leadership is not the preserve of a spontaneous generation, it is prepared through strong spiritual, intellectual, moral, physical and professional qualities. The leader must be enlightened to serve as the beacon that leads his people. The leader must transform his environment on a permanent basis and positively. Leadership in Africa must evolve through sheer paths that lead to development, to lead our countries, bogged down by enormous difficulties, towards their emergence. During the fight against colonialism, several African leaders successfully wrested independence from the colonial masters thanks to this sense of leadership, to the point that the whole African continent has today been set free from the colonial yoke.

Planning, setting specific and strategic objectives

Planning is the act of programming economic, social and cultural actions based on substantial resources to be engaged over a given period. This exercise allows for the setting of specific and strategic objectives, in important sectors of development. The contrary would be perilous, ineffective and counter-productive. In the early years of independence for African countries, this approach was adopted until the advent of the crisis in the 1990s. Donors, notably the International Monetary Fund and the World Bank replaced planning with the famous structural adjustment plans that favour great macro-economic balances, to stabilise the out-of-steam African economies, in view of reimbursing the heavy debts owed by African countries. This policy weighed heavily on public planning policies and led to the liquidation of several public enterprises, thereby subjecting thousands of workers to unemployment. It is imperative now that economic growth has returned, to once again adopt this planning approach, in order to determine priority sectors to develop, and corresponding resources needed, top among which are: education and health, agriculture, livestock, industry, tourism, diverse infrastructures, etc. Sustained efforts must be devoted to this approach for greater visibility in the short, medium and long term. Emerging countries so close to us, follow this method with the greatest rigour, planning allows for the establishment of specific benchmarks that guide the action of decision-makers and operators. It is a performance indicator that clarifies the path of decision-makers and operators. In Cameroon, the Growth and Employment Strategy Document by the year 2035 is a good step towards such strategic planning, other African counties are on that track.

Effectiveness, achievement and obligation of results

Effectiveness in an activity has as result the production of the expected effect, the best result. Anglo-Saxons have developed this virtue to the highest point, through the term "efficiency" that means, ability, competence, good output, efficiency. It is difficult to engage an activity in a mind-set other than that of seeking for positive results. Achievement of results must be obsessional, for this helps to focus all one's abilities towards this ultimate stage, it focalises all one's attention, intelligence, energy towards this exciting goal. It allows for quantification of efforts furnished to obtain the result desired. Development programmes in Africa can only yield promising and positive results if they are measured on the basis of this relentless quest for results. Achievement of results allow for progress, for a well-managed project resolves the problem raised, which enables transfer of the resources allotted towards another project, and so forth. Absence of evaluation or poor evaluation of projects programmed compromises the results expected and leaves no room for progress. It is for this reason that in Africa, one is often surprised by the fact that budgets increase every year even when effective development does not follow. That is because there is no strict evaluation that seeks fixed results.

Creation of wealth, material goods and a society of abundance

One of the most important goals of development is the creation of wealth and jobs. Wealth is the abundance of goods as is seen in the West and in other countries which have successfully created them, they have thus become strong for so long, suppliers of goods to less affluent countries notably African countries. There is no shame or evil in seeking for wealth and abundance, for man is confronted to all sorts of needs: food, dressing, housing, water, electricity, leisure, means of locomotion, healthcare, everything that contributes to the comfort and material wellbeing of man. For, when we are safe from these material and financial needs which are indispensable to natural life, we display a smiling face and the heart, the seat of feelings, is at peace. We can best develop the human when, needs are assured. Africa has also embarked on this path of wealth creation through science and technology. It is progressively entrusting this heavy task to the private sector. To succeed, growth rates of at least 7% must be achieved, if not double digit figures, to produce goods in abundance on a permanent basis and become an emerging country. The multiple constraints weighing on investment initiative as witnessed in diverse evaluations of international financial institutions (the World Bank, IMF, AfDB) must be eliminated. It is commonly admitted that the spiritual, intellectual and moral wealth that produce knowledge precede financial and material wealth. This non-reversible and irrefutable logic must be well understood by Africans if we hope to tackle, with success, the creation and production of wealth for all. For any society of abundance, a rigorous training of its citizens in true knowledge is an indispensable prerequisite, which helps to corroborate the idea whereby money does not engender ideas, but rather ideas generate money. To meet this challenge of producing wealth, Africa needs substantial financial resources: for infrastructures alone (roads, bridges, airports, electrification, water supply, etc.), the continent needs 95 000 million US dollars per annum.

When mention is made of perfect values, the fact that it is part of the constituent material of nature is often overlooked. Together with the mind, intangible substance, are the two key components of life and the universe. Material is visible and the mind is intangible and invisible. Understanding this ontological reality has direct consequences on development matters. For material is a very important reality in the universe, it is the visible part of things perceptible with the naked eye, be they the human himself, the fauna, vegetation, water, land and stars. All these visible elements are composed of atoms endowed with physical properties. This dimension of material occupies vast spaces of the universe. Water occupies 4/5 of this environment and surface land only represents 1/5 of the universe. This surface part however hosts 6 000 million living beings, 1000 million of whom are Africans. Its surface area is 510 101 103km^2, its volume 108 332 010km^3 and its mass 6.10 21 tonnes, according to the *Petit Larousse édition 2000* dictionary. This massive settlement on the land is impressive, it also includes forests, mines, precious materials, arable land in its great diversity, water which is wealth of its own and which embodies other wealth. Above land, there is the sky that is also visible to the naked eye and that contains stars (sun, moon, stars, galaxies, etc.). The latter produce light and energy. From the natural and material level, Africa abounds with enormous soil and sub-soil resources: precious wood species, precious stones and material (gold, diamond, silver, uranium, tin, cobalt, zinc, aluminium, oil, iron, phosphates, platinum, etc.), all sorts of agricultural products: coffee, cocoa, banana, cotton, groundnuts, rubber, pineapple, mahogany walnuts, tubers, all sorts of fruits, large expanses of water.

Why is it that Africa, endowed with all the natural resources known by all observers, remains under-developed and poor? Certainly because the continent has failed to sufficiently tame the forces of the mind that lead to understanding of science and technologies, transformers of material, for wealth creation and added value. The mind is thus the domineering force that overcomes material. It is the vector of science and technology and it creates monetary riches. That is why developed countries that possess this scientific and technological knowledge can easily appropriate African raw materials to transform them. For it's reasonable that development should give primacy to the mind and knowledge and not material, despite the apparent mass and their importance as we are equally observing. If gold, diamond, platinum, coffee, cotton is not transformed, what is their true added value? It is low. Material is very important, but it can only acquire real value when transformed thanks to breath from the mind, thus knowledge. The logic of primacy of the mind shows that under-developed people inject less mind, thus the force of knowledge to transform material, very few have attained 50% of spiritual power in mastery of science and technology.

In this respect, producing enough material and financial resources remains a difficult equation to be solved in Africa. Africa must address it and generate wealth for all its people and also be able to manufacture its own multimillionaires and magnates, as is the case everywhere and especially in the West and increasingly in Asia.

IX- Values of success, satisfaction, happiness, life in abundance and bliss

Success, satisfaction, happiness, life in abundance and bliss are reserved for men and societies that have acquired intelligence, knowledge and wisdom in view of the development of multifaceted wealth and the quest for a happy live, through the practice of multiple strong moral and ethical values. Certain societies have attained this level, especially in the West (Europe, the United States, and Canada) and certain emerging countries in Asia (China, South Korea, Japan, Singapore, etc.). This fundamental and implacable logic of human life must be well understood, it must be fine-tuned tirelessly and fiercely to grasp and master it, if not it will be extremely difficult for Africans to conquer the realms of a wealthy and happy life.

Truly speaking, success is an ability sought by all humans, whatever the horizons and persuasions. It is the expression of a favourable result, success, an appreciable standard of living, intellectually, morally and materially. Who would not welcome good news bearing compensation at the end of hard labour and effort? Who would not be proud of undertaking proper studies and having a well-paid and fulfilling job? This virtue must be passionately sought and fine-tuned. Success is the yardstick of efforts made to improve comfort in one's life in every domain: spiritual, intellectual, material, financial and social. It affords pleasure, happiness, and satisfaction. Africans must resolutely embrace it to become its apostles, refrain from permissiveness, fatalism, failures, and disappointments, discard the notion of a continent that never wins, that does not set the pace for others. Be winners, more than winners, must be the slogan of Africans, such that they can create viable States after a few generations have come and gone, as the emerging countries have proven. Whereas, it is the daily practice of fundamental values that leads without doubt to success. And the divine word proclaims loud and clear that success belongs to whoever finds his pleasure in the Eternal Law and deserves it day and night. It is like a tree planted near a stream, which bears its fruit at the right time and whose leaves never wither, all what it undertakes succeeds. It is thus true praise of success that depends on mastery of true knowledge. This blessing must be extended to all forms of human activities. The best organised human systems are those that create opportunities for all and especially for the best. Any country where the conditions of success are organised is a country driven by the logic of progress and for which development evolves in an obvious manner. Success leads unavoidably to happiness, material wellbeing and spiritual, moral as well as intellectual satisfaction. Any well-oriented development of society leads to happiness, for it creates all conditions necessary to achieve it. Against this backdrop of optimal quest and organisation of success, men, women and children are focused on well set objectives, whose end result is to acquire all spiritual, mental, moral, intellectual and physical material, and financial resources that lead to success and happiness. This path exists and some have found it. Africa can also do same. God said that he has offered man his own bliss such that man should be fulfilled and attain his highest level of development and fulfilment. Development is a global dimension that extends from Alpha to Omega, which is the founding axis of life that leads inexorably to happiness and bliss, for the founding axis of life contains all successes and satisfactions, spiritual and material. Many humans who follow this path proclaim it.

In this context of optimal development where the citizen attains abundance and happiness, he enters into a life of bliss. Such bliss is the expression of the quantitative and qualitative success of development. Development must have as ultimate ambition to manage abundance and not scarcity or poverty. It must produce a type of complete and fulfilled man. Happiness is thus considered in its practical aspect, and even as viewed by Greek philosophers, as an ultimate end for man, fruit of a virtuous behaviour and a fulfilled life. At this stage of development, the human enters the dimension of positive ascension further incarnating, more infinite opportunities. The sublime or in the view of Asians, nirvana or as God proclaimed, bliss and beatitudes is attained. And when one attains this level, one is endowed with the culture of perfect and optimal development, one upholds it and continues to evolve. Development is never static. All these perfect fundamental values that we have just described constitute a veritable reference system. It is a true frame of reference that can be resorted to at any moment to find solutions to multiple problems. Developed and emerging countries regularly resort to this system of strong values to undertake their development. Africa must also achieve and resort to it systematically, for we can affirm that it is a must.

This extensive analysis of themes and concepts related to perfect fundamental values, favourable to sustaining the development of Africa reflect their importance and interest. And that is why these values constitute a reference system that must always be resorted to, to solve the difficult equation of development. Some have done so. Africa has no reason not to equally do same. Africans must excel and seek the realm of the mind that breed permanent and eternal creativity.

Malfunctions hindering the drive towards perfection

It should however be noted that several breakdowns obstruct the development of Africa in its drive to perfection. Among which are: ignorance, lack of culture, corruption, illegal enrichment, indiscipline, sub-standard practice of moral and social, incompetence, degradation and depravity of morals, permissiveness and penchant for short-cuts, poverty, unemployment, circumvention of rules, insalubrity, homosexuality, below the par sustained effort, egoism, individualism, organised crime, terrorism, conflicts of interests, poor evaluation of development programmes, insufficient expertise in management of strategic files, outward-oriented and low integrated economies, poor integration of States, poor and low integrated national cultures, poor promotion of the culture of perfection, excellence and meritocracy, the will of domination, rivalries between nations, disparaging mentality, poor boosting of positive values, deficient taste for risk, disrespect of one's word, etc.

To highlight the relevance of these themes, we intend to dwell on definition, explanation and stakes of development in regard to under-development.

Chapter V

Definition and explanation of notions of development and under-development

Development and its antinomy, under-development, are several of unknown equations that this book attempts to solve. That is why it is important to equally dwell on the definition and explanation of these two capital notions in the life of human societies and particularly in Africa, a continent grappling with the complex problem of its development. In point of fact, these two aspects of life can only find ideal solutions if man appropriates perfect knowledge, which is the yardstick of everything, according to Greek philosopher, Protagoras, and as we have explained above.

I- Development, a perfect fundamental value

Our stance in this book is that the mastery of perfect fundamental values inevitably leads to development. It can, indeed, be considered that perfection is the supreme state of knowledge and action that illuminates the paths leading to development. In other words, development is nothing but a quest for the welfare of society as a whole. Considering that the perfect fundamental values expatiated lead to development, then development itself constitutes a perfect value, because it is the result or end result of all the underlying values analysed above.

Development is a theme at the centre of the agenda of discussions and concerns of Africans and African countries. The latter are constantly seeking for the most suitable means and ways of achieving it within the shortest time possible. Upon analysis, development, an evolutionary process, can certainly be achieved through dogged research, understanding, mastery and practice of perfect fundamental values for the global wellbeing of the people. For the said values embody all the values that inevitably lead to full development. Thanks to them, no aspect that leads to development is left out. They incorporate all aspects: human, spiritual, quantitative and qualitative, intellectual, moral, ethics, aesthetics, mystical, physical, material, financial, as well as political, economic, social and cultural. In this respect, development is a global knowledge process that culminates into a coherent and effective action, for the production of goods and multifarious satisfactions.

Thus, according to the *Le Petit Larousse illustré 2002* dictionary, development in general, is the process of increasing, progressing, achieving expansion, consistency. It is equally the process of evolving, attaining maturity, superiority. Such evolution leads even to bliss. It is also all the different phases completed by an organisation, a human to attain maturity, or even superiority. Development in its entirety actually begins with man himself before spreading to his environment through his action.

In economics, it is the qualitative, sustainable improvement of an economy and its functioning. It is also the state of less developed (LDC) or developing countries. Countries classified as Third World countries, in a state of economic and social under-development, embarked on a process towards development. It is the process of evolving from a perilous and poverty situation, to a satisfactory situation in view of meeting multiple needs in social life. Development is thus a complete process that involves several aspects. It is mastered progressively as the basics of knowledge and true action are mastered. It involves several phases.

Development and economic growth

The much talked about economic development, as was the case not long ago, concerns positive evolutions in the structural changes of a country or people in terms of per demography, techniques, economy, industry, health, cultural, social aspects. Such change enriches the people and improves living conditions. That is why economic development is associated to progress and transformation of social structures. Progress is associated to economic growth, which is only a component of development. That is, although economic growth increases income, economic growth cannot alone embody development, especially if growth only benefits a few. Economic growth refers to an increase in per capita income, as well as production of goods and services. Economic development involves mainly the improvement in health, education and other aspects of human welfare. Countries that raise their income without ensuring increasing life expectancy, curbing infant mortality and increasing school enrolment rates run short of important aspects of development.

By and large, development also goes along with changes in the economic structure. This is evidenced in the growing number of people who give up rural agricultural production for an urban as well as a better paid job, mostly in the manufacturing industry or tertiary sector. Any economic growth short of structural evolution often constitutes an indicator of the concentration of new incomes, in the hands of a minority. Growth situations that only benefit a rich minority of the country or foreign country, do not constitute development. Indeed, two main structural evolutions usually go with economic development. First of all, the growth share of industries in gross national product, corresponding to the drop in agriculture, and then the growth percentage of urban rather than rural dwellers.[30]

Modern economic growth alludes to the current economic period as opposed to those of merchant capitalism or feudalism. The key factor, here is the application of science to resolve economic production problems, which in turn paves the path to industrialisation, urban development and staggering demographic growth. The economic growth most often referred to may be measured by the following indicators: Gross Domestic Product (GDP), which is the sum of added values generated annually by enterprises of a country, irrespective of their nationality, whether national or foreign, operating in the said country, on the one hand, and Gross National Product (GNP),which is the aggregate GDP of a country, including the value of goods and services produced by enterprises operating outside the national territory, on the other hand. Hence the contribution of a country's Diaspora to the said country, measured in the volume of money transferred as well as other goods and services. Certain African countries have already created a ministry and/or department in charge of foreigners. GNP constitutes one of the most current terms used in estimating national income. Certain multilateral institutions like the World Bank, often term this notion Gross National Income (GNI). Gross Domestic Product (GDP) is similar to GNP, but for that it includes the entire production realised within the territory of a country, including production attributed to the country by foreign residents,

[30] Dwight H. Perkins, Steven Radelet and David L. Lindauer. *Development Economics*. Boeck Editions, 2008, Chapter devoted to development patterns, pg19-49.

excluding the production value of citizens living abroad. GDP is now a measurement criteria of national income most used by the International Monetary Fund (IMF), the United Nations Development Programme, the World Bank and other international organisations. An extensive analysis may allow for calculation of the per capita GDP. This as a whole leads to growth rate, which must be taken into account in modern time economic growth. African countries conform to this discipline in evaluating growth.

Development can only acquire true significance in its global approach.

Development in its global approach and consideration of the Human Development Index (HDI)

As a matter of fact, economic growth is no longer the only criteria to measure economic development, the latter espouses a more global approach. Reference is increasingly made to human development and the Human Development Index (HDI) or even the Happiness Index. The 1991 World Report on Human Development, published by the UNDP, affirms that the main human development goal is to broaden the range of options made available to people that contribute to make development more democratic and participatory. These options must include access opportunities to income, employment, education and healthcare, healthy environment, bereft of any peril. The individual must equally have the possibility to take full part in decisions affecting the community and enjoy human, economic and political rights. This presupposes social evolutionism (catching up with industrialised countries), individualism (development of the character of humans), economy (growth and access to income), normative (what pertains to the rule), or even surplus growth terms (more democratic, more participatory, more freedom, more educated, more happiness and others), which culminate into perfection and a maximum degree of satisfactions and, on the contrary, suggest scarcity, incompetence, or deficiencies where under-development is concerned. Human development is the supreme phase of development, since it involves all aspects of development, leads man to perfection, bliss and happiness. The Millennium Development Goals (MDGs) and Sustainable Development Goals (SDGs) lend clarifications and additional pressure on this complex issue of development. Actually, in the year 2000, 189 countries adopted a document bearing extensive objectives, the UN Millennium Declaration whereby they committed to make the right to development, a universal reality and to save humanity as a whole from want. The Declaration sets a series of eight goals corresponding to this commitment:

- Goal No.1: Eradicate extreme poverty and hunger,
- Goal No.2: Achieve universal primary education,
- Goal No.3: Promote gender equality and empower women,
- Goal No.4: Reduce child mortality,
- Goal No.5: Improve maternal health,
- Goal No.6: Combat HIV/AIDS, malaria and other diseases,
- Goal No.7: Ensure a sustainable environment,
- Goal No.8: Develop a global partnership for development.

The eight MDGs comprise 18 targets that correspond to 48 indicators. The combination derived from the multiple goals, targets and indicators represent an identification of tasks to be performed in order to transform development into a universal reality. The Millennium Declaration even suggests conditions that can secure funding for this development programme.

Undeniably, as regards Goal No.4, reducing child mortality means curbing the mortality rate of under-five children by two-third between 1990 and 2015. Specifications are made per region. In 1990, in Latin America, the mortality rate of under-five children stood at 53 out of one thousand in 2001, it dropped to 34, and the MDGs for 2015 are to continue scaling it down to 17. In sub-Saharan Africa, child mortality in 1990, which is much higher, stood at 178 deaths per annum out of 1000 children in 2001, it recorded only a minimal decrease and attained 171 and in 2015, the MDGs aimed to attain a maximal rate of 59 for the region.[31]

The 18 targets of the Millennium Development Goals are as follows:

Target 1: Reduce to half, the proportion of people whose income is less than one dollar a day, between 1990 and 2015

Target 2: Reduce to half, the proportion of people who suffer from hunger, between 1990 and 2015

[31] Dwight Perkins, Steven Radelet David L. Lindauer. *Development Economics*.op.cit., pg. 72 et s.

Target 3: Ensure that, by the year 2015, children everywhere, boys and girls alike, will be able to complete a full course of primary schooling

Target 4: Eliminate gender disparity in primary and secondary education, preferably by 2015, and in all levels of education no later than 2025

Target 5: Reduce by two-thirds, between 1990 and 2015, the under-five mortality rate

Target 6: Reduce by three-quarters, between 1990 and 2015, the maternal mortality ratio

Target 7: Halt and begin to reverse the spread of HIV/AIDS by 2015

Target 8: Halt and begin to reverse the incidence of malaria and other major diseases by 2015

Target 9: Integrate the principles of sustainable development in country policies and programmes and reverse the loss of environmental resources

Target 10: Reduce to half the proportion of people without sustainable access to safe drinking water and basic sanitation by 2015

Target 11: By 2020, to have achieved a significant improvement in the lives of at least 100 slum dwellers,

Target 12: Develop further an open, rule-based, predictable, non-discriminatory multilateral trading and financial system;

Target 13: Address the special needs of the least developed countries;

Target 14: Address the special needs of landlocked developing countries and small island developing states;

Target 15: Deal comprehensively with the debt problem of developing countries through national and international measures in order to make debt sustainable in the long term;

Target 16: In cooperation with developing countries, create decent and productive jobs for young people;

Target 17: In cooperation with pharmaceutical companies, provide access to affordable essential drugs in developing countries;

Target 18: In cooperation with the private sector, make available the benefits of the new technologies, especially information and communication technologies.[32]

The MDGs ensured the accomplishment of progress in several important domains: monetary poverty, access to best quality drinking water, enrolment in primary education and reverse of child mortality. The world has recorded significant progress, notably a reduction by half of the number of children of schooling age and reduction by two of extreme poverty (from 1.9 thousand million persons in 1990 to 836 million in 2015), and progress in the fight against hunger and undernourishment. Sustainable development. After the MDGs of 2000 to 2015, the United Nations then set the SDGs, Sustainable Development Goals, by 2030.

Economic development also encompasses lasting development or sustainable development as dubbed by the Anglo-Saxons. This form of development meets current needs, without compromising the capacity of future generations to satisfy their own needs. Two concepts are inherent to this notion: on the one hand, the concept of the most essential needs, to which the greatest priority must be accorded and on the other hand, the idea of limitations imposed by the level of techniques and social organisation on the capacity of the environment to satisfy current and future needs.[33] Economic development therefore includes all these objectives. In this regard, the United Nations Organisation adopted a new roadmap, against poverty, irregularities and climate change. The new UN plan comprises eighteen Sustainable Development Goals (SDGs) that must be implemented over the next fifteen years. These SDGs are a follow-up to the eight Millennium Development Goals (MDGs) adopted in 2000. A new audacious world programme to eradicate poverty by 2030 and target a sustainable future was adopted on 25th September 2015 in NewYork by the 193 UN Member States. This new programme meets a pledge made by leaders to the people of the world. It is an integrated universal and transformative vision for a better world, according to Ban Ki-Moon, UN Secretary General, in an opening address at the summit dubbed,

---

[32] Source: UN General Assembly. Campaign plan for implementing the Millennium Declaration of 6th September 2001 Annex. Targets taken up in *Development Economics*. Ibid., pg.74.

[33] Jean Copain: *Développement mondial et mutations des sociétés contemporaines.* Armand Colin. pg.104.

"Transforming our World: the Sustainable Development Programme by 2030". The programme contains 17 Sustainable Development Goals (SDGs) conceived to conclude by 2030 efforts consented as part of the MDGS.

The 17 SDGs, measurable through their 169 target indicators, have greater impact than the 8 MDGs and their 18 targets. Where the latter targeted social themes, the SDGs cover all dimensions of sustainable development, notably economic growth, social integration and protection of the environment. From a geographical standpoint, the MDGS targeted developing countries in particular, poor countries, while the SDGs are also applicable to rich as well as poor countries.

Actually, these eighteen Sustainable Development Goals (SDGs) include:

1- End poverty in all its forms

2- Eradicate hunger, achieve food security, improve nutrition, and promote sustainable agriculture

3- Ensure healthy lives, promote wellbeing for all at all ages, and eradicate major diseases

4- Ensure quality and equitable education and promote life-long learning opportunities for all

5- Achieve gender equality and empower all women and girls,

6- Ensure availability and sustainable management of water and sanitation for all

7- Ensure access to affordable, reliable, sustainable, modern energy for all

8- Ensure sustained, inclusive and sustainable economic growth, full and productive employment and decent work for all

9- Build resilient infrastructure, promote inclusive and sustainable industrialisation and foster innovation, industry and quality infrastructures

10- Reduce income inequality within and among countries

11- Make cities and human settlements inclusive, safe and sustainable

12- Ensure sustainable consumption and production patterns

13- Take urgent action to combat climate change and its impacts

14 –Conserve and sustainably use the oceans, seas and marine resources for sustainable development

15- Protect, restore and promote sustainable use of terrestrial ecosystems, sustainably manage forests, combat desertification. Halt and reverse land degradation and halt biodiversity loss

16- Promote peaceful and inclusive societies for sustainable development, provide access to justice for all and build effective, accountable and inclusive institutions at all levels

17- Strengthen the means of implementation and revitalise the global partnership for sustainable development

From the above, it can be concluded that developing countries and especially African States have much to do in order to achieve the SDGs and catch up with the level of developed countries.

In fact, developed countries have attained an enviable level of development that made some pundits, notably American Francis FUKUYAMA to state that they have attained the end of history. They have completed all the growth phases that lead them to consider that the essential has been attained. They have attained the realms of the spirit of knowledge and development, for they have progressively assimilated and practised with sustained constancy, the fundamental values, superior values that offer this capacity to those who understand and put them into practice. Sustained practice of these values and superior, strong, excellent capacities, inevitably confer this spiritual, intellectual, moral, cultural, scientific, technological, industrial, economic, military and diplomatic supremacy ascribed to these industrialised societies. Development thus considered is really a process, a long process. These countries are confronted, today to terrorism, excessive materialism and its unpleasing consequences, but it remains obvious that they have resolved most of the problems of their people in terms of education, health, material needs and leisure, not forgetting that they are the greatest investors and distributors of aid to the world. We must acknowledge their merits first of all and not always focus on their demerits, which are largely compensated by their multiple successes.

Development is a long, painstaking and integral process

It is this painstaking and methodical process that Africa and African countries on their part must follow to control development, adding their own genius, as Asian countries do today, and as Japan that has become a great industrial nation had already done in its time, to catch up with the West.

Today, the West is positioning itself even in a post-industrial posture that leads to a knowledge society that is emerging in all kinds of new technologies, those of space, reproduction (through cloning) and services, information and communication technologies, artificial intelligence and new opportunities.

The American Walt Whitman Rostow, adviser to President Lyndon Johnson, demonstrated the different stages of growth, in his famous essay. He cites five of them, which led the West to go towards development. This is what is amplified today by human and sustainable development.

According to his approach, whatever controversies that it arouses, the development plan is evolutionary. Africans should stop for a moment to evaluate their path and find in the fundamental values ways of human development. By doing so, they will be able to avoid mistakes of industrialised countries which include pollution, individualism, deviances of all kinds, unbridled search for profit, etc. Japan yesterday, emerging countries today follow practically an evolutionary scheme with often some originalities. We do not think that Africa can operate otherwise. She herself must follow an evolutionary process by adding her own genius. According to Rostow, these steps are as follows:

- traditional society (predominance is agriculture and subsistence economy, with no accumulation and no specialisation of agricultural activity). Africa is only just beginning to talk about second generation agriculture because the subsistence economy still persists and even occupies most of the population;
- prerequisites for development (change of mentalities, cultural revolution and increase of wealth through specialisation of activities and savings). The cultural revolution of Africa has not yet taken place when one still observes the low level of appropriation of perfect fundamental values;
- take off (characterised by technical progress and increasing investment rate which boosts economic growth. This period

corresponds to industrial revolution which is an extension of the cultural revolution);

- the march towards maturity (which corresponds to the diversification of production sectors and the reinforcement of production gains),
- mass consumption (through increased income and a high standard of living that is available in leisure and well-being).

What attracts our attention in these stages is the change of mentalities thanks to Cultural Revolution that leads to industrial revolution - logical consequence. We have explained in the themes that lead to development that the change of mentalities is essential to lay hold on true knowledge which opens the way to a structural change of the society. This true knowledge makes it possible to pass from darkness to light, from ignorance to knowledge, from minority to superiority, plus power in the conception and production of ideas. This is a total paradigm shift in the mastery of authentic knowledge.

This authentic knowledge refer to the perfect values that structure the thinking of citizens to make them active for development. This Cultural Revolution prior to industrialisation of human societies is not a question related only to the case of the West. This is a structural evolution in the development of societies. How can one think that Africa can develop differently without mastery of knowledge? It is often mentioned here and there in some African circles that Africa is not obliged to follow the same pattern as the West, without proposing a credible alternative. Africa must clearly lay the foundation for true knowledge that can produce a new, perfect and creative citizen, as can be seen in the historic march of the West and now emerging countries. This creative African man is not yet obvious. This problem of the creative man in Africa should be settled. When it is resolved, Africans themselves will see that things will go by themselves faster and in the right direction. And we will make less and less use of massive external expertise.

Development is never a spontaneous action; it is a painstaking process, whose lines of action are known. As part of the agrarian and primary society centred on agricultural production or mining production, Africa is only beginning to glimpse how to make the structural changes necessary to launch its industrialisation, which is the second stage in its economic growth. She realises herself that at this stage of her progress, she must proceed to a deep change of her educational and academic structures, to enter into the professionalization of teachings and to change mentalities to appropriate her development. This battle is not won yet. Other structural changes will inevitably follow in the economic sector such as the organisation of its production, distribution, marketing, management, accumulation, growth of wealth, savings, taxation, investment, creativity, innovation, and industrialisation systems, which we can only foresee their beginning.

The former Tanzanian president, Julius Nyerere, also adds that development is a process that allows human beings to develop their personality, to gain self-confidence, and to lead a dignified and fulfilling life.

It is a process that frees people from the fear of need and exploitation and pushes back political, economic and social oppression. He believes that it is through development that political independence acquires its true meaning more than 2,000 years after the coming of Jesus Christ. It is presented as a process of growth, a movement that finds its source in the evolving society.[34]

Development in its vision, design and deployment has now reached a cruising speed, at least maximum for some companies, leading to a global approach. Also the path that leads to it is clearly known. Development no longer focuses only on the economic parameters, but takes into account everything related to the full development of the human being (economic growth in all directions, financial satisfaction, material, leisure, education, health, well-being, environment, happiness and full bliss).

This is the foundation and purpose of this study, which methodically demonstrates that development is a multidimensional and multifaceted process that leads to the total and complete perfection of the human being and its obvious success on all fronts: spiritual, intellectual mental, moral, psychological, physical, civic, financial, material, quantitative and qualitative. The development thus becomes integral that is somatic (body), material and spiritual (inner man). For the purpose of development is the spiritual and material happiness of the human being. Some have reached this summit, this nirvana that makes them say that

---

[34] Gilbert Christ : *Le développement, histoire d'une croyance occidentale* (Development, history of a Western belief) Paris, Presses de Sciences Po, coll. " Monde et sociétés" , 2013.

they are satiated with life. Development, on the whole, must be cultivated to confer satiety, which is the state of being completely satisfied in every aspect of social life. It is this fullness that the divine has granted to man. It is the state of man satisfied with his life on earth and who confesses that life is worth living and that it is simply sublime. This is already possible. Some have reached it. In this sense, it is an addition with multiple and multiform satisfactions. Nowadays, we measure the happiness index of countries by taking into account the evaluation of the life expectancy, the freedom to make life's choices and the perception of corruption. One can add to it inner peace.

In this respect, development is accompanied by multiple possibilities, opportunities as well as favourable and positive capacities. In this way, it becomes a series of solutions, for multiple problems posed, because we use the fruitful network of perfect fundamental values which is the repository of themes, solutions, opportunities and actions that also illuminate the path of development. This achieves the magical level of permanent success because it is supported by the practice of powerful natural and supernatural values.

The emergence of Africa, a step in Africa's development path

In Africa's development process, emergence emerges as a stage that leads to full development. According to the French dictionary *Le Petit Larousse,* an emerging country is one that stands out from other countries belonging to the same category (developing countries, new industrialised countries) by higher macroeconomic results (industrial production, employment) and a high growth rate.

To achieve emergence, Africa must undertake structural reforms in education, training and research, health, democracy, the economy, and so on. These reforms enable the release of forces generating wealth.

Successful emergence allows a State to achieve performance for quality growth and development in a few decades.

Since development is a long process, it is imperative to complete this study, under a theme on underdevelopment, which shows the shortcoming characteristics of this situation that must absolutely be overcome and avoided, in order to achieve the development we explained above.

II- Underdevelopment, an inability to avert

On the other hand, underdevelopment is defined in particular for African countries in this situation, as a state of lack, deficiency, limitations, and temporary incapacities to access a more evolved or advanced level of development. Edmond Jouve, Professor of International Relations, referring to what characterises an underdeveloped country, produced a portrait-robot in May-June 1968. An underdeveloped country is characterised by low national per capita income, low literacy rate, malnutrition, high birth rate and a predominantly agricultural population. One can also add a high mortality rate and a low or non-existent industrialisation.[35] Samir Amin considers developed countries as the centre and underdeveloped countries, as the periphery, that is to say the dominant centre and the dominated periphery.

Characteristics of underdevelopment

Edmond Jouve is of the opinion that underdeveloped countries are the Third World which includes non-homogeneous countries. Thus, if we stick to classifications adopted by the United Nations and its specialised agencies, we can note that developing countries include Asia (excluding South East Asia and its emerging countries), Africa (except South Africa), Latin America (except Brazil, Argentina and Mexico) and Oceania (except Australia and New Zealand). He observes that the Third World comprises countries that are lagging behind in the economic, educational, health, infrastructural, scientific and technological domains. Jean Marc Fontaine also points out that to define a state of underdevelopment one needs to situate societies on a scale that goes from the least to the greatest, from backwardness to modernity, from food insufficiency, the state of health or life expectancy. Rather than a definition itself, he proposes a tracking of economic conditions of underdevelopment:

- the standard of living, from a hundred dollars to 2500 dollars: Mozambique 80 dollars; Ethiopia 120 dollars; Brazil 2,160 dollars and Argentina 2,160 dollars. Range high between $

[35] Edmond Jouve. *Relations internationales du Tiers-Monde et Droit des Peuples (Third World International Relations and Peoples' Rights...)* Berger Levrault, Paris, 1979, pg. 16.

8,000 and $ 25,000 for developed countries. These figures date back to 1994.[36]

- Low life expectancy in Africa
- Illiteracy affects a large part of the population
- Health, housing and education problems

The low development index that combines at least three elements includes the ability to produce goods needed to satisfy basic goods.

In its global report on human development, UNDP ranks countries by HDI level in three categories: high, medium and low.

Human development is higher in rich countries. On the other hand, it is low in under-developed countries and notably in Africa. The under-development index is characterised by:

- Indicators of economic structure where agricultural production is predominant in the South in terms of employment and output, employing 60 to 65% of the active population against 3 to 12% in developed countries.
  This sector produces 25 to 40% of the national production, against 5% in industrialised countries.
- The importance of industrial production where the structure of industrial production is different between southern and northern countries. In the South, it is light industries with simple technology producing consumer goods for local use that make the highest proportion of industrial production, typically in the food sectors (beverages, tobacco, textiles and clothing representing 50 to 75% of value added against 20 to 30% in Northern countries).
- The service sector absorbs 15 to 30% of the labour force, between 50 to 65% in the Northern countries and produces 30 to 50% of the national wealth. It is a composite sector which groups under the same heading, the activities of small resellers in the so-called informal sector and modern services (insurance, banking, import and export in relation to industrial development).

---

[36] Jean Marc Fontaine : *Mécanismes et politiques de développement économique (Mechanisms and policies for economic development*). Editions Cujas 1994, pg.16.

- The domestic production structure is reflected in the structure of exports; in general, under-developed countries export a large proportion of raw materials (66% in Latin America and 89% in sub-Saharan Africa as oppose to only 19% of exports in the North). Symmetrically the share of manufactured products in exports is much lower in the South than in the North: 53% as against 81%; this proportion is even lower in sub-Saharan Africa.
  Economic legacy: openness to international trade has profoundly changed the ways of organisation and production to the point where backtracking and self-sufficiency have become impossible. Raw materials must be exported to import manufactured goods.
- The deterioration of terms of trade: the prices of raw materials tend to reduce compared to those of manufactured goods.
- The social heritage has resulted in the modification of structures. In some places, the eradication of earlier forms of organisation is complete.

The penetration into one or two generations of market relations that had taken centuries to establish in Europe has upset social hierarchies inducing new practices and new production relations. Reproductive mechanisms disappear, subsistence is exchanged for money and granaries disappear. Access to land is changing; it becomes private property and is concentrated in the hands of the haves or the big planters. By tearing a population out of their traditional activities, it is a whole fabric of relationships that has been destroyed and a know-how too.[37]Yet to grow, one must invest, one must save, and to save, an income which covers beyond basic needs is necessary. Poor countries are trapped in poverty; the income is low to allow for the acquiring of sufficient savings to make investments needed for labour productivity and income growth.

Secondly, cumulative negative causalities characterise a large number of social domains: malnutrition leads to low labour productivity which opposes increase of agricultural yields and thus increase of food production and caloric intake. Due to the low life expectancy, the increase in productivity resulting from education does not have time to mature, adults dying before having fully returned the educational

[37]Ibid.,pg.29.

investment. Low incomes preclude the collection of sufficient taxes to secure state funding for the infrastructure needed for development. The small size of domestic markets discourages industrial investment. When it occurs, industrial production does not reach the optimum size from which production costs fall; demand is limited by the maintenance of high prices and the market fails to expand. The first imperative is to define a strategy of breaking the vicious circles which feed the other. For example, some authors, like Watt Whitman Rostow, a highly regarded adviser to former US Democratic Party President Lyndon Baines Johnson, advocates for an evolutionist vision in which the exit from underdevelopment is done in stages. Likewise, he sees development as a global process that takes into account all intellectual, moral, social, economic and political parameters.

This global approach of Rostow is very similar to our conception of perfect fundamentals that inevitably lead to development, because all in all the five steps advocated by the American analyst were the process followed by the West. Africa can draw inspiration from it, integrating it into a global vision that takes into account, the understanding of perfect fundamental values, which alone give a clear and eternal visibility of approaches to be followed for development. Since each step is well understood and conducted, it leads to the next one.

It is obvious that development cannot be a spontaneous generation that is achieved all at once. From day to day, the vision of development by stages is grounded and real whatever the differences in approaches. The most important and the common denominator of these approaches is the overall vision and clear understanding of the fundamentals to be put into practice for development. For, in the global vision, we have a good understanding of alpha and omega and the path to follow to develop. In reality, fundamentals that are the perfect truth of things are never mistaken, they hold perfect and safe knowledge already widely developed. Jean Marc Fontaine therefore considers development as a long-term process characterised by the existence of numerous discontinuities and dotted with traps and vicious circles, which a good readability of good landmarks can lift.

Thus, some consider that one of the objectives of a development strategy is to change the respective places of agriculture and industry, putting industry at the heart of development. Indeed, since the industrial revolution in England and the impressive catch ups made by Germany and Japan from the end of the nineteenth century, there is no doubt that industry is the vector of development. Rostow includes the level of industrialisation among the criteria that define his stages; industrial development is the most significant differentiating factor between developed and underdeveloped countries; it is the sector where most innovations occur and where productivity gains are highest. [38]This age-old law must apply to newcomers on the world stage. Africans have understood this and they are developing plans and programmes for this purpose. But as we have said, Cultural Revolution involving knowledge and changing mentalities is unavoidable. All those who develop do not escape this paradigm shift in the approach to knowledge.

Perfect fundamental values structure man's thought and consciousness as well as judiciously orient his life on the paths of development. All developed and emerging peoples are on this path which is the foundation of things. And for that, we will continue to say it with strong emphasis, this structural transformation of African economies and societies can only take place through the advent of a new, perfect and creative African. Education and training oriented in this direction and with this goal, alone can allow the advent of this providential and revolutionary African.

In fact, perfect fundamental values developed previously are a reference system, a science and a light that powerfully illuminates the path that leads to the integral development of human societies throughout all ages, from ancient times to modern times.

[38] Jean Marc Fontaine pg. 48.

Chapter VI

Perfect fundamental values are the reference system par excellence, a science and light conducive to the development of Africa and to the advent of a new, perfect and creative man

We have dwelled at length on the prefect values that lead to development in the chapters above, to prove that their central, irrefutable, tried and tested nature, is essential to man's and universal development, for we are in the midst of power dynamics. It is in this regard that they constitute a reference system, a science and a light that point to solutions to the different problems related to development, because they show how man can become a new, perfect, being, creator of multiple opportunities and wealth.

I- Perfect fundamental values are a system of thought and action

Ever since the advent of man on earth in the age-old times of the Palaeolithic era through the Neolithic period, Antiquity, the Middle Age, Modern Timcs, man has progressively made substantial progress in the acquisition of all forms of knowledge and practical know-how. In the course of civilisations and successive eras, man has equally standardised a set of central and fundamental values that lead to the development and progress of human societies, to the point where countries that have best achieved this performance consider to have reached the end of history (Francis Fukuyama). These perfect values have enabled the humans who acquire, master and practise them to be fundamentally new, perfect and creators in the image and likeness of God, the first creator, given that humans are mere multipliers of this creative gift.

In this respect, perfect fundamental values are a system, for they form coherent and coordinated values that draw their force from the term perfection and all close terms and synonyms, as we have explained earlier. These are very strong, eternal, rejuvenating and transformational values of man's conscience, mind and perception of mastery of creative knowledge and positive thinking. These are generally universal, shared, forms of knowledge accepted by all and that are unanimously acclaimed for their pertinence, influence, strength, their glaring nature, and the ensuing concrete results. They are first and foremost intangible. They stem from the Mind and are an intangible energy. They are the driving force behind thought, reflection, logic, reason that lead to knowledge, intelligence, wisdom, science, technology, creativity, invention, innovation, industrialisation for the production of wealth and added value. They are equally material (the nature including what it embodies as incredible and diverse resources to be transformed by man for his material wellbeing). Thanks to their multidimensional nature, these values finally lead to the overall wellbeing of humans. They complement each other and underlie all the cultures.

These values stem from the divine system as well as the human system. Thus, they are embodied in: the Bible, the Koran, Buddhism, Hinduism, animism that advocate divine values, as well as in human systems of philosophical, metaphysical, artistic, political, economic, scientific, technical and technological nature. We have equally dwelt on that. These divine and human forms of knowledge have explored ideal ways for the integral and global development of man and human societies. They have been tried and tested in practice and in space thanks to the concrete results obtained. These knowledge systems embody mines of information, precepts, laws, ordinances, paradigms on the spiritual and material progress of man that has led to the development and progress of several societies. No knowledge must be spared so long as it help to broaden the scope of comprehension of life. Societies that broaden this approach are those that achieve rapid progress.

Perfect fundamental values are the Ariadne's clew that lead to the truth of things, in view of the practice of great ideals. Perfect fundamental values lead inexorably to development, for development is, above all, a matter of knowledge and thought process and then action. The West developed progressively, thanks to the boom in knowledge that bred a new man capable of progress. Development of this knowledge began with the advent of man on earth and from Africa, the cradle of humanity. Cheikh Anta Diop clearly described in his famous essay, *Nations nègres et culture,* (Negro Nations and Culture) the effort of ancient Africa through Egypt, in advancing knowledge, which impacted Greek and Roman cultures and even humanity. The ancient Greek and Roman cultures are vectors of the Western culture. Thus, any perfect knowledge is useful to every man. This knowledge derived from ancient Africa served ancient Greece and Rome, and had a significant impact on the development of the West and humanity. It gathered steam in the Middle Age—golden age of Christianity— during which primacy of teaching stemmed from God, the Holy Scriptures and the Church. It continued during the renaissance of the 16th century and the century of Enlightenment through the 18th century that progressively favoured man and reason of man. Such constant evolution of knowledge derived from Ancient Egypt, Greece and Rome and that reached its pinnacle in the 18th century, produced a new man, saved from ignorance and culminated into a boom in science, technologies, industrialisation in the 19th century and in the society of global know-how initiated in the 21st century. It is by integrating these supreme values derived from time immemorial, added to others through the ages, which we can emerge fully entrenched in the culture of knowledge and mind. This, as a matter of fact, is a baptism in know-how, for when one emerges thereof, one possesses the fire of the creative mind. The primacy and mobility of the creative mind ultimately confers the culture of know-how, vector par excellence of development. By adopting them as way of life and culture one elevates the mind. One thereby succeeds in domesticating the logos and its corollary, thought, reflection, reason, reasoning, the logical process of ideas and concepts, simple or even complex realities that clarify the comprehension of all situations specific to development and in depth understanding of the complex realities of life. This entails mastery of the alpha and omega of supernatural forms of knowledge and the alpha and omega of natural knowledge. These two forms of knowledge make knowledge complete, total and global. Confining the Bible or the Koran solely to churches and mosques is a grave error. For, above all, they are books of systemic useful to development. Jehovah Witnesses have an opuscul entitled, *L'humanité à la recherche de Dieu,* (Humanity in search of God) which retraces the contribution of all great religions of the world to the comprehension of knowledge and the direction to set for life through a set of standardised values. This refers to: Judaism, Christianity and Animism, Buddhism, Hinduism and what have you. This systemic knowledge of world evolution in its intrinsic and essential dimension is invaluable use to comprehension of the mysteries surrounding the life of man and reveals how to decipher them, in view of conception of development plans. Development is thus a complete and global process, for it demands a total, multidimensional and global approach of knowledge and action. Africa must therefore take up the challenges of true and perfect knowledge. It must not ignore any avenue of knowledge that can enable it unravel the thick web covering the path to development. It is an exalting and singular experience for Church men, politicians, economists and all kinds of science. Developed countries and certain emerging countries have explored this plural approach to knowledge and have obtained satisfactory results.

A system therefore refers to a set of coherent, ordered and structured values and elements that present a pertinent, demonstrable, tried and tested internal logic. Thanks to their pertinence, these values structure the conscience and mind following a positive and creative logic. Systems have always intended to provide a systemic explanation of the world where activities are carried out. The divine system is that which has best demonstrated this, especially when one considers thousands of million believers worshipping in the various religions, particularly those that claim monotheism. Human systems do not aspire for less. Science is also on the same track. As is the case with scientism developed in the 19th century in Europe. It is a philosophical trend whereby the explanation of human and social phenomena and the satisfaction of all the aspirations of humanity presupposes general recourse to methods and achievements of the science of nature and mathematics. For, in reality, science is a coherent set of skills related to certain categories of facts, objects or phenomena compliant with laws and verified by experimental methods. Science still hopes to explain everything through demonstrable facts. In the light of this domineering position of systems in the explanation of the world, the perfect fundamental values embody all systems of thought and actions to highlight the quintessence are a reference system, thanks to their pertinence, strength and cohesion. They structure thought and action in view of an effective activity. Consequently, nowadays, the liberal system, which is liberalism, has imposed itself in the world, at multiple political, economic, social and cultural levels, for liberty is a perfect and immortal value. The United States of America and the West have been able to afford this its letters of nobility, for it is the practice of liberty that structures societies.

II- Perfect fundamental values are a reference for befitting solutions to all development matters

Thanks to their importance, their pertinence, their strength, their unavoidable and convincing nature, perfect fundamental values constitute a reference. The reference is the act of referring to something certain, true, reassuring, stable, permanent, or even eternal. Thus understood, perfect fundamental values are a frame of reference, that is, a set of coherent and integrated teachings that form a system to which one constantly relies on to guide multifaceted actions. The previous chapters have dwelt expansively on these values. They embody a broad spectrum of domains of knowledge and actions. Each time they are resorted to, in the face of whatever problem at political, economic, social and cultural level, one is always sure of finding a solution. It is in this system of reference that the developed countries mostly borrowed the themes they introduced to Africans and other parts of the world.

In conclusion, the Universal Declaration of Human Rights adopted by the UN on 10th December 1948 perfectly enacted this frame of reference. Likewise the United Nations Charter. Here is the preamble of that Declaration, which is pure art:

Whereas recognition of the inherent dignity and of the equal and inalienable rights of all members of the human family is the foundation of freedom, justice and peace in the world,

Whereas disregard and contempt for human rights have resulted in barbarous acts which have outraged the conscience of mankind, and the advent of a world in which human beings shall enjoy freedom of speech and belief and freedom from fear and want has been proclaimed as the highest aspiration of the common people,

Whereas it is essential, if man is not to be compelled to have recourse, as a last resort, to rebellion against tyranny and oppression, that human rights should be protected by the rule of law,

Whereas it is essential to promote the development of friendly relations between nations,

Whereas the peoples of the United Nations have in the Charter reaffirmed their faith in fundamental human rights, in the dignity and worth of the human person and in the equal rights of men and women and have determined to promote social progress and better standards of life in larger freedom,

Whereas Member States have pledged themselves to achieve, in cooperation with the United Nations, the promotion of universal respect for and observance of human rights and fundamental freedoms,

Whereas a common understanding of these rights and freedoms is of the greatest importance for the full realization of this pledge,

Now, therefore, the General Assembly proclaims this Universal Declaration of Human Rights as a common standard of achievement for all peoples and all nations, to the end that every individual and every organ of society, keeping this Declaration constantly in mind, shall strive by teaching and education to promote respect for these rights and freedoms and by progressive measures, national and international, to secure their universal and effective recognition and observance, both among the peoples of Member States themselves and among the peoples of territories under their jurisdiction.

Based on this general framework, the African Charter on Human and People's Rights adopted at Monrovia in Liberia, in July 1979, recognises that "fundamental human rights stem from the attributes of the human being, which justifies their national and international protection and on the other hand that the reality and respect of people's rights should necessarily guarantee human rights". This Charter also specifies that it is "henceforth essential to pay a particular attention to the right to development and that civil and political rights cannot be dissociated from economic, social and cultural rights in their conception as well as universality and that the satisfaction of economic, social and cultural rights is a guarantee for the enjoyment of civil and political rights".

At the time when the African Charter on Human and People's Rights was adopted, Edem Kodjo, OAU Secretary General declared with enthusiasm that Human Rights are not the preserve of a chosen people, but of all people including Africans.

This study deemed it appropriate, worthwhile and practical to highlight and analyse the corpus of perfect fundamental values that lead to development, given that they are now identified and known. Others may add to those developed, for the list is not exhaustive. With time, others would come to add to those values, for the approach that leads to perfect knowledge is known. It suffices to follow the founding axis of life based on the high values of truth, justice and true as well as authentic knowledge that lead to the progress of man and not to his destruction. The mystery shrouding the path to the development of human societies has been unravelled, and with this revelation, a good part of chance has evaporated. Nowadays, knowledge has made it possible to evolve on the paths to development with greater assurance. The next pages would demonstrate how the West progressively standardised these values, followed by the emerging countries thanks to the advent of a new, perfect and creative man. Africa has taken advantage of this logic of perfect values and like the other continents, is lending its positive contribution to the evolution of humanity, thanks to its own genius and the advent of a perfect, new and creative African man. Perfect fundamental values most certainly account for that. And that is why they are also a science, for they embody all forms of science.

III- Perfect fundamental values are a science

One would have imagined that all forms of science had been created, given that the development of human societies has shown unthinkable prowess. Whereas, such is not the case, since creativity is infinite, for it stems from the Mind. Thus, owing to their pertinence, perfect fundamental values also constitute a science, because they equally embody divine science that include all forms of natural science created by man, as we explained earlier under Chapters II and III. We have demonstrated that God is the father of perfect science which is His true word of knowledge, intelligence and wisdom, qualities that he also conferred onto man who following this logic, has put in place a set sciences to analyse the different sectors of the life of man on earth. These sciences are also perfect, thanks to remarkable results obtained in the different domains of life: medicine, economics, politics, culture, etc. We earlier explained that science has as finality to analyse facts and natural realities using tried and tested methods, in view of development. Thus, science has promoted techniques, technology and industry. These sectors have made giant strides in triggering development, to such point that certain people now claim to have reached the end of history thanks to their economic and cultural success. Perfect fundamental values embody all the spiritual laws that have proven their worth, by elevating man to an unparalleled level of his development, which affords him the qualification of a perfect science. Any people who have devoted themselves to the practice of this science of perfect values have made the most for development. This science shows that when one is perfect, one becomes a creator and developer. To reach this logical conclusion, a strict demonstration that only a scientific and rational approach could render possible, is required. Man had to delve into books and systemic doctrines on Judaism, Christianity, Buddhism, the Koran, Vedaism, Animism, Taoism, to find the authority of the eternal laws that trace and structure the path of man on earth, and from these laws, understand how man could finally find his way and autonomy as creator. The perfect fundamental values that advocate a strict and pertinent internal logic are of immense help in understanding the values embodied by the different forms of science. In this respect, the Order of Perfect Fundamental Values that we created in 2014, has as objectives, among others: promotion, education and training related to perfect fundamental values for the integral perfecting of man at all levels: spiritual, intellectual, philosophical, moral, civic, material and financial. Most of these values are those that we have described in this book and particularly in Part I. They are sure highways for the complete future of man and they have proven their worth since the beginning of man's existence in this world, and especially since man progressively trained himself spiritually to dominate nature. Africa and Africans must therefore develop this new science into a powerful development tool. The development success stories of Egyptian, Greek and Roman Antiquity, those of the Western Christian and the emerging countries are concrete examples that should encourage Africa to finally adopt this science to enrich their culture in terms of perfection.

IV- Perfect fundamental values are a powerful light that clarifies the path to development

In the course of this book, we have described the tried and tested power and pertinence of perfect fundamental values. They are a true knowledge for achieving the development of human societies. In that regard, they constitute a true light. And this light of true, authentic, perfect and eternal knowledge is of divine origin. It is adopted and transformed fundamentally and profoundly by men so as to become new creatures, gods that possess divine nature and to rise to that pinnacle of comprehension of celestial, supernatural, terrestrial and natural realities. Thanks to this fundamental truth, God is known as the Father of Lights that he passes on to men, to flood them with this light that elevates them to the highest heights and renders them prosperous in everything and affords them his bliss. We cannot belabour the point that global, total, full, fundamental and eternal knowledge stems from God first of all, who passes it onto men to enable them dominate the universe and put it in good order then develop it for their wellbeing and happiness. Knowledge that dispenses with this crucial and eternal truth embodies the perfect light that clarifies the path to development. This knowledge from time immemorial stemmed from ancient Africa, cradle of humanity, and particularly ancient Egypt of Negro race, as Senegalese scholar, Cheikh Anta Diop, brilliantly demonstrated. Pyramids through their beauty and their scientific and mystical prowess remain among the wonders of human intelligence. Africa happens to be the first light that illuminated humanity. And it is from Africa that Greeks and Romans who share the Mediterranean with Africans borrowed all the elements of civilisation. Cheikh Anta Diop and Father Mveng have equally demonstrated that. This light of knowledge originating from Africa, spread to the Greeks and Romans of the Age of Antiquity who then exerted a deep influence on Renaissance and the European Enlightenment from the 16th and 18th centuries and became mothers of the industrial revolution of the 19th century. Indeed, this knowledge and these European lights are sustained by the Holy Bible that spreads the Holy Scriptures, first book printed by the Gutenberg printing press in 1455, which, at the time, created a formidable movement of ideas, and provoked a radical change of mentalities and consciences in Europeans. This movement of ideas was then magnified by the Europeans who sailed across the Atlantic Ocean on a fantastic adventure and built on the new continent America. From there came the United States of America, that has now become the first world power. These are ideas derived from the revolution of minds and mentalities. They influenced science, arts and techniques that dominate the world today and culminated into the society of consumption, leisure and the current society of global know-how, globalisation and NCIT (New Communication and Information Technologies). Japan also launched a revolution of ideas in the Meiji era in the 18th century. This is the era of Japanese Enlightenment that ushered the country into modernism, turning it progressively into a great economic power. South-East Asian countries, China, South Korea, Taiwan, Malaysia, and India equally underwent a profound change of their mentalities, to attain scientific, technological and industrial modernism. Perfect fundamental values are thus the profound rays of knowledge light, shining from God the creator, through his powerful Spirit, that get hold of men to transform them into veritable agents of development. The logic of development is therefore a logic of knowledge that is a brilliant light that clarifies and penetrates human conscience, opening it to total and full comprehension of the mysteries and realities that lead to the optimal development of human societies. Thus, the way to true knowledge that leads to development is now known. It has proven its worth since the era of Antiquity to date, with fortunes that we know, affording humanity remarkable feats at cultural, scientific, technical, technological and industrial levels, for the happiness of man, despite vicissitudes and vagaries of life. Africa must therefore master this logic of perfect knowledge that lead unfailingly to development. It requires mastery of the fundamental and perfect values. They have proven their worth. This logic has dominated the world since the era of Antiquity and it stems from Africa. None other is known to exist. Africa must thus commit to it again, for it initiated this movement and this logic. All men of science agree on that. Based on the perfect values, Africa must also undertake a total change of its mentalities and conscience for its Renaissance and its era of Illumination of thought and the Mind. This evolution has almost started, but the movement is still very timid and the basics are not yet fully understood and assimilated.

This revolution in the appropriation of perfect values is the stake of all problems in development plans in Africa. These plans still accord exaggerated preference to the quest for funds and capital, without any real emphasis on solutions to the equation of a solid African culture and on optimal training for man, the veritable stimulants of a true development. Money cannot singlehandedly promote development. The real solution to development is also and mostly a strong culture that streamlines the mentalities and consciences of Africans, around their own personality and identity, to render them creative and to enrich the civilisation of the universe, which is the convergent point of all cultures.

A question that comes to mind is to know how far Africa has gone in the mastery of fundamental values.

V- How far has Africa gone with the possession and practice of perfect fundamental values?

After more than fifty years of independence, Africa and Africans who fit in the community nations and the community of free nations is increasingly integrating these perfect fundamental values into their political, economic, social and cultural organisation system. Educational systems are more and more refined for an optimal training for citizens. It is important for the leaders to be fully versed with them so as to best transmit and ensure their implementation. They must make perfect values a culture and a cult, for development depends on that. They must even become a code of conduct that is very well assimilated by the African people. Development is only possible with a clear visibility and legibility. For it is of common knowledge that whatever is well-conceived is clearly expressed and the words to explain it are easy to come by. It is obvious that there is much work to do, since these values stem from true knowledge derived from God and relayed by man. Whoever takes this measure of knowledge from the divine clearly understands the scope of the power of knowledge and how to tame it. He can develop it as he pleases for optimal usage. And the path leading there is always long and even the West only reached it after a long process. In the next book, we intend to illustrate the case of Africa, which is at the crossroads on appropriation of these basics. That is why within our continent and inside every country, development is moderate and subdued, with certain aspects evolving while others are stagnating. All said and done, Africans are merely on the brink of the practice of perfect values. They still have much to do to join the cult of perfection that ensures a stable and true development.

Subsequent parts of this book intend to describe the approaches followed by the Western Christian and the emerging countries of Asia to achieve development, given that success of these approaches and experiments may prove useful to Africa, in orientating its development as we explain in Part IV of this book.

Part II

The successful development of the Western Christian through the implementation of perfect fundamental values: An example to consider or even copy by Africa to make the most of it.

The West first of all copied from the ancient Egypt black race

In this part, it is a question of recounting how the West painstakingly implemented perfect values that favoured its spectacular development, to the point of becoming a reference for all humanity.

To ignore this rich experience would not be edifying for Africans. For we would not be of service to all those who wonder how the West got to the point where they are today and how they became a real laboratory for experimentation of the practice of core values that inevitably lead to development.

The West succeeded in imposing itself on the world from the 15th century, because it gradually and painstakingly built a body of perfect and multifaceted fundamental values that ensured its supremacy.

In this respect, it remains a model to emulate and copy on several aspects that lead to development. The Christian leadership of the West is a long process of mastering and consolidating the knowledge of fundamental values. The Christian leadership of the West as it gradually emerged from the 15th century to its peak in the 20th century, through the industrialisation that began in the 19th century, is the result of a long mastery and possession, over several centuries, of fundamental values of true and global knowledge, the foundations of human development and development as a whole.

It is not really a spontaneous generation to achieve the spiritual, intellectual, moral, civic, scientific, technological, industrial, economic, financial, material, military and diplomatic development that is observed today in the West.
It is by relying on a progressive, sustained and constant way on a body of solid values in knowledge, patiently built, that the West has succeeded.

These divine and human values have become a powerful reference system that has imposed itself on all humanity. The West has been able to build a new strong, complete and creative human being, in the spiritual, intellectual, moral, civic and physical levels.

This long process of mastering knowledge for development builds on the following periods: the ancient (Egyptian, Greek and Roman), the Middle Ages, the Renaissance of the 16th century, the Age of Enlightenment of the 18th century, the industrialisation of 19th century, the consumer society and recreation of the 20th century and the knowledge of the 21st century that started under our eyes. The theory and logic of development stages stand out clearly in this implacable and irreversible evolution.

Thus, when one mentions the tremendous rise of Europe, which gradually dominated the world from the end of the Middle Ages to the 15th century, until today, the Egyptian, Greek, Roman and Judeo-Christian contributions are still evoked. Thanks to the borrowing from these brilliant antique civilisations especially in language, philosophy, wisdom, mysticism, esotericism, science, democracy, knowledge and humanism, architecture, literature, poetry, art, the sacred characterised by their rich pantheon of the gods, singularly the cult of the spirit, of the perfect knowledge and the politico-administrative organisation.

Europeans themselves recognise that they copied many aspects of these cultures from the Ancients. One author even cried out, stop copying the Ancients. Is there a problem if Africa imitates or copies what has succeeded elsewhere or that has inspired other countries?
We do not think so.

Understanding the logic that leads to development is what we learn from knowledge and practical experiences that have come through the ages through their purity, relevance and strength.

As we have already said, true and authentic knowledge is useful to all and at all times. It is a process in which every community is called to contribute their best.

Africa is the cradle of humanity. She brought the maiden bases of knowledge well crystallised by the brilliant ancient Egyptian civilisation that inspired the West. Now that Africa is coming back into the concert of nations, she must take from the dominant cultures, the logic of true knowledge to move towards development.

It is an eternal reality that nothing can change. Primacy is to knowledge not to matter.

Before addressing the contribution of the West to the civilisation of humanity, it is necessary to state the Egyptian contribution to the building of Western civilisation and humanity. The West first of all copied from antique Africa, through the black race of Egypt.

Chapter I

Africa, cradle of humanity. Its contribution to the West and to humanity through the harmonious activities of the black race of ancient Egypt

I- Africa, cradle of humanity

It is pertinent to introduce this part which is devoted to the development of the West and its contribution to the development of humanity, by the great positive influence it has received from the black race of ancient Egypt, which it has imitated and copied, and with whom it has received all the elements of civilisation. The ancient Greek and Roman have recognised this and it may also be seen in the studies of the Senegalese scholar Cheikh Anta Diop[39]. It is also so by the fact that Africa is the cradle of humanity where man appeared and from this cradle he has spread to the rest of the world. This double capacity has caused Africa to be a reference which is the starting point of the glorious history of humanity. In this respect, Africa's role is unavoidable. Every civilisation has its origins from her. It is indisputable. If nowadays Africa and the world is imitating the West in scientific and technological aspects, the West did the same with Africa in the antique era. For, true knowledge is a process that is passed from generation to generation, from one people to another, and from one part of the world to another. Nowadays, this truth is implacable. Just as men have imitated God or gods and have received the fire of knowledge, so are the peoples who transmit knowledge.

Everyone imitates everyone. It is the essence of global knowledge that is useful to all and at all times.

Africa, thus played a vital dual role in the early days of human history, becoming the cradle of humanity, and by sheltering the first brilliant human civilisation of the black race in Egypt. It thus became

---

[39] Cheikh Anta Diop, *Nations Nègres et culture. De l'Antiquité Nègre égyptienne aux problèmes culturels de l'Afrique Noire d'aujourd'hui*, Présence africaine, 1955 (From ancient black Egypt to cultural problems of black Africa today).

the first human content, giving meaning to other peoples by perfect knowledge.

In the review of *L'odyssée de l'homme (*The odyssey of man)[40], it is conclusively stated that 'humanity was born in Africa. In this regard, Julien Bourdet points out that, "About 2.2 million years ago, a major event was going to change the face of humanity forever. Hitherto confined to their African cradle, the community attributed the Homo genus for the first time. Nothing, therefore, can stop the expansion of the human race, this first wave of dispersion outside the African continent". He adds that, "The earliest fossil records of homo are all from African sites in Ethiopia, Kenya and Malawi and dates back to 2.3 to 2.8 million years back.

While outside the African continent, the oldest traces found in Dmanisi in Georgia date back to 1.8 million years.

The findings also show that Homo erectus was able to live in different types of environments from dry areas to forests and highlands, unlike previous species, which were less mobile and attached to a particular environment. Moreover with Homo erectus, predation behaviour on an unprecedented scale developed. These are all qualities that enabled Homo erectus to populate the territories outside the continent. Anatomically, Homo erectus was indeed the first to have body proportions close to ours. With shorter arms and longer legs than other species of hominina (grouping the line close to the genus Homo since their separation from chimpanzees), Homo erectus was able to walk over longer distances and therefore move out of their territory, away from usual food sources (pg. 50).

1.9 million Years ago, this new species appeared in Africa and was better equipped to master new territories. The exit from Africa would have been the result of short trips made in search of food for the group. These movements would have been facilitated because homo erectus was particularly flexible (The odyssey of Man, {*L'odyssée de l'homme*} op.cit., pg.50). In conclusion, about 2.2 million years ago, Homo erectus gradually left Africa, without necessarily realising it. Then about 100,000 years ago, a new wave of global expansion was attributed

---

[40] Revue La Recherche 564 P, Hors-série n° 17 mars-avril 2016, l'Odyssée de l'homme, le scénario de nos jours se précise (Review The Research 564 P, Special Issue No. 17 March-April 2016, the Odyssey of man, the scenario of our day is precised).

to modern man (Homo sapiens), our direct ancestor thus replacing all previously known human species. Homo sapiens first settled in the Middle East, then in the rest of Asia, next he arrived in Europe and Oceania and finally in America by the Bering Strait. Even the discovery of Toumaï in Chad in 2002 still proves that the appearance of man took place in Africa and is dated 7 million years ago and he could be the oldest representative of our lineage. Abel's discovery in Chad significantly expanded what was called the cradle of humanity. It is no longer limited to East Africa (Ethiopia, Tanzania, and Kenya) but has become a large halo around the equatorial forest[41].

In September 2015, an American palaeontologist highlighted a new human species discovered in an almost inaccessible South African cave, rising star, near Johannesburg. Homo naledi, as it is referred, is a species that has a mosaic primitive human trait that suggests that it could be the first representative of the genus Homo. The precise dating of Homo naledi that will allow its classification is one of the important expectations of palaeontologists. Anne Debroise, a journalist who conducts research on the human race, says that the homo is part of the homininae, and the closest of our species is the Homo sapiens that we call today the modern man. There are some relatively well described and identified species (Homo habilis, Homo erectus, Homo neanderthalensis and Homo floresiensis). The veteran of this family is Homo habilis (skilled man). Five criteria that traditionally characterise the homo genus include; bipedalism, a cranial capacity of more than 600 cm^2; the ability to speak an articulated language; the manufacture of stone tools and the ability of precise grasping (Ibidp. 54).

The famous Burkinabe historian Joseph Ki-zerbo, analysing the course of the human saga in Kenya, Olduvai in Tanzania, Omo in Ethiopia, Chad Tropus Uxoris and Toumaï in Chad, reached the same conclusion that the first human race appeared in Africa[42].

The palaeontologist Jean Jacques Hublin developed the same thesis of Africa cradle of humanity when he declared that, "The African continent is the one in which the entire evolutionary history of the

---

[41] Yves Copens, la saga de l'humanité (The saga of humanity). La Revue Dossier pour la science n° 94 janvier mars 2017, P12 (Dossier Review for science no. 94 January March 2017, P12).

[42] Joseph Ki-Zerbo,*Histoire de l'Afrique Noire (Joseph Ki-Zerbo, History of Black Africa)*. Hatier, Paris, 1978, pg. 47.

homininae occurred until about 2 million years ago. There is a consensus on this, even if some people find it difficult to adhere to it" ("*La Revue là Recherche Hors-série – l'odyssée humaine,*op.cit., p. 6" The Review of Special Research - The Human Odyssey, op.cit., pg. 6). He recalls the discoveries concerning the first hominiae after their separation from the great apes; the orrorin, dating back 6 million years, discovered in Kenya in 2000; the Toumaï, dates 7 million years back and discovered in 2002 in Chad; the Ardipithecus, dating between 5.7 to 4.4 million years ago was found between 1990 and 2005 in Ethiopia; in South Africa the Australopitheans sediba, dating about 1.9 million years ago, was discovered in 2010 and in 2015 Homo naledi of the Rising star cave was found and yet to be dated. Everything is clear about the African origin as cradle of humanity. It is a great privilege, indeed a divine grace to shelter the cradle of humanity and to shelter the first brilliant human civilisation, whose epicentre was the black race of ancient Egypt.

II-The black origin of ancient Egypt, the first brilliant human civilisation and its contribution to the West and to humanity. Egyptian culture and spirit: spirit of knowledge, wisdom, light and perfection

The Senegalese scholar, Cheikh Anta Diop offers us the most striking testimony and the most brilliant demonstration of the black origin of the Egyptian and Pharaonic antique civilisation, in his famous work *Nations nègres et culture* (Black nations and culture). He declares, "while the European can trace the course of their history back to Greco-Latin antiquity and the Eurasian steppes, the African who through Western works tries to go back in their historical past stops at the founding of Ghana (3rd century before or 3rd century AD). Beyond, these works teach the African that it is the dark night. What were African ancestors doing on the continent during the prehistory era?" The author wonders: "how is it that they have waited so long to emerge from the shadows with a sophisticated social organisation? While the West African national can contemplate two thousand years of history, those of other regions are less favoured. For instance in the Congo and Zambezi basins in the Great Lakes region, western textbooks hardly go back without a break in continuity beyond a few centuries". He notes, therefore, that "the general problem that arises for African history is therefore to succeed, by fruitful research to link, not in a hypothetical but effective way, all these sections of the past to an antiquity, a common origin that restores continuity "(Cheik Anta Diop op.cit., pg. 27-28).

He adds, "Suppose that with modern Egyptology the Egyptians were white.

They had Greek and Roman contemporaries, who rubbed shoulders with them. They had the scientific and philosophical spirit as much as modern Westerners. They wrote about all the events of their time and particularly, they spoke about their own history and race as those of other contemporary peoples ". This means that "they were therefore well placed to inform posterity about the ethnic characteristics of the peoples who lived around the Mediterranean, and they did not fail to do so. The teaching of these testimonies seemed so right, after verification that by writing the history of Antiquity one has only copied the Ancients like Herodotus who is considered the father of history. He also visited Egypt in the middle of the fifth century BC. Diodorus (historian), Strabo (geographer), Pliny and Tacitus (philosopher) ". Now these authors, whose writings have proved to be surprisingly accurate about events and questions that are sometimes very delicate and very complex, have unanimously informed us of a fact that fell to their minds and on which they could not be deceived, the Egyptian race. Everything points to the fact that the Egyptians were blacks, like Ethiopians and other Africans. And also that Egypt civilised the world. If the modern idea in which blacks have always lived under the rule of whites and never played a role in history, is well founded, it should have been truer in antiquity. The feeling of superiority of the white ancestor of the modern Egyptologist should have been much more to accuse, no misguidance, no confusion, should have allowed the chance to find in these writings such testimonies on the Egyptian people. We can try, seriously, to mitigate the value of these testimonies, because the Ancients have repeatedly repeated them as evidence that they relied on to justify the origin of this or that custom that the Greeks had borrowed from the blacks of Egypt.

Who were the Egyptians? Such a question never arose for the contemporaries of ancient Egyptians who left us testimonies about them (testimonies of writers and ancient philosophers and the Bible). All these eyewitnesses formally claim that the Egyptians were blacks.

Herodotus, on several occasions, insisted on the black character of the Egyptians and used it to make indirect demonstrations, to prove that the floods of the Nile cannot be due to a melting of the snow. He gave among other reasons that he thought valid the following related to Egypt: the third comes from the fact that the heat makes men black there (Herodotus, book II, paragraph 2, Larcher translation).

The opinion of all the writers of antiquity on the Egyptian race is summarised by Maspero (ancient history of the peoples of the East). According to an almost unanimous testimony of ancient historians, Egyptians belonged to the African race (black), which first settled in Ethiopia on the Middle Nile, and gradually descended to the sea following the course of the river. According to the Bible, Egypt was inhabited by the descendants of Ham, an ancestor of blacks. Cheikh Anta Diop, op.cit., The sons of Ham (Genesis 10: 6-16 in the King James translation of 1948).

Cheik Anta Diop in the quest to provide details and precision adds that Herodotus after reporting his eyewitness account that the Egyptians were blacks, then demonstrated, with rare honesty (because we know that he was Greek), that Greece has taken from Egypt all the elements of her civilisation, even to the worship of the gods, and it is Egypt which is the cradle of civilisation (pg. 42).

The Jewish people at the instigation of Moses would have been open to the idea of monotheism, since Moses was sensitive to the religious centralism of the pharaoh Akhenaton who sought political centralism, since the Egyptian Empire needed a universal religion (op. cit., pp. 44-45). In the atmosphere of insecurity when the Jewish people were in Egypt, a promising God of a sure future was the irreplaceable moral support. After the initial reluctance, this people, who did not seem to have known monotheism until then, contrary to the opinion of those who want to make it their inventor, will nevertheless bring it to a considerable rate of development. With faith, Moses led the Hebrews out of Egypt. They apparently got tired very quickly of this worship and only returned gradually to monotheism (example of the golden calf of Aaron at the foot of the Sinai) op.cit., pg. 45. Cheikh Anta Diop adds that after entering Egypt as 70 shepherds organised in 12 patriarchal families, nomads, without industry, without culture, the Jewish people came out 400 years later numbering 600 000, after having drawn from this nation all the elements of its future tradition, and in particular, monotheism. He adds that the Egyptians called their country Kemit which means: black, in the Egyptian language. To him, the interpretation of "Kemit" that refers to the black land of Egypt and not simply black, and by extension the black race and the land of blacks, derives from a free imagination of spirits that are aware of what would imply an exact interpretation of that term. So it is natural to find in Hebrew: kam meaning heat, black, burned (op.cit., Pg. 46 et seq.) Cheikh Anta Diop insists however that the blacks were at the origin of the first civilisation which has flourished on the earth and to which humanity owes most of its progress. According to him, Egypt has been a cradle for civilisation for 10,000 years that is, at a time when the rest of the world is plunged into barbarism. This Egypt destroyed by successive invasions, no longer played any role in politics, but will continue no less for a long time still to initiate the young Mediterranean peoples (Greeks and Romans among others) to civilisation. It will remain throughout the Antiquity the classical land where these Mediterranean people came for pilgrimage to tap from scientific, religious, moral, social sources etc., the oldest knowledge that men have acquired.

Consequently, the new civilisations were built successively all around the Mediterranean. This was because they benefited from the multiple contributions favoured by the geographical configuration of the Mediterranean - best situated real crossroads of the world - and have evolved especially towards a materialistic and technical development, an evolution to which we must situate the materialistic genius of the Indo-Europeans who are the Greeks and Romans. The pagan impetus that favoured this Greco-Roman civilisation got exhausted towards the fourth century. Two new factors, Christianity and barbarian invasions interfered on the terrain of Western Europe to give birth to a new civilisation. This last civilisation which inherited all the technical progress of humanity, thanks to uninterrupted contacts between the peoples, was sufficiently technically equipped in the fifteenth century, to set out to conquer the world with the success that we know even if, in turn, it manifests symptoms of exhaustion (Ibid, Pg. 50-51).

Cherubini, the travel companion of the Egyptologist Champollion-le-Jeune insists on the precedence of Ethiopia compared to Egypt and recalls the unanimous opinion of the ancients that Egypt is only an Ethiopian colony, that is to say Meroitic Sudanese. It was even believed in Antiquity that humanity was born in Meroitic Sudan.

Thus, as early as Antiquity, which precedes the ordinary calculations of historical criticism, there appears a completely regulated social organisation with its religion, laws and institutions. Ethiopians boasted of having been the first to establish the worship of divinity and the use of sacrifice. Here too, the torch of science and the arts would have been lit. It is to this people that we should attribute the invention of sculpture, the use of writing characters and finally the origin of all developments of an advanced civilisation[43].

Speaking of the black race of ancient Egypt, Cherubini, who is still quoted by Cheikh Anta Diop, points out that "It is reasonable to suppose, without too much temerity, that on any point of the earth one would not have met a civilisation whose march had appeared to us surrounded by more certainty and incontestable signs of priority, since it had been revealed to us by contemporaries of these primitive trials, its progress and maturity, and when it seemed to have moved far ahead of most nations in the social aspect".

Cheikh Anta Diop emphasises that the ancient ones, the same ones who transmitted us the current civilisation, unanimously recognised, scientists and philosophers, from Herodotus to Diodorus of Sicily, in other words from Greece to Rome, that they had this civilisation from the blacks on the banks of the Nile, whether they were Ethiopians or Egyptians. From Cherubini's text it is clear that the Ancients never disputed with the blacks the role of the first initiators of civilisation.

Cheikh Anta Diop recalls the thesis of Amelineau, a great Egyptologist who is not often spoken of. Amelineau refers to "Anou, the first black race to have occupied Egypt. According to Amelineau, it is this Anou black race that probably created, in the pre-historic time, all the elements of the Egyptian civilisation which remained without much modification until the end of the later. Blacks were the first to practise agriculture, irrigate the Nile Valley, erect dikes, invent the sciences, arts, writing and calendar". They have also "created the cosmogony recorded in the Book of the Dead whose texts leave no doubt about the black character of the race that conceived the ideas. It is to this population that one can attribute without fear of error, the oldest books of Egypt, the book of the Dead and the texts "of the pyramids and consequently all the myths or religious teachings, even

[43] Cherubini, la Nubie, collection l'univers, Paris 1847, cité par Cheikh Anta Diop (Cherubini, Nubia, collection universe, Paris 1847, quoted by Cheikh Anta Diop).

the philosophical systems already known and which are still called Egyptian, as will be developed in the fourth part devoted to the glorious past of Africa.

It is certain that this people already knew the main arts as evidenced in the architecture of the tombs of Abydos, especially in the tomb of Osiris. In these tombs were found objects bearing the indelible mark of their origin.

Amelineau concludes that the Egyptian civilisation is not of Asian origin, but of African and negroid origin, although this assertion may be paradoxical. One is not accustomed to endowing the black race or neighbouring races with too much intelligence or even enough intelligence to have made the first discoveries necessary for civilisation (Cheikh Anta Diop, op.cit. , Pg 133-134). Cheikh Anta Diop argues that archaeological data did not support the hypothesis of a white race originating in the heart of Africa.

It is thanks to Amelineau that we owe the discovery of the tomb of Osiris in Abydos. This discovery showed that Osiris was not just a mythical hero, but a historical figure, a first ancestor of the Pharaohs, a black ancestor, as well as his sister Isis who was his wife. Egyptians have always painted their gods in carbon black in the image of their race, from the beginning to the end of their history (Ibid).

The Senegalese scholar Cheikh Anta Diop argues that Indo-Europeans have never created a civilisation in their primitive cradles, that is to say in the Eurasian steppes. The civilisations that are attributed to them are undoubtedly those located in the heart of black countries, on the southern part of the North atmosphere: Egypt, Arabia, Phenice, Mesopotamia, Elam, and India. He goes on to say very aptly that "In all these countries there were black civilisations at the time when Indo-Europeans arrived in the second millennium as uncouth nomads. The process consists in demonstrating that it was these wild uncivilised populations that brought, in their shaking, all the elements of civilisation and introduced them wherever they were. The question is [to know] why so many creative abilities were manifested only in contact with blacks and never in the primitive cradle of the Eurasian steppes? And "Why did these people not create civilisation at home before immigrating? If we go back to the highest antiquity, we are often obliged to look back to documents on black countries in order to explain all the phenomena of civilisation".

It would be wrong to say that civilisation was born from this interbreeding. There is evidence that civilisation existed in black countries long before the historical contact with Indo-Europeans. Homogeneous black people have created all the elements of civilisation, adapting themselves to the favourable geographical conditions of their primitive cradles. From then on, their countries become attractive poles where inhabitants of the deprived or backward regions which approached them try to enter to improve their existence. The interbreeding that is born of this contact is therefore a consequence of the civilisation already created by the blacks, and not the cause of it. Since Antiquity, all the elements of Egyptian civilisation have been created from the beginning. They remained unchangeable. We recognise with certainty the different invasions of Westerners that took place in Egypt, in historical times the Hyksos (Scythians), Libyans, Assyrians and Persians. None of these elements brought a new development in the pure sciences and even in the human sciences. "All that precedes also makes it possible to reject the explanations a posteriori which, starting from the situation of the modern world, decrees that the temperate zone is favourable, par excellence, to the blossoming of the civilisations which, all have found their origin there. Historical documents prove, on the contrary, that when the climate of the earth was already fixed, all the first civilisations existed outside this zone" (Ibid Pg. 230-231).

Cheikh Anta Diop, also quotes Jacques Weulerse (*L'Afrique Noire* [Black Africa], Ed. Fayard, 1934, Paris, pg. 11), to say that "Africa will long remain a mystery: and yet, was it not one of the cradles of history? It is a country of Africa, the millennium Egypt which still bears almost intact today the most venerable monuments of our Antiquity. At a time when all Europe was still wild, when Paris and London were only swamps and Rome and Athens deserts, Africa already had a very ancient civilisation in the Nile Valley "(Ibid). Cheikh Anta Diop even specifies that inasmuch as it is difficult to prove the relationship of Egyptian and the Indo-European and Semitic languages, it is easy to prove the deep unity of the Egyptian and black languages (Ibid).

In the fourth part, we amplify the contribution of ancient Egypt to the development of the West and of humanity. Thus, Cheikh Anta Diop defends the following themes: the black origin of the Egypto-Nubian civilisation; the contribution of the Egypto-Nubian civilisation, and therefore of the black thought, to Western civilisation in the sciences, letters, arts, the linguistic connection between Egypt and Black Africa; the delimitation of the cultural area of the black world that extends to West Asia in the Indus Valley; the training of African states throughout the continent, after the decline of Egypt and the continuity of the historic and cultural links, until the dawn of modern times; the description of the African artistic world and its problems (sculpture, painting, music, architecture, literature); demonstration of the ability of African languages to support scientific and philosophical thought.

When Cheikh Anta Diop developed these revolutionary ideas in France in 1954, it was a public outcry, to dare to assert peremptorily that it was the despised blacks in this colonial period, who in the early days of history brought all elements of civilisation to humanity, as the *Le Républicain Lorrain* newspaper headlined.

The precedence of black civilisation and its contribution to the progress of universal civilisation are also developed by the Cameroonian scientist, Engelbert Mveng. In 1971 at the Colloquium on Negritude in Dakar, he set up a typology of original researchers from Greek-Roman and archaeological sources. This is archaeological evidence of G A Beardslley in his book *The Negro in Greek and Roman Civilization: a study of the Ethiopian type (1929), the masterpiece of F.M.* Snowdena published in 1970, Blacks in Antiquity: *Ethiopians in the Greco-Roman Experience*. By relying on the exploitation of the texts of the elders such as Herodotus, Pindar, Virgil, Diodorus of Sicily, hc affirms that we find Negroes almost in all the ancient armies, in the Persian, the Carthaginian army, not forgetting the Egyptian army which was partly black[44].

In his research, he states that he has been committed to the discovery of Negro-Africans and Black Africa through the Greco-Roman civilisation. He adds that the Negro-African world and its inhabitants are not only "An artistic and literary theme for the Greco-Roman civilisation, they are one of the historical foundations. Engelbert Mveng has identified and demonstrated the contribution of negritude in the design and development of scientific knowledge of the world. Engelbert

---

[44] Jean Tabi Manga, *Des Voix... à la voie du temps. Variations sur la Renaissance, l'Émergence et la Modernité africaines*, Édition Sopecam,pp. 76 et s. (Jean Tabi Manga, Voices ... on the path of time.
Variations on the Renaissance, Emergence and Modernity of Africa, Sopecam Edition, pg. 76).

Mveng's thesis defended at the University of Paris-Sorbonne in 1970 deals with Greek sources of Negro-African history from Homer to Strasbon".

At a time when ancient Egypt was gradually experiencing its decline under the horde of Persian invaders (525 BC), Macedonians with Alexander the Great, Romans with Julius Caesar (50 BC), the Arabs in the fifth century, the Turks in the sixteenth century, France with Napoleon, then the English in the late nineteenth century, the Greeks and Romans inspired and trained in the brilliant Egyptian civilisation took over the evolution and promotion of knowledge for success we now know. The revolutionary research of the Senegalese scholar has as a result brought to light the considerable contribution of the black race of ancient Egypt to the development of sciences and arts. With this fabulous and glorious past, and its status as the cradle of humanity, Africa has undeniable assets, to find the founding axis of true knowledge, revive its Renaissance and conquer the lights of eternal knowledge, for its optimal development. It must connect to the chain of knowledge that it had initiated in antiquity and that has passed to the West and also to Asia, to play again a leading role and not follow blindly. Jean Baptiste Duroselle also emphasises that, "What counts is not only current events, but also evolution, the indispensable chain for recognising continuity, creations and the possible existence of regularities" (JB Duroselle. *Tout Empire périra.* (Every Empire will perish) Sorbonne Publications, 1981. pg.14). Other aspects of this African saga are developed in the fourth part devoted to the cultural revolution in Africa.

The origins of the rise of the West are thus posed. Other important aspects of this Egyptian contribution to the West and to humanity are developed in Part IV (Chapter II). How to understand the decline of Africa vis-à-vis the West?

III- Why the decline of Africa after its contact with the West from the 15th century?

Africa gave to humanity the elements of its civilisation since antiquity. This was possible through the black race of ancient Egypt, and all the Elders of the time, especially Greeks and Romans from Herodotus to Diodorus of Sicily, clearly recognised this fact. The Greeks recognised that they took all the foundations of civilisation from the ancient Egyptians who were blacks. Yet Africa has not been able to maintain this lead since it came in contact, in the 15th century, with a Europe that has become strong, armed with firearms and technicality.

Concerning this decline, Cheikh Anta Diop offers the best explanation. He said that, this so-called Egyptian civilisation will develop for a long period in its original cradle, then slowly descend along the Nile valley to radiate around the basin of the Mediterranean. This cycle of civilisation is the longest in history for it lasted 10,000 years. It is easy to understand that during this long period, blacks were able to gradually spread again towards the interior of the continent, to constitute nuclei which became centres of continental civilisation. These African civilisations were increasingly cut off from the rest of the world. They lived in isolation because of the enormous distance that separated them from the access routes to the Mediterranean. When Egypt lost its independence, their isolation was complete.

As much as the adaptation in the narrow, fertile valley of the Nile required a skilful technique of irrigation and dikes with precise calculations to predict Nile floods and to deduce the economic and social consequences, it was also necessary to invent geometry to delimit the inhabitants as the ground was in long flat bands and required of them to transform the palaeonegritic hoe into a plough, drawn first by the men, then by animals. So the blacks were indispensable in the valley of the Nile for material existence, all this became superfluous in the new conditions of existence within the continent. While History had broken its old balance with the environment, the black man had found a new equilibrium, different from the first one by the absence of technique which was no longer of vital importance as opposed to the social, political and moral organisation. Economic resources being provided by means which do not require perpetual inventions, the black man gradually lost interest in material progress. It is under this new state that the meeting took place with Europe.

In the fifteenth century, when the first Portuguese, Dutch, English, French, Danish, and Brandenburg merchant seamen began to establish trading posts on the west coast of Africa, the political organisation of African States was equal and often superior to that of their own respective States. The social and moral order was at the same level of perfection. There was no pre-logical mentality in the sense that Lévy-Bruhl understood it. On the other hand, for reasons already indicated, technical development was less advanced than in Europe. The black man, although he was the first to discover iron, had not built a gun, the secret of the powder was known to Egyptian priests only who used it only for religious purposes, during Mysteries of Osiris.

Africa was therefore very vulnerable from a technical point of view. It became a hanging prey, irresistible for the West who were equipped with guns and marines in the long course. The economic rise of Renaissance Europe led to the conquest of Africa, which was rapidly developing. It was at the beginning of this period that Christopher Columbus discovered America and that the overflow of the old continent poured over the new one. The development of virgin lands required cheap labour. Defenceless Africa then appeared as the human reservoir to indicate where it was necessary to draw such a workforce with minimum of costs and risks. The modern slave trade of blacks became an economic necessity before the advent of the machine. It lasted until the nineteenth century.

Such a reversal of roles, resulting from the new technical reports, resulted in master-slave social relations between Whites and blacks. Already in the Middle Ages, the memory of a black Egypt having civilised the earth had faded away from the oblivion of the ancient tradition hidden in libraries or buried in the ruins. It will fade even more during these four centuries of slavery. Imbued with their recent technical superiority, the Europeans had, at first sight, contempt for the whole black world, of which they designed only to touch riches. The ignorance of the ancient history of blacks, differences of manners and customs, ethnic prejudices between the two races that think they are confronted for the first time, in addition to the economic necessities of exploitation and so many predisposed factors, favoured the European to completely distort the moral personality of the black man and his intellectual abilities.

Being black now became synonymous to being primitive, inferior and a victim of a pre-logical mentality. And as the human being is always anxious to justify their conduct, they went even further. With the concern to legitimise colonisation and the slave trade they engendered a whole descriptive literature of the so-called inferior characters of blacks, progressively distorting the spirit of several European generations. Western opinion will crystallise and admit instinctively as a revealed truth that the black man symbolises the inferior human being. At most, one can recognise the black man's artistic gifts related to his lower animal sensitivity. Such is the opinion of the Frenchman Gobineau, precursor of the philosophy of the Nazis who, in his famous book *De l'inegalite des races humaines (Inequality of human races)*, decrees that the sense of art is inseparable from the blood of blacks, but he reduces the art to an inferior manifestation of human nature, especially the sense of rhythm is related to the emotional abilities of the black man.

Such a climate of alienation has come to have a profound effect on the personality of the educated black, who has had the opportunity to become aware of the idea that the rest of the world holds of him and his people. It is very often the case that a black intellectual loses confidence in his own possibilities and those of his race, and to such an extent that, in spite of the value of proofs exposed in this study, it will not be surprising that some of us, after acquainting ourselves with it, are still struggling to admit that we had really assumed the first civilising role of the world.

It is common that blacks of a high culture remain victims of this alienation to the point of seeking in good faith to codify these Nazi ideas of an alleged duality of the sensitive and emotional black, creative of art, and of the White man made especially of rationality.

Thus, a black complementarity literature was gradually created, to infantile and remind us of passivity. The recent remembrance of slavery which the black race suffered from has been carefully maintained in the memory of men. To the black man in particular, that has often affected their consciousness in a negative manner. From this recent slavery, an attempt has been made to build, in spite of all historical truth, of course, the legend that the black man has always been reduced to slavery by superior white races with which he has lived, wherever he may be, which makes it easy to justify the presence of blacks in Egypt or Mesopotamia, or in Arabia, from the earliest antiquity, by decreeing that they were slaves.

In the course of such transformations of the black man's relations with the rest of the world, it was becoming every day, "More and more difficult and even unacceptable, for those who did not know his past greatness, and for blacks themselves, that they could have been at the origin of the first civilisation that has blossomed on the earth and to which humanity owes most of its progress "[45].

---

[45] Cheikh Anta Diop, op.cit.,pp. 50 -57

Cheik Anta Diop also points out that to dominate a people, one must destroy their culture, take away the moral benefit of it and make them also believe that they are not responsible.

He recognises that, if the West has progressively taken its lead, it is because of its relationship with nature and its sense of materialism. He emphasises that for the Greeks "The man is master of himself and even master of his destiny, being the centre of the world, he is a god here on earth. Realising one's image with perfection constituted the ultimate ideal of the artist [...] Let us note, by the way, that anthropomorphism, materialism, development of technology will be the essential contribution of the West to the civilisation of the world".

On the other hand, all of black Africa including Egypt, will traditionally be the domain par excellence of a vitality that minimises the modest human power and will always look to benefit the intervention of extra human forces by appropriate religious means. That is how all discoveries, all material and social progress, all artistic creations will be assigned a coefficient, surrounded by an atmosphere of religiosity, from foreign spirituality to the Western mind, more inclined to materialism. When Egypt had transmitted a sacred civilisation to the rest of the world and to Greece in particular, it can only take advantage of this legacy by bringing the religiosity that surrounds it to the scale of man and nature, and it is this anthropomorphic integration of religiosity that constitutes the only palpable fact that can be remembered from the myth of the Greek miracle.

Therefore, unlike Westerners, Africa, which can secure a decent material life, will always believe that the surest way is to devote oneself to ritual practices.

Since all this conduct is inspired by the need to preserve and transmit life in the best conditions of its era, it is essentially, the materialistic instinct which is at the base, a metaphysical materialism in the sense that the African believes he can act on his destiny by relying on intangible levers.

The correction of this error must come from the West and it is the greatest advantage the African can draw from his contact with the former[46].

---

[46] Idem.

It emerges from this relevant analysis by Cheik Anta Diop, that Africa did not know how to integrate sufficiently in these early stages of human history and that knowledge, a source of progress, should be the subject of permanent development to create new dynamics of environmental domination, in order to cope with the shocks and vicissitudes of life. Moreover, the balance of mind/matter, theory/action, to have taken on concrete issues has not been sufficiently mastered, unlike the West whose capacity for domineering, conquering and concrete action was more thorough. Cheik Anta Diop humbly admits that Africa has to learn this practical side from the West. It must also be recognised that slavery, colonisation and neo-colonialism have caused enormous damage on the evolution of Africa. She was deprived of her youths and her dynamic forces deported to the West and America to work on the plantations. Joseph Ki-Zerbo notes that all slavery treaties in Africa cost the continent 100 million men and women, 50 million being the minimum[47].

Haven taken all the elements of civilisation from the black race of ancient Egypt, the foundation of the development of the West were set.

---

[47] Joseph KI-Zerbo, op.cit., pg. 218-226.

Chapter II

The contribution of ancient Greece to the rise of the West and humanity-an unprecedented experience for Africa to ponder on

In the light of this Egyptian contribution to Western civilisation and to humanity, Greek influence on the Western Christian and even on humanity is still observed today through the spirit of knowledge, wisdom and of intelligence obtained and developed in philosophy, poetry, humanism, sciences, arts, the Greek language, democracy, myths, gods and heroes.

All things crowned in a brilliant and dominant culture. This domination of ancient Greece spread throughout the Mediterranean from the conquests of Alexander the Great from 331 to 146 BC and goes even beyond this period. That is why the Mediterranean is recognised as a great cradle of civilisation. It is in this space that the three great monotheistic religions that dominate the world today were born: Judaism, Christianity and Islam. It is also recognised that Africa is the cradle of humanity and the first great civilisation, where man was born. These are sacred and realities dedicated to the universal plan.

I- Greek culture and spirit: spirit of knowledge, intelligence, wisdom and perfection

Initially, we noticed that the characteristics of Greek culture are identical to those of ancient Egypt, since Greeks themselves acknowledge having drawn all the elements of civilisation from Egypt. The Greek spirit is summed up in the perfect values of knowledge, intelligence, wisdom, perfection and beauty. In reality, it is a spirit that praises the good and handsome man, bearer of the highest ethical values. Thus we develop the power of the word, as a means of gathering men and government, the efficiency of the thought which, developing in itself and for itself, makes it possible to act on the real like the sophists, the goldsmiths of the word, of the good formula, and great philosophers of whom ancient Greece has the secret. Finally, there is the importance of physical exercise, essential to ensure the beauty of the body and allow competition between men.[48]

The conquest of the East and the Mediterranean by Alexander the Great, son of Philip of Macedonia, promotes the spread of the Greek spirit. It brings on board philosophy, mathematics, poetry and the arts without omitting language. Greek then imposed itself as the lingua franca of the entire East and the Mediterranean, an idiom indispensable to trade or relate with the administration. The Greek city became the model of the new cities of which Alexander the Great and later his generals built their Empires on, and the most famous was Alexandria of Egypt which exists to this day in this African country and the Middle-East. Other cities followed suit and built gymnasiums, theatres, acropolises (the highest part of Greek cities). Greek architecture also imposed itself. Hellenisation was transformed into a true cultural conquest. The Hellenistic world remains Greek and it is in the Greek language that non-Greeks will make known their history and culture, under the leadership of Saint Paul, the Jewish apostle of the chosen people of Israel, who spoke Greek. Christianity first spoke and thought Greek.

The New Testament is even written in Greek. This grip of Greek culture lasted until the Middle Ages, a continuous influence of over a thousand years, as we will discuss in the section on European Renaissance of the 16th century. This cultural hold found a place among Jews, Christians and Muslims. Even today, at a time when philosophy wants to be a way of life, it is again towards Greek thinkers, Epicureans or Stoics that the modern man seeks wisdom, or Sophia as the Greeks put it.

Pierre Lanares in his wonderful book *Qui dominera le monde* (*Who will dominate the world*) Editions SDT France, 1982, recognises the importance of Hellenism in the contemporary world. To him, in the history of humanity, Hellenism holds a considerable place and we can say that we still live the civilisation it created. What is called humanism is nothing else than Greco-Latin culture and Europe has not yet found a way to replace it. This brilliant culture is illustrated by great Greek minds in philosophy, history, poetry, mathematics, science and oratory.

[48] *Le Point Références*. July–August 2011, La sagesse grecque, les textes fondamentaux, p.8.

We can quote in philosophy the renowned Socrates, Plato, Aristotle, Pythagoras, Zenon of Elea, Epicurus, Zenon of Kiton and also historians such as Herodotus, Thucidides, Hesiod (poet) and Sophocles (playwright). Pythagoras considered that numbers are the principle and the source of all things. Pythagorean arithmetic, limited to integers, included a theory of proportions. He is the inventor of mystical mathematics. The Pythagorean philosophical school founded by Pythagoras believed in the reincarnation of souls (metempsychosis). Many of these great Greek minds were trained in Egypt.

Socrates (470 - 399 BC) He did not leave books as such. For, he had the reputation of spending most of his time with his young disciples discussing in the streets, gymnasiums and other public places, to make them discover that which they knew. This method of seeking knowledge is known as Socratic maieutic. Plato was his disciple. He made Socrates one of his actors in his work *The Banquet*. The essence of his philosophy consists in his faith in human reason by which man can attain knowledge.

Plato (418-347 BC): the thought of this philosopher has sustainably and profoundly influenced the West. He founded a school of thought, the Academy. His work gave birth to Platonism characterised by the dualism body/soul and the primacy of the idea on the sensible world. His work consists mainly of dialogues, including the banquet, in which, especially through the personality of Socrates, he tackles the great metaphysical and philosophical problems in a language often poetic and of a great literary quality.[49]Christianity better expresses the primacy of the word, of the spirit on matter.

Aristotle (384-322 BC) He studied with Plato in Athens where he founded, around 355 BC, his own philosophical school, the High School. He had encyclopaedic knowledge. His system was based on a rigorous conception of the universe. His philosophy was one of the pillars of Western thought. He was the author of a large number of works, among others, physics, logic, politics, biology (composite anatomy, classification of animals), metaphysics, and Nicomachean ethics. The complexity of his thought provoked a crisis in Europe, calling into question the omnipotence of theology.[50]He played his decisive role in the debates of science and philosophy of Islam. The

[49]Ibid., pp. 101-102.
[50]Ibid., p. 98.

academy and the high school as elevated places of knowledge have become essential, as unsurpassable legacies of the Greek spirit up to today.

Solon was an Athenian statesman and a learned. His name is attached to the social and political form that provoked the rise of Athens. He laid the foundation for what was later known as the Athenian democracy, from Clisthenes (late 6th century BC). The Greeks venerated wisdom and erected seven wise personalities, hence the seven sages, each of whom had their own slogan: the two most famous, the philosopher Thales of Miletus and the Athenian legislator Solon. Plato adds the five others: Chilon of Sparta, Pittacos of Mytilene, Bias of Priene, Cleobulus of Lindos and Corinthian Periander. The sage Thales of Miletus, who is included in the presocratic thinkers, is an astronomer, and is said to have predicted the solar eclipse of 28 May 585. We owe him the invention of the geographical map and the sundial and we know his interest in biology. He would have had the intuition that the appearance of man probably resulted from a long evolutionary process. He reported of Egypt and Babylon the elements of geometry and algebra. He is credited with the first exact missive of time and knowledge of the relationship of angles with the triangles to which they belong, as well as the calculation of proportions (Thales theorem). For him, water is the primary element of the universe.

Zenon of Elea (about 480-420 BC) was a philosopher. According to Aristotle, he is the inventor of the dialectic, a philosophical method adopted by Plato that still remains famous today. Dialectic comes from the Greek word "dialegein", which means to distinguish and "dialegestha", refers to dialogue. It is the codified art of philosophical dialogue, it is the art of questioning and answering, as oppose to eristic (of eris, quarrel) where participants try to impose fixed views. In Socrates, the dialectic consists in dissipating false knowledge in order to reach the truth. Aristotle sees in it a method which makes it possible to identify, on all subjects, the commonly accepted ideas in order to draw the probable reasoning from them ". Among the sophists' verb artists, it designates formal and artificial reasoning that makes it possible to prove everything. The thought so much floats among Greeks that they took up the divine term logos, a Greek term that is difficult to translate, used today to designate the search for rationality that emerges in ancient Greece. And in Greek, depending on the context, the word logos can mean: speech, tongue, language, word, reason, intelligence, foundation, principle, reason, proposition, calculation, report, relation, narrative, thesis, reasoning, argument, explanation, statement, proposition, sentence and definition.[51] It is thus a very rich term which imposes itself in the scholarly language. The Old Testament and the New Testament also develop this term which means the word of God.

Epicurus (341-270 BC) is a philosopher. Hence Epicureanism which is a school of thought whose purpose of life is to achieve the happiness it defines as an absence of physical pain and moral disorder (ataraxia).

Zenon of Kiton (3845-264 BC). He is the founder of the stoicism which maintains that wisdom and happiness reside in living in agreement with the reason which governs the soul and the universe. Today, the word stoicism has become popular and means indifference to the pain and vicissitudes of life.

Theophrastus (370-285 BC). He is a philosopher. He was first Plato's disciple before becoming that of Aristotle who gave him the nickname of Theophrastus meaning "He who speaks like the gods" (his real name was Tyrtamos). He was a Botanist who was at the origin, especially, of the theoretical separation between the animal and plant kingdoms and left an important history of the plants, as well as a paper on the causes of the plants in six books. He also presented papers on physics and psychology, especially through the characters, from which the French Jean de la Bruyère (1645-1696) got inspiration.

Homer: He is the poet who inaugurated the epic genre with his mythical titles: the Iliad that describes the Trojan War and founded the genre of the epic, the odyssey that tells the return of Ulysses to his island of Ithaca after the Trojan War. The epic is a poetic narrative or prose that narrates the exploits of a hero.

Thucydides (about 460-395 BC). He is the first of Greek historians. He is the author of the history of the Peloponnesian War. He tells the facts with rigour and tries to explain the causes. He gives economic and social facts their true importance.

Herodotus (about 484-420 BC): Greek historian and considered the father of history. He is the author of the stories that tell the decades-long battles between the Greeks and the barbarian world (non-Greek foreign world in the first place the Persians). He is one of the Greeks,

[51] Ibid, pg. 43-103.

with his fellow historians Diodorus of Sicily and Geographer Strabo, to recognise that the Egyptians founded the first brilliant human civilisation and were blacks. And Herodotus recognises that Greece has received from Egypt all the elements of civilisation even the worship of gods and that this nation is the cradle of civilisation[52].

Protagoras (486-410 BC): A Greek philosopher. He says that man is the measure of everything.

Hesiod (8th-7th century BC). He was a poet. In his work, "the theogonia", he recounts the genealogy and the origins of the world and gods. In another poem "Works and days", he describes farm work and delivers some autobiographical elements.

Demosthenes (384-322). He was a politician and great Athenian speaker. Through tenacity and study, he managed to overcome his speech difficulties and acquired a remarkable talent as a speaker.

Plutarch (50-125 AD): Greek writer, he travelled to Egypt and Rome. He has written a great number of papers which have been divided since Antiquity into two groups: moral works and parallel paths. His work had a great influence, from Montaigne to Rousseau and the French Revolution.

Sophocles (495-405 BC): He was a Greek playwright who was close to Pericles and influenced the destiny of Athens from 460 to 431 BC. His tragedies, considered as masterpieces of the Greek spirit, show how men are led despite their loss.

Hippocrates (about 460 to 370 BC). He is also a Greek, father of medicine and the most famous doctor of ancient Greece. Western medicine, which has remained humoral until the end of the eighteenth century, was dominated by the Hippocratic conception. This approach is philosophical and considers that the human body is a set of organs from which four body liquids flow: blood, phlegm or slime, yellow bile and black bile (which are associated with four elementary qualities (hot, cold, dry, wet and all four seasons). Good health is the balance between these four moods that vary from person to person and the same subject depending on the season. The predominance of one over the other in an individual determines his temperament, that is to say his nature and the type of diseases to which he is likely to be subjected to.[53]In the Greek

[52] Cheikh Anta Diop.op.cit.,pg. 42.

[53] *Le Point Références*, La sagesse grecque, les textes fondamentaux, op.cit.,pp. 31 -33

spirit of the beauty of the soul, the Hippocratic Oath, pronounced by doctors, recommends, among other things, purity of the soul of those who enter the medical profession. The Hippocratic Oath has remained unsurpassable until today and a universal reference because of the fundamental and perfect value of purity.

Isocrates (436-338 BC) was a great Professor of eloquence having been to the school of sophists, good talkers. He opened his own school of rhetoric that teaches not only the art of well-being, but also morals and politics. He put all his acquired knowledge at the service of practical life. In his writing entitled, "Who are the truly educated men?" He provides this definition. For him, he establishes the comparison between gymnastics (for the body) and philosophy, understood as a culture of intelligence, which underpins the ambition of an education with a moral aim as complete as possible (body- mind). To him still, to speak properly is the certainty of a right reason, and a language in conformity with reality and justice is the image of a beautiful soul and in whom one can trust the word directs all the actions of our thoughts.

He continues that, education builds a learned man. The outcome of this education that includes the body, spirit, and soul is to be an accomplished man, knowing how to think well, to speak well in order to live well. In his last speech (panathenaic), Isocrates offers his fellow citizens his vision of the wise man as complete, endowed with all the virtucs in his private and public life, capable in all circumstances of deciding according to a fair opinion and to find the best course of action. With a pleasant and easy conscience, he knows how to accommodate the best of the world of the characters of those with whom he is in contact. His equality of soul is matched only by his rectitude of judgement, the education of his epoch is the search for a constant moral perfection, going beyond the city alone. He has been an undisputed master of oratorical periods, phrases with admirable constructions, where everything is opposed, with symmetry and harmony. His quest for a good man, steeped in humanities, ideally prefigures the worship of the honest man dear to the seventeenth century.[54]

[54]*Point Repères*, juillet-août.op.cit.,pp. 82 -83 (Point Repères, July-August.op.cit., Pg. 82-83)

The beauty of the body and mind

In the same vein, we find one of the major characteristics of the Greek spirit, that is to say, the desire to seek the beauty of the body and soul held to be inseparable. An accomplished man is qualified as handsome and good. His body may be pleasant to look at, but this physical beauty must be inseparable from irreproachable conduct. Ancients do not distinguish between beauty and goodness. Plato goes even further, since beauty becomes the privileged means of access to being. To him the things that surround us are only images of real realities that are found elsewhere, and the soul alone is able to achieve beauty. Beauty is the red thread that allows us on the way to the bottom to go back to the top of reality. Socrates in *the banquet* thinks that one must pass from beautiful bodies to beautiful souls, the only ones to be able to produce beautiful speeches and beautiful actions. It is physical education and learning of literary and musical culture that must lead to this goal and above all allow the soul to contemplate beauty in itself. We are thus beyond aesthetics and metaphysics. It is understandable why beauty is so much present in Plato's work, which reiterates a belief prevalent in Athens, and of which he makes a philosophical instrument that allows him to unify all levels of reality. Beauty leads to interest in the soul and moderation. It is this moderation that renders living together acceptable and makes the soul available for research on what goes beyond the body. The Greek word "deinos" translated as wonderful, is ambiguous, it means wonderful, extraordinary, but also terrible and scary. The Greeks understood this in all in these two senses, which lead back to the questioning of man capable of the good, the bad and the interrogation of all tragedies.

Greeks do not dissociate the body from the spirit. They make physical beauty a moral value, hence the importance given to the education of the body in the gymnasium, where training takes place. The Greeks are interested in games of which the most important are those instituted in Olympia in 776 BC, the founding date of the Greek chronology. Olympia is a religious site of ancient Greece, where all the Olympic Games (every four years) were held from 776 BC. These are the ancestors of modern Olympic Games.

For the Greeks, beauty goes beyond aesthetic considerations, because it merges with good, and for Plato, it gives access to true reality, which for him is not that of the senses, but that of the soul and the intelligible.

Sophocles (485-405 BC) affirms in a peremptory way that between so many marvels of the world, the great wonder is man.[55]Sophocles is a Greek tragic poet. He renewed the form of tragedy. He changed the meaning of the tragedy, making the evolution of the hero and his character an essential part manifesting the destiny of the will of the gods.

The importance of matter in Greek culture

Nature has been one of the favourite subjects of many Greeks since the 6th century BC. Many lost Pre-Socratic writings deal with physics, nature, hence the word "physics". It is also one of the fundamental works of Aristotle. Put together by students from his lectures, physics marks one of the summits of Greek thought, anxious to explain natural phenomena otherwise than by mythology. Aristotle's universe is therefore a finite world in motion, but without beginning or end, therefore uncreated. It is, however, moved by a first motor, God, pure form, but without matter that gives it its order (kosmos).[56]

The philosopher Martin Heidegger (1889-1976) described Aristotle's physics as the basic book of Western philosophy. It was a great success until it was dethroned in the seventeenth century by the modern science of Galileo and Descartes. Aristotelian science tries to make sense of what seemed natural and gives a rational explanation to the world. His monumental "cause of plants", work in several volumes, devoted to the analysis and classification of plants is considered the first botanical treaty. It is one of the most influential products of Aristotelian science and like physics, a reference work for Antiquity and the Middle Ages.

Mathematics from Pythagoras to Euclid.

The Greek spirit is a new view of nature, that of science. It is a view that looks behind appearances, harmonious and stable structures of an ideal reality and capable of expression in mathematical language.

Pythagoras (580-495 BC) is one of the first Greek philosophers and mathematicians.

[55]Ibid.,p. 74.
[56]Ibid., pg. 34.

In one of his theories "Two lines do not close the space", he describes the metaphysical architecture of the universe, starting with two ultimate principles: the monad, pure unity and the dyad, formless matter.

The monad applying on the dyad gradually generates numbers, points, lines, surfaces and five solids which are for him the five elements (water, earth, air, fire and ether) that the physical universe is composed of, a theory found in Timeaus by Plato which narrates the creation of the world. It was at the end of the fourth century that Greek mathematical science reached full maturity with the Elements. It was composed in Alexandria around 300 BC by the mathematician Euclid (25-265 BC) and his disciples on the basis of previous works. They present in a rigorous form, almost all the Greek geometric knowledge of the time. It is a question of building from the first elements of the geometry (points, lines and surfaces), the five Platonic solids. These objects and their properties are described by various propositions and the method used by Euclid referred to as axiomatic was of great rigour.

The author starts from certain propositions considered as primitive and irreducible to logically deduce all the others: the definitions characterise a geometrical object by a property, the postulates describe the properties of space, most of the time by construction operations (by the ruler and the compass) that can be done, for example in definitions: the point is what has no part, or the line is a length without width, the ends of a line are points, an area is what has length and width only.

The postulations (demands): to lead a line from any point to any point, from any point and any interval, to describe a circumference, all the right angles are equal to each other. Finally, the common notions (or axioms) govern the numerical quantities present in all sciences (for example, the quantities which are equal to the same quantity are equal to each other).

This proves, among other things, the Pythagorean Theorem: "To right triangles, the square of the side which supports the right angle (hypotenuse) is equal to the squares of the two sides". Several important mathematical theories are used: a form of geometric algebra, the important theory of propositions resulting from the effort of the Pythagoreans to reduce everything to numbers or numerical ratios.

Finally, ancestor of the infinitesimal calculus, the method of exhaustion aims to measure the surface of a shape by successive approximations.

The elements of Euclid had an immense influence and became, the most printed text after the Bible in the modern West. A philosopher like Spinoza (17th century) discovered an ideal rationality. As for the five so-called Platonic solids, they are found in the modern theory of groups, massively used by quantum physics.[57]

II-Other aspects of Greek culture: democracy, politics, the city, the force of law

Greek democracy is based on fundamental values, some of which are still recognised today and have been adopted by the Western Christian and even the rest of humanity. They include freedom, equality, righteousness, debates, civism, responsibility, education of citizens etc. It participates in Greek wisdom.

Greece is known as the cradle of democracy born in Athens around the 6th century BC. Aristotle began the Athenian democracy from the political, social and economic reforms of Solon (640-560 BC), a poet, legislator and one of the seven sages of ancient Greece. Solon was the mediator of the rivalry between two political parties, aristocrats and the common people. He defends the idea of a social life based on generosity and righteousness, in fact on the beauty of man and his soul, cherished by the Greeks. He has faith in human progress and in law, this human justice rests on the only strength which triumphs over abuses. To him, it is necessary to follow the ideal good order to smooth out dangers. He considers the judgement of the poet Hesiod, whereby, among the useful virtues, order is the first and disorder is the worst of ailments. After drawing a sinister picture of human weaknesses, he proposes to refer them to a higher order, the law. The law alone can restore order and harmony as well as restrain evil. Solon advocates a perfect measurement for the rich and the poor and the equality of rights which he wants to guarantee, hence the principle of isonomy (equality before the law for all) which is the origin of political democracy that the Greeks decline in many forms: equality of speech, of votes, of birth, and of rank. These civic and moral characters, put at the service of the community, made this legislator to be praised by Plato and Demosthenes (Athenian politician).[58]

---

[57] Le Point références juillet-août (The point references July-August). 2011.Ibid., p. 36.
[58] Ibid.,pg. 44.

Moreover, the ephebic oath is an act of commitment of the Greek citizens towards their city. The term "ephebe" refers in a broad sense to young men from 15 to 20 or 18 to 20 years old. Ephebes is a probationary period of two years which is equivalent to a military service. It corresponds to the age of legal majority confirmed by an examination called "dokimasia". On this occasion, the young people take an oath before the ecclesia, the assembly of the people. This prestigious oath obliges the person who pronounces it not to fail. It expresses a double function, marking the commitment of the young person in the future and enumerating his civic duties which include loyalty to the fatherland, religion, human and divine institutions. It is at this price that the future citizen nurtures in him the innate sense of the State, men and gods. It is a true profession of faith by which the citizen marks his belonging to his sovereign city. It reinforces the democratic bond at the same time a passage rite that marks the entry into adulthood.[59]In reality, it is an initiatory rite to move from one level to another, from one age to age another.

In addition, the 5th century BC marks the golden age of Athens and the apex of its democracy. It is also called the century of Pericles, because it was marked by him. Pericles was an Athenian statesman (495-429 BC) and leader of the Democratic Party in 461 BC who was re-elected strategist for thirty years. He attached himself to the democratisation of political life, opening to all access to the high magistracy. Around him was a group of artists like Phidia, his friend. The works of these artists endowed Greek art and brilliant intellectual life earned, the name of Pericles at that time.

On the occasion of a funeral oration that remained famous in honour of the dead during the conflict between Athens and Sparta, Solon praised Athens and its political regime: democracy, the power of the people (demos, the people and kratos, power). This very solemn speech aimed at enhancing the city for which the soldiers gave their lives. Athens is presented as a model for Greece, the school of Greece. The speaker stresses many times on the originality of Athens, its superiority in all areas, the fundamental values it venerates: freedom, intelligence and balance. His political system is just, all citizens are equal before the law, by virtue of the principle of isonomy, a capital rule for the city. It is merit that makes it possible to become a magistrate and not the social

---

[59] Ibid., p.58.

status. It's a public responsibility and no one is prevented by poverty, because towards 450 BC, Pericles himself created misthophoria, an allowance compensating the loss of salary of citizens who exercise political functions and sit at the Bouli (council) or the Helie (popular court). Any citizen may alternatively occupy the functions of governor and governed: meaning legitimacy and trust are based on the principle of rotation of duties obtained by a draw. This mode of designation is spreading and replaces elections. In addition, because of a great moral perfection, according to Pericles, there are added exemplary citizens. Tolerance governs private relations; the city does not recognise anger or vexations. Concord exists between citizens. Harmony in depth therefore, balances between the word, the logos, the action, the praxis, the importance given to discussion, to speech, characterise the Athenian culture.

Education is an effective instrument of action. Pericles insists on the power of the Athenian imperialism based on the navy and the money, which exposes itself in a monumental way in the acropolis temple which he built. This eulogy resonates like a hymn to the glory of the city thought, dreamed, remodelled, which constitutes an ever-current source of reflection on democracy. The Greeks think of their life as politics according to the city (in Greek: polis). Plato seeks to build an ideal city through the Republic and the laws.

For Aristotle, politics is the supreme end of human action and of man who is a political animal. He explains this in his book *Politics.* For him, the city is what man tends to by nature. Bees are also described as political animals since they are grouped together like men, except that they are not endowed with words and reason like men through whom there is real politics. The city is the supreme goal because it allows the form of autonomy and well-being that man seeks. As for a citizen, he is a free born man who can partake in the political life, thus having the right to be part of a city. Yet in the Athenian democracy, slaves, foreigners, women and children, an overwhelming majority of the population are not citizens and therefore do not participate in politics. The city will remain for centuries, including for the Romans, the ultimate model for thinking politics. Aristotle's book on politics is still today a contemporary reference.

Greek democracy, however, has some defenders, and not the least, in the person of Plato, who considers that the city is like a ship. The crowd can never intelligently stir a ship nor a city.[60]

To conclude, Alexander the Great exported the model of Greek mainland cities to the Near East and Middle East and Egypt. These regions also had their theatre, their council, their temples dedicated to gods. It is also the time when Greek was the common language. In Hellenistic courts, kings surround themselves with officials, doctors and intellectuals who all speak Greek. As for their gods, they are also part of the city.

Rome itself fell under Greek charm, because the Greeks sold to the Romans the idea that they shared the same vision of the world: Alexander, the great conqueror thus coupled with Caesar, the conqueror of the Gaul and Demosthenes the great orator of Athens to Cicero, Roman master of eloquence. "Parallel lives", seeks to demonstrate that famous characters, whether they are Roman or Greek, belong to the same world. The Romans themselves were quickly convinced of this, and they began to speak and read Greek. Cicero translated into Latin Greek writers, created the Latin philosophical vocabulary from the Greek and even sometimes wrote Greek.[61]

III- Gods, myths and heroes in Ancient Greece

Greek wisdom and the brilliance of its universally recognised ancient culture stems from its gods and myths.

Greek gods

Ancient Greeks already have a notion of sacredness in relation to deities. They are very religious and pious, which adds to their seriousness and discernment of things. For, this sacredness shows that there are things that one must take very seriously by following deities that are an integral part of their daily lives. What is sacred in Greece is the presence of thousands of divine powers that haunt the world and make it what it is. Greeks honour them with rites and prayer. They have faith in connivance between the mortal man and immortal deities. There is a continuous intervention of the gods in the life of men. Greeks have no right to be atheists, under pain of exile, or even death. The

[60]Ibid., p.65.
[61] Idem.

philosopher Socrates was forced to drink hemlock for not honouring the gods of the city, his accusers declared. Each city had its own deities, often the same as those of its neighbours and organised its own religious events. Athens, every year, celebrates the Panathenaeans (religious festivities of Athens) in honour of Athena, goddess of Athens and Dionysus (god of wine, inspiration and ecstasy). Religious feasts regulate the lives of citizens who are required to participate in rites. This civic cult imposes itself in a somewhat restrictive way as a State religion. Religion is therefore a factor of social cohesion. All Greeks recognise themselves in the use of a common language and in submission to the same gods, celebrate the Pan-Hellenic feasts and Olympic Games in honour of the gods.

This Greek religion contributed to the social cohesion of a vast Empire over a long period of three millennia, from the Mycenaean period around 1500 BC to the fall of Constantinople in 1453 AD. It spread throughout the Middle Eastern and Mediterranean world.[62] Greek spirit and culture are strengthened by this relationship with the divine and the sacred. There is always this relationship of man with the divine, an inseparable relationship that has elevated the West to the perfect understanding of supernatural and natural realities, and hence to the mastery of knowledge leading to integral development unfolding before our eyes.

The twelve main gods of the Greek pantheon include:

Zeus- He is the most powerful god of the pantheon, the king of gods and reserves the right to rule the universe. His court is located at the top of Olympia (religious site of Ancient Greece, which comes from Olympia, the highest peak of Greece, deemed to be the residence of gods).

Hera- goddess of wives, symbolises the home, often protective of political communities.

Athena- One of the great deities of Olympia and one of the most sacred of the Greek pantheon, goddess of intelligence, patroness of skilled workers, protector of Athens.

---

[62] Le Point Références : juillet août 2012 (.The Point References: July August 2012.) Greece and its myths. The fundamental texts.pg. 10 -11

Apollo- god of light, poetry, music and arts. He is represented wearing the bow or lyre, sometimes crowned with laurels and surrounded by muses (goddesses) to whom he teaches sciences and arts.

In Hesiod's theogonia, their attributions are precise and override the different forms of poetry.

Artemis: goddess of hunting and wild nature. It is associated with the moon as Apollo is to the sun. It is represented by a quiver and arrows.

Aphrodite- goddess of beauty and love. She has the features of a young woman of great beauty,

Ares- god of war. Cruel and violent, he has a tall stature and a booming voice.

Poseidon- god of the sea and the legendary element.

Demeter- god of religion.'

Hephaestus- god of fire, volcanoes and blacksmith and heroes,

Hermes- god of eloquence and messenger of all the deities of the main pantheon.

Hersh- goddess of the home. She is considered the oldest of the twelve Olympic deities. It is a symbol of prosperity, continuity and presides over the rites of integration into the family group, including marriages and the representation of the new-born in the family home.

Greek mythology

Mythology is a set of myths and legends proper to a people. A myth, according to *Le Petit Larousse illustré*, 2002, (a French dictionary), is a popular or literary narrative featuring superhuman beings and remarkable actions, expressed under the guise of legends, principles and values of such and such society. It is also a symbolic representation that influences social life.

In Greece, the land of mythology, the narrative, the "logy" (in the sense of logos) does not cease to tell stories such as the stolen fire of Prometheus and the song of muses. In the West, for three millennia, this tradition continues to enchant the imagination of people. Western tradition has made mythology one of the fields of its knowledge and thought. For two centuries, the enigma of mythology fascinates philosophy and anthropology, because a myth is a language, a thought, both have been inseparable since the eighteenth century. The Jesuit

Joseph Francis Lafitau (1681-1746) believes that fables and myths testify to a first civil religion. To him savages and Greeks would commune in a religious thought beyond the Bible and Christianity. For the philosopher Fontenelle, the similarities between the fables of the ancients and the myths of the New World (America) provide proof that in the centuries that do not yet speak the language of reason, humanity invents fabulous stories, because it is curious to account for phenomena and a world around her; two approaches that mobilise both thought and language, but whose major challenge is religion, is essential in the West. Lafitau wants to discover in mythology an infantile thought before reason and its enlightenment. He intends to put religion at the origins of humanity, even if he observes degradation in fables and myths. Fontenelle likes to show that so many absurd and senseless narratives are the first sketches of what will become religion for the ancients, and for the savages and barbarians of yesterday and today.

In addition, some authors, especially in Germany in the eighteenth century, applaud the genius of Greece (archaeologist and historian Johann Winckelmann, Novales, Ludwig Tieck and Schelling). For those authors who are literary, intellectual and aesthetic of Romanticism (as opposed to the Romanticism of Enlightenment), it is in the Hellenic nation that the idea of freedom and beauty emerges as well as absolute mythology; that which is rooted in the authentic depth of the spirit. This is the spirit of an exceptional people by its language, its thought and its stories. Thought is the first language of humanity.[63]

Mutation of myth to reason is a question of substance for the best minds. The great anthropologist Lévi-Strauss recognises that myth is a language. He points out that savage thought proceeds like Western thought i.e. by the ways of understanding. It must also walk in the direction of abstraction as it happened in ancient Greece. Structuralist anthropology posits that in its march towards abstraction, mythico-savage thought itself draws the strength to move from myth to concept, from narrative to thought. Levi-Strauss considers that this upheaval is at the frontiers of Greek thought, where mythology is in favour of a philosophy that emerges as the precondition for scientific reference.

[63] Le Point Références juillet –août 2012, La Grèce et ses mythes, Les textes Fondamentaux pp. 88-90 (Le Point References July-August 2012, Greece and its myths, Fundamental texts pp. 88-90).

And this, one could add, as a prerequisite for technological thinking for invention and creativity.[64]

Some famous Greek myths include Prometheus, it is one of the main Greek myths supposed to have explained the world.

The myth of Prometheus- In Greek mythology, Prometheus is the name of a titan that means one who thinks before and gave men fire against the will of Zeus. The titans precede by their reign Empire of the gods of Olympus presided by Zeus. This opened their way to higher knowledge, that of the gods. In punishment, he is chained at the summit of Mount Caucasus, where an eagle is supposed to eat up his liver but this exercise was regularly postponed. Heracles, the hero, killed the eagle and delivered him. Very popular, he often passes for having taught men all the knowledge necessary for civilisation such as writing, science of construction and domestication of animals.[65]

The myth of Pandora- This myth is mainly known by the Greek poet Hesiod (8th-7th century BC) who speaks about it in his two poems, theogonia, works and days. The latter has for its major theme, justice which consists in enriching itself by the honest work of the land, the only form of labour considered honourable by the Greeks. The popularity of Hesiod's work in ancient Greece is comparable to that of Homer and, in a way, his poems constitute a common base of Greeks' religious and mythological culture. From these texts, it appears that before the creation of the first woman, humanity existed and lived in a kind of golden age where all pain and suffering were spared from men. The god Zeus decided to create Pandora, the first woman in a rage against the men to whom Prometheus brought fire. The Pandora myth relates with that of Prometheus in three ways. Firstly the anger of the god Zeus turns against men because of the theft of fire committed by Prometheus for the benefit of humanity. Pandora is a beautiful misfortune (beautiful appearance, formidable by her invisible defects). Finally, if Prometheus is the one who planned and sought to help humanity, his brother Epimetheus, who became Pandora's husband, was stunned and thought late. By his improvidence and clumsiness, he brought misfortune to humanity by accepting the dreadful gift sent from the gods. Pandora by opening the jar (from the European Renaissance became the box, hence the expression Pandora's box), frees the

---

[64]Ibid.,pg. 90.
[65]Ibid.,p.36.

misfortunes that were there. This myth is the founder in many ways. The condition of the first woman established the human condition. It is only from the moment that it existed that the men knew the various evils which were attached to it. Firstly men were forced to work to feed themselves and also condemned to reproduce. With her, it's not just a woman, but the race of women that is created. The Pandora figure is therefore very ambiguous, since it is at the same time because of her, as a prototype of all women, but also thanks to her that human species can survive by reproducing itself. A similar ambiguity is found in her name, from the words pan (all) and dora (the gifts), it can mean, the one that the gods have given to men, as Hesiod proposed, the one in which all the gifts have been placed by the gods, or else the one who brings all gifts to men.

Finally, Pandora is the archetype of the fatal woman, responsible for the ruin of men from which she profits and abuses but nonetheless adored by her victims.[66]

Cassandra prophecies- In Greek mythology, Cassandra is a pretty princess who has visions of the future. However, she announces such terrible misfortunes that no one believes her. She is accused of madness, kidnapping, rape, illegal detention and slaughter. It is the sad fate of Cassandra that Homer in the Iliad says is similar to Aphrodite (Greek goddess of beauty and love), she is as beautiful as Helen, wife of the king of Sparta, this myth refers to the complex Cassandra, which refers to the inability to persuade others of imminent danger.

The myth of Penelope, the faithful woman- The image of Penelope, the one that posterity has preserved, is that of the devoted wife, virtuous, faithful to her husband, even though he has been absent for more than twenty years, like the virtuous woman of Proverbs 31 verse 10-31. Her story is found in the odyssey of the poet Homer, vast epic of the eighth century before Christ who sings the long and tumultuous return of Ulysses from the Trojan War. Ulysses went to the Trojan War, Penelope never wanted to marry another, although twenty years have passed since the departure of Ulysses, she still awaits and watches for any sign that can consolidate in her hope of knowing if he is still alive. This explains why she does not hesitate to talk to the person she believes to be an old Cretan beggar, in fact Ulysses himself disguised, who claims to have known her husband. At the end of her

---

[66]Ibid.,pp. 54 -55

strength, she confides in him and tells the tricks she is forced to deploy to repel her marriage which horrifies her. Thus she proclaimed that she would remarry once she had finished weaving a shroud for her father-in-law, Laertie, before she was finally denounced by one of her maids. This trick was inspiration from the goddess Athena.

By doing so, Penelope postpones her remarriage, and symbolically the death of her father-in-law. She acts not only as a perfect wife, but also as an ideal daughter-in-law. She symbolises the image of a housewife par excellence. For the Greeks, it is up to the woman to take care of house chores, to supervise the work of her servants and maids, and, the man to spend his days spinning and weaving, but Ulysses being away, Penelope also exercises some of his prerogatives. She has the keys to the treasury where the goods of the house are piled up. The cunning nature she demonstrates is also a mark of her exceptional character. Penelope is indeed described as the most intelligent of women.[67]

The myth of Oedipus - the inexorable law of destiny

This Greek myth has become today the Oedipus complex which is a boy child's tendency to be closer to his mother than to his father, and a daughter more interested in her father than her mother. To the psychoanalyst Freud, particularly in the interpretation of dreams (1900), which he calls the Oedipus complex, it is the unconscious desire of a child to sleep with the parent of the opposite sex and to eliminate the other.

Of all Greek myths, Oedipus is probably the most famous and certainly the one that is still very common in modern times. This myth is handled by a large number of mythographers (those who transmit and compile myths such as Homer, Hesiod and Ovid who are the most famous). Oedipus grows up at a Corinthian court ignorant of his origin and has to kill his father and couple with his mother. This is indeed what happens, for he commits parricide and incest. He reveals himself as husband and son of the woman who gave birth to him[68]. Understanding that he is parricidal and incestuous; he burst his own eyes, while Jocasta his wife and mother commits suicide. Oedipus leaves his country for a long wandering with his daughter Antigone born out of incest, who leads him into the suburbs of Athens where he dies. This myth inspired

---

[67]Ibid., pp. 64-65.
[68]Ibid.,pp. 74 -75

Corneille (1659), Voltaire (1718), Hölderlin (1804), Cocteau (1927 and 1934), Gide (1931) and Robbegullet (1953).

The myth of Sisyphus - Sisyphus is the son of Aeol, a mythical founder of Corinth. According to Homer, who does not explain the reason for this punishment, Sisyphus is condemned to roll a heavy rock on the top of a mountain in the underworld to see him eternally fall back. He inspired Albert Camus, in his book the myth of Sisyphus where his hero rolls a stone on the hill and still falls, illustrating the eternal beginning of things in life, or the logic of inevitability or absurdity of life. Albert Camus was awarded the Nobel Prize for Literature in 1957.

The myth of Ulysses- Ulysses is a hero, the most cunning of heroes and a protégé of the goddess Athena. He participates in the expedition of the Greeks against Troy and contributes greatly to the victory through his skill and courage. But it is his return fraught with pitfalls to the Isle of Ithaca, where his patient wife Penelope waits for him, which is the best-known part of the legend, recounted in the Odyssey of the poet Homer.[69]

The myth of Ulysses has witnessed a considerable fortune. The Middle Ages saw in his cunning character a brand of deceit, worthy to be decried. His return to grace is seen with the English playwright William Shakespeare (1564-1616) who in his Troilus and Crussiola (1602) indicated his exceptional intelligence. From the nineteenth century, Ulysses again became a legendary character of the first order. Many works for both youth and adults use it to address more contemporary issues. Thus, more than a sum of extraordinary adventures, the story of Ulysses is above all that of a man faithful to his fatherland, his family and ultimately to himself. Nothing, not even the immortality promised by Calypso, the nymph, diverts him from his duty.

Heroes

In this long line of gods, myths that convey values, principles and knowledge that are a common background of Greek culture, and shape the consciousness and behaviour of Greeks, we cannot forget the

---

[69] The Trojan War is a legendary war traced by Homer's Iliad opposing the inhabitants of Troy in Asia Minor, to a coalition of Greeks, referred to as the Achaeans. It must have taken place in 1200 BC.

heroes, considered as demi-gods, who transmit and reinforce this cult of great values proper to ancient Greek culture. Some of the most prominent heroes include:

Achilles symbol of warrior bravery, his mother soaks him in the waters of stigx (underground river of hell) to make him immortal. Only the heel by which she held him was not immersed. It is only through this heel that he became vulnerable. In the Iliad, he distinguished himself as the most valiant warrior during the Trojan War before being wounded to death by an arrow shot by Paris to his heel (hence the expression Achilles heel, the point by which one is vulnerable).

Heracles: very popular throughout the Greek world. He is the son of the god Zeus and Princess Alcmene. He is known for his strength and bravery. He is confronted with impossible tasks that he manages to overcome, including bringing back from hell, Cerberus, the terrible dog with three heads that keeps the gates (hence the term today Cerberus, to talk about someone one who is wicked and dangerous).

Theseus: The mythology of Theseus is one of the richest in the Greek world and was built over more than a millennium. In his parallel lives, the Greek Plutarch compares in two pairs a famous Greek and a Roman. Theseus is one of the kings who helped the founding of Athens. He is associated with Romulus, the mythical founder of Rome. His greatest achievement is his victory over the Minotaur, a monster half-man, half-bull, held captive in a labyrinth by his father, the king of Crete Minos. He killed the Minotaur and found the exit thanks to the thread that Ariadne gave him (hence the expression Ariadne's thread that we use. This is the way that allows someone to find an orientation, a track to reach a goal). He is a kind of Athenian national hero, whose multiple achievements make him almost equal to Heracles. In the course of the fifth century BC, the character of Theseus is recovered by the Athenian ideology that makes him the true founder of Athens, its religious calendar, its main religious holiday panathenaic and even democracy.[70] This is why the Athenians have created the proverb "nothing without Theseus".

In summary, the study of this brilliant Greek civilisation, philosophers, men of culture, science, statesmen, gods, myths and heroes, illustrates the fundamentals that have gone down in history and

[70] Le Point Références juillet-août 2012. op. cit.p.52. (Le Point References July-August 2012. op. cit.p.52).

have shaped Western culture and reached other civilisations even African: the sacred, the relationship with the divine, religion, spirit, spiritual elevation, holiness, perfection, mysticism, language, the reign of knowledge, humanism, wisdom, intelligence, perfect education, logical thinking, excellence, sense of measurement, taste for science, heroism of the mind, beauty of the body, beauty of the soul, beautiful, great beauty, goodness, honesty, research and practice of the values: of the good, well-being, love of nature and arts, moral rectitude, righteousness, aesthetics, equality, justice, courage, patriotism, of civism, sense of duty, family, fidelity, prosperity, freedom, rule of the law, heroic life, taste for research for fundamental values of life. And as the French philosopher Luc Ferry says: of good life, and to achieve it, one must know the world, mobilise the sciences to get a complete idea of this order of the universe where everyone must find their rightful place. It is not surprising that with the knowledge and practice of these perfect values, ancient Greece has built a brilliant civilisation whose realities are still noticeable today.[71]

Marie Dominique Porée goes further to speak about the Greek miracle, reconciling the love of beauty, the art of the word, sense of measure and feeling of concord around the divine and rational spirit, the human ideal and the spirit citizen, guarantor of sustainability.[72] That is why the great Greek spirits are still relevant today and have had a considerable influence in Europe and the West, and have come to us thanks to the humanist values they have developed. From Greek wisdom, we can see how in ancient times science, mathematics, astronomy, physics and biology are strictly inseparable from the great philosophies within which they are absolutely integrated. We therefore understand why the development of human societies is first and foremost a question of multifarious knowledge, wisdom, intelligence, knowledge, rationality and logos which are gradually acquired. One draws from it that, to develop, one must bathe, immerse oneself in knowledge, live from within to be impregnated and come out completely renewed. Development, therefore, is baptism in global knowledge. It is immersing oneself in the complete knowledge that totally releases from ignorance, superstitions and sterile traditions, to know-how to be, know-how and know- how to become perfect and

---

[71] Le Point Références juillet-août 2011. op. cit.p.15. (Le Point References July-August 2012. op. cit.p.15).

[72] Ibid.,pg.11.

awesome. This central truth since ancient times is still valid today, for it is perfect knowledge that is the foundation of life and development. Africa must also appropriate permanently this eternal truth and rise to the level of perfection as did the Greeks of antiquity and even European countries from the 16th century. In reality it is in perfection that one discovers the levels of true knowledge and effective action. It is this knowledge that has been part of the history of time since ancient Africa (Egypt, ancient Greece and the future), which swells to decline in technical science, technology and ultimately industry to produce the development of human societies that we see today.

Ancient Rome is part of this growth of life and perfect societies.

Chapter III

Contribution of ancient Rome to the rise of the West and humanity, an original experience for Africa to ponder

Next to ancient Greece, which has brought a lot to European civilisation and the rest of humanity through Sophia, her spirit of wisdom, her love of knowledge, beauty, ethics, aesthetics, perfection and democracy, is added the contribution of the ancient Rome which enriches this civilisation and the humanity, by its sense of the organisation of the State and city, through its scholars and its humanism.

I- Organisation of the State of law

Ancient Rome bequeathed to Europe the sense of organising the State. She knew how to organise the vast Empire which she had conquered in the West and in the East. Indeed, the Roman Empire succeeded the Greek Empire and lasted six centuries, from 146 BC to 476 AD and far beyond, thanks on the one hand, to talented politicians such as Pompey, Crassus, Julius Caesar, Octavian Augustus his nephew, Trajan, Constantine I The Great and on the other hand, to a remarkable political genius. The Roman power secured the domination of the world. Under Trajan, Roman Emperor from 98 to 117, Rome governed a territory covering 2 800 000km^2, in Europe, in Great Britain, in Eastern Danube, in Asia, as far as Chaldea in Mesopotamia, in Africa, Egypt, Numidia and Mauritania. It is a regime that demonstrated values such as courage, discipline and organisation. These helped them to control this vast territory.[73] Rome modelled communities, by providing them the Latin language, a monetary system and a legal organisation that survived well after its end. Europe constituted the essential part of the Roman Empire ruled by the Antonines (Roman emperors from 138 to 161). It included 80 million inhabitants, distributed as follows, 42 in Europe, 16 in Africa and 22 in Asia. This

[73] Pierre Lanarès : *Qui dominera le monde.*Éditions S.D.T. Paris, 1982.p. 40. (Who will dominate the world. Editions S.D.T. Paris, 1982.p.g 40).

vast territory constituted the Roman Empire. Pierre Grimaldi stresses that this entity is the geographical and legal framework within which the most prestigious changes ever occurred to human societies whose consequences of all kinds have not yet been exhausted after more than two thousand years.[74]

The Roman Empire and the imperium

The term Roman Empire or imperium romanum designates not only the space within which Rome exercises its power, but this power itself. The imperium is a creative, orderly, transcendent force, capable of acting on reality, making it obedient to a will. In the etymology of the word, one finds the idea of a setting in order, of preparations that one makes with a view to an end conceived by the spirit of the one who commands. This power in Rome, since the time of kings, belongs to a god who possesses the supreme level of this Empire. It is worshipped under the name of Jupiter, to which is indissolubly linked two epithets: that of "very helpful" or "very effective" (optimus) and very great or the greatest (Maximus). It is around him, under his gaze that the city is ordered and he resides on the Capitol, the high place that dominates the valley of the forum. He is not only the visible symbol of the Roman State, but the power that maintains its unity and guarantees its vitality. He is the holder of the imperium, the power. He communicates this power to the king who has direct relations with him, thanks to the omens that he receives, when the king consults him. Then when the army of the city has a victory, it is to him that this same king comes to give thanks, at the ceremony of triumph, clothed in the garment of the god himself.

After the kings who were expelled from Rome at the end of the fifth century BC in 509, their successors retained the same divine power, this imperium which they were authorised to ask from the god when the people had chosen them. Romans possess absolute political supremacy (the maiestas), but the exercise of power is linked to the imperium. One of the essential Jupiterian values is the establishment of the rule of law and a stable political order. In a city at war, the imperium belongs to the official in charge of leading the army. The conduct of a military campaign requires that the soldiers be totally subjected to their leader. Never will the sanctity of the imperium be erased. As a result of victory, the leader acclaimed by his soldiers receives the title of imperator like

[74] Pierre Grimaldi : *L'Empire romain*, Éditions de Fallois, Paris, 1993, p.7.

Jupiter. The words imperium and imperator have a mystical aura that emanates from a god. The almost automatic possession of the title of imperator by the prince, the first personality of the city, his driver and his guide, from Caesar and then Augustus confers on him a particular prestige, if not that of a deity, at least a predestination to become a god. It is the recognition in him of a nature already divine or superhuman, which asserts itself in the course of the sacred if he does not let his power degenerate into tyranny as well as if he makes justice, order and peace to prevail within the Empire and on its borders. When he dies, such an emperor is regarded by all as a god. He is awarded the honours of the apotheosis (official recognition by the Senate of the deification of a deceased emperor) which puts him among the number of divinities recognised by the official religion. The Senate recognises Caesar's title of perpetual conqueror, which means in practice the name of imperator that his nephew Octavia Augustus will later take. The various Jupiterian functions are united in a single personality, at once perpetually warlord and supreme civil magistrate, thus possessing at the same time the civil imperium and the military imperium.[75]Today, we refer to the Head of State and Supreme Commander of the Armed Forces. It is a legacy from Rome. This Empire is felt, we have said it is as a desired order and guaranteed by the god of capitol. To this supreme god are indissolubly linked the moral and even metaphysical values which condition not only personal behaviour, but the whole policy of the city. This order desired by the god is unalterable. Therefore, next to the temple capitol is a sanctuary dedicated to Dius Fidius the Jupiter of oath, patron of good faith, fidelity to the sworn faith. It is he who ensures the duration of a State in the universe, once and for all. And this is a major innovation and a profound originality of the Roman spirit. This state of the universe is not the result of violence that would make the strength of victors last, but of the given word, of a commitment made once and for all, both by citizens themselves and by neighbouring peoples with regard to Rome, by which one and another renounce violence.

Paradoxically, the imperium romanum expresses a desire for peace. The peace desired by Rome is the establishment of an ideally peaceful order, not the annihilation of the vanquished or their spoliation, but their coexistence with Rome, their survival within the framework of their

[75]Ibid,pg. 12.

own laws, as far as they are not incompatible with the Roman peace (a kind of indirect rule).

This primordial desire to create a stable order also manifests itself in the capitol. In the temple of Jupiter sits another divinity, conceived as a masculine force, referred to as Terminus. He guarantees the stability of things between domains belonging to such a group of citizens, but also between the cities as well as between the laity and the sacred. Terminus sanctifies a state of the universe that Jupiter wants unalterable and subtracts it from arbitrariness. The management of the Empire is wisely conducted in order to obtain the support of conquered peoples. The conquered regions are those held by magistrates appointed by the emperor. The Roman Empire derives its strength from the practice of core values which include the sacred, the power, the organisation of power, honour, fidelity, the divine nature, the recourse to god, peace, order, stability, fidelity, the art of governing, in one word wisdom.

The reign of laws

Next to the imperium, we find laws. They are two sources of power, parallel and complementary. The law voted by the people is a rule accepted once and for all. It refers to certain situations and imposes solutions. The imperium does not replace the law whose authority rests on the people. This conception, which goes back to the very origins of the Roman State, was still alive at the beginning of the Empire. It was formulated by Tiberius, about a case that occurred in the eighth year of his reign in 22 AD: "Rights, (i.e. rules fixed by the law)" he says, "are diminished every time power increases, and one must not resort to imperium when it is possible to decide according to the law ". There is a very strict distinction between what an imperium is and what law is. Freedom of the citizens is protected by the different legal provisions (the iura) contained in the laws. The privileges conferred by these laws cannot be questioned by any holder of the imperium. This philosophy of strong power enabled the Roman Empire to stand for six centuries because the whole territory was divided into provinces headed by governors. The senate which is a meeting of peers holds the power from which great leaders emerged from time to time. The Roman imperium even extended to Africa, to the point that a second province took the name of Africa Nova.[76]

---

[76]Ibid,pg. 33.

Ultimately, the organisation, structuring and philosophy of power conceived by Rome are very modern and fixed around perfect values. They include the constant relationship with the sacred, with gods, to mysticism, to the spirit that inspires leaders and populations aware of belonging to the same spiritual universe. The concentration of sacred power, civil and military in the hands of a strong man, the divine status given to leaders who have distinguished themselves by acts of bravery, the sense of honour, majesty, prestige, greatness, fidelity, sworn faith, the sense of leadership of the rulers, the consummate art of directing and governing men and peoples, conquered in a spirit of peaceful coexistence, the spirit of peace, order, freedom, justice, respect for the laws, the rule of law and a stable political order, social organisation around high moral values, in a nutshell the intelligence, wisdom, essential values to achieve the development of sustainable societies.

II- Roman humanism

The imperium goes in the direction of Humanitas (a name derived from *homo,* human being) implying the recognition of spiritual particularities peculiar to the human being and consequently, the respect of them in others. This is why Romans admire Greek civilisation and are inspired by it on certain precise points such as theatre, sculpture and architecture. A general feeling leads them to believe that they are relatives of the Greeks. Romans sought from Greek cities, yet subjected to their domination, the knowledge and practice of rhetoric as well as philosophy. A famous letter of Cicero to his brother Quintus, governor of Asia, sums up this feeling of Romans towards this country of very ancient civilisation, cradle of humanity, towards which the conquerors or rather the suzerains have an immense debt of gratitude. [77]

Roman humanism did not have the same splendour as its Greek counterpart, since the Greek language was widely used alongside Latin. It is under the reign of Octavian Augustus, baptised "Century of Augustus" emperor from 63 BC to 14 AD that the human spirit reached the highest summits. This reign is culturally animated by poetry, written prose, rhetoric, philosophers, arts, town planning and a taste of the sacred.

[77]Ibid,pg. 25.

A century of poets

In fact, the century of Augustus marked the peak of Latin literature that was to become its classicism. Latin experienced a certain growth and showed that it could lend itself to the expression of love. The great representatives are Virgil, Horace and Ovid. A tradition of two centuries required that poets go close to a great person. These poets clung to the protection of patron (in Latin cains cilnius Macienus 69-8 BC), personal friend of Octavia Augustus. Nowadays, the term patron is given to those who support artists. Virgil published three important works: the Bucolics (42-39 BC), the Georgians (39-29 BC) and the Eneide, founding myth of the new Rome. In the work of Virgil, Italy is present, an Italy gathered around Rome. The force that animates the poet corresponds to the great movement of thought to which the Emperor Octavia Augustus gives body, to the metamorphosis that goes from Italy dominated by Rome, to an integrated political system within an imperium accepted by the peoples who become aware of belonging to the same spiritual universe. Virgil's influence was immense on Latin and Western literatures, and a whole legend was formed around his memoirs. There is also Terence (185-159 BC) a comic poet and freed slave. He composed six comedies based on psychological analysis. He became a model for French classics especially for Molière. Terence is the author of the maxim "homo sum: humani nihil a me alienum puto" (I am a man: nothing that is human is foreign).

As for Horace (65-8 BC), he was a friend of Virgil and Maecenas and a protégé of the Emperor Octavia Augustus. With Horace, poetry reached its peak. It expresses what is deepest in the Roman soul and ceases to be a game of the spirit. Horace is a moralist poet. In the sermons, that is to say the satires and the epistles, he uses in his evocations people and manners of realism close to that of the portraits of contemporary sculpture from the Italian tradition. He was a free mind and refused to be the private secretary of the emperor who asked him. He defended his independence vis-à-vis Maecenas his benefactor. His participation in the moral revolution around him is explained by a voluntary membership. He composed lyric works in which he celebrated the traditional virtues recognised and practised by the Romans which include courage, patriotism, the sense of discipline, and above all virtue, the inner energy which alone is the guarantor of freedom. He expects Jupiter to restore this ideal. He invited Romans as Augustus who started doing so, to restore the sanctuaries in ruins, to find the spirit of traditional religion and revive the worship of the gods who made the greatness of the Empire. These are the major themes developed in his moral codes. He adheres to the revival of Rome close to him and that Virgil sings still with him.[78]He was held by the humanists and French classics for the model of classic virtues of balance and measurement.

If Latin poetry reached its peak under the reign of Augustus, it is due to the fact that genius poets (Virgil and Horace leading) were able to capture spiritual forces.

The advent of the principate is not only a political revolution and the expansion of the ruling class, as well as the participation in power of men from more distant provinces. It coincides with the emergence of new forces in the field of culture.

Written prose

If it is true that the age of Augustus is par excellence that of poetry, literary prose was also present and its peak was attained with the work of Cicero. He is a speaker, lawyer and politician. He had brought eloquence to its highest level. His pleas and speeches served as a model for all Latin rhetoric. With the loss of prominence of eloquence prevail more durable written messages, and likely to exert a deeper action on a larger audience. Cicero and Caesar used it. We realised that historical genre is the one that lends itself best to political analysis. Making a last resort to eloquence, history persuades better and more surely. **Titus-Livius** (59 BC-17 AD) is the historian par excellence of this century. He was the author of a history of Rome (from the origins until the 9th century) unfinished in 142 books of which only 35 are preserved. In this masterpiece the author used, besides the work of earlier historians, ancient annals of Rome and strived to revive in a living style the Roman past. As for Cicero, his philosophical papers (Di Finibus, de Officius) have acclimatised in Greek literature Greek metaphysics and morals. This power of recognising quick writing led to the development of an intense cultural life, more widespread than before.

The rise of the library

Emperor Caesar had already begun to build a library inaugurated after him in 35 BC. It was partly double, having Latin and Greek libraries. In dedicating to him this library, Pliny, the elder, wrote that

---

[78]Ibid.,pp. 80 -81

he had placed the genius of men at the disposal of all. Libraries multiplied afterwards and Emperor Octavia Augustus also built them. Libraries have become part of monuments that make up the Roman city both in the West and in the East.[79]This heritage of libraries has survived until today for the great happiness of scholars and lovers of knowledge.

Rhetoric (rhetoricians)

Rhetoric and eloquence, despite their loss of speed, have still maintained a certain topicality. Coming from Greece, the Romans adopted them. The masters of rhetoric teach their students, first to think, to discover ideas, to build righteous reasoning, then to expose all this in the clearest and most effective order, and in the purest language. All this practice is supposed to lead to real practice, to train lawyers able to defend any cause before the real court. This rhetoric, despite its name is derived from speakers, is an art of writing and also of thought or even spoken. It gives access to the expression, a universality to which we could not claim until then. In this respect, it is close to poetry, whose ambition of eternity it shares.[80] Seneca (60 BC) is one of the eminent rhetoricians. His controversies and declamations are a precious document on public education in the first century. The thought of this Stoic as well as his concise and lively style had a great influence. His son Seneca is a philosopher (4 BC to 65 AD).

Philosophers and humanism

Roman philosophy did not reach the density of its Greek counterpart, since in Augustus' century the latter remained the philosophical language. The philosophers around Augustus and his sister Octavia were Greeks. Their language is inseparable from the content of their thought. Romans practised both languages. The Emperor Marc Aurelius (161-180) published the thoughts, a philosophical essay that marked his adherence to Stoicism. Thus, between the Hellenistic world and the Latin world, there is no deep opposition. This persistence of Greek as the language of moral life helped to unite the two halves of the emperium, the East and the West. There is a cultural harmony. Greek works are in libraries with those of the Latin language such as Homer and Virgil, Demosthenes and Cicero regarded as the Fathers of Humanitas. Humanitas derives from the notion of homo, a human being, involving the recognition of spiritual peculiarities of the human

---

[79]Ibid., pp.82.
[80] Ibid.,p.86.

being and, consequently, the respect of it in others. Humanitas leads to humanism that puts man above all things. There is an immense impulse towards the things of the spirit and it is one of the most remarkable features of this Empire.

III- Roman town planning

In the Roman Empire, the city was becoming more and more a reality. The city reflects a more ideological than material conception; it is not just a collection of houses and buildings that have sprung up and assembled hazardously over the centuries, but a spiritual being. The temple of Jupiter at the capitol is the mystical centre. The Roman city is therefore a material and spiritual entity, an originality that Renaissance Europe took over. Everywhere, one finds a capitol, a place for the official religion and symbol of unity of the Empire under Constantine 1 (emperor from 306-337). Rome, therefore, became the major city of Christians. Constantine built a basilica in the Vatican on the right bank of Tiber, which was to mark the central point of the Christian religion. Another basilica devoted to Apostle Paul was built on the left bank of the Tiber. Constantine, master of the Empire built a second capital in Byzantium in Asia outside Rome, which took the name of Constantinople, to better monitor the border of Danube and the Persians. Inaugurated on 11 May 330, Constantinople quickly became the political, religious and intellectual capital of the Byzantine Empire. In 325, he ordered a council in Nicea, to consider the church as a support to the State. In 312, he decided the triumph of Christianity.

There is a curie for senate meetings, another place around which public buildings are orderly arranged as well as buildings constructed which serve as stock exchanges for commercial transactions and court meeting places. He built gymnasiums and theatres. Thus, a civilisation of Augustinian town planning was born which does not develop at random. This city foreshadows the modern city. Rome bequeathed to the West aqueducts, roads, pavements and drainage techniques. In this respect, the genius of Agrippa, Minister of Octavia Augustus, made a decisive contribution. To carry out these works, which are admired by the historian Denys of Halicarnassus, who considered them the most prestigious material achievements, Rome has a rigorous financial administration, subject to exact controls. Budgetary discipline is one of the benefits of the Empire.

IV- The Pantheon of Roman gods

Roman pantheon includes gods who are Greek gods, with different names. This pantheon of gods refers to the sacred, mysticism and contact with the supernatural.

Respect for the sacred

In ancient Rome, respect for the sacred, for the divine, for the religious, is considered essential in the human community. It is considered that negligence of the sacred is the sign of a perversion of morality which announces the decline of the cities and the progressive loss of their souls. It is considered that what the gods bring to men is not a series of miracles, but a continuous inspiration which raises them to the Lord. Augustus understood it. The restoration of ancient sanctuaries is a moral imperative, essential for its policy that tends to reform manners, to restore the values of the past. Rome is covered with temples, chapels, and shrines of all kinds. Each recalls the ancient times when the virtues of citizens made the greatness of the State. These constructions add to town planning. He ceded to Europe the mysticism found in Judaism and Christianity, the taste for rigour, discipline and knowledge.

One of the characteristics of the Roman religion is the difference it establishes between religion and superstition. Religion is what has adherence to tradition and laws. This forbids any innovation, any sudden inspiration that seizes this or that spirit and leads to unpredictable acts. Religion in relation with the gods, that is to say with forces that men cannot control, is similar to the law of relations between men themselves. It is religion that establishes peace and calms anguish before the unknown. It knows that there is a law that regulates relationships with the gods. Thus is tamed all mysticism which is a level of understanding of very high and perfect realities. Thus, the Roman pantheon includes gods who correspond to the Greek gods with different names:

Jupiter: king of the gods, god of heaven and thunder

Junion: goddess of wives

Minerva: goddess of intelligence and craftsmen

Apolon: healing god, protector of music and poetry

Diana: goddess of hunting, protector of slaves

Venus: goddess of beauty and love

Mars: god of war

Neptune: god of the sea

Ceres: goddess of the harvest

Vulcan: god of blacksmith, god of fire

Mercury: god of commerce

Nesta: goddess of the home

Bacchus: god of the vine and fire

Under Constantine I (emperor from 306-337) the sacred reached paroxysm with the construction of a basilica in the Vatican, and especially with the triumph of Christianity that became the State's religion.

In reality, the strength of this Empire came from its desire to reconcile social life, strength and law. The force of arms is material constraint. The law is also a constraint, but of a moral type. It creates an order acceptable to all that engenders peace, that is to say, a state of a desirable world, in which personal ire have the possibility of unfolding themselves with a sufficient margin to the aspirations of sensibility. This is the meaning of the famous Ciceronian formula inviting arms to fade before the toga, the glory of the soldier to be only second before the esteem of the citizen.[81]Caesar Augustus realised this ideal in which it is not an issue to hide the military, but to set limits. As President Obama also said, the United States military force should not allow them to do anything they want. The force must be a transitory means, not an end in itself. This duality, this couple formed by two aspects of social life (force and law), is symbolised by the title of monarch to whom the State is entrusted: imperator, that is to say, absolute master of the force. He is at the same time the one who creates the law and observes it.

Rome has bequeathed to Europe and humanity a rich cultural legacy based on the organisation of the State, productive town planning, literature and renown names such as: Horace, Virgil, Titus Livius, Cicero and Seneca. In a word, Rome has bequeathed to Europe and to humanity perfect fundamental values of the spirit, intelligence, wisdom and organisation of the State, organisation of the city, sense of direction to politicians of the State, the sacred, mysticism, ethics, humanism, etc.

[81] Pierre Grimaldi.op.cit.,pp. 178 et s.

One of the causes that followed and accelerated the end of the Empire was the breach of this rule of wisdom. The Roman Empire throughout centuries remained a legally ordered system. The severe Emperor Alexander (222-235) read the Republic of Plato, as well as that of Cicero, which shows that States are living beings.

During his State visit to Italy from 20th - 22nd March 2017, President Paul Biya magnified the brilliant culture that ancient Rome has bequeathed to humanity. It was on the occasion of the reception of a gold medal awarded by the Conference of Rectors of Italian Universities, to acknowledge his many contributions to the development and promotion of culture and education. He recognised the secular humanism of this culture: "Rome is the undisputed cradle of the Greco-Latin civilisation, created in 8th century BC. This city is the bedrock of Judeo-Christian humanism from which it has laid the philosophical foundation ... many artists, thinkers, lawyers, architects, speakers, strategists from which the world has been inspired for centuries emerged from Rome. He pays homage to these monuments of history." in *Cameroon Tribune* of Thursday 23rd March 2017, pg. 5. President Biya adds that it is indeed "Rome that has transmitted to us, through the vicissitudes of history, the Greco-Latin culture that has marked the world. It is from her that our philosophy and politics, and therefore of democracy, of law and even of vocabulary, originate for the most part. Both Latin and Greek have strongly influenced most languages of the world". This is why Rome will remain the eternal city. He adds that "Roman Sapientia is linked to the African wisdom of measurement, listening to others and conciliation. Both learn to debate without fighting" in *Cameroon Tribune* of Tuesday, 21 March 2017.

Another aspect of this historic Roman culture is the Quirinal Palace, the official residence of the President of Italy. This palace has a surface area of 110,500 m^2 and contains 1,200 rooms. It is the sixth largest building in the world in terms of surface area. The Quirinal Palace was at a moment the residence of 30 popes, from Gregory XIII to Pius IX and of the royal family from 1870. It was built in 1583 on the initiative of Pope Gregory XIII, Pope from 1572 to 1585. In it are found collections including tapestries, paintings, statues, old carriages, clocks, antique furniture and porcelain. A fantastic story, worthy of a fairy tale and still inspiring humanity with its glory and beauty, and thus adding to the splendour of Rome's town planning in which ancient Rome was a great inspirer.

Chapter IV

Contribution of the Middle Age to the West: the primacy of God, Christianity and the Church in social organisation. An era that rigorously structured the mind set of Europe and the Western society

We began to develop the centrality of the Bible and other divine schools of thought in the progress of peoples in general. In this chapter, we demonstrate how knowledge from the Bible has concretely structured the Western society. Africa may wonder in the light of this successful experience of the West if it meditates the Scriptures in their depths for a structural transformation of this underdeveloped continent. For development is first and foremost a question of a very structured spiritual conception, and the Bible teaches how to achieve this solid structuring of the mind around perfect values.

The tremendous growth that Europe gradually experienced since the Middle Ages derives its strength from the development of knowledge, especially on the religious level, despite the aspect of feudalism. In fact, it was during the Middle Ages that the West became Christian thanks to the primacy of Christianity and the Church in the social organisation.

The Middle Ages extends over a period of almost a thousand years from the 5th century in 476 during the fall of the Western Roman Empire, to the Eastern Empire of Constantinople in 1453, in the 15th century. This is the period of world history between antiquity and modern times. Jacques le Golf situates it, from the fourth century of our era to the eighteenth century with the beginnings of the industrial revolution and the great French political revolution in 1789, when the Church and royalty cease definitively to dominate the social and intellectual world, as if to signify the end of a long cultural cycle.[82]

---

[82] Le Point références, Comprendre le Moyen-âge, Les textes fondamentaux, novembre-décembre (The Point References, Understanding the Middle Ages, The Fundamental Texts, November-December). 2011.p. 11.

I- The Centrality of God and the Bible in the medieval society. The construction of cathedrals, a high place of aesthetics, mysticism and exaltation of the divine presence in its splendour and power

1- The centrality of God and the Bible as a reference book in medieval society

The Middle Age is said to be Christian, because the values and ideas of Christianity dominated in the realm of faith, social organisation, moral life, the conception of nature and the world. Christianity is even an official religion of the Roman Empire since 380, decreed by King Constantine I. Society sees itself according to a hierarchy which places at its summit those who are devoted themselves to God. Political thought is dominated by thinking about the relationship between the temporal and spiritual powers, between faith and reason. In the order of thought, theology is the queen science. Philosophy, the sciences of nature and experimentation must come to terms with it, because they must be considered in the light of God and the divine sciences. This dimension of Christian values will profoundly influence and structure the consciences of men and women of this time and beyond.

That is why it is accepted that European civilisation is in essence Judeo-Christian, that is, from God, hence the power of the Spirit which is its central element and a stimulant of true and authentic knowledge

We understand why this long period which lasts a thousand years (10 centuries), structured rigorously and upward, the thought and mentalities of the European man, marks the beginning of his spiritual awakening and the revolution of his thought. In the European, it gradually marks the deepening of true knowledge.

The Bible in Greek, La Biblia, the book of books, is the first book in Europe, taken out of the printing presses invented by the German Gutenberg in 1455. Education was based on clericalism. Schools were opened in every diocese and monastery. The university itself is an ecclesiastical institution. In the same way, the fathers of philosophy, Plato and Aristotle were not forgotten; their writings were taken into account in this elevation of the mind in the quest for perfect knowledge. Plato especially, with his myth of the ascension of the soul through the sky to the intelligible and the light of the intellect, to contemplate beauty in itself. Thus in his book *Le Banquet* (The Banquet), Plato refers to the stages of spiritual initiation through the Little Mysteries and Great Mysteries. The latter being reserved for certain initiates who had access to the perfect things and likely to be seen (epoptika). In the Banquet, the guests celebrate Eros, god of love and beauty. In the end, Socrates shows that Eros does not seek only visible beauty, but above all irreversible beauty, that of the soul and real realities.

Socrates describes the rise of the soul of beautiful bodies towards the incorporeal beauty. The initiation of this ascent consists in rising in steps from the sensible to the intelligible through beautiful bodies, beautiful souls, beautiful words and beautiful actions, in order to contemplate self-beauty and beauty.

In this context, sacred objects are real realities, forms that are visible only in the light of the intellect. The philosophical experience then merges with the religious experience, insofar as both have as objective the invisible. Plotinus, who uses Plato's vocabulary, goes even further. The soul once identified with the intellect and therefore with the intelligible unites through the latter to the One. For Christians, the mystical ascension leads no longer to forms or to one, but to the Supreme Being that is God.

In reality, the Bible and Greeks have not only fed Christian mysticism in examples and conceptual frameworks, but have enabled it to develop a way of accounting for mystical experience, using rhetoric (art of speech) that is both pagan and biblical. This is based on the manipulation of a symbolic and poetic language that allows us to communicate the experience of the unspeakable. Fathers of the Church have resorted to the vocabulary of eminence through multiplication of adjectives of favourable meaning such as unspeakable, ineffable, inexpressible, unpronounceable, inexplicable, beautiful, fabulous, majestic, wonderful, celebration, admiration, great, divine, blessed, holy, very holy, hyper and essential. Thus, the Fathers of the Church invented a new rhetoric that allowed them to express the inexpressible. Christian mysticism magnifies God, man, love, purity, perfection, happiness and wisdom. The Christian Kabbalah is developed as a result of the Jewish Kabbalah which is the deepening of the study of the Holy Scriptures. This Christian myth of the holy word is observed in the construction of cathedrals, a high place of aesthetic construction and adoration.

2- Cathedrals, high places of architectural construction, aesthetics, mysticism and exaltation of the divine presence in its splendour and power

The Middle Age, which is the epoch of God's centrality in European society, conveys the language of cathedrals, which are a real field of spirituality. Most European cathedrals date back to the Middle Ages. They also bear the mark of a daring, aesthetic and sublime architecture, characterised by Gothic architecture, which follows the footsteps of Roman architecture, all related to the sacred such as the Paris, Chartres, Amiens, Cologne, Vienna and Milan Cathedrals.

Gothic art uses the daring techniques already experimented, sublimating them, using them at the same moment and carrying them to their extreme as in the buttress, the broken bow and crossed vaults. These techniques have the advantage of raising and lightening buildings. Gothic art also privileges the light, the image of God and His son Jesus Christ "The work shines with a noble light. May its brightness enlighten the spirits so that, guided by the true light, they reach the true light where Christ is the true door "(*Les cahiers de science et vie. Histoire des civilisations*, (The books of science and life. History of civilisations) No. 164 of October 2016. Pg. 32)

There are many who see the Gothic cathedral as the architectural translation of the theology of light dear to the Neo-Platonists. If the designers bring more light into the buildings, it is because the light is an emanation from God, and by receiving it, through the church, the spirit of men is enlightened and their souls rise. Gothic architecture benefits from technical progress to exalt this quest for light in the proportions never reached before.

Moreover, there is a true evolution of dogma in the relationship between God and His creature. Until then, Christianity insisted on the humility of man, as can be seen in the book of Job. However, in the middle of the twelfth century, gradually the power of man was exalted. If Roman art celebrated the triumphant Christ, its Gothic counterpart represents a passionate Christ exalting His humanity, while the church opens more widely to members. To express the outrageousness of the era of cathedrals, historians refer to this striking comparison: from the twelfth to the fourteenth century, France extracted more quarry stones than ancient Egypt in three thousand years of history. Thousands of churches saw the light of the day together with them, eighty cathedrals, during the Pharaonic undertakings that spread over several decades and even over centuries. (IBID. Pg. 36)

These buildings are truly to the glory of God. They drained an entire economy and technical expertise through the use of professionals such as carpenters, masons, stonemasons, blacksmiths, glassmakers and even the unskilled. They also put in place original means of funding in the likes of donations, patronage, legacies and public quests.

The Gothic iconography (sacred image) of the cathedrals is serene and shows a peaceful union between the creator and the creature. Iconography also expresses the transformation of the participating material of the splendour of God which includes painters and sculptors going to the forests, fields, gardens and orchards to copy the great work of nature as well as to testify the wonder that all men must experience before this creation of God. The set of images offers a summary of the world as God created it. Entering a cathedral under the benevolent gaze of hundreds of angels with outspread wings is for a layperson of the last centuries of the Middle Ages to enter another universe and have a foretaste of paradise. The cathedral is presented as the archetype of the heavenly Jerusalem, this walled city of gold with constellations of precious stones. It is presented in the first century by Saint John in Revelation (Chapter 21) as responsible for promoting faith through seeing. The media that is a cathedral offers a very rich iconographic programme. Nothing that touches the sacred history (Genesis, Prophets and other key figures of the Old Testament, the life of Christ and Holy Mary, Apostles, Revelation, last judgement, paradise and hell) escapes the scissors of stonecutters, brushes with squirrel hair, or painters' badger with gold and silk threads of tapestries. Gothic art rehabilitates manual labour hitherto despised in the name of inferiority of mechanical arts over liberal arts.

Thus, three great types of universe ordinarily coexist in iconography: the world of revelation (the world of men in which the prophets, Christ, the Saints lived and proclaimed the divine word), the celestial world (beyond the court where God is surrounded by angels, elects, saints) and the underworlds (indeterminate worlds evoked by ancient geographers and populated by fantastic animals). Each of these worlds occupies a privileged location in the cathedral (Ibid, pg. 58).

Thus, the gate, a super significant element of the building since Jesus proclaims "I am the Way" in the Gospel according to Saint John, is very frequently consecrated to Christ, the virgin and the Patron Saints of the diocese. In the same way, many sculptures of the gate stage portray the last judgement while the statues, columns typical of the Gothic art glorify prophets, apostles and evangelists. Truly holy comics, stained glass windows, which are read from bottom to top, take pleasure recounting the life of great men who helped to build Christendom and considered example of good kings (the Emperors Constantine, Clovis and Charlemagne). Others represent a multitude of characters from the Bible. Others cultivate allegory in which feature the seven liberal arts (the intellectual disciplines regarded as the basics like grammar, rhetoric, dialectic, arithmetic, geometry, music and astronomy). Stained glass windows show willing craftsmen at work by transforming the participating matter from the splendour of God. The set of images that adorn the house of God testifies to the opulence and power of the Church on earth and encourages the flock of the faithful to obey God. A cathedral gate looks like a triumphal arch planted in the heart of the city that houses it. Very concerned about heresies (Cathar, Waldensian, etc.), the ecclesiastical authorities also mobilise the iconography of cathedrals to block these non-conformist religious movements. The Marian image is one of the main anti-heresy weapons. By cultivating the analogy between the virgin that artists do humanise, and the Church, the former gives herself the image of a caring mother and a reassuring protector. She relates with the faithfuls through feelings by telling them that just as Mary is the mother of Christ, the Church is the mother of Christians.

But the iconography of the carved, glazed or painted decoration of the cathedral has, above all, an educational function. At a time when the majority of the population is illiterate and only the clergy have access to sacred texts, is the image not the Bible of the illiterate? (IBID). The sciences of Antiquity seem to have inspired in part the builders of cathedrals. The statues of sages such as Pythagoras, Aristotle or Euclid, represented alternately with the disciplines of liberal arts, Trivium (grammar, rhetoric and dialectic) and quadrivium (Astronomy, music, arithmetic, and geometry) in the arch (vaults) of the royal gate of Chartres testify to this (Ibid.pg 42).

In short, in Gothic cathedrals there is a direct link between moral perfection and architectural perfection. Cathedrals express the Bible in all the practical splendour of God, in all His perfection and sublime beauty. Cathedrals are a hymn and a song to the glory of practical knowledge, intelligence and wisdom.

II- Medieval mysticism in social life

In this atmosphere of the prevalence of theology and the science of God in medieval society, there are mystical thinkers such as:

Saint Augustine (354-430) - his thought has sustainably marked Western thought. In his book *Les Confessions (Confessions)*, he speaks directly to God. It is under this gaze and asking for his help that he recounts the itinerary that brought him to baptism, before narrating his experience as a bishop, confessing his sins, but also praising him for all his gifts. The book evokes the contemplation or ecstasy of Ostia near Rome between his mother and him. This scene emphasises the strength of experience of these two. The starting point is a possible exchange between Monica and Augustine on eternal life, an exchange that arouses a burning desire for the source of life (Psalm 36:10), an extension of the whole being to God. A step by step ascension: first outward, then within oneself and finally beyond oneself. Outside, rising from earthly bodies to celestial bodies; within oneself by going beyond the dreams and visions of imagination; and finally the soul itself, beyond oneself to eternal wisdom above all.

Ascension is described a second time as a silence that imposes itself on all creation: silence of the things of the world that are signs of the creator, then silence of the soul in itself, so that it can hear God himself speak. The summit of experience is evoked as a contract in a supreme impulse of the heart: the attainment of wisdom. Then, follows the return to everyday life and the vain limit of the lips, which is out of proportion to the immutable word; that is to say, the divine word itself. The experience nonetheless has the effect of highlighting the first fruits of the mind. The phrase suggests that the upper part of the human spirit, the leading edge of the spirit is anchored to the shore it has just reached. It remains fixed in God, stretched towards Him, while daily life lays hold of its rights. This moment is a foretaste of heavenly life. If it were prolonged and absorbed the soul entirely in joy, it would be eternal life. The experience is Christian is the word creator, wisdom and life, that is here attained in the silence of all creation.

The following quote describes this elevation towards God: "Our conversation had led us to the conclusion that, in the bliss of such a life, the delights of our carnal senses, no matter how great, no matter how much body light they radiate, bear no comparison or even a mere mention of the delights of that life. And then, raising us with a more ardent impulse towards the Being himself, we traverse, step by step, all bodily things and even heaven".[83]

Anicius Manlius Severinus Boetius alias Boethius (480-524)

Hinge thinker between philosopher and Christianity, between antiquity and medieval thought. He authored consolation and philosophy, his masterpiece. He wonders in this work, if the happiness to which all men aspire resides in glory, wealth and the pleasure of the senses. No, it exists only in the pursuit of good, the supreme good (it is God), the divine providence and the rational order that God has impressed on the world. The world obeys rational laws desired by divine goodness. There is freedom, he answers, for whoever raises their thought towards God and frees themselves from links with the events of the world.[84]

Benedict of Nursia (480-547)

Future Saint Benedict, founder of the Benedictine order. According to his biographer, Pope Gregory I (540-604) was disgusted by the dissolute ways of Rome and it is for this reason that he decided to abandon everything and to devote himself to God. He wrote in 503, the rule of St. Benedict that bears his name. This brief and clear text describes the spirit and rules to be followed by monks in their daily life: obedience, chastity, and poverty, precise schedules of the day shared between prayers, manual work and study of sacred texts as well as hospitality.

Bernard of Clairvaux (1090-1153)

He was a nobleman who became an Abbot of Clairvaux. He had a decisive impact on the history of mysticism, notably by his famous sermons on the hymn of hymns. In his sermons, it is the word, the word of God which, by means of love, takes the initiative of the spiritual life

---

[83]Le Point Références, Janvier-Février 2012 op.cit., pp 28-29, in « confessions », Saint Augustin (The Point References, January-February 2012 op.cit., Pg. 28-29, in "confessions", St. Augustine.

[84]Le Point Références, Novembre-Décembre, 2011. op.cit., pp.16-17, in « consolation de la philosophie, livre I, vers 524 (The Point References, November-December, 2011. op.cit., Pp.16-17, in "consolation of philosophy, book I, about 524).

and leads it. It is not a mystic who reaches God by their own strength, but it is God who goes to the mystic to bring them to him. The art of seeking God is a sign that God attracts us. He also innovates by making the spousal relationship (between spouses), between Jesus and the soul of the Christian, the norm in matters of mysticism. Saint Bernard generalises the spiritual experience. For the mystic to make progress and teach they must read the book of experience. He learns to distinguish the divine presence in him as a light breeze intermixed with his thoughts. The verb leads directly or through monastic obedience in a long itinerary consisting of fasting, vigils, frequent and persevering prayers performed in calm and silence. At the end of the journey is the rapture of the soul, which is a mystical union. The sermons of Saint-Claivaux had an immense impact. There appeared a mystical spousal (union with God) which was to dominate the coming centuries at the risk of giving an exclusively feminine turn to mysticism.[85]

St. Francis of Assisi (1182-1226)

He is creator of the Franciscan order. He proposes the evangelical counsels which include poverty, chastity, obedience, gentleness and love of nature. This Franciscan spirit will deeply permeate mentalities, especially the art of the fourteenth century. He wrote a letter to all the faithfuls who glorify God and exalted nature, entitled "Praise be to God for our glorious brother the sun".[86]This hymn is of the beauty of the world and also called the hymn of creatures. He glorifies God and his son Jesus in these eulogistic words "Oh! How glorious and holy and great to have a Father in heaven! Oh! How holy and beautiful it is, magnificent and admirable, to have in heaven a husband! Oh! How holy and dear, pleasant and humble, soothing and sweet, kind and desirable more than anything to have such a brother and a son, who gave his life for his sheep. For them, I sanctify myself so that they may be sanctified together as we do. And I want, Father, that where I am, they should be with me, so that they may see my splendour in your kingdom".[87] This radicalism in faith attracts countless disciples to Saint Francis of Assisi,

---

[85] Le Point Références janvier-février 2012 op.cit.,pp. 38-39, in, Sermons sur le cantique des cantiques, de Bernard de Clairvaux (The Point References January-February 2012 op.cit., Pg. 38-39, in, Sermons on the Song of Songs, by Bernard of Clairvaux.

[86] Le Point Références, Ibid., pp.42-43, in, « cantique des créatures » de François d'Assise.

[87]Ibid,pg. 42 (Le Point References, Ibid., Pp.42-43, in, "Hymn of creatures" of Francis of Assisi Ibid., Pg. 42).

in search of a new spirituality, at a time when the church is in a state of delinquency, sensitive to the struggles of power more than salvation of souls. This call to poverty echoes the criticism of the Cathars, a religious movement, in search of absolute purity. To train his disciples and reassure the Catholic Church, he wrote in 1221 a proposed rule, then a second and more sober one, approved by the Pope in 1223. Like all the monastic rules, this one prescribes the observance of the evangelical counsels like poverty, chastity, obedience and it also imposes a life of total destitution, alms and obedience to the pope. The hymn of creatures, written by him, is the most beautiful of Italian poems.

In this mystical flight, Francis sings the fraternity of man with his sun brother, his sister the moon, the mother nature, but also with the wind, the clouds, water, for a Church that is accustomed to consider that the moderator is in the power of evil. We remember especially in this great mystic, the call to an intense spirituality.

Saint Bonaventure (1217-1274). He was proclaimed doctor of the church in 1587. In his book, *L'intineraire de l'esprit vers Dieu* (The Spirit's Journey to God), he aims to reconcile the demands of the rational mind with the ardour of the mystical soul. It is to a true pilgrimage that he invites reason. Starting from the sensible, it must return in itself and lead to the contemplation of God and mystical ecstasy. The Christian rationality that he proposes rests on three ideas: first, only divine grace, operating from baptism (a sacrament that allows one to become a Christian) can generate reason. Baptism thus allows reason, initially bowed to earthly things because of original sin, to return to God. Then, its practice must be part of a life based on prayer and the exercise of virtues. Finally, it must be preceded by faith, which is defined as a joint act of intelligence and will. This act of prior faith, that is posing the existence of a transcendent God decides the gaze of man on the world. Christian revelation then makes it possible to rely on philosophical reason to form the mirror that makes it possible to represent divine realities. For Saint Bonaventure, whoever wishes to rise to God must, after having avoided the sin which disfigures his nature, exercise the divine powers to acquire by prayer, grace which reforms, a holy life, righteousness which purifies, meditation, the science that illuminates, and by contemplation, the wisdom that makes perfect. But just as no one comes to wisdom except through grace, justice, and science, so too one only reaches contemplation by a deep meditation, a pure life, and a fervent reason.

Thus, one must begin by praying, living well, applying oneself to attentively consider the truth wherever it is offered to one's gaze, and finally endeavour to ascend gradually until one arrives at the elevated mountain, the holy Zion where the God of gods will manifest His glory to us.[88]In this pure and holy life, we come to the eternal model in which all things derive the relationship and the sequence which unites them according to the rules existing to the divine model. All the light of human reasoning has its source in this truth, since it is only in this light that we can embrace the truth with certainty.

St. Thomas Aquinas (1225-1274)

He is a scribe of the Church and major philosopher of the Middle Ages. He is of the order of the Dominicans. He wrote a memorable book entitled: *La somme de théologie (The sum of theology).* This book claims to present the whole of Christian doctrine. Thomas Aquinas is convinced that all truth comes from God. He builds his theology on biblical revelation and Christian tradition, but also on Greek thinkers, especially Aristotle as well as Arab and Jewish. He renews theology thanks to the great value he gives to human reason, in that he is already a forerunner of Renaissance and the era of European Enlightenment. The second part of the theology, the most original, deals with the moral life of man. It expresses a great confidence in human nature. Man being in the image of God possesses an intellectual nature, acts freely, and discerns the goal and the means to achieve it. The freedom of man is constitutive of his being; God himself must respect it so that He may not destroy His own image. The very condition of an authentically human existence is for the person who qualifies by will and intelligence. However, this freedom cannot be expressed without God. For Thomas Aquinas, God alone can fill the desire for knowledge, love and happiness that the human being is carrying. To reach this end, man must act according to the dignity of his nature created in the image of God. For Thomas Aquinas this image is not reduced to an imprint, but to a dynamism and a resemblance to perfect. He devotes a great deal of his morality to showing how human passions regulated by reason are at the

[88]Ibid., pp.46-47, in « Itinéraire de l'Esprit vers Dieu », de Saint Bonaventure (Ibid., pp.46-47, in "The Way of the Spirit to God", Saint Bonaventure)

basis of virtuous dynamism, enabling man to blossom and become fully fulfilled.[89]

With regards to power, he reveals that: "Both spiritual and secular powers are derived from the power of God, and therefore secular power is subject to spiritual power only with regard to the salvation of souls". In this field we must obey the spiritual power than the secular one, but with regard to the city's good, we must obey the secular power, as it's written in the Gospel, "Give to Caesar, what is Caesar's, and to God, what is God's".[90]

Master Eckhart (1260-1328)

He is one of the most recognised medieval writers and a major thinker. Sermon 71 brings out the conversation of the apostle Paul struck by a heavenly light and the call of Jesus on the road to Damascus. When the Acts of the Apostles (9: 9) say that he was overcome, he got up and with his eyes open, he saw nothing. For him, this nothing was God. He does not deny God who is this divine nothingness, since he multiplies the usual names of God: light, absolute Being and totality. He opens the space of contemplation which alone embraces the infinite.[91]

Gregory of Palamas (1296-1359)

He was a monk of Mount Amos in Greece. He was the spokesman of the Hesychastes, the orthodox monks followers of a prayer to Jesus, repetitive (Lord Jesus Christ, son of God, have pity on me), punctuated by breath, while the gaze of the praying man remains fixed on the heart. For this mystic and the hesychastes (hesychasm is a school of spirituality of the Orthodox Church based on the contemplation and the repeated invocation of the name of Jesus Christ), the true knowledge of God consists in fact in direct experience, which passes through the vision of the uncreated light (which exists without being created) and divine, as it was manifested during the transfiguration of Christ (Mark 9: 1-10). The transfiguration is the episode of the life of Jesus on the summit of Mount Tabor (present-day Israel), before the disciples Peter, James, John where Jesus shines with deity, his clothes became

---

[89] Le Point Références, Novembre-Décembre. op.cit., 2011. P.56 (The Point References, November-December. op.cit., 2011. p.56).

[90]Ibid., p.57.

[91] Le Point Références, Janvier-Février . 2012.pp. 52 -53 (The Point References, January-February. 2012.Pg. 52-53)

dazzlingly white, and he was surrounded by two prophets: Elijah and Moses. Verse 3 is more accurate in saying that Jesus' garments became dazzling white, whiter than anyone in the world could bleach them. For Palamas, this vision of uncreated light is not a vision of the nature or essence of God, but divine energies that radiate from its nature, the latter being unknowable. Palamas justifies this mystical experience on the theological level, by asserting that there exists in God a distinction between his nature or essence and his energies, a distinction which is not a separation and remains inexpressible, because it's appropriate to God alone. Palamas thus wished to highlight two truths concerning the divine experience: on the one hand the reality of the union of man with God, and on the other hand the transcendence of God, that is at the same time knowledge and unknowable.[92]

In the writings of Palamas, he speaks of prayer, as an act of the spirit, that is to say, the superior faculty of the soul by which man can unite with God. But this understanding must not make us forget the human body, essential for its participation in prayer and the acquisition of grace. Mysticism can be considered as that which is based on the incarnation of God. But the spirit is the receptacle of the grace of the Holy Spirit also called intercessor or comforter (John 16:7). By this method, the mind abandons all passions and arrives at the state of hesychia (silence and peace). For Palamas, prayer and ascetic life are only means to open oneself to divine grace. The reception of the divine gift is an act of God alone. There is no longer a subject or an object in this divine contemplation. There is only light. He says it even more clearly: "The contemplation of this light is a union although it does not last in the imperfect. But is the union with the light anything other than a vision? And since it is accomplished with the cessation of intellectual activity, how could it be accomplished except through the Holy Spirit? For it is in the light that the light appears and it is in the similar light that the visual faculty is found". Since this faculty has no other way of acting, having left all other beings, it becomes entirely light and assimilates what it sees. "It unites without mixing, because it's light. If it looks at itself, it sees light. If it looks at the object of its vision, it is also light. This is the union. Let all be one, so that he who sees does not distinguish between the means, nor the goal, nor the essence, but that he is only conscious of being light and of seeing a light distinct from all

[92]Ibid., pp. 52 -53

his creature "[93]. This light is God, the source of all things and life. The Apostle Paul himself expresses this rapture in the vision of a delighted man up in the third heaven to the point that he was taken away to paradise, where he heard inexpressible things that no one was allowed to express (2 Corinthians 12: 1-5). In this contemplation, Paul is united with the Holy Spirit and through Him he has the opportunity to unite himself with Him after having come out of created beings and became Divine Light by grace. This higher elevation in knowledge can only impart the perfect understanding of natural and supernatural things. It thus promotes man's progress and ability to understand everything through the mind and the intellect and to attain perfect wisdom.

Juliana of Norwich (1342-1416)

She is a Benedictine (of Saint Benedict) from the central west region of England. Her short book *The Revelations of Divine Love*, alongside the works of the hermit Richard Rolle (1295-1349) or the spiritual manual "***The Cloud of Unknowing*"**, return to the rich mystical tradition of medieval England. Juliana's *Revelations of Divine Love* is the story of a mystical experience, surprising in its freshness, clarity and spontaneity. In the book, she recounts how she was favoured in a strange illness through supernatural revelations transmitted simultaneously by the senses (the sight of the suffering Christ), by a mental discourse and by an indescribable spiritual intuition. In response to her own doubts and anxieties, these revelations relate to the deepest mysteries of the Christian faith which include the knowledge of God, Trinity, sense of creation in genesis (the first book of the Bible that recounts the creation of the universe by God), the origin of man and the Hebrews, the problem of evil, universal providence, the influence of God or the gods on the course of things. An idea links all the steps that Juliana goes through: the centrality of divine love which constitutes the metaphysical unity of reality and humanity. Metaphysics is considered as the part of philosophy which studies what is common to all beings (Being, Beauty, Truth), beyond the specific sciences, or the rational knowledge of transcendent things, or even the search for first principles and root causes. This divine love guarantees that everything will end well; everything is good for eternity because of the perfection of this all-powerful love. This message of love and divine is summarised at the end of the story: "Will you want to know what your Lord meant? Know

[93] Idem.

very well, it is the love he had in view".[94] In short, her message relates the divine love that constitutes the metaphysical unity of humanity and allows us to rush towards the being, the beautiful, the truth, the righteous, the perfect and the good.

Catherine of Siena (1347-1380)

She is a Dominican nun and one of the greatest Italian mystics, peculiar by the abundance of her visions and her generosity, as an expression of the selfless love of God. This love through which He wants to renew His friendship with men. The spiritual life found in the purification of human love in contact with this heart, its transmutation, in a pure and selfless love lead to the perfect love, key to eternal happiness. In the natural state, man is full of self-esteem rooted in pride. He loves only his own interest and loves neither God nor his neighbour, two loves which are united to one another indissolubly. It is necessary for those who seek eternal life to love without calculation, for affection seeks a higher object. Then, by persevering in virtue and prayer, meditating on divine goodness, the soul reaches the second step from the point where its affection begins to be purified and its virtue consolidated. Its intelligence presents the free love springing from the heart of Christ. It becomes attached and transforms itself into a freed and faithful servant, though less attached to God than the gifts. The third state is that of the perfect. Stripped of their egoism and their own will, they have inner peace.[95]

St. Teresa of Avila (1515-1582)

She is unanimously recognised as one of the great mystics of Catholicism. In her major text, the Castle of the Soul, considered as the founder of modern Catholic mysticism, she conveys her spiritual experience. The work is based on an original conception of the soul, raised by God in a vision where it appears as a magnificent crystal globe shaped like a castle with seven mansions. In the seventh, placed at the centre was the king of glory. The text emphasises the extraordinary beauty of any soul compared to a wonderful diamond castle made in the image of God or as a very clear diamond much larger than the whole world. It strongly emphasises the constant, though invisible, presence

[94] Le Point Références, janvier-février, 2012, p.50, in « Révélations de l'amour divin », de Juliane de Norwich (Le Point References, January-February, 2012, p.50, in "Revelations of Divine Love", by Juliane de Norwich)
[95]Ibid.,pp.54-55.

of God Himself in the central home of every soul, even that of the great sinner. From there, God illuminates Jerusalem with the book of Revelation that illuminates Jerusalem, the righteous of Psalm 1 which is like a tree watered by the waters of divine grace. Through a subtle game of comparisons, derived from the Bible and her mystical experience, she intends to make comprehend all the richness of the spiritual realities, invisible to daily conscience. She defends the intrinsic dignity of the soul and the presence of God in it. She adds to this fundamental mystic the miserable state of the soul in a state of sin, which is the case of most people. Returned to the world, to all its passions and worries, the soul ignores its own beauty and that of the divine master who lives in it. And the mystical life, precisely, has the purpose of bringing back the soul in itself so that it discovers God there.

In prayer, the soul spends some moments in silence and comes in contact with God through contemplation of the humanity of Christ. Exposed to His influence, the soul purifies itself gradually and goes from member to member, finding Him at the centre of her soul. It is then the stage of mystical marriage, traditional theme of Catholic mysticism, symbol of the stable union of the soul with God. The influence of Teresa, proclaimed doctor of the Church, has been enormous.[96]

All these examples highlight the centrality of God in the European society of the Middle Ages, which shapes, formats and structures in the right direction the consciences, mentalities, behaviours of people at that time. This culture of high divine values is at the basis of the social advancement of Europe at that time and even today, despite some relaxation, because the base of this culture is Judeo-Christian. It is therefore a powerful culture with sure markers, because it is illuminated by the word and the divine spirit.

III- Emergence of school and university

This very advanced spiritual experience promotes knowledge, develops human reason, emergence of school with the advent of scholasticism that seeks to harmoniously reconcile the Bible and Greco-Latin knowledge. School is progressively taking shape with lessons taught since antiquity which include grammar, rhetoric and dialectic (the art of philosophical dialogue).

---

[96]Ibid., pp. 62 -63.

Latin is the language of education. In 789, the great reforms of Charlemagne and clericalism of education took place. Schools were opened in every diocese and monastery, so that children should learn to read, write, count, sing and master Latin grammar to understand the Bible. Similarly, we do not leave aside the fundamentals of humanists and we seek to reconcile the love of letters and the desire of God. The ninth century brought back the dialectic as well as authors such as Virgil, Horace, Seneca, Cicero, Plato and Aristotle. In the year 1000, humanist values were pushed even further. The seven liberal arts were deepened notably arithmetic, geometry, astronomy, music, rhetoric, dialectics and grammar. Science started making progress. Schools flourished in Paris, Chartres, Tours, Angers in France, and also in England, Italy and Germany.

The culmination of this profound cultural change was the birth of universities in the late twelfth and early thirteenth centuries. Today we speak of higher education. The university is an ecclesiastical institution, but some great people and Lords also arrogate the right to open a university. The universities were born in Paris with the Sorbonne founded in 1253, in the 13th century, Oxford and Cambridge (England), Bologna and Florence (Italy), Lisbon (Portugal), and in Germany. This is a real revolution in the European education system. Universities teach medicine, law, theology and the seven arts listed above. Architecture is not left out. The best cathedrals date back to this time with Gothic art.[97]Apart from these subjects taught, there is also morality which is the milestone of good education. There are countless number of papers, books on vices and virtues as well as works on good manners.

The creation of universities places knowledge at the heart of medieval society. Latin favours communication, since cultured people use it as a means of expression. All this positive evolution takes place despite the difficult beginnings of European Middle Ages, because of the feudal organisation of the society, with its attendant servitude for the poor, completely subject to the Lord. In this respect, medieval Europe already forms a set. The students of Paris go to study in Germany, England, Italy and vice versa. These movements allow rich cultural exchange which is the origin of European culture. Universities

[97] Read on this subject the wonderful work of Christian Jacq, *Le message des constructeurs de Cathédrales* (*The message of builders of Cathedrals)*, Éditions du Rocher, 1980.

open up individual paths to success and social uplifting. The Middle Ages despite its flaws and weaknesses, sought to elevate man to the divine dimension, using his faith and reason.

IV- Emergence of cities

This spiritual, mystical, intellectual and scientific effervescence is increasing and promoting innovation in Europe. Especially with the emergence of cities that are hotbeds of creativity, science, technical and economic progress. It is in the cities that the first educational institutions appeared. Moreover, it is in cities located near communication nodes, in particular fluvial as Paris and London, or on ports like Marseilles, Venice, Amsterdam, and Genoa that the first credit institutions and first currencies were established.

Finally, it is in the cities that political life also increased and that democracy begun to be practised, that is the participation of citizens in the affairs of the city. Athens in Greece and Rome in Antiquity remained the models of genre. Closer to home, the development of democracy is linked to the liberation movements of cities for, new ideas take shape. In reality, cities, by rubbing shoulders with men (communication of wealth, ideas) as well as forming nuclei of wealth accumulation and teaching centres, promote initiatives, innovations, entrepreneurship and the evolution of societies in the direction that make European, American and Japanese societies among the first in modern times.[98]

V- Middle Age develops divine and human themes which progressively promote a New European Man

Although the Middle Ages was a difficult period for Europe, that of feudalism marked by the exploitation of man by great landlords, poverty, epidemics, etc., it was already preparing the advent of a new man through the teachings of the Bible.

In fact, the Middle Ages develops strong, perfect, powerful themes that constitute the spiritual, mystical, intuitive, rational, scientific,

---

[98] Jean Sauvy, *Initiation à l'économie des pays en développement*, Institut international d'administration publique, Paris,1968, p.149 (Jean Sauvy, *Initiation to the Economies of Developing Countries*, International Institute of Public Administration, Paris, 1968, p.149).

intellectual, moral and cultural framework of Christian Europe. Most of these elevation tools come from the divine sphere as we have emphasised above.

These are themes that revolve around God, the absolute Being, the man, Christ, the Bible, the divine word, Christianity, the Holy Spirit, beauty, the righteous, the truth and perfection. From this rich Christian theme, the human is completely renewed in his intelligence and fit for any good work. In fact, it is gradually a new birth with completely renewed paradigms and analysis grids. With this enlightening light of the mind, the human mind opens to more knowledge to improve its earthly life. He creates new themes of the human sphere that reconcile God with man and the latter becomes aware of his own abilities and his acting rationality.

To Thomas Aquinas, man descends to earth and feels himself associated with the divine work of creation. He must act and create in turn. Hence an increasingly creative human theme such as: human rationality and reason, humanism, art, architecture, secular power, the development of man, the development of sciences, schools, university, progress, techniques, economic development, trade, political life, development of cities, development of communication routes, communication between men, the creation of credit institutions, first currencies, the accumulation of wealth, the circulation of goods, the production of books, ideas, democracy, the State, sovereignty, the spirit of enterprisc.

The man trained in the school of God and his perfect values takes off; he is actually born gradually into true knowledge. He can become a creator. This profound change allowed man to operate a true baptism of knowledge. He has immersed in the depths of mysteries that open to him the light of true and authentic knowledge.

To sum up, by the combination of divine perfect values and those of men, the first part of this reflection, the human being progressively leaves the darkness of ignorance and progresses in true knowledge, or to say like Kant, he leaves his minor for his major. In this respect, the Middle Ages, contrary to certain popular ideas and despite its feudal character, marked an important point and laid an indelible mark in the progress of Europe and of humanity, because knowledge does not only benefit those who discover it but everybody. The proof is, this knowledge has reached us today and serves us as well.

Jacques Le Golf, the greatest medieval historian, summarises the importance of this period: "The Middle Ages was an essential period for the training of our society and our culture, perhaps the most important. It is indeed in the Middle Ages that the fundamental element of our collective identity, Christianity, is truly established. [...]. I believe that our birth occurred in the Middle Ages, that this is our genesis. But we must not forget its shadow part." (Journal *Le Monde* Thursday, 3 April 2014, pg.16).

We see how the chain of true knowledge is built progressively. We started from Africa, cradle of humanity to ancient Egypt, ancient Greece and Rome, to arrive at the centrality of God in the European society of the Middle Ages. This centrality of God in the life of man marks a very important stage in the appropriation by man of the light of eternal knowledge. This opens the perspectives for scientific, technical, technological and industrial knowledge that will follow, as well as the knowledge of the society of today. The spirit of the new and more enlightened European man is already emerging.

At a time when Africa is seeking its path for its development, it must revisit this initiatory, edifying and laborious journey of acquiring perfect knowledge, as the West did in its time. It must avoid making the Gospel a simple reality limited to Sunday activities in churches or mosques for the Quran.

The European Renaissance offers another dimension of this evolution in the perfect training of the new European.

Chapter V

The contribution of the European renaissance from the 15th to the 17th centuries to western development that turned into Christianity: A cultural revolution of the mind, mentality and the central role of the new man in the European society

It will not be an exaggeration to mention this step in the European evolution. It always demonstrates to what level the systematic evolution of knowledge is indispensable to man to lead the development of human societies. The example of Europe is a case study worth reviewing.

In its lengthy walk towards its development, the era of renaissance of this continent marks an important step. It arises after the European middle age of which the last decades already announce this rejuvenation. Yves Hersant estimates that this period extends from Christopher Columbus who discovered America in 1492 to Galileo (1564-1642) who founded modern science. The latter defends the idea of the rotation of the earth and the planets around the earth (heleocentrism). This period inaugurates a true cultural revolution of minds and mentalities and of the central role of man in the society. This is contrary to the Middle Ages where God and the Church occupied the central position.[99] The profile of the European man is much more projected.

In the 15th Century in Europe, intellectuals, artists, patrons and princes developed the conviction to live a new age. It is a true spiritual crusade which brings about a true revival of mentalities and consciences. This spiritual movement is a synonym of regeneration, change, transformation, energy and restoration. It is in effect a complete renewal of man in a spiritual, intellectual and moral dimension and a profound and not a shallow transformation. So many terms or metaphors by which European elite, especially Italians formulate a giant project. The project to reactivate ancient times to open the way to

---

[99] Le Point Références, la renaissance Mars-avril 2011, Textes fondamentaux, Yves Persant. P.7. in « L'Aurore de l'Europe », Yves Herseint.

modern times, the retrospect in order to advance. To get into the ancient school, not only Latin and Greek considering them as a model for initiating creativity. This renewal is that of intense thinking through learnedness, education, curiosity, aspiration for beauty and humanism. This era is inspired by the great thinkers of the Greeko-Romanian Antiquity. They include Plato, Epicurus, Zeno of Kition, Zeno d'Elée, Aristotle, Heroditus, Parmenide, Pythagoras, Hippocrates, Holme, Archimedes, Galileo, Euclid, Plutos, Porphyre,_Democrite, Ciceron, Horace, Virgile, Ovide, Salluste, Tite-Live, Tacite,Senec, Suetonius and Pline l'Ancien. It is a period of the outburst of humanism which is a demanding philosophy, which renders man a conqueror. Humanism seeks to place man at the centre of all debates in the European society. It is the outcome of a true Copernican revolution of the culture which, from the Middle Age studies moves from that of humans to be focused on the "me" and the "I" of Montaigne[100]. Is equally the period of reforms, which is a generic term referring to the effort of the renewal of faith and Christian practices, which give birth to Protestantism. This is in response to Catholicism and the all-powerful papacy. Rebirth is a cultural revolution of minds and mentalities. It marks the beginning of colonization, capitalism and political absolutism. This revolution originated from Italy and gradually engulfed Europe, affecting Arts, letters, sciences and the habits. It is followed in the first place by the spectacular development of cities, trips, exchanges, through the accrued circulation of goods and talents, then, increase consumption by the vitality of Europe whose economic strength counterbalances the rest of the world. This revolution is manifested by a world that has been largely spread out by Christopher Columbus, Vespucci, and Magellan of which the discovery of America and India, and other regions brought affluent to Europe. They brought gold, spices, perfumes and wood. Commerce then develops and the world expands from the Mediterranean to the Atlantic. Portugal and Spain share the new world amongst themselves. This situation will be contested in the 17th Century by France and England. The great discoveries lead the Europeans to clearly define their characteristics, contrasting them to those of others. The European idea is a legacy of rebirth[101].

---

[100] Ibid. p.82.

[101] Révolution intellectuelle et scientifique, la renaissance marque ainsi le début de la colonisation, du capitalisme et de l'absolutisme politique.

This spectacular revolution could not have been carried out without the scientific curiosity that characterises renaissance and without the advanced techniques that were recorded in that era. Cartographic and mathematical studies improved the tools of navigation. Apart from the compass known in the Mediterranean since the beginning of the 14th Century, sailors also use the astrolabe and the quadrant to calculate the latitude, which enables them to easily distant themselves from the coasts. The ships are also modernised.

On a scientific framework, discoveries have invaluable consequences. They prove the roundness of the earth, permit the discovery of new civilisations and offer new fields for evangelisation to the church. It is on the economic and political framework that the impact is stronger. With the new commercial route through the Atlantic and the Indian Oceans, the Mediterranean ports (Genoa and Venice) lose their intermediary role in the commercialisation of spices. On the other hand the Atlantic ports develop as follows Lisbon, Cadiz, Bordeaux, Amsterdam, London and Anvers. They benefit from business with colonies and certain business men enriched themselves with the slave trade. The conquests and the discoveries affected the entire Europe because products like cocoa, coffee, sugar cane, Irish potatoes, maize and precious metals were brought in great quantities from America. Financial techniques were developed and true fortunes were constituted. These capital affluent profoundly overturns the economic structures. The industries gradually replace the artisanal. The peasants' lives improved due to an increase in prices and the workers were getting poorer and poorer because of a drop in wages. As for the bourgeoisies, enriched by their commerce and industry, they took a lead in landed dignity which became a court nobility at the service of the dominant.

Humanism aims at valorising speech and languages, restore the rhetoric, aestheticize life and strengthen human dignity in order to compete with the divine. In broad terms, to regenerate civilisation and cease it from barbarism and decadence they pulled intellectual and moral energy from Antiquity. The scheme was to offer to man a complete life model by which he will compete with himself.

It is also in the course of the renaissance that the idea of a Europe that has a conscience of cultural belonging emerges. Italy, France and Germany play an important role within it.

I- The place of Italy in this cultural revolution

Above all, with the discovery of Latin and Greek Antiquity in Italian cities, then came the amazing outbreak of European Renaissance at the beginning of the14th Century. This renaissance or Second Birth is that of a splendid past. For Medieval Latin Europe, these are the Centuries of the Roman Empire (chapter II). A fairly brilliant history which is akin to a far constellation, but whose brightness, perceived at a close range brings shame to the darkness of barbarism of the after-Rome.

Italy was the Metropolitan of the Western Roman Empire. It is in Italy that the Roman history entered into myth and legend. Italy was the first and the most effervescent laboratory of this European take-off, known as the Renaissance. The Italians rediscover the beauty in Greek texts and started to study other ancient languages like Hebrew, Arab and Chaldean. A bourgeoisie was developed in Italy. The Italian Merchants who were the financiers of Europe were the greatest innovators of this era. Francis of Assisi the son of a rich businessman is converted to Christianity and takes as mission to evangelise this urban society.

Francis Petrarch (from Italian Francesco Petrarco) makes Roman splendour and the meditation on its ruins a principle of a renovation of a civil modern city. His experimentations, poems and correspondences make him a great European writer. He is the first to model it on that of the great authors of the golden age of Latin, the first century before Jesus Christ. This was like an absolute model of Cicero, in prose and Virgil in epic poetry. Petrarch primarily took a position similar to that of the restorer of the classical civilisation as well as the founding father of humanism, which initiates the Renaissance era. Petrarch was up-to-date with the strong Aristotelian tradition that was developed by the University of Padua in Veneto, which placed scientific and technical knowhow above the Antiquity tradition of the church fathers like Saint Augustine. This humanist approach entails the measuring the logic of unalterable splendour and the indispensable centrality of man[102].

Latin Renaissance is also Greek. Medici bankers, patrons of the Hellenist Marsile Ficino, render Florence the capital of Neo-Platonism (philosophical doctrine of Plotin, a disciple of Plato. It gives a specific importance to the first principle, one and its outcome, the multiple

---

[102] Ibid. pp. 17-19.

assimilation of assets) and an academic city where artists work with Greco-Roman ancient collections. Masacio, Donatello, Michel Ange arise to reconnect with the Greek geniuses of the Arts. Music also undergo a big boom with the principles of harmonisation and the tonal melody of Monteverdi, which was adopted by the entire Europe. He is considered as one of the founding fathers of opera. Greek scientific literature, brought to Italy by Archimedes, Ptolemy, Euclid, Diophantus is commented, translated and published by humanists. It causes a giant step in European science.

- Archimedes (287-212 BC) is a scientific Mathematician and a Greek engineer who is considered as the father of statistical mechanics. He is the inventor of the catapult and the pulley.
- Ptolemy (100-170 AC) is a Greek mathematician, an astrologist and a geographer whose presentation of the world, with a fixed Earth at the centre of the universe, remained unchallenged up to the 16th century.
- Euclid (300 BC) is a Greek mathematician who had lived in Alexandria in Egypt, author of geometric elements who put together and organised the knowledge of mathematics in his era. Through this essential text, he becomes the founder of the said Euclidian geometry, which defines mathematical properties starting from axioms.
- Diophantus of Alexandria is a Greek mathematician who is believed to have lived towards the 3rd Century AC. His most famous work is a combination of thirteen works of mathematics[103].

It is Galileo, a geometry teacher at the Florentine Academy who was the first to draw the conclusion of this scientific revolution, as being an emancipated daughter of the Italian Renaissance. Galileo (Galico Galileo, 1564-1642) is an Italian servant, serving Medici of Florence and who introduces mathematics in the description of physics phenomena: the law of pendulum movement, the law of free fall of objects in a vacuum and stated the law of inertia. In 1609, he invented a glass, which permitted him to discover the rotation of the sun. He had wanted to back the principle of double revolution of the planets and the

[103] Ibid., Le lexique pp. 96-99

earth around the sun like Copernic, but in 1633, the inquiry, the tribunal which fought against heresies forced him to renounce it.

Italy prides itself with Florence governed by the family of Medici who contributed to the humanism of arts. Florence is a republic which carries the standards of communal liberty. It considers itself as the heritage of the Republican Rome, a city whose people are sovereign and conquering. This awe-inspiring image is not only political but as well cultural. This city claims to be the proponent of a new civilisation nourished with the best of antiquity, whereby arts holds a fundamental position. Florence is ennobled by her painters, architects and sculptors. From the Mid13th Century, the town was filled with magnificent public edifices. They began the reconstruction of the Santa Maria cathedral which was later decorated by the architect Filippo Brunelleschi into an enormous dome, revolutionising the art of architecture. If Florence is not viewed from within, it won't be possible to conceive the extent of its beauty. There are no streets that are more beautiful of more sparkling than others, it is the entire town in all its corners which shines. For the ornaments are spread out through the whole city. The leaders of the city, the Medicis are the patrons, the surround themselves with the learned and sculptors like Michel Ange. They proceed to the exportation of artists and tables towards Italian courts, in the likes of Leonardo Da Vinci. This painter and engineer who works in Florence, Milan and Rome incarnates the spirit of Renaissance for his incessant researches, notably in the domain of picturesque techniques, the depth and the mystery of this table (the last scene) and his creativity modifies and ameliorates many machines. It's same for his compatriot Michel Ange (1475-1565). The latter is an Italian sculptor painter, architect and poet who is famous for his sculptures: David, Pieta, Moses, the grave of Jules II, as well as the painted frescos on the ceiling of the Chapel Sistine in the Vatican. The architect also conceives the Saint Peter dome of Rome. All these participate to the spread of the new style of the Renaissance.

The diplomacy of the era is also artistic. There is correspondence to request for a painter, an architect or to inquire of a talent.

Among Italian artists, Raffaelo Sanzio, popularly known as Raphael is called by Pope Jules II (1443-1513) to participate in the decoration of Vatican rooms alongside prestigious artists like Lorenzo Lotto (1480-1556) or Le Perugin (1448-1523). The pope then confines the decoration of his apartments to Raphael alone. It's from this intellectual and artistic emulation that he takes his inspiration[104].

In the same domain of art, Giorgi Vasari (1511-1574), the political communicator of Cosimo 1 of Medicis and the Duke of Florence from 1537 to 1574, plays a determining role in princely sponsorship in 1563 by creating "the Academia delle Anti Del Disegno". This was at the service of painters, architects and sculptors. He is also the author of the Vite (lives). This monumental text is a collection of portraits from 160 artists of his time. There is therefore an imposed conceptual posterity of an envisaged Renaissance that appears as a confrontation of geniuses that is a dramatised rivalry around three major personalities: Leonardo Da Vinci, Michel Ange and Raphael.

Elsewhere, John Picus of Mirandula (1463-1494) publishes his major work on the dignity of man. He renders an account on the significance of man. This one receives the privilege to be what he becomes and to become what he is. God created him as creator for himself, craftsperson of his own destiny. His immense learnedness and tolerance make him one of the greatest minds of the Renaissance. Without quoting Picus of Mirandula, John-Paul Satre says in his own way that existentialism is humanism, whose existence precedes the mind and man is called to be free. It is in this era that Niccolo di Bernardo dei Machiavelli of Florentine publishes his pamphlet *The Prince* in 1513, on the manner in which politics should be done and men be led. This book underwent an extraordinary success. Today, it is still considered as the manifesto on which modern political science, as an autonomous discipline is based, away from subordination to theology or moral community. In chapter 18 of *The Prince* which has about 20 chapters, Machiavelli presents an animal symbol which becomes a legend. Here he affirms that to take Florence and Italy out of the miserable state in which foreign invasion has left them, the Prince must possess the qualities of a lion who in his imagination possesses the brutal force (in politics and military force) and that of a fox, to be tricky (the capacity to manoeuver political and diplomatic activity). He assesses that the practice of moral virtues is a good thing (compassion, faithfulness to your word, honesty and religiosity), that is, a humanist

[104] Ibid. pp. 46-51, in « Le clan des Médicis, entre Humanisme et violence » et « La Création selon Raphaël ».

or humane politics. In a world that does not practise these virtues, to cling to them is madness[105].

This assertion is recalled in the following terms: "Everyone knows how praiseworthy it is, in a Prince, to keep faith, and proceed smoothly, and without finesse, but the experience of these times shows that he did not do great things, only to the princes, who have little regard for their word ... instead of those who have proceeded loyally, they have always been wrong at the end". And he adds that: “It is therefore to know that there are two ways to fight, one with the laws, the other with force. The first is that of men, the second is that of animals. But as often as the first, which is that of men, is not enough, it is necessary to resort to the second”[106].

Italy remains an elected land of the Roman Church. It was spared by the reforms of Luther and Calvin. It proved itself capable of a Renaissance whose contagion changed the face of Europe, then of a prodigious religious movement, also called a Catholic counter-reform, which developed in Europe from the sixteenth century to counter the progress of Protestantism.

II- The place of other countries in this Cultural Revolution.

The Renaissance is not just an Italian affair: everywhere in Europe other artistic and intellectual centers are born, where other approaches to Antiquity and Humanism develop. These include France and Germany.

France

In France, this cultural renewal is manifested with the invention of oil paint, musical renewal, the development of vernaculars with the defence and the illustration of the French language by Du Bellay. If there is a place in the world which can legitimately claim to be the mother of arts, arms and laws, it is Rome.

To raise France to the place of Rome is to clearly indicate the direction of history. If France has Caesars, he also needs the Virgil. The transfer of political power must also be accompanied by the transfer of knowledge. Du Bellay defends this theses on developing local

---

105 Ibid., pp.30-42.

106 Idem

languages and especially French, because at that time, Latin was the international language of knowledge found in all serious publications. According to Bellay, Greek and Latin are powerful languages because they have been developed by the Greeks and the Romans. He assesses that if the ancient Romans had neglected the refinement of their language, it is certain that it wouldn't have become important. He also thinks that when France will be like Rome, the reindeer of the world, its language can also take on a real scale and can match Latin and Greek, producing like these two languages, the Homers, the Demosthenes, the Ciceros and politicians of the classes of Pericles, Nicias Alcibiade, Themistocles (Greece) and its Caesars, Scipio, Octavian Augustus (Rome). This reality challenges Africans today, like the French at the time, to develop their national languages in order to convey their culture for a better control of knowledge and their African culture.

Francois Rabelais (1494-1553) is also a prominent figure of the French Renaissance. He's a great novelist. Like the humanists, he seeks to go through the encyclopaedia of knowledge, to make it have a complete tour. In complete swing compared to the expectations of the time, he presents a radically new conception of the reading of the texts and challenges the interpretative tradition of the Middle-Ages, based on the distinction between four levels of reading: literal, allegorical, tropological and eschatological. He believes that the truth of a book, even his, is not posited in advance by the author. This substantive marrow that is this truth is to be elaborated by the reader himself at the end of an investigation to be carried out. Rebirth goes further in the search for polysemy (search for the plurality of meanings of a text), and does not stop with the interpretation inherited from the four-way Middle-Ages. Literal, is attached to the strict sense of the text. Then allegorical, which is the expression of an idea by a figure endowed with symbolic attributes (art for example) or by a developed metaphor (literature). Furthermore, tropological (a trope), which is a figure of rhetoric which consists in using a word in a deviated sense (veil for a ship, the light of the spirit). Finally, eschatological (eschatology), which is a set of doctrines and beliefs about the ultimate fate of man and the universe.

The tropological sense consists above all in seeking representations of the stages that the human mind must travel in its ascension to God. Rabelais and other humanists like Erasmus and Guillaume Budé think that other meanings can be found. Rabelais will be revived in the nineteenth century by Victor Hugo who annexed the romantic Middle-Ages and made him one of the wizards of the French language, then by the scientific current of the 20th Century that admires in him the man of science. Two of his most important books are Gargantua and Pantagruel. In short Rabelais, monk, doctor, botanist, and diplomat is the perfect model of the humanists of the Renaissance who fight with enthusiasm, to renew the light of the ancient thought, that is, the philosophical and moral ideal of his time.

As for Montaigne (1553-1592), he is a pure product of the Renaissance, of which he embodies the best aspects. With him, the humanist is pushed to the extreme. What interests him is not only the man in general, it is himself, he is the very subject of his book *Les Essais*. It is therefore the culmination of a Copernican revolution of culture which, from the study of the divine in the Middle Ages, passed to that of the human, to focus then on the ego. The Montaigne publications is the triumph of the "I", the prototype of autobiography, memories, confession and introspection. The center of the world was God, now it's “me”. Montaigne cultivates an art of living on earth. This life is no longer the pilgrimage through the valley of tears presented by theologians, it is a long stay that must be made as pleasant as possible. This hedonism (a doctrine based on the pursuit of pleasure and the avoidance of pain) is a refined Epicureanism that measures pleasure and extracts all its substance. He recognizes that he has been spoiled by fate. He is an artist of happiness. He spiritualises and intellectualises pleasures by splitting them. Montaigne understands that the source of pleasure is the brain. By becoming aware of the enjoyment, one reaches a higher level that can be described as happiness. To be happy, you have to know who you are. Montaigne rehabilitated the pleasure and the will to enjoy life reasonably. This is one of the great revolutions of the Renaissance. Pierre Charon, his disciple, by his book of wisdom, is an extension of the publications. Despite criticism, the future is Montaigne, whose credo of the pleasure of life is shared by the honest man of the 17th century and the Enlightenment, in search of earthly happiness by the knowledge of the self. Voltaire, writer of lights, praises the charming project of Montaigne to paint himself as he did. Contemporary self-satisfaction finds its roots in it[107].

---

[107] Ibid., pp.84-85, in, “Les Essais de Montaigne”

In another register, Montaigne evokes the relativism of cultures. For him, the cannibal (he replaces barbaric by this term), is no longer one who knows neither the language nor the customs of the civilized people, but the representative of another civilization. He says so, in order to oppose European civilization to that of America which has just been discovered. For him, one world has just found another. He finds that civil wars ravage France, bringing the most barbarous of Catholics and Protestants to the brink. Go, after that, defend the European culture against the barbarism of the Americas. Nice lesson of humility and honesty[108].

Finally, Calvin is a man of the Renaissance by his ambition to regenerate the Church. He returns to the source of the Scriptures, as the reformers Ulrich Zwingli and Luther wished, despite some differences on the mode of the presence of God in the Eucharist (the holy one) and the organisation of the Church. Calvin thus participates in the European renaissance, by the role he will play in the evolution of the French language. In 1541, he translated his work from Latin into French, making it the first scholarly book written in this language. By the remarkable precision of his words and his clear style, the theologian consequently favoured the development of French literature in the 16th century[109].

Germany

In Germany, it is the invention of printing by Johannes Gutenberg that accelerates the circulation of information and the effects of the reform. From its positive consequences, this invention is compared to a miracle of God. This reform is led by a German priest Martin Luther among others. He believes that a priest, a bishop or a pope cannot impose the law on men and cannot even help them find their salvation before God. The Church of Rome is not the mistress of this world as it explains to the German Christian nobility in 1520. It condemns the system by which the Catholic Church makes pay to lighten the sentences of Purgatory. He advocates the return to the Gospel message of love, modesty and denial that contrasts with the splendor of the Vatican.

---

[108] Ibid., pp.84-85.
[109] Ibid., pp.53-85.

He thinks that only faith can obtain the grace of God. Luther reproaches the Romanists, that is, the popes and their consequences and urges them to rise above the temporal power of the princes, claiming the monopoly of the explanation of the sacred texts, and the exclusive right to convoke the general council of the Church. These three walls prevent reforms without Rome being judge and jury. There is already the fight on secularism and the place of the Church in public life and the state. In this logic of reform that leads to Protestantism and a handover of the hegemony of the Roman Catholic Church, John Calvin appears after Martin Luther as a major player. At 26, he publishes a capital book that occupies his whole life: *Institution de la religion chrétienne* (Institution of the Christian religion). Calvin clearly states the religious principles of the reform. It invites to organize the Catholic Church, because the religion that it claims is universal (in Greek, katholikos: universal). He reproaches his adversaries for confounding the Church of God and uniting the community of believers with the Church of Rome. To him, reform does not mean to create a new church, it rather refers to this invisible church bringing together all true believers. It gives impetus to the Reformed Church of France and the Presbyterianism of Scotland and the United States.

III- Other great spirits of the Renaissance

Other great humanist minds who enriched the Renaissance include Erasmus, born in Rotterdam around 1469. It starts from this rebirth that magnifies man and undermines the impact of original sin on his nature, in this respect, he gives an essential place to education. According to him, education must begin early before vicious habits are established, he believes that the good possession of a language depend on judgment and knowledge. Mastering the language is the basis of culture. We know things only by means of words. The Erasmusian pedagogy will open a new era in education through the European Jesuit colleges, these elite trainers will be inspired.

The Spanish humanist Luis Vives defends that the love for the neighbour must inspire the human right by which everyone is actively fulfilled in a society.

Nicholas Copernicus. He is of Polish origin (1473-1543). In his book *Des Révolutions des sphères célestes* (Revolutions of the Celestial Spheres), he makes a major contribution to the Renaissance and modern science, questioning theCosmos of antiquity where all bodies revolved around the earth (geocentric), to be replaced by a universe where the planets, including the earth, revolve around the sun (heliocentric).

Thomas More (1478-1535). He is of English origin, in Utopie (Utopia) he brings a great innovation in the revival of political ideas, thanks to the trust that is granted to the human capacities which allows the imagination of an ideal world, a world we hope that will one day be realized. In his utopia, the inhabitants are trained in the control and discipline of war, in order to be in a state of being capable to practice it if it becomes indispensable. The utopia, published in 1516 marks a decisive step in the secularization and justification of war and the use of military force. Machiavelli himself in The Prince, exposes the advantages of judicious recourse to war. Utopia opens the way to realpolitik[110].

Henrich Cornelius Agrippa (1486-1535) publishes *DE Occulta Philosophia* (*occult philosophy*) which is a book on magic, because it will fascinate the people of the Renaissance. According to him, there are three worlds. Firstly, the elemental world, that is, the world below which include the natural bodies consisting of four elements (earth, water, air, fire). Then the celestial world, that is, the heavens and the stars and finally the intellectual world, that of higher intelligences, called angels, spirits, and demons, where each lower pavement is governed by a superior thing, and receives the influences of the forces of that superior power, so that the Archetype and supreme craftsman himself, by the angels, the heavens, the stars, the elements, the animals, the plants, the metals, the stones, spread the powers of his omnipotence over the humans , for the service for which all these things were created. Therefore, the magi (those who are trained in occult, hidden things and magic) think that man can rise through his degrees, through each of these worlds up to the Archetype himself. Artisan and primary cause of all things, from which all things exist and from which all things proceed. That we cannot only benefit from those forces which are in the noblest things, but also, in attracting top news from them. Thus the magi seek the forces of the elemental world through medicine and natural philosophy using various mixtures of natural things.

Then they connect the heavenly virtues to these by the rays and influences of the celestial world following the rules of astrologers and

[110] Ibid., pp.60.

disciplines of mathematics. Finally, they strengthen and strengthen all these things by the powers of the different intelligences by means of sacred religious ceremonies.

He adds that the magic discipline that has received many powers, with high mysteries, embraces the deepest contemplation of secret things. These include the power, quality, substance and power, as well as the knowledge of nature as a whole. The magic discipline learns how things differ from each other and how they agree, producing from it its wonderful effects. That is, they proceed by uniting powers of things by the application of things to each other, that is, to those which are adapted to undergo their actions and by uniting and relating things inferior to the contributions and superior powers. He believes that it is the highest and most sacred philosophy, it is the absolute fulfillment of all the noblest philosophy. He considers that the perfect rationality of magic must embrace three disciplines: physics, mathematics and knowledge of aspects of the configurations of stars and theologies. Physics shows the qualities of things where the occult, hidden properties of each being are revealed. The mathematics and the knowledge of the aspects and configurations of the stars, reveal the power and the sublime property of each thing and as for theology, it shows the immaterial substances that distribute and direct all things.

In reality, Cornelius Agrippa exhibits perfect knowledge that takes into account the natural and supernatural, human and divine, terrestrial and celestial realities. From these laws stem the divine science, the natural sciences, and the various sciences. These laws, when mastered, they produce miraculous and prodigious results, because the perfect magic, as Agrippa so aptly puts it, leads to this understanding of optimal laws and realities described above. This is because the perfect magic is the constant practice of good for the purposes that we propose and exceptionally for the complete development of man. The achievements in the field of development that have led humanity to levels never equaled emanate from magic and high knowledge. What man has achieved in all areas is simply magic: cultural, scientific, technological, industrial, economic. On the other hand, the constant practice of evil also leads to negative magical effects, which is why we talk about the magic of goodness and the magic of evil as effectively defined in the French dictionary *Le petit Larousse* éditions 2000.

Leon the Hebrew (1465-1525) is a physician, philosopher, and poet. He is credited with one of the most interesting works between Judaism and Platonism. He is the eldest son of the great biblical commentator and councilor of princes, Isaac Abranavel. In his work *Dialoghi d'amore (Dialogues of love)*, published in 1535 in Italian, he stages two characters with evocative names: Sophie (of Sophia, wisdom), eager to increase her knowledge and philon (philien, to love), who answers questions of his beloved on the nature of love, eros, on his definition in the world of creation and on his divine origin. The power of eros is magnified there, it unites the inorganic elements, connects between the living beings, causes the movements of the stars, governs the angelic intellects, and animates the divine life. For this author, love is dynamic. It's the creative and transformative energy that travels through the chain of beings from divinity to chaos and goes back the same way in the opposite direction. Leon considers that the very existence of the body is good because it is conceived by God for the reproduction of the species. For him, he rejects Plato's dualistic anthropology and advocates an organic conception of the individual, even of creation. For him, matter, body and pleasure find their place in God's plan.

Man grasped in these dimensions the trace of the presence of God in creation and not the sign of remoteness or its absence[111]. This idea will resonate with other modern thinkers, such as Giordano Bruno and even more Baruch Spinoza who will go to identify God with nature.

Paraclèse, by his real name Philippe Aureole-Theophraste Bombast of Hohenheim (1493-1541). He is of Swiss origin and was one of the most daring doctors of the sixteenth century, he proposes a medicine that is new, compared to that of antiquity until the Renaissance. In his book La Grande Chirurgie, published in Germany in 1536, Paraclèse defines man as a small universe (microsome) and each organ of man corresponds to a planet. In reality, the correspondence between man and the universe is found in medicine from antiquity to Renaissance. Thus for the fathers of Western medicine, the Greeks Hippocrates (406-356 BC) and Galen, the universe and man are composed of four elements (earth, water, air, fire).

In man, these elements are associated with four fluids: moods, blood, yellow bile, black bile or phlegm. The state of health depends on the balance of moods in the body, and on the other hand, a disease is caused by the breaking of this balance. Paraclèse refutes this idea of the composition of the body by these moods. For him, man and the universe

[111] Le Point Références, mars avril, 2011, op.cit., pp 70-73.

consist of three chemical principles: sulfur, salt and mercury. And each individual has an (archaic) mind that regulates body functions and health. Every mineral, vegetable, or animal being has an analogy or correspondence with the stars of heaven. The doctor who knows his correspondence and who manipulates these substances through experimentation can find good therapies for his patient. For example, an alchemical preparation based on iron, a substance linked to the Mars planet and rich in sulfur, is the analogous remedy for blood, which is in harmony with this planet. This quest for analogy, typical of the Renaissance, may seem odd, but it allowed to overcome old therapies, based on the use of natural remedies such as herbal teas and invasive maneuvers, such as bleeding or surgical procedures. Paraclèse requires the doctor to produce drugs himself, he is considered the source of homeopathy and chemical medicine, which uses non-natural drugs to fight against diseases. He was considered the Luther of medicine. From 1580, a flourishing of publications of his works, translated from German into Latin and Latin into vernacular languages, fueled the debate between the different medical schools, particularly in France, where in 1666 the Faculty of Medicine of Paris accepted the most famous chemical remedies, antimony for its emetic virtues and purgatives[112].

This epic of the humanists of the 16th century continues with the Brussels physician Andreas Vesalius (1514-1543). Andreas Vesalius marks the history of ideas, like Copernicus, by his book in anatomy, entitled La fabrique du corps humain(The Making of the Human Body). His book changes the way of practicing dissection forever and reveals to the anatomical doctors the true way of grasping, the true structure of the human body. It is the first work of anatomy based on the personal observations of a doctor and not on the transmission of book knowledge. Before Vesalius, anatomical knowledge was based essentially on the reading and commentary of the anatomical works of the Greek physician

Pergamon Galen (129-210), considered with Hippocrates as the founding fathers of Western medicine. However, Galen had not dissected human bodies. He based his observations on the research of the doctors who preceded him, as well as on the dissection of animals, including monkeys, pigs and dogs. Galen attributes to human bodies,

---

112 Ibid., pp.74-75.

what he finds in the bodies of animals, hence errors transmitted to the anatomists of the Middle Ages and the Renaissance. Vesalius corrects more than two hundred errors of Galen. Despite criticism no one will be able to continue practicing anatomy through books, at the risk of not being credible anymore. Vesalius teaches doctors to seek the source of knowledge in the nature of the body. Realdo Colombo and Gabriel Fallope are two of the famous anatomists who continue his work by describing the main structures of the human body. It was also after studying at the University of Padua (Italy) where Vesalius taught in 1628, that William Harvey (1578-1657) published his major work on blood circulation. The factory of the human body of Vesalius is rich in image. One of the errors that Vesalius corrects concerns the structure of the liver. He opposes the tradition that the liver is divided into five lobes by demonstrating that Galen attributed to the human liver the structure of the livers of the dog and the pig that he dissected[113].

The Renaissance operated in Europe, a major cultural revolution that has enabled this continent, formed to the perfect divine culture and the centrality of God in society, to move to the centrality of man and his reason in the social life. Beautiful evolution. Humanism and its fundamentals observed in Greek and Roman antiquity find the letters of nobility and progress even more. It is the renewal of the man and his thought. Man relies on the knowledge acquired in the Holy Scriptures, and the ancient Greco-Roman culture, to pass to deep human, academic, artistic, scientific and technical knowledge. This is a Copernician revolution, because science takes a real boom in medicine and economics. The omnipotence of the Church and the Papacy is beginning to crumble for the benefit of man and the idea that man has intrinsic qualities and potentialities to assert. Hence the accelerated development of education and scholarship. This movement is gaining momentum in the Enlightenment era.

---

[113] Ibid., pp.78-79.

Chapter VI

The contribution of the Enlightenment of the 18th century to the rise of the Western Christian and humanity: the triumph of the reason of the new, perfect and creative Man. An experience to be meditated by Africa

As we have already said, all tested knowledge is useful at all times. The century of European Enlightenment remains a period of reference in the evolution of knowledge. It still illuminates humanity today with its powerful impact.

The Revolution of knowledge that began in the middle Ages and the Renaissance, grew in the 18th century through the Revolution of ideas and the primacy of human reason. This evolution of man in knowledge is very lengthy. It is spread over millennia. It nevertheless takes an acceleration from the 15th century by the decisive contribution of the Holy Scriptures that fix the man in strong themes for a perfect training on the meaning he must give to his life. From a powerful divine spiritual base, man takes his flight to be master of his destiny and become more and more creator of various riches for his well-being. We have explained in the first part of the book that the true light is in God Himself, and this is what He gives to the man who communicates with Him by his word of truth. The century of European Enlightenment is an extension of this life of light that began in the fifteenth century. It is this divine light that opened the boulevard of knowledge that followed (chapter I, paragraph on the Bible and the supernatural knowledge God is light). According to Emmanuel Kant, the Enlightenment's motto is: "Have courage to use your own reason".

The 18th century, in Europe corresponds to the century of the Light. It continues and amplifies the spiritual, intellectual and cultural movement which vibrated Europe since the end of the 15th century. It is indeed a movement of the thought and the Lights of the mind. This movement is a long work of undermining the very foundations of traditional society and its dogmas. The lights of the mind, thought and knowledge still govern the world today.

The Enlightenment corresponds to a period of synthesis and not entirely original intervention. It absorbed the legacy of a thought that began in Europe since the end of the Middle Ages and whose ingredients were affirmed during the Renaissance. It emphasize both rationalism, empiricism and Epicureanism. Empiricism is a philosophical doctrine which places sensible experience at the origin of knowledge. Its main representatives are British: Francis Bacon, initiator of modern science, John Locke, Berkeley Gorge, David Hume[114].

Rationalism, on the other hand, is a doctrine which considers that all that exists has its reason for existence and cannot be considered in itself as unintelligible. It is also a doctrine according to which human knowledge proceeds from principles that are a priori independent from the experience of the senses. The rationalism that can be absolute (Plato, Descartes) or critical (Kant) is opposed to empiricism. It is a conception which admits in religion only that which is compatible with reason Petit Larousse (French Dictionary). Epicureanism is the doctrine of the Greek philosopher, Epicurus (342-271 BC). For this doctrine, the purpose of the blessed life is to achieve the absence of physical pain (aponia) and moral disorder (ataraxia).

The Enlightenment preaches the knowledge of the eternal laws, the history of peoples, affirm the plurality of cultures and the uniqueness of civilization. At the same time, they defend reason and passions, body and spirit, arts, sciences, artifice and naturalness, permeating all areas of intellectual creation: from philosophy to science through literature, law, and painting. It's a real revolution in ideas and knowledge. What is new is that ideas leave books to find their application in everyday life. A logical evolution of things, from theory to practice. This passage in the late 18th century will take the explosive forms: War of independence in America (1776 for the United States of America) and the French Revolution in 1989[115].

Thus, knowledge with a capital "K" emancipates from all ideological control and the dogmas of religion. Autonomy is self-assertive, everyone must be able to manage their private and collective lives as they wish.

---

[114] Le Point Hor-Série, n°26 Mars-Avril 2010, Des Lumières, les textes fondamentaux. P. 8.

[115] Le Point Références n° 26, Idem.

The sovereign people can formulate the laws, the fundamentals that will govern their lives and choose the people who will conduct the affairs of the country. Because of this plurality of autonomy, the powers within a state must prevent each other from becoming absolute[116]. Individual freedom restricts popular freedom and the opposite is also true. The concern for the common good restricts the aspiration to personal satisfaction. At the same time, the requirement of autonomy is not absolute. It is limited on one side by the finality attributed to public action: to serve the well-being of the population by the principle of universality. That is, the recognition of a dignity equal to all the members of the human species, which are called human rights today[117].

I- Understanding the Enlightenment movement in the development of man

To understand what the Enlightenment movement was, we must go back to the foundation of Europe in the 15th and 17th centuries. It was a strictly hierarchical society, where power was monarchical and beliefs dominated by religion. Science, culture and education were held on a leash by dogmas that reduced the scope of debate and innovation. The economic system was rigid and very unequal, because the main resource, the land was controlled by a powerful aristocracy. The majority of the population lived in a state of obvious subordination. The law protected privileges first. It was necessary that these dogmas be challenged by the majority. It was this extraordinary movement that we called the Enlightenment, powerful in its significance, and whose consequences were unique in their magnitude. It still governs the world today. This order is based on a set of shared rights and fundamentals: individual liberty, democracy, gender and race equality, freedom of the press and expression, and on the principle that the state exists only to ensure the well-being of the majority. It is clear that it is the opposite of the legal system that prevailed in the 17th, 18th, and even 19th centuries.

This upheaval leaves the Renaissance, the reform and the cultural, spiritual and intellectual, industrial revolution far behind.

It is the conjunction of several factors: religious tolerance, the impact of new scientific discoveries, particularly those of Copernicus and

[116] Ibid., pp.8.
[117] Idem.

Galileo, on the rotation of the planets around the sun, the first rebellions to the royal tyranny. The Enlightenment philosophers affirm the falsehoods of the concepts with which the majority considers the fundamental things of life. They say that revising them could significantly improve human existence. Society would thus be more stable and tolerant, which is the main concern of Bayle, safer and more stable to Hobbes, more rational in his approach to Descartes, and also more distinctly oriented and fairer in his treatment of minorities and the weakest. Spinoza goes further in the revolution of the spirits. His philosophy challenges the principle of a divine order, a fixity of species. For the first time, it gives supremacy to science and reason. From its concepts, society will be better able to withstand religious manipulation, autocracy, oligarchies and dictators. It can become more democratic, freer and more egalitarian. He is the first philosopher to proclaim that the Democratic Republic is the best political organization. He will oppose philosophy to theology, the existing world that would be the best in the future world. All these contributions make him the most outstanding figure of the radical Enlightenment[118].

At the end of the 18th century, the gap between the respectable Enlightenment that tries to find a balance between faith and reason and the radical Enlightenment that claims that only reason directs the world, widens. The most important thing in the Age of Enlightenment is this remarkable evolution in the appropriation of perfect fundamental ideas and values that free man from ignorance. The divine is not discarded, it also leaves room for the assertion of man as God's indispensable partner in the future of the universe where his role is vital. It is really a period of synthesis between the divine knowledge and the human knowledge, the one where the man discovers that he has a capital role to play in the future of the world and that it is not the product of the forces which handle it. It is this new and creative man completely renewed in his intelligence and abilities who is the powerful actor of the development of the Western Christian. This basic logic remains valid until today for any country struggling for its development. He must absolutely fight for the constant improvement of the man.

[118] Ibid., pp.112.

II- The Principal Philosophers and Thinkers of this time

The Principal Philosophers and Thinkers of this period are: Hugo Grotius and Samuel Pufendorf defenders of the School of Natural Law, Spinoza, Leibnitz and the cult of reason, the British John Locke with religious tolerance, George Berkeley and David Hume with the empiricism, Adams Smith with the moral foundations of liberalism and market freedom, the French Montesquieu and the spirit of the laws, Diderot and Alembert or the spirit of the encyclopedia, Voltaire and the philosophical dictionary portable. There is Rousseau and the social contract, the Germans Christian Wolff and Kant (on the systematization of the reason and the criticism of the reason), Italy with the Illuminismo, the right with Beccaria, and the history with Vico.

Hugo Grotius, a Dutchman, the father of the law of nations, and Samuel Pufendorf, a Saxon, are the greatest representatives of the School of Natural Law, whose influence has been considerable on Enlightenment philosophy. The law of war and peace, which is Hugo Grotius's main work, is an impressive attempt to base international law (the law of nations) on the modern theory of just war, while recognizing sovereignty States, this thesis tries to limit the use of force. He is also at the origin of a coherent conception of law that introduces modern elements into a traditional framework. He proposes to think natural law in its relations with other forms of law. Natural law is distinguished first of all from that which it calls human, resulting from the conventions of men, but also from divine voluntary law. The latter raises commands from the divine will alone. These do not derive from nature itself, and contrary to the principles of natural law, they cannot be discovered by reason alone. Natural law, on the contrary, is founded on reason and is immutable, explains Grotius, for God himself cannot change what is right by reason. He adds that even if God does not care about human affairs, or if he does not exist, the principles of law should be held to be true. This is a Stoic doctrine and Grotius is classic on this point. Since Stoicism comes from the Greek "stoapoikile", named after a portico of the agora of Athens, where the followers of this movement met.

He argues that wisdom and happiness lie in living in accordance with the reason that governs the soul and the universe. But his thought takes on a new significance in the 18th century: he seeks to free himself from religion revealed for a natural law, established by a watchmaking God who rules the world.

Samuel Pufendorf (1632-1694) is another great theorist of natural law and close to Grotius, but his doctrine takes into account to a greater extend, the thesis of Thomas Hobbes (1588-1689) who considers that there is no absolute disagreement between the search for personal interest and the respect for the law. He demonstrates this in his book, *Du droit de la nature des gens, (The Right of the Nature of People (1672),* where he affirms the primacy of selfish self-love. This self-sufficiency is partially compensated, according to it, by a natural provision and desires for oneself at the same time following a logic that can extend to the whole humanity. This synthesis of sociability and self-love allows Pufendorf to place men and women at the center of the law. Widely distributed, the works of Grotius and Pufendorf announce many themes of Enlightenment philosophy. If they accept the absolutist state that still reigns at this time, they are already putting the rights of individuals first. They bind the natural law to the divine will, without absorbing it. They temper the theory of the social contract of the natural sociability of men, and thus make possible a distinction between the state and the society. This will flourish in the political economy[119].

Baruch Spinoza, born in Amsterdam in 1632, and Gottfried Wilhelm Leibniz of German origin exalt the power of reason, because the Enlightenment carries this value to its highest level, to give man the ability to take control of his own destiny. In 1670, Spinoza published his *Traité théologico-politique (Theologico-Political Treatise), L'éthique (Ethics)* in 1677. Spinoza poses the themes that will upset Europe and constitute the world of Enlightenment: the freedom of individual judgment and its expression, the denunciation of superstition, the conception of a political right based on the distinction between the public and the private. The Treatise ends with an apology for freedom of thought and religious tolerance. Spinoza is already sending the project to enlighten the people so as to get them out of servitude. For him, liberation first passes through the freeing vis-à-vis the religious authorities. This is why the *Treatise* proposes a new method for interpreting the Bible. It is a question of fighting against those who claim to derive from the sacred text that human reason is fundamentally corrupt and therefore cannot lead to the truth or to the salvation of the soul.

[119] Le point Références. Ibid., pp.14-15.

In *Ethics*, Spinoza demonstrates the opposite: reason alone can lead us to bliss. He defends natural light. The reason against obscurantism and religious fanaticism. He holds the liberty for the dearest and the sweetest of goods.

Leibniz opposes the interpretation mechanism of the universe in vogue at the time in favour of a rational explanation of things. It is to him that one owes the formulation of the famous principle of reason, according to which a thing or an event must necessarily have a sufficient reason to account for its existence if not, it does not exist. Leibniz imagines God as a sort of supreme monad (from Greek Monas, unity). Leibniz likens the monad to a soul that would arrange all the movements of the universe in a pre-established harmony according to reason. In front of the infinity of the possible worlds, God chose the best of the worlds, ours. The rationalism of Leibniz will become a school in Germany and will prevail as a model to the German Light. Martin Heidegger (1889-1976) will see in Leibniz, the most German of German thinkers and in the principle of sufficient reason the body that implicitly governs philosophy since Plato[120].

The British **John Locke (1632-1704)** is one of the great inspirers of the Enlightenment, not only his theory of knowledge but also his political philosophy, he is also the most important theoretician of religious tolerance that will be at the heart of the fights of the 18th century. Locke writes in a Protestant England where the Anglican churches tolerate dissidents badly, and the rival churches or sects are not more tolerant than they are. Most believers believe that it is the duty of the state to defend religious truth. Locke argues from the dual point of view of political philosophy and religion to show that while the state has no right to constrain consciences, true religion has no interest in exercising such a constraint.

But above all, in his conception of the role of the civil government, what legitimizes the latter to act is that it has been established by men in accordance with the natural law which fixes its ends and limits.

Men accept political authority because it guarantees their security and allows them to peacefully enjoy the goods of this world by protecting them against what violates the rights of others. But they have not given up what is obvious, which cannot lead them to give up what

[120] Ibid., pp.16-17 et pp. 24-25.

they consider necessary for their salvation. England and the United States have illustrated a tolerance based on the coexistence of Protestant religions.

Adam Smith (1723-1790) is the founding father of economic liberalism. The Enlightenment is to a great extent synonymous with freedom. That is, political freedom against absolutism, freedom of worship against intolerance, freedom of the press against censorship, economic freedom against monopoly, protectionism and corporatism. The champion of this freedom is Adam Smith, Scottish economist and philosopher, author of the famous book, *L'enquête sur la nature et les causes de la richesse des nations* (*The Inquiry into the Nature and Causes of the Wealth of Nations) 1776*. Before Adam Smith, the liberal doctrine had never been so systematically and strongly argued. The most famous thesis of the investigation is that the market self-regulates in order to coordinate all the requests and all the offers coming from the private interest, as the men were directed by an invisible hand. This metaphor is that, private interests, while working to satisfy themselves, serve the same public interest, even if they do it without knowing. Adam Smith links the effectiveness of economic exchange to the pursuit of private interest, and that is why this research must be allowed to proceed as freely as possible, without constraining it too much by the State. As Adam Smith's other great book, *La Théorie des sentiments moraux (The Theory of Moral Sentiments)*, teaches, the search for interest necessarily involves sympathy with others, which leads to moral evaluation. Even if the market must remain so free, he needs the state to accomplish, according to him, three indispensable duties: national security, civil peace and the burdens of public utility. Today, we can speak of the sovereign duties of the state (security, education, infrastructure construction, health, etc.). "*L'enquête" The Inquiry*, was quickly considered a reference work for economic thought, and its success steadily increased in the 19th century. The capitalists of the industrial revolution found their justification, while the lights of the classical school, like David Ricardo (1772-1823) or Jean Baptiste Say (1767-1832) found their inspiration. Today, this book continues to feed the economic thinking of the neoclassical school at the Chicago School.

More generally, "*L'enquête*" (The Inquiry) feeds contemporary discussions on the opposition between socialism and liberalism, the development of the third world, globalization, and the reliability of economic prescriptions. He stimulates intellectual exchanges[121]. It emphasizes that: "It is obvious that every individual, wherever he is, is much more able than any statesman or legislator to discern the kind of activity his capital can support in his country and whose product will undoubtedly have the greatest value"[122].

The Enlightenment is also animated by the French:

Charles Louis de Secondat, Baron de la Brède et de Montesquieu (1689-1755). He occupies a singular and atypical place in the French lights. He has always defended parliaments where most philosophers rely instead on absolute monarchy to advance the cause of the Enlightenment. He is a staunch opponent of the spirit of uniformity that impels his contemporaries to impose the progress of reason against the diversity of customs. In his major work, *DE L'esprit des Lois (The Spirit of the Laws)* (1748), he defines these as the necessary relationships that derive from the nature of things. Montesquieu gives a large place to human freedom. But the necessity that Montesquieu talks about, plays in the human world in an original way that distinguishes it from God and at the same time from the material world. On the one hand, divinity has established an order that it has no reason to transgress since its laws express its perfection. On the other hand the material world is governed by laws that are inherently invariable. Between the two there are men, intelligent and sensitive beings who enact the laws which aim at correcting the fallible nature of man and who understand the laws of the religion, that is, the moral and the political and civil laws. Made to live in the society, the man could forget the others, the legislators returned to his duties by the political and civil laws[123].

Count Buffon, born Georges Louis Leclerc (1707-1788) was a child of the Enlightenment by his diversity, and also by his desire to transmit knowledge accessible to the cultured minds of his time. He successively studied law, botany and mathematics. He was admitted to the Academy of Sciences in 1734. In 1739, the king appointed him steward of the garden of medicinal plants and the cabinet of natural history (the current plant garden of Paris). He designed major redevelopment and extension works to make this botanical garden a place of research.

---

[121] Ibid., pp.50-51.
[122] Idem.
[123] Ibid., pp.60-61.

He planted species from all over the world and enriches the collections of mineral species or species of animals brought back by the great explorers. The garden is a digest of the whole of nature and serves as a foundation for his great work "*Histoire naturelle" (Natural History)*. The ambition is to embrace all the objects of the universe, coupled with a rationalist ideal that bears the mark of the encyclopaedic Enlightenment project. Natural history will be divided into four groups: general and particular natural history, natural history of minerals. This is a monumental sum of thirty-six volumes. Despite numerous errors, his classification will be revolutionary and foundational in the study of natural sciences. Innovative as well, his reflection on the origin of the species that he reunites in families prefigures the works of Charles Darwin on the evolution of the living species revolutionized the biology. Natural history was one of the great successes of the 18yh century. He became Count of Buffon by decision of Louis XV in 1773, and beneficiary for the cabinet of the king, of the gifts of the sovereigns Catherine II of Russia (1729-1796) and Frederick II of Prussia known as, the Great (1712-1786), who all admired the Enlightenment. At his death, he is one of the most illustrious representatives of the Enlightenment's spirit of scientific discovery.

Diderot (1713-1784) and Jean Rond d'Alembert (1717-1783) are responsible for preparing and publishing the Encyclopaedia, a radical and daring project. Diderot is already known as the author of sulphurous texts and famous for their impiety. On the contrary, D'Alembert appears as a scientist with undisputed legitimacy. Their ambition is to bring together in a single work the body of knowledge acquired by man. This venture will require the participation of over a hundred writers and will ultimately represent a set of seventeen volumes. This gigantic work of compilation and popularisation translates into itself an almost absolute confidence in the powers of the human mind as in scientific and technical progress. The authors do not content themselves with describing knowledge, but try to submit it to the critical mind. The editors turn the encyclopaedia into a weapon of battle to question the main foundations of the Ancient Regime. Articles give rise to attacks on superstition and intolerance. Other contributions are an opportunity to denounce absolutism and to praise the English parliamentary monarchy.

In his article "political authority", Diderot asserts that the sovereign is bound to his people by a tacit contract. According to him, when a prince fails in his duties, he loses all rights he has over his subjects. Faced with these attacks by the monarchy and Catholicism, the publication of the Encyclopaedia is suspended twice in 1752 and 1759. D'Alembert tired of these incessant attacks abandons the direction of the book. Finally, Diderot managed to publish the Encyclopaedia and the last volumes appeared in 1772, after twenty years of fierce battle. He is supported by the head of the royal censorship, Chrétien guillaume de Lamoignon de Malesherbes.

The encyclopedia has a decisive influence on intellectual life in France and in Europe. Voltaire sees in it a movement of the human spirit[124]. The encyclopaedia has become a major work in the pantheon of the Enlightenment. It allowed Diderot to develop a radical and strictly materialistic thought, resolutely atheist, while most of his contemporaries Voltaire and Rousseau adopted a deism more or less detached from orthodoxy. Deism is a belief in the existence of a personal God, which cannot be revealed.

Voltaire (1694-1778) is the author of the portable philosophical dictionary. This pocket dictionary mode allows him to continue the fight against superstitions, abuses of religious power. He blames the Encyclopaedia for being too cautious. This dictionary is a synthesis of Voltaire's political thought. Articles discussed, devoted to religion (atheism, fanaticism, miracles, superstitions, tolerance, persecution) attest to an anti-clerical party. Contagious as it is, this denunciation never goes to athcism. Voltaire also recognizes the existence of a creative principle, while believing that this architect of the universe, this great watchmaker does not exert influence on the march of the world. The portable dictionary is a veritable war machine directed against religious authorities. The choice of the portable proves the relevance of the choice of Voltaire.

Jean Jacques Rousseau (1712-1778) published in 1762, his most famous work, *Du contrat social (The social contract)*. The chapter on the social pact makes it possible to understand why we saw in Rousseau an authentic individualist and the founder of modern democracy.

For Rousseau, just as Thomas Hobbes (1588-1679), the social contract that succeeds to the state of nature is not a historical hypothesis on the beginnings of society, but a means of conveying the meaning of

---

124 Ibid., pp.66-67.

the political condition. For Hobbes, the state of nature was a state of war, that is, all against all, a state born with the absence of a common power, and the main function of the state is to guarantee peace and security. For Rousseau, the state of war springs from human nature, for man is naturally good, but he is not naturally social: men are born free and independent of each other and are led to live in society only by an external necessity, as soon as they live together and begin to compare with each other, the state of war becomes inevitable and it is necessary, says Hobbes, that a political power restores peace. The big difference with Rousseau is that this power also preserves freedom, which is possible only if it is not separated from society and if everyone takes an equal part in the elaboration of the law. Rousseau intervenes in this historical process as a radical individualist for whom the individual submits to the political authorities only because in uniting with all he obeys only himself and always remains free. He accepts the total alienation of each partner with all his rights. Rousseau seems foreign to the liberal tradition, whose main concern is to protect the rights of individuals especially against the state and not only to guarantee the state of rights. Rousseau's thought was associated with the French revolution as an implementation of the ideas of the social contract.

The Germans **Christian Wolff and Emmanuel Friedrich Hegel** fuel the European Enlightenment with an emphasis on reason.

Christian Wolff (1679-1754) gave a real framework of thought to the Enlightenment, through his monumental work of forty volumes. That which Hegel refers to as a practical wisdom, proposes to conceive philosophy as an operational wisdom reflected in action but also as a worldly wisdom (Weltweisheit in German) capable of attracting a large public in German universities. He advocates a rationalism closer to common sense than that of Leibniz, his compatriot. He recasts the notion of being, of ontology by taking again the principles of sufficient reason without contradicting of Leibniz. He treats ontology according to the scientific method, the only way capable of building a real system to put the truth in full evidence. He believes that the principles of ontology direct the understanding in the knowledge of the truth. He brings back the confused notions of Scholastics to fruitful notions, by drawing the general principles of knowledge, using the demonstrative method.

Moreover, he considers that Chinese morality, nourished by the philosophy of Confucius (the 6th century BC), opens up a veritable field of experimentation to validate his rationalist approach. For him, there is no need for divine commandments to this atheist people, which shows that recourse to reason is sufficient to build a moral life. It is only a question of achieving a distinct knowledge of good and evil by examining the nature and reason of things. It reveals, for example, the approach of Tsem Tsu, one of the most distinguished disciples of Confucius, who proves that the main occupation of the wise heroes of antiquity was to perfect their reason from day to day, that is, their faculty to think, to judge well and discern, to seek wisdom.

Emmanuel Kant (1724-1804) in his article to the magazine Berliner Monatsschrift, titled *Qu'est-ce que les Lumières, (*What's The Enlightenment), gives an answer that will become canonical. From the first sentence, he defines the Enlightenment as the exit of man from his minority of which he is himself responsible. By minority, he understands the state of guardianship in which men rely on others. To engage in the Enlightenment, requires the courage to use one's own understanding.

It is not by chance that the Enlightenment has revived the slogan of the Latin poet **Horace** (1st century BC) "dare to know". This is, according to Kant, the motto of the poet of the Enlightenment. For him the Enlightenment cannot develop where there is no freedom to do what he calls a use of reason. Liberty, which consists for the scientists, to be able to write and to be read. It is therefore the public use of reason. He adopts a phrase of his monarch, Frederick II of Prussia: "Reason as much as you want and on what you want, but obey." Kant develops this conception of the use of reason in the criticism of pure reason. Instead of starting from objects to find the reason, we must examine how they regulate our reason. An approach that involves giving up any claim to know what is beyond our experience (God or the immortality of the soul). Thus with Kant, reason becomes critical of itself, and no longer conceives as a treasure held by an enlightened elite, but as a process of public and open construction[125].

Towards the end of the Age of Enlightenment, Hegel, George Wilhelm Friedriech (1770-1837), German idealistic philosopher, in his system he claims that absolute knowledge is achieved by a reconciliation of thought with reality. His philosophy identifies the being and the thought in a unique principle, the concept (intellectual

---

[125] Ibid., pp.88-101.

representation of an object conceived by the mind), of the latter, Hegel describes the development by means of the dialectic (continuation of rigorous reasoning), of which he makes it a rational method of thought and the very life of the concept and its history. He is credited with among his works: *Phénoménologie de l'esprit* (Phenomenology of the Mind) 1807, *La science de la logique* (The Science of Logic) 1812-1816, *Encyclopédie des sciences philosophiques* (Encyclopaedia of Philosophical Sciences) 1817.

III- Italy is distinguished in the Enlightenment with the Illuminismo

Two Italian thinkers emerge: **Cesare Beccaria (1738-1794)** and **Giambattista Vico (1688-1744).** Beccaria is distinguished by his book published in 1764, Dei delitti e delle pene (offenses and punishments), it is to this book that the Western world owes the gradual remission of torture and the death penalty. It poses the problem of the right to punish for a just city. In order for the judges not to consider the crime as a sin any longer, he advocates the secularisation of norms to definitively separate the religious from the penal. He claims the decriminalization of homosexuality and suicide, develops a plea for the accused, the abolition of judicial torture, torture and capital punishment for ordinary crimes. It requires a legal codification of offenses and punishments and advises the prevention of crime through egalitarian rights and education. Beccaria sets out the paradigm of criminal modernity, which will lead to the rule of law in France with the adoption of the first Penal Code in 1791, which inspired Leopard II. A law that abolishes torture and capital punishment by introducing penalties proportional to the offenses. Having placed the reason and the social contract before God and the kings to renew justice according to the Enlightenment, the criminal humanism of Beccaria founds the ethics of the right to punish indispensable in democracy.

Giambattista Vico is a jurist and historian. It is marked by Plato, Tacitus, Grotius and Francis Bacon (initiator of modern science by his principles of an inductive and experimental method). His major book is *scienza nuava.* Vico develops a comparative historical method which returns to the past in the prism of the present. The finality of knowledge is not, according to him, erudition, but the good government of the city. Vico sees history as a cycle at three periods: age of the gods, age of heroes, age of men who trace the evolution of humanity, from barbarism to civilization, progress of peace over war, laws, commerce, and government. Rational facts rather than metaphysical speculations explain human history. His physical thought is similar to other Enlightenment philosophers, sensitive to progress in history such as Montesquieu, Rousseau or Diderot[126].

The European Enlightenment of the 18th century marks a very important articulation in the history of humanity, because the Western man shakes and jostles the dogmas, the superstitions, the gravities and the authorities (powers of the monarchs and the Church) in which he was enclosed like in a tight gangue. He seeks to free himself by his own reason and his own intellectual faculties and aspires to progress. He also gradually aspires to the era of modern science. As Kant so aptly puts it, he goes out of his minority to reach his spiritual, intellectual and moral majority. It is really a new and creative man who emerges from this long growth. He aspires to all the freedoms and the aspiration of a clear social contract between the governments and the governed, according to the relevant theories of Thomas Hobbes, John Locke, Rousseau and all those who claim it. It is this liberating and enlightened vision of the man that still dominates the world today.

The Age of Enlightenment develops a body of fundamental values that have been gradually codified to become universal and dominate the world: the lights of the spirit, the divine values, knowledge, science, technique, reason, logic, perfection, the perfection of man, the affirmation of man, peace, the dignity of the human species, creativity, innovation, human rights, freedom, plurality of opinions, the people sovereignty, freedom of worship, religious tolerance, economic freedom, liberalism, equality of race and gender, the rule of law, the debate of ideas, the social contract, democracy, the republic, the man as master of his destiny, security, peace, idealism, dream, powerful ambition, matter, good, progress, discernment of good and evil, schooling and radical change of mentalities.

This new reading of things has opened the door to global and total knowledge for the progress of man. It completely undermined the foundations of the old order in the West: the unique thought, the spirit of inequality, uniformity, arbitrariness, authoritarianism, absolutism,

---

126 Ibid., pp.106-107.

obscurantism, domination, exploration of man, superstition, dogmatism, intolerance, persecution, and evil.

Development therefore proceeds from knowledge. This is a long chain that each human race, each era, each culture enriches by its contribution of the perfect fundamental values . These values, which are specific to a given culture and which are imposed by force and relevance, enrich and serve all humanity engaged in a common destiny. Ancient and pre-colonial Africa, ancient Egypt, ancient Greece, ancient Rome, the Middle Ages, the European Renaissance, the European Enlightenment operate in this long chain that inherit the centuries that followed, until our days. Africa must connect to this logical understanding of knowledge, for Africa has been the first in the chain in ancient times, to appropriate and contribute to strengthening it, by its fruitful contribution in all areas: culture, science, technology. There is no fatality that suggests that some people are producing ideas and systems of thought conducive to development and not others. The faculty of thought conducive to development and not others. The faculty of thought and reasoning is innate in man, it belongs to each people to develop it powerfully, understanding very well the fundamental axis of the knowledge of the life and the future of the man which pushes him to perfection, a stage that inexorably leads to development.

The Enlightenment of the Spirit allows man to assume his divinity and humanity in a fruitful and dynamic synthesis. In sum, we see how total and perfect knowledge gradually triumphs for the integral development of man and human societies. The West has long shown the way, thanks to its successes in the spiritual, scientific, technology, financial and material domains. Africa had also begun this salutary path, unfortunately slowed down over several centuries by slavery and colonization.

With the liberation of thought, energies, intelligences, social forces, happy evolutions could only progressively take place by the spiritual, intellectual, scientific, cultural and moral revolution of the 15th, 16th and 18th century's revolution. Then from the 19th-century consumer and leisure society and knowledge, to the information and communication technologies (ICT) of the 21st century and other dramatic transformations of the next centuries, thanks to the always abundant and triumphant knowledge. We find that true knowledge comes from God, the original creator of the heavens and the earth, to man who found his way which led him to the development that we observe with admiration.

IV- The lessons that Africa can draw from this revolution of knowledge

Africa therefore has before it, clearly exposed, the path that leads to global development. That is, all spiritual, intellectual, moral, civic, scientific, technical and technological knowledge. Africa must not neglect any knowledge. For divine knowledge is at the beginning or even at the end of knowledge. She is the alpha and omega of all truth. It must be taken as a measure and basis of knowledge in order to grasp the logic and the full range of man's intelligence, wisdom and perfection. This long evolution of knowledge shows how the West has gradually adapted to it, in order to understand that it is a logic and a global process. The West itself has taken the true measure of the knowledge of God in the Middle Ages, to reach that of man through the great minds and thinkers of Egyptian, Greek and Roman antiquity. This allowed him to understand the alpha and omega of heavenly and earthly things, divine and human. From these perfect and sure fundamentals, his progressive supremacy over the rest of the world has become logical and understandable. It is this laborious and perfect logic that leads man to the light of knowledge which is the basis of European, American and even Japanese development. This must also inspire the African continent, adding his own genius, as we can see in the approaches of the emerging countries of Asia and Latin America, for their development.

Progressive perfect knowledge was therefore a prerequisite for the economic take-off of Europe and the countries that followed, such as the United States of America and Japan. The dominant features are the habit of logical reasoning, the scientific mind, interest in material wealth, hard work, ambition, competitive spirit and many other fundamental values. The practice of logical reasoning, associated with the study of nature, of the human body, of natural phenomena, has led Europeans to build modern science, that is, a co-ordinated body of knowledge that makes it possible to describe and classify the beings and objects that we encounter in the world (science of geology, botany, anatomy, the atom, etc.) and which makes it possible to describe and explain the functioning of the mechanisms offered by nature or created by man.

Science could only be constituted because it was able to rely on the writing that preserves the acquired knowledge and to transmit it to a large number of men of the same generation or of subsequent generations. It has found a field of dissemination which is constantly enlarged by the development of teaching, and has been extended into practical achievements (measuring instruments, apparatus and mechanisms) which have made it possible to verify hypotheses, establish a back and forth between theory and reality, and to allow science to make new progress[127].

In fact, the development of science and that of its practical applications (steam engine, machine tool, and electricity) have evolved together, so that industrial societies have been characterized by a considerable expansion of what is still called today the technical progress. This evolution has on the one hand allowed greater control of man over the world. It has also considerably increased the means of man's struggle against sickness and death, and it has made available to men, numerous and varied material wealth.

This long evolution of knowledge and techniques consequently led to the birth of industries in Europe for the optimal transformation of the goods therefore, added value.

[127] Jean Sauvy. Op.cit., p. 146.

Chapter VII

The Industrial Revolution, a logical consequence of the mastery of perfect fundamental values by the Western Christian world. An example that should serve Africa

The industrial revolution in the Western Christian world is the logical consequence of the cultural, human and social revolution that has been taking place in Europe since the 16th century. This Cultural Revolution profoundly transformed the mentalities of the Europeans. It allowed certain countries, such as England, France, Germany and also the United States of America, to start the industrial revolution. Japan without though not a Christian country has also achieved its cultural and industrial revolution.

These Christian European countries profoundly transformed their traditional mentality which was characterised, as a primitive underdeveloped space by ignorance, obscurantism, immobilism, serfdom, superstitions, and dogmas, exploitation of man, gravity, and inequality. This salutary transformation was effected by the combined action of great philosophers, men of science, and men of the Church. The knowledge of God, revealed by the Bible, the Hebrew law and the Christian law, has been a decisive contribution to breaking human ignorance. To the point that from the end of the 15th century and afterwards, a body of spiritual, intellectual, moral, civic, scientific and technological values was built, which produced a new and creative man capable of becoming a total master of his destiny. It is the combination of divine and human values that has been the essence of this tremendous spiritual revolution and mentalities. The Western Christian, by a happy combination of circumstances and divine grace, is the repository and incarnation of these values, both divine and rational, which have founded all modern history. We will discuss the cases of England, pioneer of the industrial revolution, the United States, which has masterfully assimilated the perfect fundamental values to build a great nation in the new continent, and Japan, which, without being Christian, but of Buddhist culture, has assimilated these scientific and technical values. Thus, the transformation of mentalities through the revolution of knowledge, ideas and techniques has led to the industrial development of Christian Europe. Begun in 1850, more than a century and a half ago, the industrial revolution has profoundly changed the practises of the world, marking it with the seal of inequality. The minority of countries and human beings who accomplished it has grown considerably and developed decade after decade. In 1870, the most prosperous country on the planet was nine times richer than the poorest, a century later the gap was multiplied, this ratio has increased to 45 (Jeune Afrique from March 15 to 22, 2014).

I- England, pioneer of the industrial revolution

The long evolution of divine and human mastery of knowledge made possible the industrial revolution in England. This revolution was a radical transformation in production techniques, thanks to the steam engine and electricity.

In the 19th century, England became the workshop of the world and the mother of the industrial revolution. This happy revolution was possible, as we have said, thanks to the appropriation of the perfect, sure values which have made man the master of his destiny. They are values of truth, dignity, justice, liberty, humanism, intelligence, wisdom, research, creativity, innovation, ambition, faith in man and his organisational skills, hard work, risk and daring, competitive spirit, desire to succeed and lead a better life, willingness to improve oneself and to do better, taste for the discovery and control of one's environment, etc. This conquering spirit and action in the transformation of the world, was embraced by the Christian Europe and England. They made it a weapon to establish the industrial revolution.

Indeed, the discovery of the steam engine and the innovations in the textile, iron and coal industries permitted, for the first time in history, the increase in the production of goods while reducing the painful laborious forms of production by human and animal[128]. England had the most capital and dominated the overseas trade. England was in all the four corners of the world thanks to the mastery of the seas. She had the most advanced credit techniques, so she was the country best placed to take advantage of these new technologies and consolidate her dominance over the world[129]. She also had control of the seas, which

[128] Eugène Nyambal. Op.cit., p. 1113.
[129] Idem.

allowed her to disseminate goods all over the world. England occupied India, part of China and Africa, Canada, Australia and the part that will become the United States.

Eugene Nyambal dwells on Hojoan Chang's excellent book Renverser l'échelle: les strategies de développement dans une perspective historique,(Reverse the ladder: development strategies from a historical perspective). The author recalls that during the first decades of its industrialisation, England practiced a voluntarist policy to promote strategic industries for a long time. This policy combined customs protection and lower tariffs on inputs, sometimes the ban on importation of textile products, as well as the attraction of skilled European workers and the limitation of technological flows to competing countries. It was based on the development of infrastructure including the construction of a system of canals and roads to facilitate the distribution of goods across the country. Finally, it relied on the modernisation of the shipbuilding industry and the adoption of laws obliging any country wishing to trade with England to use English ships[130].

Eugene Nyambal notes that England only adopted the rules of free trade in the middle of the 19th century after having acquired its technological superiority, sheltered from protectionist barriers, in order to widen its markets and prevent the emergence of competitors? This attitude provoked a rejection reaction in Germany, where economists urged the authorities to adopt a systematic policy of protecting infant industries on the pretext that free trade only benefited countries with the same level of development[131].

Germany also relied on a system of infant industry subsidies, as well as the creation of universal banks such as Deutsche Bank or Dresdner Bank to finance industries, oversee their performance and promote innovation. Consequently, Germany managed to accelerate the process of industrial catch-up on England. In fact most of the European countries used the same scheme that allowed them to acquire a certain technological base, in view of their industrialisation.

---

[130] Idem.

[131] Idem.

II- The tremendous success of the United States of America or the laboratory par excellence of the practice of perfect fundamental values

The United States of America is a typical example of the country that has practiced the perfect fundamental values in their fullness, rigour and strength. This led them to the position of first world power for three centuries today, that is from their first installation on the Massachusetts Bay in 1650, in the east coast of the territory which launched the adventure of the conquest of a vast space from East to West. The American dream of building a society where freedom, success, prosperity and happiness reign has become a reality that feeds every generation. This dream enabled the founding fathers and people to build strong political institutions, a prosperous economy and a vibrant culture. This success is the combined action of the practice of strong divine and human values, and the powerful ambition of a people sure of themselves. Elected by God (a chosen country), it is animated by the revolutionary ideas of the century, the European Enlightenment. This country has an area of 9,364,000 km² and has a population of more than 300 million inhabitants. The man who built the United States of America was this new man from Europe who had perfect knowledge and who developed it in the new continent. He even went further, because he maintained its paroxysm, a constant and durable spiritual rigour. The development of the United States of America has relied on strong institutions, freedom of enterprise in economics and a strong cultural identity.

1- Strong institutions

The constitution is the solid building on which the organization of American society is based. It was written in 1787 and adopted in 1788, more than a century after the occupation of the United States. For the first time, a constitution gives primacy to the people: "We the people", which replaced the British monarchy by the republic which is secular. This solid constitution has survived wars and crises. She makes success and happiness (pursuit of happiness). It instituted a society of freedom, democracy and a system of balance and separation of powers between the executive, the legislature and the judiciary, the famous "checks and balances", a system of weight and counterweight[132]. This idea of

---

[132] Le Point Hors-Séries, Faits et mythes n°1, Le Rève américain, avril, 2012, p.13.

balance of power was dear to Montesquieu, a French philosopher of the European Enlightenment. In the United States of America, according to this principle, each power controls the other, to the point that there is a blocking of powers between the executive and the legislature. The judiciary is independent of the executive and the legislature.

The judicial system is capped at the top by the Supreme Court which is the guarantor of the rights and liberties against the runaways and the tyranny of the majority. We often talk about the government of judges, to refer to the authority of justice. This well-oiled institutional machine has made some say that the constitution is of divine inspiration, to evoke a certain idea of mysticism that surrounds it, Americans are so proud of it. And for more than three centuries, it has only undergone 17 amendments since 1791. Despite weaknesses related to the blocking of relations between the executive and the legislature, the Senate and Congress (Gridlock) and between Republicans and Democrats. It is often difficult to come to a compromise, the Americans have trouble agreeing to reform it. It is necessary that two-thirds of the assemblies be approved in 38 states out of 50. It is true that the constitution was drafted for 4 million inhabitants circulating at the time on horseback. The founding fathers had not foreseen either the rise of the media or the size of the administration and the military apparatus. Their concern was above all to prevent the return of the monarchy and the tyranny it represented. For Prospect Magazine's Harold Meyerson, the gridlock is actually part of the power-balance system.

With its complicated architecture, the constitution is a constituent element which is exceptionally American. It is the subject of what must be called a cult in that, in the face of this situation, some believe that the system will evolve towards a strengthening of presidential power like the Gaullist type. The distinctiveness in the election of the American president. The latter is elected, not by direct universal suffrage, but from the states that designate the electors (527 in total) who must elect the president of the majority of 280 electors. He is elected for a four-year term renewable once.

The only exception was the case of President Franklin Delano Roosevelt elected four times in 1933, certainly to face the raging WWII, from 1944.

Land of resilience by its ability to manage its contradictions, the United States of America, slave and segregationist country, managed, thanks to this same constitution, to elect a president of black origin for the two mandates: President Barack Hussein Obama. He was elected in 2008 and 2012 successively, thereby giving him ability to exceed. Obama was solemnly sworn in as president on January 20th, 2013 at the Capitol, for his second term. This corresponds to a historic day, that of the respective feast of Martin Luther King, a fervent advocate against racial discrimination against black Americans and the President Abraham Lincoln who abolished slavery. President Obama swore on the Bibles of these two personalities that he admires. A strong symbol for this democracy of more than two centuries old.

2- The US economy based on freedom of enterprise

Americans have based their democracy on the sign of freedom and freedom of enterprise and private initiative. The British who land on the new continent are brave Christians fleeing royal absolutism and religious persecution. They dream of founding a society of freedom and a prosperous economy. They are mostly Puritan Protestant Christians animated by strong religious and moral values. These religious fervent, chased from England by religious persecution and royal authoritarianism are efficient, pragmatic, ambitious managers. They want to create a new world, to build on earth a kind of paradise where men would live free according to their puritanical ethics. The land is immense and incredibly rich, the frontier was constantly going west. The future was open[133].

Gradually, the dream of a little Protestant paradise turned into a bigger, crazier ambition. That is, to build the biggest, the most powerful, the most admirable country in the world, by the spirit of entrepreneurship where people would be stronger, more beautiful and healthier. A place where those who would bother could be successful. And it worked. In three centuries, America has become the world's leading power by its currency, the dollar, the compass of the universe[134]. This original ethic was also made of hard work, belief in God, family ethics, sense of good and evil, hope and optimism, denial of lies. America has become the country of winners, life in abundance, opportunity to succeed, and opportunities of all kinds. Americans have never doubted the accuracy of their ideals, because creativity is at the heart of their economy. They excel in scientific research and technology

---

[133] Ibid., p.84.

[134] Idem.

(Internet, Twitter, Facebook, and Silicon Valley). The American writer Douglas Kennedy did not fail to say that "the American century was the twentieth"[135]. This country loves success stories, such as the extraordinary fortune of Rockefeller, Bill Gates and many other fortunes. This country despises losers.

3- The United States of America, artisans of the second industrial revolution: that of the big multinational company

This entrepreneurial spirit allows American companies to be competitive. This success is also built on the emergence of big businesses. The United States is the architect of the birth of the multinational company. It was after the Second World War that American industrial supremacy was acquired. The United States of America has become the champion of trade liberalisation.

Eugene Nyambal underlines that large modern companies have appeared in large numbers in the USA because they feed on a pioneering spirit, a large and growing domestic market, a continuous development of technology, an enabling environment for the execution of contracts, physical, economic and financial infrastructures and intense competition in a large domestic market[136]. But the United States could only benefit from this internal market with the revolution of transport, communications, and electricity.

Eugene Nyambal notes that: "like the Africa of today, American companies were small before the 1840s. There was little innovation because the population was small, mostly rural and living on self-consumption, where the process of production and distribution depended on traditional sources of human, animal or wind energy that did not allow for mass production". Note that, "the lack of infrastructure between the different regions of the United States did not permit the constitution of a sufficiently large market for a company. According to Alfred Chandler the big company in its modern form appeared with the arrival of modern means of transport and communication around 1870".

[135] Ibid., p.91.

[136] Eugène Nyambal. Op.cit., p. 116.

A new system of production, distribution, maintenance, investment credit and management, in an integrated approach

In production, a new breed of pioneers exploited these technological innovations to set up a production system capable of transforming raw materials into finished products on a large scale to take advantage of market expansion. It was in this context that, from the 1880s, most of the big companies that still dominate their sector today, like Procter and Gamble in the soap and consumer chemical industry, General Electric and Westinghouse in electrical equipment, soon followed by German firms Siemens and AEG.

To bring mass production to the final consumer, the Americans organized a mass distribution system. New companies that still dominate the sector in the US today, such as Sears or Reebok, emerged, using new infrastructure to coordinate the purchase of a large number of agricultural and industrial products for a large number of consumers , at a speed and regularity to improve productivity and reduce costs.

In industries whose prices remained beyond the reach of customers, particularly in agricultural machinery, companies such as MC Cornick Harvesting Machines and John Deere, began mass production and set up a distribution, maintenance and repair system, credit to facilitate the sale of machinery to farmers. The American experience was later imitated by most European countries, which still share today with the Americans, the main industrial sectors at the world level.

To grow, companies had to produce in large quantities and sell the products as quickly as possible, in order to reduce costs, make investments profitable and dominate their sector of activity. To ensure the efficiency of the production process, it was necessary to strengthen the capabilities of companies by investing in complementary production, distribution and management. The first groups of American, European, Japanese or Korean companies that made these investments still dominate their global business sector today.

The first level of investment was investing in technology and building plants large enough to exploit the high-volume production potential of new technologies, and reducing costs through economies of scale. The second level was to operate this plant optimally by recruiting a team of professional managers capable of administering these investments and coordinating the entire process. The third level involved setting up a national and international distribution and marketing network to sell mass production. The combination of these capabilities helped lower prices, sell more products, strengthen innovation capacity and conquer new markets.

It is this integrated approach that makes the success of sectors such as telecommunications, breweries or tobacco ... "Such an organization is in total contradiction with the logic of the white elephants who have left to Africa oversised factories, with no outlets , nor adequate technological and managerial capabilities and unable to cope with international competition "[137].

Eugene Nyambal summarizes this dynamism in these words: "protectionism would not explain the dynamism of the American economy nor even less constitute a management mode to produce for nations facing globalization. Large companies have appeared in large numbers in the United States and elsewhere because they feed on a pioneering spirit" which will be manifested later through "a large and growing domestic market, a continuous development technology, a legal environment that allows for the execution of contracts, quality physical, economic and financial infrastructures and intense competition allowing companies to deploy their resources in the vast market"[138]. It is the application of the rules of clear play and observable by all. There is no room for confusion.

This efficient organization of the economy has enabled the United States to achieve full employment for a very long time, because all human, spiritual, moral, scientific, technological, managerial fundamentals have been intelligently used. This rises to the point that the United States is the first country in the world to count the largest billionaires in dollars.

Today, the economy of the United States has entered a certain decline because of unbridled liberalism that leaves room for market forces, opening the way to all sorts of stock market and banking speculation. President Barack Obama, elected for the first time in 2008, led the state to put a semblance of order into this unbridled liberalism. He promised to tackle the huge national debt and the budget deficit. But thanks to the creative, scientific, technological and managerial capacity, the USA has the means to revive victoriously the economy which

---

[137] Eugène Nyambal. Op.cit., pp. 116-118.
[138] Ibid., p.115.

remains always the first in the world, in spite of the stiff competition on them from China, Europe, and Japan.

In economics, the Americans have shown how one can master the stages of development by developing the infrastructure needed for this development: roads, railways, telephone, telegraph, electricity. How do we organize production, distribution, credit, promote great managers? All thanks to this pioneering spirit, enterprise, rage to succeed, efficiency, rigorous justice to fulfill the commitments made. It is these capacities of moral ethic, scientific, technological and managerial organisation that are indeed lacking in Africa. It is cruelly lacking roads, railways, electricity, technology, high-flying managers and in large numbers.

To achieve these spectacular and exceptional results in terms of institutions and the economy, the United States has developed a genuine and solid cultural identity, the bedrock of this success.

4- A strong American cultural identity.

Whether we love the United States or we do not like it, we must recognize that no other country has been able to impose itself on the world as they have managed to do thanks to the fundamental values. That is, the belief in religious values developed by early American colonists in the seventeenth century who were Puritans. They founded the first theocratic colonies in Massachusetts Bay east of the United States. They were rigorous and uncompromising in applying these values. This religious commitment remains today the entitlement of American society. When America feels threatened, the model of the pioneer Wasp (White Anglo-Saxon Protestant) regains its appeal because it is synonymous with entrepreneurship, hard work, love of the homeland. A true asceticism. The first settlers wanted to establish on the virgin lands of this vast territory that they discovered, the heavenly Jerusalem, a paradise on earth, the city on the mountain. A whole mystique of perfect values, very high values, in short, the best human cities in the world. This puritanical mentality means that Americans do not tolerate lies, especially in politics. These heroes and founding fathers also brought the freedom that allowed for the establishment of a vibrant democracy, perhaps the first in the world. They have made personal and individual success a real social lift.

Religious passion, a characteristic feature of American culture

This religious fervour is accompanied by some ethics for life that should be exemplary, the respect of the family and the established authority. This assurance that the United States is a blessed country of God, is inscribed on the dollar "In God we trust" (we trust God). This motto has become that of the whole country. This country is convinced of its scientific, technological, political, economic, financial, military and diplomatic superiority. He believes in his unity, his culture, his dream, the American dream of a life of happiness, success, abundance, perfection and excellence. He knows how to question himself. As a slavery country, it has overcome this incongruity by establishing a multiracial and multicultural society (black-white, Hispanic, Native American, Asian). This attachment to divine values does not prevent it from being a secular state. The true guardians of American secularism are inspired by Jefferson's old formula that the First Amendment erects a real dividing wall between Church and State. The first amendment of the constitution prohibits any official church and any manifestation favouring a particular religion, or particularly religion with respect to irreligion.

This great country has built its success on a culture and a true mystic values strong, well assimilated and practiced by the vast majority of citizens. This people developed a strong mental and moral framework. It's the bottom of his world leadership. In short, it is the laboratory par excellence of perfect fundamental values of divine and human origin. He knew how to make a happy synthesis between God and man, inspired by the European Enlightenment. From the first part of our research, it appears that knowledge derives from the divine sphere and the human sphere. The United States, a secular state par excellence, is very well illustrated and their success, built on this indestructible spiritual base is indisputable. It is carried especially from generation to generation by the American dream, because the dream is at the very heart of the spiritual reality, it explores all that it wants: God and the man, the natural and the supernatural, the visible and the invisible.

Africa for success also must first emulate countries that have experimented with values that have proven and continue to do so. It must proceed with its cultural, mental, spiritual, intellectual, political and economic revolution by producing a new man capable of doing so. These are the fundamental values that are unanimous among the peoples of the world that make this revolution possible. It is this founding spiritual axis that has led the world since the 18th century. And it is the Western Christian that laboriously put it in place, as recognized by Jean Tabi Manga in his excellent book: *Variation sur la Renaissance, l'Emergence et la modernité africaines(Variations on the Renaissance, Emergence and African Modernity)* Sopecam edition, 2015.

III- The lessons that Africa can draw from the development experience of Europe and the Western Christian

To the reality of all the above, Jean Tabi Manga, thinks that the European Renaissance can inspire Africa when it notes that: "the trajectory of Africa, especially the black subcontinent, should be enlightened by experiences received from other civilizational areas such as Europe, China, Korea ...»

Middle-aged Europe faced, like Africa today, innumerable problems whose solutions could no longer be found within the narrow framework of the cognitive, political, economic and societal paradigms that described, explained, and justified the medieval order.

The medieval intellectual and political order was no longer up to the demands, expectations and hopes of the new European society which was already maturing its parturition. Obscurantism and religious, political and intellectual autocrats encroached on medieval European society. In addition, other great calamities of the time paralyzed the functioning of the whole social body. These calamities were named the black plague, famine, war and misery.

This particularly cumbersome social, intellectual and political climate characterised by demobilising and defeatist consciousness resembles, mutatis mutandis, Africa's dramatic living today. Africa, like medieval Europe, is suffering from the debt burden of structural adjustment policies. Although it is true that it has, in many cases, exceeded what economists call the sustainable debt threshold. Africa, in terms of health, is literally devastated by pandemics, endemic pathologies, and recurrent diseases reminiscent of the Black Death in view of the extent of social damage.

Africa is struggling with her education. Overall, universal schooling is still a myth. Many African children of school age do not have the opportunity to know a complete schooling. Technical and vocational training is in its infancy. As a result, unemployment everywhere reigns as a true social cancer. This exposes African societies to permanent socio-political convulsions that threaten to break the fragile political stability and prevent ambitious and legitimate programs from building real, long-term, law-based political communities.

The evolutions on this point are hazardous and chaotic because of insufficient appropriation of the democratic culture, the rule of law. This culture, itself Western in nature, is not related to the political culture of ancient Africa such as to construct lines of convergence from the angle of legal and political anthropology in order to create a cultural basis for a democratic culture.

Europe had to impose itself a step of cognitive rupture to be reborn in modernity. By historically finding its founding source, it has been able to find adequate answers to the structural problems that beset it. In solving these problems and calamities, Europe fought victoriously against the unreasoning religiosity that had plagued the popular classes by frequent recourse to the marvellous and the miracles. The new Church, called "awakened", maintains this climate everywhere in Africa today, thoroughly operating the marvelous in its function of producing prodigies for cathartic purposes.

Africa lives and experiences daily a metaphysics of consolation that plunges the social conscience into a deep lethargy, while at the same time weakening the powers of knowledge and creativity by the triumph of magico-religious. Europe has managed to recover to face this defeatist conscience by taking again in hand its destiny. It is to this task that Africa must work to prevent emergence from being a simple and banal punctuation of political rhetoric.

How has Europe achieved its ideological transformation? What should Africa do to achieve its transmutation with regard to the European course? The European Renaissance is a deep movement. It is global because it is at once cultural, philosophical, intellectual and social. There is a historical dynamic and a willingness to revitalise and rediscover the founding cultural values to create something else, another state of mind and to imagine other possible "ways" of development, according to the sense that Edgar Morin employs concerning this.

This cultural renewal in Europe in the 15th and 16th centuries was a reasoned return to the sources of antiquity through philosophical research that allowed the renewal of poetry, literature, science and art. Philosophically, the founding source of Europe is not an essence, it is a rediscovery, a reinvention which has been the subject of an updated hermeneutics.

Europe has reinvented Indo-European as a structuring schema of thought, of European civilization. This schema of thought is based on what philologists call the tri-functional ideology of G. Dumézil. This intellectual schema rigorously reconstructed from comparative philological studies has justified the social organization of the Greek, Latin, German, Asiatic, Germanic, Baltic and Slavic peoples.

To this founding foundation is added the Hebrew complementary source which will legitimize the spiritual and religious rebirth that will carry the Protestant Reformation movement.

From Renaissance come the great values that make Europe modern and fascinating. These are the values of freedom, democracy, the rule of law, and the will to progress, conquest and domination. A new relationship to scientific knowledge. In the same vein, Europe has impacted both the world and humanity thanks to its great movements of philosophical thought that have given meaning to humanism. One should also mention its great scientific theories and the modelling of its social revolutions that inspired and nurtured so many liberation struggles.

This is the first requirement imposed on the African conscience by the power of evidence alone. Philosophically, impose a cognitive revolution by intellectually building a refounding and regenerative source of cultural values that will fertilize its global emergence. This cultural source would play the same role as the ideology of Indo-European, enlightened by the historical and philological works of G. Dumézil and enriched by the Hebrew component.

This philosophical research based on comparative linguistics has favoured the emergence of rational thought, and by intellectual reconstitution, a centre of common civilization in Europe and India. This refers to Indo-European, source of modern Western culture. The comparative study of Indo-European languages and myths has unveiled a common schema of social organization which is symbolized by what is called the tri-functional Indo-European ideology represented by the

Capitoline triad on the divine plane Jupiter, Mars and Quirinus. (G. Dumézil). Jupiter represents sovereignty on the divine and political levels. Sovereignty, that is, the imperium which, in the Indo-European, Greco-Roman imaginary, represents the highest value. Mars, god of war, represents one of the sacred values for the man "Vir". It is courage, virtue from (virtus). Quirinus, the third deity associated with the Capitoline triad, represents happiness. "The search for the prosperity of the people will lead Europe to cultivate entrepreneurial value. The desire to create wealth "(Jean Tabi Manga, op.cit, p. 44-48 and 83). The development experience of the United States of America is very enlightening and is in the same conquering logic as that of Europe.

Chapter VIII

The Japanese Success Model, the Buddhist tradition in the footsteps of the West, an example to be meditated or even copied by Africa

I- The Japanese Cultural Revolution in the Meiji Era (Era of Japanese Light): Willingness for Reform and Westernization while Maintaining its Buddhist Culture and Traditions of Group and Family Spirit

Japan is an East Asian country made up of four islands, covering an area of 373,000 km^2 with a population of more than 125 million people. Japan, without being a Christian country, achieved a pattern of development similar to that of Christian Europe, assimilating the spirit of perfect fundamental values into a different cultural context. In this Japan relied on her polytheistic but strongly Buddhist culture, which favours the logic of the group, respect for the elders of the family and order. In a word, wisdom. This Japanese culture has been open to transformations from the so-called Japanese Enlightenment era or enlightened politics, Meiji Tenno, posthumous name of Mutsuhito, Emperor of Japan (1867-1912) inaugurated the Meiji Era in 1868. He proclaims his desire for reform and westernization in the charter of five articles. He suppresses the shogunate and the feudal system. In 1889, he gives a constitution to Japan. Japan proceeds to its industrialization by imitating the Western Christian in a culture different from his own. The state played a vital role in this revolution through the strategic leadership of society and the economy. It is rather recognised that people of the West have a linear conception of time and of human action. They devote to the primacy of the individual to the community and have different modes of social and cultural organization. Japan favours the group and the family as in Africa.

This desire to imitate the West while remaining oneself is well developed in the excellent book of Pierre François Souyri, entitled *Moderne sans être Occident. Origins du Japon d'aujourd'hui* (Modernisation without Westernisation. Origins of today's Japan). Gallimard Editions. 2016. He nuanced a common historical place with long roots, according to which the Japan of the Meiji Era would be transformed in a radical way and throw herself into a slavish imitation of the West. Pierre Souyri's book shows that things are more complex. He exposes a perception of modernity from a Japanese point of view. In this perspective, modernisation is far from being a Westernisation. The years 1870-1880 were pivotal years marked by the freedom of speech and passionate debates that electrified the Japanese society. They try to translate some Western concepts (a Japanese mission travels through Europe from 1871 to 1873), but a reintegration of the Japanese tradition into play. To emphasize the originality of this Japan of the Meiji Era, Pierre François Souyri describes the commitment of women in the movement for freedom and the rights of the people that develops from 1870 to 1885. For the first time, some women dare speak and claim the right to vote. This was at least for those women who pay taxes. A woman like Kishida TOSHIKO, unknown in the West and where the cause of women and still stammering at this time, defends bold positions. She refers to Confucianism by questioning its most widespread interpretation that women should obey men.

All in all, the author paints a living portrait in a complex, chaotic, contradictory way with which Japan has modernised, or rather "civilized", as the protagonists of the Meiji era said. It demonstrates very convincingly that this modernisation was never a pure and simple Westernisation. A way of saying that the laws of progress are better assimilated than a solid culture that shows the way.

In this respect, Africa must continue to consolidate its culture to give itself reliable benchmarks that allow it to be itself, to preserve its originality while enriching itself with the contributions of other cultures as they complement each other, particularly in the domains of science and technology, with a view to its industrialisation.

II- The role of the state in the cultural and industrial revolution of Japan

The so-called Meiji Era of the Japanese Enlightenment, which corresponds to the popularisation of knowledge and openness to the West, favoured the industrial boom. The state played a vital role in this evolution, in the absence of a strong private sector at the beginning. As a result, the state embarked on an unprecedented program of reforms in the country's history, and primary education became compulsory with a particular emphasis on the scientific questioning of nature. The goal was to introduce Japanese children to phenomena such as nature, electricity, magnetism and measuring instruments such as the thermometer, the barometer using images adapted to the local culture. In the same vein, the country had a critical mass of engineers and technicians capable of taking over from foreign technical assistance. The process used in the Western world[139].

III- Japan's industrial revolution through strategic leadership and the creation of the National Agency for the Promotion of Science and Technology

This desire for Westernisation of Japan led him to domesticate and improve peoples of Judeo-Christian tradition. It is a technological catch-up model for non-Western peoples. In its quest for industrialisation, this country had to overcome most of the challenges that Africans face. Japan is known as a country that has achieved its development thanks to the dynamism of its industrialization, its technological and industrial success.

Through its technological and industrial success, Japan served as a model for several countries such as Korea, Taiwan, Singapore, Malaysia and to a certain extent Mauritius in Africa. Its commercial surpluses remain colossal and it continues to invest its savings in the rest of the world, as Eugène Nyambal points out. It reveals that three complementary factors contributed to the emergence of Japan's technological and industrial power. First, the state created an environment conducive to access to advanced technologies and corporate finance. Then, the intense rivalry between companies in the domestic market fostered innovation. Finally, the density and rivalry of the associative and institutional network facilitated the diffusion of technological innovation[140].This modernising vision of the Meiji Era was amplified after the Second World War, considering technological mastery as a key factor in economic development. With this in mind, the Japanese government, in consultation with the private sector, started

[139] Eugène Nyambal, Ibid., P.120. also read Pierre François Souyri, *Moderne sans être Occident. Origins du Japon d'aujourd'hui (*Modernisation without Westernisation. Origins of today's Japan). He demonstrates that before opening to the western world, Japan had engaged in a proto-industrialisation process and that Japan was already a pre-modern civilisation. (1603-1867).

[140] Ibid., p.119

making steering strategies. Here the entire economy was considered as a portfolio of activities to develop or abandon, depending on the development potential of each of them. The promotion of strategic industries was carried out as part of development plans setting ambitious targets for channelling the energy of all stakeholders. To this end, the government put in place mechanisms of financial and fiscal incentives and other supports to improve the quality of products, the development of new ideas on these products and the boosting of their sale abroad[141].

The government also promotes research and development. Contrary to what happened in Africa in 1990 with the privatisations, the Japanese public companies were sold to the big commercial families like that of Mitsui or the founder of Mitsubishi, and the State framed them to ensure the technological and industrial modernisation of the country. The government also set up a policy to facilitate the transfer of technology. It also pushed companies to buy licenses or copy foreign technologies, to invest in developing capabilities to absorb technologies.

In terms of technological leadership, the government created the National Agency for the Promotion of Science and Technology with relays across the country. Its role was: to identify, in consultation with the private sector, the technologies to be acquired, to advise the government on the introduction of standards and techniques of mass production in companies, to promote vocational training, to set up productivity centres funded by the government, large enterprises, foreign aid and control the quality of products. This agency worked in collaboration with a network of public research institutes and research laboratories of major universities which focus on applied research in new technologies, new products and production processes, research on problems identified during business surveys. These institutes made the results of their research available to enterprises[142].

This intelligent vision of the diffusion of technology was provided at three levels. The role of the central government and its specialised research institutes was to engage in advanced projects aimed at implementing the country's technological and industrial ambition. Next, local authorities aimed to respond to local needs for wealth creation and employment and to ensure the mastery of technology, through research

141 Idem.

142 Ibid., p.122.

institutes, professional associations and their permanent development. Finally, enterprises on their part were to constantly develop the ability to import, adopt and improve imported technologies in order to remain globally competitive[143].

Added to this frame was a dense and decentralised associative and institutional level set up by the government. The aim was to encourage local innovation, disseminate information on new technologies, test them and adapt them to existing production systems. This system was based on close links between local authorities, research centres and local technical schools and professional associations under the coordination of the central government.

This large-scale technological development that extends to the whole country, allowed Japan to have some of the largest companies in the world in the following sector of activities: Toyota, NTT, SONY, Mitsubishi, Sumitomo. Like American companies, they have achieved the three types of investment required for market dominance, particularly in production, management and distribution[144]. This technological efficiency has enabled Japan to establish itself in the computer industry as a major player after the United States of America by giving another turn to the second industrial revolution.

In the end, as Tessa Morris-Suzuki showed in her book entitled: *The technological transformation of Japan: From the 17th to the 21st century*, Japan's modernizing ambition would have been in vain if it had not benefited from a favourable social and cultural environment. An environment with logical groups, family, respect for authority and elders, sense of discipline and seriousness, taste of effort and knowledge, desire to catch up with technology, to crown all that, attitude of wisdom.

In the Japanese model, as in the case of the industrialised countries, technological success or simply success, rests on the practice of a corpus of fundamental values that are perfect over a long period of time.

This modernizing ambition was also based on a series of conferences, seminars and symposia at the national level bringing together representatives of all the laboratories to exchange information on the most recent technological initiatives. It also encouraged the

---

143 Idem.
144 Ibid., p.124.

systematic participation of companies in international fairs and the regular holding of industrial fairs in the country, with a view to promoting local products. This system was stimulated by the establishment of competition mechanisms between inventors, innovative projects within each region and intense competition between regions in areas that the central state wanted to promote[145].

Apart from the Western Christian and Buddhist Japan, emerging countries offer another example that can inspire Africa, because these countries apply the fundamentals that lead to development, whose mastery of knowledge is the founding axis.

IV- Lessons that Africa can draw from Japan's development experience

Following the reminder of Japan's brilliant development history, Jean Tabi Manga stresses that: "The renaissance of Japan is an example of a trajectory that can inspire Africa effectively. Indeed, the political framework of Japan's awakening to modernity is not unlike the historical situation in Africa. In-depth study of the Japanese approach can provide Africa with strategic keys to its emergence". From this experience and this strategy, Africa can conceptually build a winning tactic for its modernity.

The challenge of Japanese elites is original. It was to succeed in the westernisation of their culture and even globally through all the East under the Meiji Era. These elites were sent to Europe from the angle of modernity. Great treatises on Western philosophy were literally translated into Japanese before being exhibited in China. Thus, the East experienced a period of Westernisation through the mediation of Japan. Japan's challenge was to achieve a living synthesis endowed with strength, an operational capacity between traditional and modern Nipponese and the modern and conquering western world.

The Japanese renaissance consisted in constantly cultivating the art of being oneself while integrating the power of the other with its intelligence in order to renew its vital force.

This operation presupposes the fullness of self-knowledge. The art and science of Japanese battle have been applied with intelligence and mastery. Japan has had a rigorously realistic vision. The world is a field

[145] Ibid., p.121.

of war where nations fight to conquer political, economic, cultural and military hegemony. It is appropriate as in the martial arts to make use of the strength of the opponent's intelligence in favour of his own vision and interests. So Japan has used Western technology to modernise its culture and build an image of power. Japan had to die in itself to be reborn in modernity. This is the effort that Africa must accomplish by giving itself a culture of post-colonialism. For this, Africa must carry out another preliminary task like Japan. Great social and political innovations are needed to welcome this new culture and put it in motion and action.

This is, for example, the case of the education training sector which needs to be renewed in order to boost the dynamics of innovation for social progress. The African university must evolve structurally in its mandates and modes of operation. She is more than fifty years old and has corresponded to a type of society which gradually left the colonial yoke to start a life within the institutional framework of independence. Today, it must change configuration due to a new contextualisation of the data. This is how, under the Meiji Era that corresponds to the Japanese Enlightenment, social institutions evolved to achieve the rebirth of Japan.

The renaissance of Japan is within reach for Africa. It is in fact to make of one's own cultural, intellectual and philosophical resources effective instruments of the mastery of the other through knowledge. To make the other an integral part of oneself through socio-educational investment. This process leads to a transmutation of global society and modernity (Jean Tabi Manga, op.cit., pp. 49-52).

Following the successful experience of the development of the West that has inspired humanity since the 19th century and Africa since the independence of its states, we believe that the experience of emerging countries can also be useful to Africa.

Part III

Correlation between perfect fundamental values and development: the development model of emerging countries of Buddhist and Confucian faith, another example worth considering, emulating, or copying by Africa

Knowledge that leads to development through a thorough understanding of perfect fundamental values, inter alia, culture, education, training, science and technology is gaining more ground. A similar cultural, scientific, technological and industrial pattern followed by the so called emerging countries in East and South-East Asia such as: South Korea, Taiwan, Singapore, Hong Kong, Malaysia, Indonesia, Thailand, China and other countries like the BRICS: Brazil, Russia, India and South Africa. To buttress our point, this part shall focus on some Asian countries like: South Korea, China, Malaysia, and Singapore. These countries are considered as the Asian dragons.

Chapter I

South Korea or the Korean dragon miracle

South Korea followed a classical pattern that leads to development by emulating Japan and Western countries, through a cultural, mental and industrial revolution.

I- Cultural and mental revolution of South Korea beneficial to the country's development

Western Christian countries as well as Japan, a Buddhist country, had to undergo a cultural revolution, that of mentalities and knowledge, to achieve their industrial revolution. South Korea did same. The country had to control its thinking to best chart the course to its development.

Alain Faujas provides a perfect illustration of this successful development[146]. South Korea is an East Asian state with a surface area of 99 000 Km^2 and a population estimated at more than 50 million inhabitants. The South Korean miracle was made possible by the fact that, in no less than four decades, starting from 1960, this country evolved from a subsistence society to an affluent society. Before then however, South Korea was at the same level as certain African countries. Its remarkable economic boom and development encouraged the country to organise the G20, the club of industrialised countries, which includes a few emerging countries, in November 2010, at Seoul, its capital. In the view of Alain Faujas, the sacred ingredients of these performances include:

- Proclivity for order and discipline: Confucian ideals derived from China glorified hierarchy and family (Christian, evangelical and animist values par excellence), but were unfairly applied in Africa, it must be admitted. Values that gave rise to "Chaebols", great ultra-competitive family business conglomerates, the best example is Samsung.

---

[146] Jeune Afrique, No.2585 of 25 - 30 June 2010, Article entitled, "*Le Maghreb et le Dragon*".

- Proclivity for the future: according to the author, Japan alone tops performance in the field of research and development, and the need to protect itself against invasion by North Korea compelled South Korea to invest heavily in information technologies.
- Proclivity for openness and modernism: it revealed that South Koreans are "cultural sponges". They blended religions, to the extent of even inviting Christian missionaries to complement traditional Confucianist and Buddhist principles, they copied the best from Western technology.
- Africa equally received Christianism whose contribution to Western development is irrefutable, without applying its best ideals to its development process. Many in Africa considered the gospel as a story good for listening only on Sunday in church, after church, African Christians usually resumed with their natural customs. Hence, the confusion noted in the behaviour of Africans, which makes it difficult to distinguish between a practising Christian and any other ordinary citizen. It stands out how some people splendidly imbibed the source of fundamental values, to undergo spiritual, moral, intellectual, scientific transformation into enlightened subjects, skilled to develop whatever is good, beautiful, true, durable, which, inter alia, constitute the path to development. Max Weber, a German economist and sociologist underscored the role of Protestantism and its values in the economic success of Europe.
- Proclivity for knowledge: Alain Faujas emphasises that enrolment rate in higher education institutions surpasses that of Japan, its labour force is the best trained in the world. This entails that funds allocated to education are substantial and employed effectively to produce such results.
- Spirit of adaptation: Alain Faujas adds that South Korea lost, owing to its increased standard of living, benefit of its extremely low salary costs, it dropped its bottom-of-the-line exporter model and turned to added value products, such as shipyard building, car or computer manufacturing. Alain Faujas advises Africa to retain these few lessons of the success-story accomplished with pump and fanfare: namely the passion for success, promotion of personal initiatives in what it holds as spiritually, intellectually and morally fulfilling, refusal to withdraw into oneself in the event of any crisis. This economic and industrial success of South Korea is equally

described in the collective book, *Économie du Développement (Development Economics),* referred to above.

II- South Korean industrial revolution and emulation of the West in science, technology and finance

According to Alain Faujas, this recognition is only fair, inasmuch as the country's development had been incredible. He recalls that back in 1950, at the wake of the war that resulted in the partition of the country and that caused 2.5 million deaths, 70% of South Koreans were peasants. Cities were mostly composed of swampy slums. Per capita GNP stood at 70 dollars. Thanks to a fierce determination and American assistance, they undertook reconstruction, trowel in hand, transforming their country, first of all, into a dragon, and then into a developed country. A comparison of its evolution with that of African countries is striking. In 1980, the classification stood as follows: Algeria recorded the highest per capita GNP, 2 251 dollars, ahead of South Korea (1 704 dollars), Tunisia (1 354 dollars) and Morocco (1 075 dollars). In 1990, South Korea shot to the top and attained 17 591 dollars per inhabitant (about 12 000 Euros at the time) in 2008, and Algeria, in the meantime, recorded 4 900 dollars, Tunisia, 3 966 dollars, Morocco, 2 673 dollars, and sub-Saharan African countries, stood at an even lower level than the Maghrebian countries. Even without natural resources, South Korea was able to multiply its wealth by 10. None of the crises encountered could cast doubts on its liberal approach: neither the 1979 oil shock, nor the 1997 Asian debt crisis, or let alone that of the 2008 *subprimes* in the USA. Better still, its GNP is by far higher than that of the entire sub-Saharan Africa. Its exports are also higher than those of all African countries south of the Sahara thanks to its technological and industrial boom. Alain Faujas adds that, Samsung and Hyundai are now competing with their Japanese rivals, Sony and Nissan, and unsurprisingly, it is the South Korean consortium, "Kepco", that sold nuclear reactors to the United Arab Emirates, under the nose of the world number one in the sector, the French group, Areva.

Conversely, South Korea proved particularly aggressive as it caught up with Japan by appropriating, the Japanese industrial and technological development model. In this regard, the country recorded success in the electronic industry, and even in mastery of the high-speed train technology. Thanks to this resolute determination to develop its technological and industrial sector, South Korean multinationals like

Samsung, DAEWOO, Hyundai, in the automobile secteur, and others acquired world fame.

The State played an active role in the development of the electronic industry by adopting, as early as 1969, a long term plan designed to transform this sector into one of the vectors of exports. This plan relied on the creation of a fund for promotion of the electronic industry, with subsidised loans and subventions.[147]

In this way, France had to make important concessions in terms of technology transfer to win this contract. The corresponding technical documentation on the manufacturing of the high-speed train, the TGV was transmitted to the South Koreans and more than one thousand South Koreans were trained in France.

III- The South Korean development experience may be extremely beneficial to Africa

Jean Tabi Manga equally admits that the South Korean experience may serve Africa as he observes that: "South Korea achieved the same inspiring and enviable result thanks to a unique experience, actually rooted in a particular socio-political and economic background. This experience is that of a cultural identity movement termed 'Saemaul'".

Saemaul is the philosophical, cultural movement that propelled and legitimised all South Korean aspirations to their political, economic, cultural and social renaissance.

Saemaul is a compound word in the Korean language. It is composed of the term "Sar" which means "new", while "Maul" signifies "village". For Koreans, the term "village" symbolises the basic unit of life and any human society.

The adjective "new" embodied by the term "Sae" refers to the will to get rid of the old, to be emancipated from the past, from tradition. Saemaul therefore obtains as a notion of change, a desire for reform and modernisation.

In Korean belief, since the village is a unit of basic social life, it must be reformed to improve living conditions in rural areas. Through a metonymic effect, the term "Saemaul" ultimately applies to Korea as a

---

[147] Eugène Nyambal.op.cit.,pg. 128.

whole and what was initially not an intention to reform, change becomes a vast movement of Korean renaissance.

The socio-political, cultural and economic context warranted this national awakening. The etiologic and unpublished documents given to me by officials of the Korea Foundation at the end of my mission to Seoul testify that Korea of the 60s was a country “devoid of hope”.

The Saemaul movement began its development activities in 1970, at the request of president Park Chung-Hu, soon after he took stock of the miserable and deplorable conditions under which his country was languishing. At political level, the Korea, occupied by foreign forces at the beginning of the 20th century, was marked by internal divisions, political differences and conflicts.

Korea in the 60s was essentially an agricultural country, though living conditions in the rural areas were extremely agonising and difficult, food production as a result fell short of sustaining the cities. Thus, a new concept was necessary to pave the way for the advent of “new villages”.

Besides, the educational system was not effective. Reports and unpublished documents obtained from the Korea Foundation reveal that rather than attend school, children were made to go to farms in the mountain and assist their parents in performing farm duties. Famine was widespread, rural-to-urban migration on the rise, cities suffocating and thc society as a whole had become exceedingly instable.

Whereas, without stability in the country sides, it was difficult to hope for sustainability in cities and the country. At the same time the country’s resources were not enough and the government wasn’t equipped to singlehandedly ensure development in the country.

A revival was therefore necessary, a bold determination of the people as a whole to kindle hope and get out of the endemic poverty through a long process of economic emergence. This process required a renovated lay out of the villages to create new social and cultural conditions. Farmers, just like city-dwellers, have the right to enjoy incentives and leisure of the cultural life they desire. That is what the “Saemaul” movement targeted. In this light, the first reflex was to combat the defeatist mood overwhelming the entire Korean population within an atmosphere marked by resignation, abandonment and lack of confidence in self and others. This is confirmed by the unpublished documents. The damage was in the Korean psyche:

This is a fight against our concepts and prejudices rooted in us such that "we remain forever poor!" or "we cannot do that".

Saemaul therefore posits a national psychological surge by reinventing positive values that forge a new personality, a new Korean identity.

In a nutshell, it is a drive towards reform, modernity whereby moral values and satisfaction are sought, in a new spirit, thanks to an active participation for development of the village.

Other than trust in oneself, capacities, virtues and qualities, another positive value to cultivate, so as to curb poverty in South Korea, was working with community solidarity spirit:

There is nobody to help me: you and I, are in difficulty: so in that case, what can be done? The village, as a whole must come together as one and strive resolutely and earnestly, in a spirit of independence and collaboration. Those are the three fundamental spirits!

This lengthy quote teaches us that, besides the belief in hard work, the Korean Saemaul spirit is a spirit of sacrifice. Koreans must work hard and earnestly to considerably improve the general situation of Korea today and for future generations.

Africa, in its quest for full emergence, must draw inspiration from that as well as from "the spirit of independence". The spirit of independence, as the term posits, is a spirit with which man must singlehandedly perform his work, having in mind his personal progress and his own destiny bearing in mind that everything depends on him therefore he most employ his best efforts.

The spirit of collaboration is a spirit of truth whereby togetherness is stronger than the individual. We must share our joy together, we must help each other whenever the other lacks something, encounters difficulties, and we must strive for a solution together. This is a spirit whereby we must, above all, consider the moral virtue of each other.

This spirit of collaboration means pooling resources, convergence of spirits and skills to avert misery and cultivate wealth for or through development.

Thanks to the Saemaul movement, within a short period of just twenty years, South Korea, hitherto a poor agricultural country, devoid of everything, became a very advanced industrial country owing to its rapid economic growth. The assessment is clear and true. The transformation of South Korea had been rapid and remarkable.

In the 70s, South Korea was extremely poor. And by the end of the 70s, the term 'Miracle of River Hana' emerged, and then from the 80s, South Korea featured as a dragon among the four Asian dragons. Were one to exaggerate the growth rate of Korea, one can state that it is a creative rate that evolved from Nothing to Existence. There was no experimental model. Believe could be placed in one thing only, the efforts of people and their skills. That is the national and public concept of solidarity.

A review of these patterns is enlightening. These patterns show the path that Africa must take if it wants to achieve its emergence, and if it hopes to fulfil the prophecy of Thabo Mbeki, which portends that the 21st century shall be African. Mr Sévérino espouses the same theme when he talks of "temps de l'Afrique" (likewise Jean Tabi Manga).

Chapter II

China's outstanding development

China initiated its cultural and mental revolution and emulated the West and Japan in the fields of science, technology and industry to achieve its economic development.

I- Cultural and mental revolution of China and emulation of the West in scientific, technical and industrial areas

Another example of a dazzling development comes from China. It is a country that covers a 9 600 000 Km^2 surface area and has a population of more than one billion inhabitants. It represents far more than one-fifth of world population. With such a large population, China nevertheless succeeded in laying a solid groundwork for its development as Bechir Ben Yahmed acknowledges.[148] The country relies on its true cultural assets and a solid State organisation machinery founded on the Chinese communist party.

Thus at cultural level, performance of the Chinese political, economic and social system, as well as success of the Chinese miracle can be attributed to revived Confucian values. These fundamental and sacred values promote: the mind, order, discipline, authority, the family, hierarchy, hard work and relentless effort, wisdom, education, the culture of savings. A Chinese ambassador to Cameroon, once declared on the eve of a congress of the Chinese communist party that the ruling organs intended to lay emphasis on development of the mind, as a driving force behind thought and triumphant action.

In reality, other than the Confucian values, revisited above, the Chinese success and miracle stem from a strict and permanent application of perfect fundamental values in all aspects of social activity, inter alia: passion for entrepreneurship and success, political institutions, State and economic stability, a clear vision of the objectives to attain, the economy as a national priority, reaching the objectives

---

[148] Jeune Afrique, No.2604 of 11 December 2010, in an article entitled, "*un exemple venu d'ailleurs*" (an example from elsewhere).

targeted, passion for knowledge and wisdom, promotion of science, technology and innovation, modernity, permanent quest for excellence and perfection, recognition of the merits of leaders, senior officials and populations, glorification of the works of Mao Tse Toung and Deng Xiao Ping where Deng XiaoPing himself admits that Mao was 70% good and only 30% bad, promotion of leadership mentality and self-confidence.

All in all, China undertook its spiritual, cultural, Promethean and Copernician revolution, which opened gateways to the world of perfect and true knowledge that inevitably leads all those who embraced it, to full development. China performed its renaissance and fully embraced the realms of the mind, just like Western countries and Japan had done earlier, emulating them in the fields of science, technology and industrialisation, following the footprints of Japan and South Korea in the yesteryears.

These palpable successes in terms of development clearly indicate that the patterns that lead thereto are paved by knowledge, full knowledge and strict application of the scientific, technological and industrial values derived from illuminations of the mind, thought, reflexion, rational thinking, and above all, intelligence and wisdom.

Conversely, the country's political organisation matches this Cultural Revolution. It is an expression of the wisdom of Chinese leaders.

II- China's political revolution

Thus at political level, Bechir Ben Yahmed reinforces the fact that this country has been governed for more than sixty years (since 1949 with the advent of Mao Tse Tung to power), by a single, communist party. In this land, there has been no room for open elections. Even though after witnessing a period of disorder in the 1970s, leaders of the party holding the reins of this country developed a formula that they have consistently applied for thirty years now. This formula has enabled the Chinese communist party to conserve power, all powers, and its leaders to follow one another at the helm of the party and State, without any hitch, as regularly like clockwork. Such succession at the helm of the State jelled after the death of Mao Tse Tung in 1976. This State organisation around the communist party ensures State stability.

After Mao, Deng Xiaoping took over from the 11th congress of the communist party held between 12th and 18th August 1977. He went on to put order in the party and the country. This gave birth (from 1978) to a China of the Post-Mao Tse Toung era, marked by an opening to the world, to reforms and to the socialist market economy.

Political, economic, military and judiciary power is exercised at the pinnacle of the country by the Chinese communist party. Within the communist party, power is shared between well-known organs, such as the central committee, which is a kind of parliament for the party, and at the centre and at the head of the edifice is a permanent committee of nine members.

The advent of new leaders at the helm of the State, during the 18th congress of the communist party, marked the 5th generation of rotation at the summit of the State. This involved President Xi Jinping and Prime Minister Li Keqiang. They replaced President Hu Jintao and Prime Minister Wen Jibao respectively. Nevertheless, the consequences of the amendment to the constitution that suppresses the limitation of the presidential mandate, beneficial to President Xi Jinping who may now be re-elected as many times as he so desires, are still to be perceived. Some pundits considered this as a return to old ways and are fearful of an absolute power like that wielded by Mao Tse Tung. This change took place on 11th March 2018 during Chinese parliamentary session. That cultural and political revolution provoked an economic revolution.

III- China's economic revolution or the Chinese miracle

After Mao, Deng Xiaoping acceded to power. At economic level, Deng Xiaoping initiated the socialist market economy, subsequently implemented with success by all his successors. To him, it does not matter whether a cat is grey or black, so long as it catches the rat. In other words, what matters in economy, is the performance of the approach adopted, whether capitalist or socialist. This economic policy enabled China to record extraordinary economic results with a double digit growth rate. Bechir Ben Yahmed, adds that this thrust into orbit by Deng Xiaoping has in thirty years become, thirty glorious years. Thus, the Middle Empire regained its rightful position that it had held right up to the end of the 18th century.

Deng Xiaoping introduced the policy of 4 modernisations: science, agriculture, industry, military, a policy already attempted by Zhou En Lai, former prime minister of Mao. As from the Deng era, China witnessed an exceptional economic progression. Deng laid the theoretical bases for reforms by positing that Marxism must be adapted to the realities of China. He defended the idea that communism does not mean sharing poverty, making the economy a national priority. Most of the economic reforms were, to begin with, experimented at local level, and then, if proven positive, spread to national level, a testimony of the intelligence and wisdom of the Chinese rulers.

IV- Chinese miracle via an open door policy, reforms and socialist market economy

What is the secret behind the Chinese miracle? Li Junru, researcher and Vice-President of the Forum on Reform and Open Door Policy, advocates the following fundamental capacities: research and innovation, objectives and a perfect direction, with the best drivers. This include specified long-term strategic objectives, with short-term planning and execution. This form of economic development is well-oriented and planned, just like the development policy and that of all other sectors. The communist party officials are properly trained to become good drivers, capable of wheeling the steering towards the set strategic objectives and phases. He adds to this a State macro-control that ensures functioning of the economy in its role as stop-gap system against crises. He believes that Chinese economy is a macro-controlled market economy and a free market economy. This was confirmed, Li Junru states, during the fight against the Asian financial crisis in 1998 and the fight against the world financial crisis. He equally alludes to the capacity of transmitting information to facilitate coordination of various social functions. The results are self-illustrative. This open-door policy and reforms are now extended to all regions owing to its performance.

Lu Shaye, Director General of African Affairs in the Ministry of Foreign Affairs explains that in Deng Xiaoping's view, to reform is to free productivity. To accomplish development with a sturdy and rapid economic growth, obstacles to the development of productivity must be eliminated. Any sector where factors obstruct productivity must be reformed to stamp out such counter-productive factors. For instance, he added, if counter-productive factors exist in political, economic, cultural and social domains, those factors deemed unsuitable to a sustainable productivity must be eliminated.

In the economic domain, China introduced market economy reform by associating it to socialism, because it understood that all developed countries in the world practise market economy. Lu Shaye states that China does not automatically transpose a foreign model, even if it has recorded success. He adds that the reforms introduced in the different sectors go hand-in-hand. For example, reforms in the political, economic, social and cultural sectors are coordinated and not contradictory. He reveals that Western countries consider economic reforms in China to have progressed too fast, while political reforms are slow. Lu Shaye thinks that such criticism stems from the fact that the West do not understand Chinese reality, since in his view, reforms in the political sector have always been far ahead of economic reforms, given that if the concept of planned economy had not been discarded, socialist market economy would not have been possible. This criticism from the West is due to the fact that China has not adopted the multiparty democratic system. Lu Shaye stresses that for Chinese rulers, practice is the sole criteria for truth. And the open-door and reform policy must be judged from results.

Innocent Bannassoubeck, a Cameroonian working in one Chinese banking institution, adds spices to this evaluation of the Chinese miracle. To him, the Chinese economic boom is attributable, inter alia, to the boom in industrial activities and exports that propelled the Middle Empire to the position of second world economic power. This resulted to an exceptional double digit growth (10.4%) in 2010, and then 9.2 in 2011 with a GDP standing at 75 000 million dollars in the same year. A slowdown in the activities owing to the world crisis that somewhat reduced foreign demand, compelled China to make efforts to boost domestic consumption, by raising the living standards of the people, increasing revenue, while controlling inflation. He believes that the fundamental assets in this success are: hard work, a strong resolution to attain set objectives, overcome difficulties and self-confidence. Therefore since 2008, China has become the first trade partner of Africa with trade exchanges amounting to 66 000 million dollars in 2011. The China-Africa Summit of July 2012 earmarked a package of 20 000 million dollars for the execution of major projects: roads, ports, hydro-power, agricultural infrastructure, etc. These are job-creating projects that Africa must capitalise on to master the know-how, technology and science. Its import-export bank, the China Exim Bank, is the secular arm of its financial ventures in Africa, where it funds all sorts of projects in all African countries: roads, railway, dams, electrification, and telecommunication networks, construction of cultural exhibition centres, cities, mining, facilitation of loans, to confessional terms, etc.

Moreover, a well-structured report on China, published by the newspaper, Cameroon Tribune, on 4th December 2012, retraces the path that led to the Chinese miracle. It relates that Dong Guan is a world factory where computer equipment is manufactured and which ranks among the first three in world sales and the Canton Tower, with its 600 metres height, and finally its fast-track train with 350km/hr as maximum speed. The fast-track train is a combination of technologies from French ALSTOM and German SIEMENS and a special touch from Chinese engineers and technicians. Another symbol of the Chinese miracle, Shenzen, a modern metropol close to Hong-kong, is the showcase of major projects executed as part of the open-door and reform policy. Its economy, based on innovation, is founded on four pillars: finance, high level technology, logistics and cultural industry. With a population of 10 million inhabitants, Shenzen's Gross Domestic Product (GDP) which ranks it 4th among all Chinese cities (17 000 dollars per annum and inhabitant). Shenzen has become an international trade hub and bears little ressemblance to the small fishing village of just thirty years ago that was inhabited by some 30 000 souls. And for good reason, Shenzen has reaped the benefits of a special economic free trade zone since 1980. It is thus a pioneer that served as laboratory for political reforms, open-door policies, freedom and development of productivity, introduction of market economy, acquisition and application of knowledge from the West under the guidance of Deng Xiaping. Thus, to pay a glowing tribute to him, his statue sits on the peak of Mount Lotus at Shenzen: brisk step, seemingly in a haste and his gaze focused on the metropole he dreamt of as a visionary and conqueror.[149]

It is obvious that this flattering picture had shortcomings that the Chinese themselves denounce, notably and mostly corruption of the rulers, some of whom have enriched their pockets. Others believe that, in its cooperation with Africa, China is looking only after its own

---

[149]*Cameroon Tribune* of 4 December, 2012. op.cit., pg. 17.

interests, for mass purchase of certain African raw materials: oil, gold, iron, timber and others.

It must indeed be admitted that there is an ongoing debate on this diplomacy of the Yuan, the Chinese currency. China also targets the raw materials abounding in Africa for its industries. Criticised by the West in this respect, China retorts that it is offering Africa a win-win partnership, which is to the satisfaction of Africans, especially now that Western funds are rare due to the crisis in Western economies where there is a strong propensity to subject economic assistance to democratic and human right issues.

V- Can the Chinese development experience be beneficial to Africa?

Here again, Jean Tabi Manga only perceives the advantages for Africa to emulate China as he describes the success of the Chinese experience: "the Chinese renaissance espouses a similar approach to that of Japan. This demands an effective cultural synthesis that paves the way for the advent of modernism. It must be pointed out that the time of the Chinese renaissance is ancient. It was influenced by intellectual bustling and reforms undertaken in the Meiji Era". It must be recalled that in the said period, Japan had launched a controlled westernisation of its culture, drawing largely from martial arts techniques.

In the Chinese mind at the beginning of the 20th century, the West had expressed its strength and power in the military field. Such power was obvious during the conflict between China and Japan, where despite its numerical superiority, China was defeated in the 1894-1895 war. During this war, China lost the greatest part of its fleet and South Mandchuria was occupied by Japan. Japan scored this victory due to the modernisation of its military machinery and as a result of its "enlightened policy". That is the literary translation for the word Meiji.

Thereafter, China opted to open up to the West. Such open-door policy was also controlled thanks to Japanese mediation. Indeed, towards the end of the 19th century, westernisation of the East was being done through Japan. Japanese mediation was simply done in writing, as such Western thought concepts were translated into Japanese. Written in the form of ideogram, they seemed de-westernised in their form. Such skilful disguise favoured their adoption and appropriation in China. A good number of Chinese on training in Japan were influenced intellectually by Western philosophy. The early influence of Western culture on Chinese culture largely inspired the revolutionary movement of 4th May 1919.

This movement, though complex from the onset, according to J.C. Guillebaud (2008), provoked street manifestations, designed to protest against the Versailles Treaty that granted Chandong province to Japan. Owing to its magnitude and echoes of complains and demands, it evolved quickly into a national revolutionary movement. The young Chinese students leading it demanded a modernisation of China and an abandonment of hardened mandarin traditions derived from the Confucian culture. The slogan at the time that sustained the movement was: let's shut down the shop of Confucius.

These young intellectuals fervently and ardently embraced the blend of European philosophy through a Japanese dressing. In their eyes, Japan already incarnate the modernism to which they aspired.

The movement of 4th May 1919 had an obvious and far-reaching impact on the mind of Chinese youth, for the philosophy of this movement reappeared in speeches which, in the 80s, fomented the criticism of the Mao Tse Toung communism. The Chinese students of the "Beijing Spring", while radicalising their movement, echoed the 4th May 1919 calls for promotion and dissemination of "Chinese enlightenment" to combat the hardened and authoritarian Maoïsm they considered as a retrograde force. These students were machine-gunned in 1989 at Tienanmen Square in Peking. However, they had clearly expressed their resolution to re-appropriate the European philosophy of the Age of Enlightenment in the 18th century.

Chinese renaissance is a policy for modernising the country while effectively blending traditional Chinese culture, Confucianism and Western culture. Deng Xiaoping completed the modernisation of this philosophy that led to the country's emergence policy within the view of mondialisation. This philosophy was expatiated through the concept of "market socialism". Theorists of market socialism then identified four vectors of modernisation, namely:

- Training education,
- Economy,
- Military,
- ICTs.

Combined and decisive actions performed within the framework of these four strategic priority sectors propelled China into modernism, enabling it to reach exceptional levels of knowledge (Jean Tabi Manga, op.cit., pg.52-55).

Chapter III

Singapore's development model, steered by Prime Minister Lee Kuan Yew

This is an island located in South-East Asia that forms a State in the Far Southern part of the Malasian peninsula. It covers a surface area of 618km2 and a population of more than three million inhabitants. It has as spoken languages English, Chinese, Malay and Tamil.

The development of Singapore is the work of a strong-man, Lee Kuan Yew, who acceded to power in 1959 and retired in 1999. In 40 years, this great builder, on leaving power, bequeathed a wealthy country, whose revenue evolved from 400 dollars to more than 21 000 dollars.[150]

At the time this country gained independence in 1959, nobody could bet on the economic viability of this former commercial and military warehouse of the British Empire South-East of Asia. Singapore has no raw materials. Confronted, from the onset by the British army in 1965 that accounted for close to 20% of the GDP, the new leaders were compelled to build a nation from scratch. This new State had to contend with mass unemployment and lack of housing. Faced with this situation, Lee Kuan Yew could opt either for international aid or put in place an ambitious income-generating policy. He explained to his compatriots that they must not rely on international aid and that their survival depends only on hard work. He chose to transform Singapore into an industrial, commercial and financial centre in the sub-region, so as to make the most of the strategic position of their country, located between China, India and Europe. He put in place quality infrastructure and a better social organisation. In this way, he transformed the former military bases of the English army into industrial zones.

It was difficult for Lee Kuan Yew to put in place such a programme within an environment plagued by mass misery, widespread corruption in all walks of life. Thus, he gathered a strong team and opted to work on three fronts.

---

[150] Eugène Nyambal, op.cit., pg181.

He then decided to build up the credibility of institutions, with a view to gain the confidence of the people. He did this by making the fight against corruption within the government an absolute priority, and by forging in public opinion, an environment where corruption is considered as a threat to society. Next, he created enabling conditions to improve the well-being of the people through the creation of jobs, construction of modern infrastructure, schools and hospitals, and by easing access to housing property, thanks to a compulsory savings system. Finally, he encouraged the emergence of meritocracy by offering opportunities to the greatest number, entrusting management of enterprises and administrations to the most brilliant individuals of their generation, trained in the best Western schools. Moreover, he cultivated within the population values of integrity, hard work, discipline, the desire to learn and love for knowledge and competence,[151] fundamental values par excellence.

Lee Kuan Yew and his team also embarked on an industrialisation of Singapore. They set goals to be reached in terms of development, promoted investment, forged partnerships with foreign entrepreneurs. There was also the emergence of public enterprises in industries such as steel, air transport, ocean freight, etc. where the private sector was lagging. He protected burgeoning industries like the assembling of refrigerators, air conditioners, radios and televisions, in hope that these products will later be manufactured on the spot.

In view of promoting investment, Singapore attracted businessmen from Taiwan and Hong Kong in light industries (toys, textile). The leaders equally put in place an enabling environment to attract multinationals to high value added sectors, while encouraging local entrepreneurs to manufacture products for local consumption. This ambitious and bold policy enabled investment to account for 30% of Gross National Product (GNP) over a long period, and a growth rate in the tune of 8.2% between 1960 and 1990, representing thirty years. This policy alleviated and eradicated widespread poverty.[152]Eugène Nyambal best demonstrates that the economic and social success of Singapore is due to several fundamental factors and values: firstly, the calibre of the leaders who knew how to take advantage of the political and social stability of the country to speed up economic and social development. In reality, this country witnessed a continuity in terms

[151]Ibid., pg 182-183.
[152] Ditto.

policy direction and vision of development over more than three decades. On this basis, the leaders mobilised the population around a long term development vision and strategy.

Secondly, Singapore benefitted from quality institutions and relied on a solid strategic coordination at the summit of the State, as well as on close ties between the different agencies to ensure a methodical attainment of the objectives. This institutional set up is founded on a meritocratic public service, heavily involved in strategic choices and benefitting from a high social status. Thus, Singapore has the peculiarity of having reached a high level of development thanks to foreign investment, as well as to the quality of the men who managed public enterprises and administrations, bound by an obligation of success as strict as in the private sector.

Thirdly, the leaders managed to uphold a consensus around the development strategy, by associating representatives of employers and workers in the elaboration of development and social policies, creating general access to housing, education and health. Finally, the leaders constantly sought, train, employ and promote new talents.[153]

Singapore practically resorted to the same pattern to attain its development, that of effective and optimal application of the fundamental values. This include solid and stable political and State institutions, the skills of the rulers, priority to the economy and industrialisation, education and training of human resources, satisfaction of thc people's expectations, promotion of honesty, meritocracy, competence, hard work, judicious use of financial resources. This, in a nutshell, illustrates the success of a wise development policy.

---

[153]Ibid., pg 183-184.

Chapter IV

Malasia's development model, steered by Prime Minister, Dr Mohamed Mahathir

This is a Federal State found in South-East Asia, composed of the mainland (Western Malasia or peninsula) and insular part (Eastern Malasia).

Eugène Nyambal in his excellent book, '*Créer la prospérité en Afrique. Dix clés pour sortir de la pauvreté* (Creating wealth in Africa. Ten solutions to overcome poverty), describes the evolution of this South-East Asian country towards a fast-track development, just like China and South Korea. The author considers Malasia to be an example for Africa. This country covers a surface area estimated at 330 000 Km^2, smaller than that of Cameroon and has a population of more than 25 million inhabitants, who speak five main local languages, with English used as official language. Malasia is a tropical country facing similar ethnic and cultural challenges to those of many African countries. Such challenges include consolidating national unity, ensuring political and social stability, while satisfying the economic aspirations of the people. As a former British colony, this country gained independence in 1957 and succeeded to rise, within thirty or more years, starting from 1981, to the rank of the fifth Asian dragon, behind South Korea, Taiwan, Hong Kong, and Singapore. This was under the charismatic leadership of Prime Minister, Mohamad Mahathir, who acceded to power in 1981 and reigned right up 2003. Eugène Nyambal reveals that his style of government was a blend of economic nationalism, democratic authoritarism, social conservatism, technological and industrial vision, founded on the Japanese model and concrete openness to exchanges with the outside world. He adds that in the face of the Asian crisis in 1997, Dr Mahathir mustered the courage to defy the entire international finance community, by rejecting the structural adjustment policies recommended by IMF and rather opted for an internal adjustment whose positive results fanned a debate on performance of the crisis policies posited by donors. Prime Minister Mahathir retired in 2003, after transforming Malasia, from a country exporting a few basic products (palm oil, rubber, timber) into a technological and industrial power, producing manufactured products such as: electronic equipment, air conditioners, textile, steel and cars, and occupies a leading position in the transformation of raw materials (palm oil, rubber, timber). For several years now, Malasia has become a major investor in Africa in the domains of telecommunications, oil or agriculture.

To illustrate the staggering success of this country, Eugène Nyambal asserts that in 2003 its GDP stood at 103 000 million dollars, 4 times, the wealth of countries like Cameroon, Côte d'Ivoire, Ghana. Widespread poverty has been alleviated. Per capita income stood at 3 780 dollars in 2004, enrolment rate at 93% and the health system is of excellent quality.

With a view to develop the economy and accelerate industrialisation, the prime minister opted for privatisation in the 1980s to attract national industry magnates, capable of serving as model for the people. In 1991, he launched his grand "Malaisia Project": 2020 Vision". Thirty or more years to match the living standards of the industrialised countries and thus, turn Malasia into a full-developed country, with regard to economics, politics, social and cultural aspects.

The prime minister promoted a new national identity, by strengthening the sense of common destiny within a population psychologically freed, proud and distinct from others, through a quest for excellence, or even perfection. He created more space for a more active civil society, a tolerant, consensual society, driven by strong moral values. He strove to build a wealthy, an equitable and open economic society, by resorting to innovation, technology, high productivity, and high professional conscience, in order to reduce poverty and enable the emergence of a vast and enterprising middle class. This dynamic and ambitious vision of the society was conveyed on the media, in schools, enterprises and associations.

To match living standards in Malaysia with those of industrialised countries, GDP was doubled every ten years between 1990 and 2020. In this respect, an economic growth rate of 7% per annum over 30 years was targeted. This vision was sustained by a series of five-year development plans founded on 10-year strategic plans that defined priority sectors necessary to increase competitiveness. Regarding this broad brainstorming and coherent actions, the State, in conjunction with the private sector, put in place a general incentive mechanism, in view of realising the 2020 vision.

Thanks to a stable political and economic environment, a volontarist industrial and technological policy, driven by the determination to turn Malaysia into the main technological, industrial and service centre of South-East Asia, Prime Minister Mahathir launched major projects designed to take Malaysia into modernism. Top among them is the construction of the first world multimedia corridor at Putrayava and Cyberyava to challenge Silicon Valley in California, construction of the two tallest buildings in the world by Petronas, a National company, construction of tourist centres, making Malasia one of the prime destinations of the region. To add, the production of entirely national vehicles by Proton, a national company, in view of developing technological capacities and mastering the car building technology.[154]

Therefore, thanks to these multiple assets crafted by Prime Minister Mahathir: a stable political and economic environment, a voluntarist industrial and technological policy, quality infrastructure, high savings and foreign investment rate, quality administration, a well-trained labour force and an incentive system driven towards realising the 2020 vision, Malaysia was able to evolve into a wealthy society, which is more economically and culturally balanced.[155]

Malaysia, just like developing countries espoused all the fundamentals that enable political, economic, social and cultural success. That is, an extremely good quality educational and health system, clear and specific objectives at economic and social level, the vision prescribed for the future, hard work, the quest for excellence and perfection, innovation and creativity, general interest, the desire for modernism, taking hold of their destiny, national pride, emulation of best development practices from developed countries, courage in providing leadership, sustenance for a long period in this appealing dynamism, strong and exceptional moral qualities, power of the mind, the will to succeed at all course, the quest for all sorts of opportunities and patience.

After a lengthy description of the processes that lead to development such as conducted by the West and emerging countries, thanks to a revolution of thought, culture, science, technology and industries and

[154]Ibid.,pg. 181.
[155] Ditto

to the advent of a new Man, who is perfect and creative, we turn our focus to Part IV. This is based on this double experience, to provoke the cultural revolution of Africa. Such Cultural Revolution must also pave way for the advent of a new African, expected to be perfect and creator of development.

Part IV

Africa's cultural and spiritual revolution and African renaissance for the advent of a new African, who is perfect and creative, capable of achieving an optimal development of the African continent.

In this way, Africa may finally and positively take off

In the parts above, it was extremely essential to recollect the methods employed by the Western world and Asia to achieve their development. This is because in reality their experiences can be very valuable to Africa, in the same way as the European experience was for Japan and Asia. This is because the error we often commit, is to assume that development stems from nothing and that everyone may kick-start theirs without drawing from what has been done before but that is not how it works. What had been done before and successfully done is very often useful to others, especially given that true knowledge, tried and tested by concrete facts is the genesis of development. We have eloquently described the way ancient Greece and Rome borrowed all elements from the Negro Egyptian civilisation. Something they even admitted. It is obvious today that Africa must turn towards the West and Asia to gather elements of knowledge and modern civilisation.

This extensive overview of the evolution of development issues in the world since Antiquity has clearly illustrated the importance of culture in awakening the consciences of people to the perfect values of true knowledge. This approach is involved in rolling back, or even overwhelming darkness, ignorance, dogmatism, superstitions and obstacles to development. Such evolution that led to a revolution in mentalities, highlighted intelligence, wisdom as well as true and pure knowledge as inevitable vectors in the quest for development through creative and inventive minds. Africa cannot therefore neglect this rationale of spiritual and cultural revolution in perfect knowledge that constitute the only path to development. Such spiritual and cultural revolution is all the more obvious in Africa's Renaissance, just like it was the case in Ancient Negro Egypt, Europe and Japan at that time and Asia nowadays under our eyes. The spiritual and cultural revolution of Africa must enable the continent to assimilate all divine and human knowledge as well as their concrete and positive fallouts. The divine system has the advantage of providing answers to major life issues such as we posited above, because, contrary to all expectations, religions set the pace for humanity.

African renaissance, like that of other continents before it, must undergo a revolution in appropriating pure knowledge at many levels: spiritual, intellectual, mental, moral, ethics, aesthetics, civic, behavioural, scientific, technical, technological and industrial. Such complete spiritual knowledge would brood bliss, a complete, perfect and accomplished Man. A complete change in mentalities must be undergone for enlightenment and the power of the Mind to flourish. In a nutshell, African renaissance must produce a new, complete and superior being who incarnates the perfect fundamental values and who is emancipated in his Mind, because he is mature and capable of clearly grasping the intricate challenges of development. This is a superman according to the terminology of Nietzsche and a superior Man according Bergson. The African being a product of such Renaissance, must be a complete creative actor of development, for he has, thanks to true knowledge, successfully assimilated the complete process of development, given that this process is global and must be understood as such in all its dimensions (alpha to omega), particularly now that all the values leading to it are known. In reality, development, above all, concerns man himself who must accede to this stage, before transposing this reality in his environment.

Having attained such a high level, this African must form the critical mass that can jump-start development, by propelling the rest of the society to the top. Jesus rightly said to Nicodemus, a doctor in Hebraic law that what is born of the flesh is flesh and that which is born of the spirit is spirit. He who creates must change to become more of spirit than flesh, for it is in the spirit that the creative energy is found.

The intent of this part is therefore to follow and call to mind the initiatory course that must influence Africa to once again embark on the spiritual revolution that leads to knowledge. Just like the other continents had to, Africa must revisit its glorious ancient past that continues to shine like a splendid diamond, and Pan-Africanism which remains a great source of inspiration for African Renaissance, crowned by the Charter of African Cultural Renaissance and by the advent of new, perfect and creative African.

From this perspective of radical regeneration and transformation of the mind, mentalities towards positive and creative thought, Africa is on the right track and may once and for all embark on its development. At the dawn of independence, it must be admitted that adopting perfect fundamental values as an obvious approach to the development of Nations was yet to be realised by Africans. All this influenced René Dumont to declare that Africa is on the wrong footing. With a progressive assimilation and practice of perfect values, Africa is on the Broadway, a door to happy prospects for its development. And it can finally embark on a genuine path to development as described in the next book.

Chapter I

Necessity for a revolution in the Mind, knowledge and a mastery of perfect fundamental values, a springboard to African Renaissance

Perfect fundamental values constitute a reference system and structured science, thanks to their multiple prowess across the ages. We have illustrated this in the first 3 parts.

European Renaissance between the 16th to 18th centuries posited the acquisition of perfect knowledge. Firstly Japan in the 19th century during the Meiji Era then East and South-East Asia in the 20th century. These values enabled these continents, to emerge from the gloom of feudalism, ignorance, obscurantism, poverty, instability, from an archaic and traditional society. This evolution, a real revolution, was made possible by the formidable movement of knowledge, ideas, thought, awakenness of consciences, mind and creativity, or in a single word, by the far-reaching revolution in fundamental, spiritual, intellectual, moral, mental, ethics, aesthetics, civic, scientific, technical, technological and industrial knowledge. In short, this new form of cultural movement gave birth to a new man who has undergone a complete transformation in his paradigms and reading and understanding of the scales of life, his environment and thc universe. Man found himself equipped with new spiritual, intellectual and mental capacities to conquer the obstacles and difficulties of life and development. This powerful drive to master natural and supernatural knowledge, rational and intuitive thought enabled those parts of the world to attain their industrialisation and development. This was the case of Europe and the United States of America in particular, which became, major hubs for the spread of science, technology, fundamental skills and practices leading to the development of man the creator. It led to development for production in abundance of intangible, tangible and financial wealth. For, as we have stated, there can be no development without that of man as creator in the first place, key actor in any concrete positive action. We have shown how Asia, by relying on its cultural specificities and its own genius, was able to emulate the West, to bridge its scientific, technological and industrial gap. The West itself, through ancient Greece and Rome, had already imitated Africa by scouring the prowess of ancient Negro Egypt, to extract all elements of civilisation.

Africa, in its evolution towards Renaissance and following the example of these regions, must again undergo a spiritual, ontological change in its cultural revolution, like the West and Asia, and as was the case in ancient Negro Egypt. This requires appropriating the fundamental values cultivated in this venture that, alone, offer a global, total, circular, powerful, panoramic, permanent, perfect and transcending vision, which provide insight into the alpha and omega of all natural and supernatural realities, in their lucid, intuitive, creative, essential, or even magical dimension. This rational approach of the mind that constitute the power of creative thought opens the door to a comprehension of superficial and hidden meaning of things. Such spiritual, moral, intellectual and mental revolution must enable Africa to also become a source of ideas, themes, symbols, values, norms, benchmarks, paradigms, direction and dynamic references, as was the case far back in the era of Antiquity. It is at this level of knowledge that Africans may also become creators of development. This well-trained man who has become creator would then influence development. These values are of divine and human origin. Divine values concern: God and the qualities He has generously offered to man created in his image and resemblance. Such qualities include a creative and enlightened mind, power and strength, perfection, purity, holiness, intelligence, wisdom, knowledge, truth, probity, justice, goodness, love, virtue, peace, dignity, honour, majesty, nobility, eternity, force and other similar values. Africa received the gospel and Christianity, the Koran and Islam, and turned them into major religions that convey values of knowledge and elevate consciences to the peaks of learnings. Christianity and Judaism formatted the consciences of the Western people to afford them the logic of true knowledge, the logic of thought, reflection and reason, transforming them into new superior beings in terms of elevation of thought. It is not therefore admissible that, having constituted the cultural bedrock of development for Western Europe, these religions should not produce a similar result in Africa. It is thus necessary for Africans and Africa, to take the study of Scriptures to a greater depth in order to draw the quintessence and become new and creative beings. It is a fact that the gospel preaches New Birth, to a New Mind in view of gaining access to the universe of illumination and of true and pure knowledge, which is a divine universe, within which are found revelations on the different mysteries and problems of life. This is also known as Christian cabala or Jewish cabala that represents efforts towards deepening the study of the Holy Scriptures to understand their real meaning as liberator and creator. The West had to submit to this discipline of mysticism that places man in intimate contact with God to reflect on the innermost realities of things. The centeredness of God and the Church in the medieval society offered enormous advantages such as forging a new enlightened man who was at the origin of the European Renaissance and Enlightenment in the 16th and 18th centuries and of the ensuing industrial revolution. Despite scientific, technological and industrial developments in Europe, the continent continued to acknowledge that its culture is of Judeo-Christian origin. The United States of America, the number one world power since the 20th century, still resolutely adheres to the Christian values that constitute the spiritual bedrock of their culture. In this regard, Americans are still profoundly religious. Africa must refrain from practising a timid Christianity and Islam that would ultimately not allow the continent to grasp the essence of the Christian and Koranic philosophy that sets man free from ignorance and fatality, and that opens avenues to bliss and happiness. This greater understanding of the gospel or the Koran also paves the way for a better appropriation of the natural bases of human knowledge. It equally provides vitality to the African animist religion that submerges the African into his Africanity. Such Africanity revolves around values of the sacred, spiritual, freedom and community solidarity. Africa must perfectly appropriate knowledge of human origin founded on the principles of intelligence, wisdom, perfection and excellence. To accomplish that, Africa must also master science, technology, industry and creativity, which are principal avenues to an optimal transformation of the natural resources abounding in its soil and sub-soil, to overcome poverty and under-development, and plan its political, economic, social and cultural success. To do that, Africa must emulate, or even copy the industrialised countries in Europe, as well as the burgeoning Asian countries that are conducting a successful economic and industrial experiment based on their Buddhist and Confucian culture. This privileged culture is like that of Africa: respect for the family, elders, parents. In addition to values of order and discipline, respect of hierarchy, love for the future, courtesy, wisdom and intelligence as well as hard work, is the rage to win and succeed, and also mastery of science, technology and industry copied from the West.

Africa must soar to the mystical, magical, miraculous and prodigious realm of knowledge that consists in seeing the superior dimension of visible and hidden thing. This is in order to break obstacles to the bloom of a creative mind, catalyst of thought and all what is intelligible, to produce a man that is mature and superior in his intelligence. For this, he has to adopt the platonician initiatory approach that leads to the unravelling of little and major mysteries, an approach found in books and practices of wisdom: the Bible, the Koran, Confucianism, Buddhism, Hinduism, animism, etc. Africa must join this powerful spiritual movement that governs the world, by drawing from great African thinkers like: Kwame Nkrumah, Martin Luther King, Cheik Anta Diop, Léopold Sédar Senghor, Houphouet Boigny, Julius Nyerere, Nelson Mandela, King Njoya, Hampâte Ba, Engelbert Mveng, Ebénézer Njoh Mouellé, Marcien Towa, Bernard Dadié, Achille Mbembe and many others.

African wisdom also comprised similar germs that helped it to evolve from a primary level through knowledge to a superior level as has been explained above. Unfortunately, the trauma caused by slavery, colonisation, the different debasing imperialisms, derailed the African continent from its positive evolution. That notwithstanding, the African continent is the cradle of humanity and provided a base for the first great human civilisation, ancient negro Egypt for more than three millennia as Senegalese scholar, Cheik Anta Diop, demonstrated. Africa needs to rebuild and redevelop, relying on its glorious past that began since the Palaeolithic, Neolithic eras right up to ancient Egypt and pre-colonial Africa with the Great African Empires on the one hand, and on all perfect fundamental values acquired and cultivated by the different human societies and which have become a universal heritage on the other. They then enabled humanity to take an unprecedented giant step towards its development.

Africa must rebuild itself spiritually, structurally and positively in a coherent way of thinking that influences its fundamental options for the development of its people and societies. The perfect fundamental values that enlighten thinking lead to that. Mbog Bassong describes this desire to structure the coherent thinking of Africa in his book, '*La pensée africaine. Essai sur l'universisme philosophique*', Éditions kiyikaat, 2012. This glorious past must animate Africa and constitute its pride as was the case in ancient Greece and Rome and Europe. Especially given that Africa was the first laboratory where the perfect fundamental values and all elements of civilisation were experimented, as the ancient Greeks and Roman admitted.

Chapter II

The Resurgence of Africa's glorious past for African Renaissance. Africa, pioneer experimental laboratory for perfect fundamental values by ancient Negro Egypt

Ever since the Palaeolithic, Neolithic eras and for a long while, it was believed, by Western researchers in particular, that Africa was a land of the past, devoid of any history and culture. But as a result of ground-breaking studies carried out by Senegalese scholar, Cheikh Anta Diop, in his famous write-up, *Nations nègres et culture* (Negro Nations and culture), to demonstrate in a brilliant manner the anteriority of negro civilisations, this simplistic vision of African history was shattered. A similar feat was performed by studies of Burkinabé scholar, Joseph Ki-Zerbo, in his book, *L'Afrique Noire,* Éditions Hatier (Black Africa). Africa has now learned to live with its history. A history where Africa was the pioneer human civilisation and a cradle for humanity. Africa then set the pace in history and in its own history in the first eras of life on earth. This dates as far back as the Palaeolithic periods (early periods of the Stone Age), Neolithic (later periods of the Stone Age), Antiquity with Ancient Negro Egypt, right up to the Middle-Age and modern times. The Great African Empires, clearly demonstrated a logic of life and knowledge in Africa, to the extent that the first experimental laboratory for perfect fundamental values was Ancient Negro Egypt and the Great African Empires. Greeks, Romans of the Antiquity and even the first European explorers encountered it. Long before the arrival of whites, Africa was already conscious of knowledge.

Hampaté Bâ, the great Malian writer of African oral literature, skilfully demonstrated African superiority, as portrayed in his poems, Kaïdara. In this poem, each symbol embodies one or several meanings. In reality, Kaïdara explores the theme of wisdom, like we related in the paragraph on animism and African wisdom.

This tale is described as initiatory, because the history narrated leads to quest fraught with obstacles for aspirants and also leads to knowledge hidden from the eyes of the common man but revealed to anyone who shows proof of their ability to receive wisdom. Kaidara is a genius of knowledge and wisdom as we underscored above in reference to African wisdom.

Is this initiatory approach in the quest for knowledge different from that of the gospel and other religions where believers are expected to implore through prayers, reading of the holy scriptures, meditation, or practice of fundamental virtues, for access to knowledge and bliss? This saga clearly demonstrates that African culture encompasses all the ingredients of wisdom, transmitted orally. It may have been lost, strengthened in this regard by the traumatic effects of slavery and colonisation. What could have prevented this character, Kaidara, from becoming a Buddha, a Confucius, a Lao Tseu of African wisdom? This text, like any other literary work of Amadou Hampaté Bâ, offers us an inkling of the cultural heritage of West Africa and Africa as a whole.[156] This approach in the quest for wisdom clearly recalls the one advocated in the Holy Scriptures: "But seek first his kingdom and his righteousness, and all these things will be given to you as well", Matthew 6, verse 33, or even "Blessed are those who find wisdom, those who gain understanding, long life is in her right hand; in her left hand are riches and honour", Proverbs 3: 13, 16.

Likewise, in the five orphanages found in the fantasy tales of the Sahel, Marie Baron describes, in a tale of the exploits of Auta, an orphan who enjoys the spiritual protection of his defunct mother and intelligence traits attributed to certain West African divinities and their last offspring. Legba, the youngest son of Mawu, god of heaven, Bade, youngest son of Sogbo, god of thunder or Aflekete who occupies an important place in the pantheon of divinities of the sea.[157]Auta, through, his exploits is expected to be a civilising hero. Marie Baron was obliged to extend the end of the tale with a moral lesson: we must always heed the advice of our fathers and mothers who transfer common sense and wisdom.

Africa, like other regions of the world, must rediscover and rely on its myths, legends, tales that are bearers of great wisdom through the lessons conveyed. Archbishop Victor Tonye Bakot provides us with a

---

[156] Le Point références, L'âme de l'Afrique, Épopées, Contes et Légendes, novembre-décembre 2012, pg. 82.
[157]Ibid.,pg.84.

beautiful analysis and scope of Bassa proverbs[158]. Africa must rediscover the magical and mystical universe in its noble and not pejorative and obscurantist dimension. Even the other continents followed this path to true and global knowledge, for, actually, the spiritual world has realities accessible only to those with a superior mind and who have cultivated it. Indeed, magic is defined in its noble sense as a set of practices founded on belief in invisible forces immanent in nature or supernatural and aimed to master and conquer these forces in order to do good, fundamental and principal value of action of whoever employs this procedure. That is positive magic whence springs miracles, prodigies, singular and novel realities. Witchcraft in its positive dimension produces the same effects. Likewise, mystic derived from mysticism, considered as a spiritual attitude that affirms the possibility of a perfect union with God or the absolute, to grasp realities beyond appearances alone. This approach also requires intuition as well as reason. We have discovered that the pharaohs of ancient Egypt were revered as gods, they were powerful and endowed with mystical powers, and some of them were Blacks. It is no surprise therefore that they were able to build a prosperous civilisation, whose effects still dazzle humanity today. The Bible itself mentions this power wielded by the pharaohs. Even the kings of African Empires were venerated as gods. The Great Nations they built illustrate this power they wielded thanks to their proximity to divine realities. We cannot disregard inventions of the famous Bamoun monarch, Njoya in Cameroon, reputed for his inventions, architectural constructions and a political destiny that placed him at the crossroads of the German, English and French Colonial Empires. He invented the "Ka U Ku" writing and the shumum language. He wrote a history book of laws, the Saa' ngam, books containing religious and medical prescriptions. Unfortunately, the French colonial administration halted his amazing evolution by proscribing his teachings and forcing him into exile. A colloquium held in Yaounde in November 2013 on the manifold work of this genius.

In reality, some African wise men were equally mystical. They forged an intuitive and close relation with the spirit world. Reverend Father Placide Tempels explores African mysticism in his excellent book, *La philosophie bantoue* (Bantu philosophy). Wisdom and intelligence can only be rooted in this spiritual depth. This glorious past

[158]Victor Tonye Bakot, *Les Proverbes Bassa,* Éditions du Schabel, 2017, 199 pg.

is seen and observed in African prehistory and the Great Black Empires. The first laboratory elaborating perfect fundamental values has its cradle in Africa as is illustrated in the developments below.

I- African prehistory or the golden age of Africa in the Palaeolithic and Neolithic era

Africa, the cradle of humanity

In point of fact, Africa was one of the first civilisations and cradle of humanity. We expatiated on that in Part II, Chapter I. African origins of humanity have been extensively explored and relayed by famous authors like the great burkinabe historian, Ki Zerbo. In his famous book, *Histoire de l'Afrique* (History of Africa), he states, without beating about the bush, that, all that is linking us to the farthermost ancestors of man are found in Africa and in Africa only, particularly on the Eastern and Southern plateaux. The ancestors or rather the presumed parents of man are found in Africa.[159] He cites the famous English author, Darwin, who wrote on the evolution of human species, and who equally states that it is possible that the first parents of man lived in Africa rather than elsewhere. This fact is confirmed every day by new discoveries. Teilhard de Chardin wrote that: "it is in the heart of Africa that man appeared for the first time".[160]

The review, *'la Recherche',* Hors-Série No.17 March-April 2016, pg. 6-7, entitled: 'l'odyssée de l'homme. Le scénario de nos origines se précise' revisits the African origins of man. This review observes that since the 1980s, progress in genetics has allowed for a reconstitution of the evolution of our ancestors. The French palaeontology researcher, Jean-Jacques Hublin, demonstrates that hominins (grouping close descendants to homo gender since their separation from chimpanzees) found in Africa: Orrorin dates back to 6 million years, discovered in Kenya in 2000, Toumaï to 7 million years in 2001 in Chad, ardipithecus from 5.7 to 4.4 million years between the 1990s and 2005 in Ethiopia. He adds that it is in the African continent that all evolutionary history of hominins occurred some 2 million years ago. There is consensus on that, even if certain critics find it difficult to

[159] Joseph Ki-Zerbo, *Histoire de l'Afrique Noire*, Hatier-France, 1978, pg.44.
[160]Ibid.,pg.45.

accept. Homo sapiens, the present human appeared in Africa some 200 000 years ago to replace the other species in the world.

Ki-Zerbo illustrates that African prehistory during the Stone Age era was one of the most brilliant periods in the history of Africa and humanity. It was one of the longest as well, given that it lasted more than one million years. All over Africa, it left carved stones, using techniques progressively fine-tuned by humans who step by step became men: Australanthropians and Archanthropians.[161]He even estimates that Australanthropians constituted the first human race.

In regard to stone or similar tools of this era, Africa possessed an overwhelming superiority over the other continents. It is in Africa that the most patent and regular progress was witnessed in the evolution of these tools. According to many scholars, African hominians invented the first tools and spread them to the other continents. Prof. Van Riet Low believes that it is from Africa that man, after many millennia and trials and tribulations, conquered Northern Europe, Eastern Asia.

In the same way, the Eastern plateaux of Africa enjoyed clear advantages during the Palaeolithic era, just like the Sahara seem to have been an extremely attractive zone, in the Neolithic era. Tens of thousands of multifaceted testimonies of human life in prehistoric stations or villages sometimes situated hundreds of kilometres away from current watersheds.[162] The Palaeolithic era corresponds to the first period of prehistory, marked by the appearance and then development of the stone industry and through an economy of predation, corresponding to hunting and gathering.

Africa, cradle of the first agricultural or Neolithic revolution

This brilliant evolution continues in the Neolithic era that paves the way to a new era with the polished stone: Neolithic (from Greek, Neo = new, lithos = stone, it is the new era with the stone that is henceforth polished). This affords man a new and more advanced tool for inventions and practices. An evolution was witnessed during the Neolithic era, as from -10 000 years, from hunting and gathering to cattle rearing and agriculture, which brought together the current settlement of the continent.

[161] Ibid., pg.47.
[162] Ibid., pg. 53.

In Neolithic Sahara, wheat, barley and textile plants were grown. Sahara, in that era, constituted a vast world under one tenant where the circulation of men, techniques and cultures seem to have been intensive. Neolithism is even closer to us than Palaeolithic, it corresponds to the technical phase of development in prehistoric societies (polished stone, ceramics) and their accession to a productive economy (agriculture, livestock).

In support of A. Chevalier, a botanist, Ki-Zerbo adds that Negroes of the savannah invented agriculture all alone, but similar to that of inhabitants of Mesopotamia, East Asia and the plateaus of Mexico and Peru. As early as the 6th century and the 5th millennium, these inhabitants of the Niger upper valley selected and grew plants like Sorghum (Sorgum Vulgare), pearl millet (penisetum), certain varieties of rice, sesame, fonio, and furthermost in the South, yam (discrorea), oil palm (elacis guinensis), kola and a variety of cotton.[163]

And while these discoveries were spreading to the North and North-East from the Nile valley, the former welcomed and added them to they found in Mesopotamia like wheat, barley, onions, lentil, pea, melon, fig, while sugar cane, other varieties of rice and banana flocked in from Asia, Ethiopia even started growing coffee. Thus, prior to the American contribution borne by the Portuguese, Africa had known such a convergence of agricultural discoveries that we can actually talk of a **revolution**. Some of these cereals or tubers, in more or less improved forms, still feed Africans nowadays. They helped men to settle down, something without which there can be no progressive civilisation.[164] A positive evolution of Africa was really underway during this period. In the wake of Ki-Zerbo, we can conclude that during this distant period, Africa was at the origin of the first **agricultural revolution** of humanity since Negroes of the Antiquity invented self-sufficient agriculture.

Invention of pottery and painting by Africa in the Neolithic era

But the most important contribution of African Neolithism is the invention of pottery that is among the sources of domestic economy. Ki-Zerbo again states that in Neolithic Africa, one consequence of production increase (which is a partial cause) is population growth, which influenced migrations and trading. On the other hand, the organisation essential to farm work triggered a process of social

---

[163]Ibid.,pg. 56.

[164] Idem.

differentiation whose effects would be observed in the Nile valley. Such differentiation broadened the scope of occupations and possibilities. The Palaeolithic man had no choice. His job orientation was automatic: hunting or fishing. But the Neolithic man had greater possibilities. Finally, these technical transformations were followed by inherent changes in conscience and thinking.

Prehistoric Africa would then play a crucial role in art. Artistic sensation is one of the most elementary and most characteristic of man, to the extent that we can state that where there is art, there is humanity and vice-versa.

Ki-Zerbo reveals that our African ancestors invented artistic forms of an originality so profound that it is still leaving a visible impression on current productions. And researchers who discover paintings dating back to several millennia in caves and shelters found in the Sahara or Southern Africa, have identified the same African artistic inspiration.

As the most important continent in prehistoric evolution, where human populations right back to hominins were the oldest, greatest in number, busiest and most inventive, it is no surprise that African prehistoric art should by far be the richest in the world, and that in its time it has asserted a domination as influential as that of music of Negro-African source in the world of today. Africa is the richest prehistoric museum that exist.[165]

Regions that have preserved the greatest number of these precious relics are those that played the greatest role in designing and disseminating techniques, equally those where conservation of old relics was the easiest due to weather conditions, and where research had been most extensive: South and East Africa, as well as the Sahara, Egypt and the Atlas upper plateaux. The plains and great river basins of Africa offer less resources. The area bordered by the Zambezi and the Zaire rivers on the one hand, the Atlantic and the Indian oceans on the other, alone contain more paintings than all world prehistoric sites.[166] These are either chiselled engravings, with relief effects or polychrome paintings, whose styles are multifarious. What is striking in these creations is the vigour and natural movement. The engravings are often accentuated by a large trait showing contours, while the object itself is either polished with care to feature curved relief, or quilted with fur that

---

[165] Ibid., pg. 57.
[166] Ibid., pg. 58.

represent animal strips, a technique subsequently used in Ife art in Nigeria, and even nowadays in Africa to portray all hairy spots of the human body.

In Bechuanaland as well as in the Republic of South Africa, roosting cattle and elk are painted with great attention to anatomical detail, sketched as vivid as the true natural attitude. Sometimes on the contrary, like a bathing scene of young women or of a porpoise game, here the movement primes, bursting and teeming with vibrancy and joy, but still subjugated and controlled by the artist thanks to the unfailing precision of the perspectives, boldness of style and refined purity of the feature.[167]

Prehistoric engravings and paintings of the Sahara constitute another world equally as rich and wonderful as in South Africa. In Western and Central Sahara, and particularly in mountainous refuge zones (Hoggar, Tassili, Tibesti, Fezzan), tens of thousands of paintings and engravings appear featuring sixteen different styles that reflect a progressive and very long evolution. In a nutshell, the period of hunters, shepherds, cattlemen (-3500 years), of the horse (-1200 years), of the camel (beginning of the Christian era) stand out. Certain paintings date as back far as 8000 years at least. We can identify a more frequent style in the North, which portray hunters and then cattlemen, while in the South, the scenes illustrate Negroid aspects. Many hunting parties are always represented in an extremely vivid style involving elephants, giraffes, antelopes, ostriches, all animals found in the African savannah.

Though, as much as these early representations reflect the turbulent and passionate life of those who were trying to carve out a living, in the midst of wildlife, often resorting to the magic of masked and paroxysmal dances, paintings of the time dubbed the bovidian phase depict a profound pastoral calm. While the early representations are unique in their style, the most recent enriches them with numerous elements where transcends a naturalism marked by patient observation.

The colours of all these paintings are still remarkably fresh. The palette is, however, limited for it generally comprises only red, brown, yellow (which are ochre obtained from iron oxides), white (obtained from bird or kaolin droppings) and black derived from charcoal, wood, charred and crushed bones, smoked or burned fats. Exactly the same shade as those of paintings made by Pharaonic Egypt or many black

---

[167] Ditto.

people nowadays, like the Bobos of Burkina Faso. These ingredients cleverly crushed with a stone or wooden pestle in mortars were blended with melted animal fat or the marrow of cooked bones. That spelled the beginning of oil painting.[168]

From these exceedingly rudimentary methods and elements emerged: the passionate or epic peaceful fresco paintings, found on the walls of shelters and caves, as well as activities and emotions of our prehistoric ancestors.[169]

In this cultural saga and epic, ancient Egypt constitutes a strong moment, still sparkling today through the magical ingenuous architecture of its pyramids.

This saga relating the marvellous evolution of Africa peaked through ancient Egypt and the Great African Empires much later.

II- Ancient Negro Egypt, pioneer laboratory for perfect fundamental values or the Egyptian miracle

The vital contribution of the Nile to the growth of the brilliant Egyptian civilisation

Within the 4th millennium B.C., the Nile valley witnessed a multifarious and phenomenal development in the people who planned the first historical civilisation, that of Egypt ruled by Negro Pharaohs. Why Africa? Because we remember the fundamental role played by this continent during the Palaeolithic and Neolithic periods. Egyptian civilisation only crowns the leadership that Africa provided uninterruptedly for the first 3000 centuries of human history, representing 300 000 years (Joseph Ki-Zerbo even talks of a million years). This is simply fantastic. Neither ancient Greece nor ancient Rome, or even the civilisations that followed achieved such longevity. This is a record held by Africa, and Africans must know so as to use it and build their future. Sociological laws shed light on the origins of the Egyptian boom and miracle. Sahara has progressively ceased to be a park swarming with life to become an arid area. Neolithic people were skilled farmers. Whereas from 3500 B.C., due to weather conditions, the climate of tropical Africa deteriorated. With drought becoming

---

[168]Ibid.,pg.59 Read the 'La revue historama' No.56 October 1988. 'Les pharaons de l'aube', pg. 33-53.
[169] Ditto.

more severe, especially as from the beginning of the 3rd millennium, water tables declined. That is why Neolithic villages witnessed a gathering of people around rare watersheds in contrast with the scattered settlement that characterised Neolithic Sahara. It is then that the Nile in a verdant Sahara, hitherto of little interest, assumed the substantial economic value that it has maintained since then. Its terraces emerged, abounding with fertile lemon.

In just a few centuries, the banks of the Nile witnessed an exceptional demographic density. Harvest became superabundant and spurred the demographic boom. The people had to organise themselves to address the needs of the clan: leaders, priests, servants. A complete diversified and complex new society sprung up from the fertile lemon of the river. To the extent that Herodotus made this famous declaration: Egypt is a gift of the Nile. Of all this evolution, Egypt emerged from the darkness of prehistory as a mature and powerful people, ruled by the pharaoh, a demi-god. It became the cradle of one of the most brilliant and most lasting human civilisations. For 3000 years, it illuminated the Nile valley and witnessed the rule of 500 kings, especially those from the 1st to the 20th dynasty, many of whom were Blacks. Their fantastic history is recounted in the Bible in the book of Exodus, Chapters V to XV.

Within this period, pharaohs took turns at the helm of this great and brilliant civilisation. The 3rd to the 6th dynasty under the Ancient Empire lasted from 2778 to 2260, representing 618 years, it is renowned for the great pyramids of Gizeh, Kheops, kephren and mykerinus, those built by queens are smaller. Under the 17th dynasty, Joseph in the Bible was invited by one of these kings to serve as minister, a presence that swelled the Jewish colony in Egypt. During the period of Antiquity, the greatest pyramid, that of Kheops was one of the Seven Wonders of the World, 147m high and 277m wide. It covered 5 hectares. This enormous mass was composed of about 2 300 000 limestone blocks, each weighing at least 2 tonnes. This construction kept 100 000 men working for 20 years. The 18th and 20th dynasties under the New Empire (1580-1085) constituted the era for constructions of monuments: the temple of Karnack devoted to the god Ammon, the temple at the heart of the largest set of religious edifices in the country. The temple presents the canonical plan of the temple of pharaonic Egypt with pylons, a courtyard bounded by a portico whose roof lies on 32 pillars. Under the New Empire with Thebes as capital, Egypt was the most powerful in the Middle-East. Under the rule of Thoutmosis III,

Amenophis IV, initiator of the cult of Aton (under the name of Akhenaton, the one who pleases the Sun-god) and Ramses II, the Empire witnessed an unprecedented artistic bloom with the construction of a series of architectural Karnak edifices, the funeral Temples of Hatshepsout (Queen of the 18th dynasty, 1520-1484 B.C, wife of Thoutmoisis III), Ramses II and Ramses III, royal Hypogeums (tombs) in the Valley of the Kings, architectural culmination of the divine temple (Louqsor). Wall painting reached its peak. Realism and sensuality characterised the sculpture of the queen of Akhenaton (bust of Nefertiti, her wife from the black race). Certain pharaohs were Blacks: Tutankhamon of the 18th dynasty, Ramses II, Kephren, founder of the 4th dynasty (Ancient Empire). He ordered the construction of the second pyramid of Egypt, Thutmosis, son of a Sudanese, known as Napoleon of the Antiquity, he founded the 12th dynasty and inaugurated the era of Egyptian imperialism, the Sudanese pharaoh Taharqa. Cheikh Anta Diop also presents the bust of Namer, a typical Negro, first pharaoh of Egypt who united upper and Lower Egypt. Cheikh Anta Diop stressed that pharaoh Namer was neither an Aryan nor an Indo-European, or a Semite, but indisputably a Black. He also mentions the monarch Tera Neter, proto-historical character of the Negro race of Anou, the first inhabitants of Egypt. The different busts of these black characters are related in the book of Cheikh Anta Diop (ibid, pg 73 to 82). It presents the statue of god Osiris who was a Black.

The pyramid itself is a great monument, rectangular at the base and of four triangular facets. It is the royal burial, which is pharaonic tomb of ancient Egypt. It was under Amenophis IV, pharaoh of the 18th dynasty who adopted the name Akhenaton (the one who please Aton the Sun-god) that a single God was experimented (monotheism) under the influence of his wife, Queen Nefertiti. Pharaohs bearing the name Ramses (1580-1320 B.C.) of the 19th and 20th dynasties, were among the most famous including Ramses I who founded the 19th dynasty. This dynasty witnessed the reign of eleven pharaohs.

Egyptian civilisation succeeded in asserting itself through its socio-political, religious, cultural, scientific and artistic organisation. Pyramids bear testimony to that. The practical science used in constructions revealed by these monuments is vast and has never been topped. The funeral chambers and interior corridors have borne millions of kilos for millennia without any mishap. These final resting places for pharaohs are real eternal houses. They were built by slaves and mostly peasants driven by genuine faith, with stone and wooden tools forged using techniques whose secrets have often disappeared, or maybe vanished maybe during the burning of the Alexandria library by the Romans. Each city had its divinity. Ancient Egypt was deeply spiritual. The religion of the Egyptians was centred, above all, on the cult of the sun and the Nile, the two sources of life in the country. The Egyptian pantheon had a multitude of gods and sacred places. Osiris was the god of the Nile, divinity of fertility and husband of Isis, Rê was the Sun-god, worshipped by Heliopolis. Aton, god of Thebes, represented by a solar disc, participated in elevating this city. In Thermopolis, the citizens worshipped the moon, the deity protector of mathematicians, scribes and the wise.

Egyptian art per se reached unparalleled summits, and architecture, sculpture, engraving, painting witnessed a good number of styles. This art was mainly inspired by religion. Temples are the principal expression. These edifices are like buildings that fit together starting from the esplanade of pylons right to the open chapel that contain the image of the god. The walls of the temple are covered by representations of rituals and images, the statues bear hieroglyphic formulas. All that has as intent to revive the good forces represented by god. Egyptian art is also inspired by the funerary. Beyond appearances, it is one of the religious symbols that guide the defunct through rites of passage to eternity. Egyptian religion is at the bottom a vitalism.

Contribution of Blacks to the brilliant Egyptian civilisation

In this brilliant civilisation, Ki-Zerbo highlights the contribution of blacks in the Nile Valley, using geographical, anthropological and cultural arguments. He concludes that Blacks must have formed the majority population of the ancient Nile Valley, at least in the early stages of protohistoric and historic eras and in southern zones. They played a decisive role in building the Egyptian civilisation. And a good number of great men in Egyptian history were blacks. Nefertiti, queen of Egypt and wife of Pharaoh Amenophis IV, Akhenaton from 1372 to 1354, was Black. She played a key political role. She is mostly known for being at the origin of a religious revolution that impacted her time. As worshipper of Aton, a god represented in the form of a solar disc, she convinced her husband to institute a single divinity. According to the British Egyptologist, Cyeril Aldred, she sow the barleycorn from which grew the great religions of Moses and Jesus (Jeune Afrique

No.2555-2556 of 27th December 2009 to 9th January 2010. An article written by Leila Sliman, entiled: Nefertiti, Queen of Egypt, Great Wife of Akhenaton), a thesis defended by Cheikh Anta Diop (in his book, '*Nations nègres et culture*', Présence africaine, 2015). In his book, he presents statues of the Blacks of Ancient Negro Egypt: a very common hairstyle for young girls in black Africa (it is found at the Louvre Museum in Paris), the Egyptian woman, the butcher, 2nd dynasty, a cook, an Egyptian functionary (Ancient Empire, 6th dynasty): a young Egyptian girl, 18th dynasty, the hairstyle of this young girl shows that Egyptians were totemists. It is the hairstyle preferred by all young girls in Senegal up to the age of puberty. It can be observed that hairs were frizzy, an Egyptian priestess (the tradition of priestess was widespread in Negro Antiquity: priestesses of Thebes, Jupiter Amon (Libya), an Egyptian (Ancient Empire, 6th dynasty), and Egyptian heads of the Middle Kingdom deemed too Negroid. He presents hairstyle as an Ife art in Nigeria, to illustrate its resemblance with that of the pharaoh of ancient Egypt (ibid).

Senegalese scholar, Cheikh Anta Diop, devotes this quest of Blacks for emancipation and universal knowledge in '*Nations Nègres et Culture*'. A book in which he demonstrates the anteriority Negro-African civilisations. The civilisation is struggling in an environment where the European intelligentsia develops a radically hierarchizing concept of humanity, from which it is assumed that black Africa cannot and must not have a history, that it cannot constitute an intelligible historical field, to use the words of the British historian, Arnold Toynbee, that it could not have created any civilisation.[170]

One of the ultimate goals of the important and revolutionary task of Cheikh Anta Diop is to restore the historic conscience of the African, which is the conscience of having a history. Théophile Obenga, a Congolese Egyptologist and disciple of Cheikh Anta Diop, explains what the concept of historic conscience embodies: "greater awareness of the depth of the world that he has experienced, and also acquire a conscience to participate in history, to create history". Historic conscience is synonymous to awakening to the possibility of an option that is freedom. Accidents in history (slave trade, colonisation, economic, political, cultural, psychological traumas) have rendered

[170] Cheick M'backé Diop, Cheikh Anta Diop, *L'homme et l'œuvre*, Présence africaine, 2003, pg.16.

black people amnesic: the collective memory of African people was severely affected. Cheikh Anta Diop took on the fundamental task of restoring the historic conscience of Africans.[171] Cheikh M'baké Diop concluded that the challenge is formidable, for it means understanding the present in order to commit without much ado to the daily construction of a planned, envisioned, dreamed future, chosen in absolute intellectual, social and political freedom. And this can only be fully achieved through an appropriation of the perfect fundamental values that have become a universal heritage, since the world is now a global village that shares similar values.

Concerning African Renaissance, Cheikh Anta Diop published an article titled, "*Quand pourra-t-on parler d'une renaissance africaine*" (when can we talk of an African renaissance). For the first time, he affirmed the need to build African classics based on ancient Egyptian platform, like the Graeco-Latin (Greek and Latin) that form the basis of European classics. Development and employment of African languages in all fields of the life of Negro-African people constitute a cornerstone of this article that equally dwells on art and music.

For Cheikh Anta Diop, the history of Africa in the long run becomes an essential issue formulated in new words: "How is African history perceived? As we can observe, while the European may trace his history right back to Graeco-Latin Antiquity and the Eurasian steppes, Africa, through Western books, in trying to retrace its historical past, stops at the foundation of Ghana (3rd century before or 3rd century after Jesus Christ)". Beyond that, "is a black void according to these books. What were these ancestors doing on the continent since prehistory? Why is it that they took so long to emerge from the darkness with an advanced social organisation? Have they always lived in Africa or did they migrate from elsewhere?"[172]

All these questions about the past gave birth to the four books published at '*Présence africaine*' that constitute the foundation of the historic work of Cheikh Anta Diop:

- *Nations nègres et culture. De l'Antiquité négro-égyptienne aux problèmes culturels de l'Afrique Noire d'aujourd'hui - 1954*
- *L'Afrique noire pré-coloniale, 1960*

---

[171]Ibid., pg.20.
[172]Ibid., pg. 40.

- *L'unité culturelle de l'Afrique Noire, 1960*
- *Antériorité des civilisations nègres, mythe ou vérité historique, 1967*

This emboldened Cheikh Anta Diop to carry on, for it is his multidisciplinary approach to the history away from a Western racial hierarchy prejudice. For instance, the study of names of places (toponymy), the study of names of human groups (ethonymy), the comparative study of languages on the entire continent provide elements to concretely and vividly confirm his initial working hypothesis on existing links between the various people of Africa.

The themes developed by Cheikh Anta Diop in his books in light with putting Africa back into perspective in point of time and space are many:

- *L'origine africaine de l'humanité,*
- *La délimitation de l'aire culturelle du monde noir qui s'étend jusqu'en Asie occidentale dans la vallée de l'Indus*
- *Les deux berceaux culturels septentrional et méridional : étude du patriarcat et du matriarcat,*
- *Le peuplement de la vallée du Nil,*
- *L'identification des grands courants migratoires et la formation des ethnies africaines,*
- *La véritable origine du monde sémitique,*
- *La parenté linguistique, culturelle entre l'Égypte et l'Afrique noire,*
- *L'apport de la civilisation égyptienne, donc la pensée nègre, à la civilisation occidentale dans les sciences, les lettres et les arts, le droit, la religion, la médecine, la philosophie, etc.*
- *La caractérisation des structures politiques et sociales,*
- *La formation et l'organisation des États africains dans le continent après le déclin de l'Égypte et la continuité du lien historico-culturel, jusqu'à l'aube des temps modernes,*
- *La description de l'univers artistique africain, sculpture, peinture, musique, architecture, littérature, etc.*
- *La démonstration de l'aptitude des langues africaines a supporté la pensée scientifique et philosophique, et partant la première transcription non ethnographique de ces langues.*[173]

---

[173]Ibid.,pg. 43 et s.

In his views on colonialism, talking about Negro Nations and culture, Aimé Césaire admits that this book is essential to the awakening of Africa. The aspect much criticised is that of the belonging of ancient Egyptians and the brilliant civilisation they built in the Negro-African world. The significant contribution of ancient Egypt to Greek civilisation was unanimously pointed out by ancient Greeks themselves. The decipherer of hieroglyphics, Jean François Champollion (1790-1832), known as Champollion le jeune, recalled this intellectual heritage: "an interpretation of the evolutions of Egypt will better highlight the Egyptian origin of science and the main philosophical doctrines of Greece, the Platonician school nothing but Egyptianism".

Jean Marc Ela acknowledges that Cheikh Anta Diop did not wait for specialists to give him credit before stating that ancient Egypt was Negro and expressing his view on the cultural unity of Black Africa.

In 1956, subsequent to a lecture delivered by Cheikh Anta Diop, a French newspaper, '*Le Républicain Lorrain*', shrewdly wrote: "two centuries of erudition under attack": a young Senegalese historian declared that, "Western civilisation is legatee of a black civilisation that originated from the Nile".[174]

Cheikh Anta Diop claims that the Western intellectual failed in his duty of transferring knowledge without any distortion, stating that: "when imperialism reached its peak in modern times in the 14th century, the West discovered that it was rather black Egypt that provided all the elements of civilisation to Europe, and this truth could not be revealed, that is the reality".[175]

He further points out that: "And all scholars were equally not willing to reveal this truth unequivocally". For that reason, the community of scholars break up into two groups:

- Bonafide scholars who mustered the courage to face the truth, Volney included.
- And all the line of Egyptologists who twisted the history of humanity generation after generation and who committed the greatest crime against humanity.

---

[174]Ibid.,pg. 47.
[175]Ibid.,pg. 48.

Among these Egyptologists, "there has been a much more reasonable school that tried to postulate a more or less disguised truth. From misrepresentation to misrepresentation it was finally declared that Egypt was an accident in Africa and that any mention of Egypt, rather refers to the East. Egypt is not the East, it is Africa".[176]

In the wake of this scientific and historical approach of Cheikh Anta Diop, Jean Marc Ela demontrates that scientific objectivity also constitutes a strategic challenge. "Working on the first general book on African history written by a French-speaking Black, Cheikh Anta Diop ensures that the quality of his research as much as his scientific effort fall within the purview of a struggle. The African historian is too conscious of the challenge facing his research to commit the same errors he is combating".[177]

Cheikh Anta Diop expresses a pressing need for Africa to regain its memory, its historic conscience, by restoring its history, to find keys to an in depth understanding of the structures and evolution of human societies in general and African societies in particular, identify the position of the continent in the historic evolution of humanity. He quickly understood the fact that the only salutary way of restoring enabling creativity conditions for Africa is to unlock the creative mind, such as to allow Africa again to participate in the progress of human civilisation, and not bear the brunt. He understood very early that history and language are the components essential to the development of people.[178] How do we know where we are going if we don't know where we are coming from? That is the necessary link between the past, the present and the future of Africa made by Cheikh Anta Diop.

In this respect, Cheikh Anta Diop disagrees with Léopold Sédar Senghor. While Senghor speaks of negritude, Diop advocates African Renaissance from the pharaonic Egypt heritage and promotion of Negro-African languages. He considers Senghor and his friends as African foreign language writers. He is not convinced that their writings constitute the foundation for an African culture. While Senghor asserts that emotion is negro, reason is Greek, Diop denounces the alienation of Negroes of high intellect that seek to standardise these Nazi ideas into a supposed duality of the sensitive and emotional Negro, creator of

---

[176] Idem.
[177]Ibid.,pg.49.
[178]Ibid.,pg.50.

art, and of the white mostly driven by rationality. According to him, Senghor uses negritude to destroy true African culture.

According to Cheikh Anta Diop, it is difficult to apprehend the people who compose humanity on the basis of supposed differences in intellectual abilities, reasoning skills, for these qualities are same for all humanity: reason is universal. In other words, reason is not only Greek and emotion specifically Negro. The human being as a whole embodies the two at once. The author of '*Nations Nègres et Culture*', believes that knowledge of the past constitutes a security shield for a community against cultural or physical genocide. Such knowledge equally forms a solid foundation that the community may and must use to choose new institutions and formulate a genuine development policy.

In 1956, the rector of the University of Haiti, chair of the first international Congress of Black Writers and Artists, held in Paris at the Sorbonne, from 19th to 22nd September 1956, most opportunely affirmed that: "Despite the diversity of views and variety of themes discussed, all our concerns boil down to a similarity in conception, meaning that all men are human and, but for some latitude and conditions they experience, they deserve the respect and consideration of all other men because all have in them a bit of this divine essence through which the distinguished human dignity is expressed".[179]

During the second edition of the International Congress of Black Writers and Artists, held in Rome, Italy from 26th March to 1st April 1959, Georges Gurvitch, a sociologist, in a letter addressed to Alioune Diop, founder of the *Présence africaine* publishing house declared: "Negro-African culture has shown to the entire world an extraordinary example of vitality and vigour. All religious as well as philosophic vitalist conceptions stemmed from this source. The civilisation of ancient Egypt would never have been possible without the great example from the Negro-African culture, and it was solely sublimation".[180]

A whole generation of African and Caribbean intellectuals and politicians graced this period: Hampâte Bâ, Aimé Césaire, Léon Gontran Damas, Gabriel d'Arboussier, René Depestre, Amady Aly Dieng, Alioune Diop, Mahjemout Diop, Saint-Claire Drake, Boutros Boutros Ghali, Cheik Fall, Frantz Fanon, Keita Fodeba, Édouard

[179] Ibid, pg. 62.
[180]Ibid., pg.63.

Glissant, J. Price Mars, Abdou Moumouni, Ahmadou Mactar M'Bow, Ruben Um Nyobe, Houphouet Boigny, Rabemananjara, Assane Seck, Bakary Touré, Abdoulaye Wade, Joseph Ki-Zerbo, Paul Hazoumé, E.L. Losebikan, Édouard Andrianats, Laniaro, Davidson Nicol, Horace Mann Bond, Ben Enwonwu, Richard Wright.[181]

All espoused this truism whereby every people have a history and Black Africa, contrary to many views, has a glorious past, inspired by scholarly research works undertaken by illustrious Africans and mostly by the Senegalese scholar, Cheikh Anta Diop. Thus, the latter and other Africans took part in writing the general history of Africa, published by UNESCO and even the history of cultural and scientific development of humanity.[182]

Africa's legacy to humanity is therefore real and confirmed by many research findings. Thus, the legacy of pharaonic Egypt, scientific (mathematics, astronomy), architectural, religious, philosophic, moral, legislative and legal, artistic (sculpture, painting, music), ludic, linguistic, to the Western world, has been underscored by a majority of ancient Greeks themselves. Jean Philippe Omotunde gathers in two books: '*L'origine négro-africaine du savoir grec* et *Les racines africaines de la civilisation européenne*', Eropean sources of the cultural legacy of ancient Africa to ancient Greece.

Théophile Obenga describes this contribution in his book, '*L'école d'Alexandrie, la Grèce ancienne et l'Égypte pharaonique*'. The geographical location of the Alexandria Library in Egypt on African soil (around 295 before our era under Ptolemy I) is very significant, the same applies to the Alexandria School, which fed on Negro-Egyptian intellectual and spiritual legacy for many centuries, under Ptolemy and the Roman Empire. The burning down of the Alexandria Library that contained hundreds of thousands of documents (from 400 000 to 700 000) inflicted an inestimable loss of intellectual and spiritual memory to Black Africa and humanity as a whole.[183]

On his part, Martin Bemal, a researcher of English origin, from Cornell University (the USA), in his book, *Athena-afroasiatic roots of classical civilisation*, lambasts the Greek miracle, condemning the

---

[181]Ibid., pg. 60 et s.
[182]Ibid., pg. 101.
[183]Ibid., p. 215.

Euro-centrist vision of Antiquity that plays down Egyptian and Semitic influence on classical and hellenistic Greece.

Thus, archaeological findings, linguistic Egyptology studies, molecular biology and genetics studies, material culture studies, philosophical thinking, oral tradition have confirmed the remarkable fertility of historical research opened as early as 1954 by Cheikh Anta Diop with '*Nations Nègres et Culture'*. Added to that are a series of new works that contribute to restore and re-examine the input of Africa in human civilisation and to encourage African men as well as women in the domains of science, medicine, historians, sociologists, jurists, economists, artists, craftsmen, sportsmen, architects, philosophers to appropriate this immense legacy bequeathed by the civilisations of the Nile Valley, by those of the continent as a whole. We also include the legacy of the University of Timbuktu, built in 1325 during the great Sahelian Empires or even Muslim Arab contribution to Europe. The work of Engelbert Mveng, a Cameroonian scholar, also dwells on anteriority of the Negro civilisation and its contribution to humanity through his thesis defended at the Sorbonne in 1976 on the theme, "*Les sources grecques de l'histoire négro-africaine depuis Homère jusqu'à Strabon*".

III- Contribution of Ethiopia-Nubia and ancient Negro Egypt to human civilisation

In this respect, Cheikh Anta Diop underlines that according to undisputed testimonies from ancestors, Nubians and Ethiopians first fashioned and disseminated all civilisation elements to an extraordinary level of development, followed by Egyptians, while other peoples, especially Eurasians, were still grappling with barbarism. The explanation can be found in the material conditions under which geography had, by sheer luck, placed them at the beginning of time. For man to adapt to this environment, he had to invent science to which he added the arts of religion.

He further states that we cannot be too expansive on all what this world, and especially the Hellenic world, owes the Egyptian world. Greeks merely borrowed and often developed Egyptian inventions to an extent and their materialistic predilection pushed them to strip these inventions bare of the religious, idealist armour that served as their shield. Thus, when Greeks borrowed the Egyptian god who was a true god in the real sense of the word, he could only understand and adore the god by bringing this deity down to the level of man. In this way, the Greek adopted pantheon is a mere human. Such anthropomorphism, in this particular case, is nothing but extreme materialism that characterised the Greek mind. The Egyptian scholar considers that the Greek miracle at intellectual level per se never occurred, if we were to discuss the acclimatisation process to Egyptian values in Greece. According to him, Greek genius owed essentially to the influence of Eurasian steppes and their pitiable religious disposition. This religious disposition made possible among them, the existence of a secular science taught in public by equally secular philosophers, once they borrowed Egyptian values, instead of this science being the prerogative of a sacerdotal corps who could guard it jealously, without spreading it among the people, such as to spare it from getting extinct in social upheavals. The power and dignities of the mind running their invisible Empire everywhere else, alongside the force of arms was neither wielded by priests or functionaries in Greece, but by researchers and thinkers. The latter could, as was obviously the case with Thales, Pythagoras, Plato, Aristotle, Epicurus, Zenon of Kiton and Empedocles, become the centre of a circle found between the congregation of a school, an academy, and the community of an order closer at one time to one and sometimes to the other, setting the scientific, moral and political goals and interlinking them to form a philosophic tradition (Ernest d'Astir: '*Histoire de la philosophie, traduction*', M. Belvianes, Payot, 1952 pg.48) cited by Cheikh Anta Diop. Scientific, philosophical teaching was provided there by nonbelievers not different from the people, if not for the intellectual level or their Aristocratic rank. No halo of holiness surrounded them. Plutarch, a Greek writer who travelled to Egypt and Rome, in *Isis and Osiris*, recounts the story of all Greek scholars and philosophers who were brought up by Egyptians, stating that the latter never desecrated their science: Solon, Thales, Plato, Lycurgus, Eudoxius, Pythagoras, encountered difficulties before their initiation by Egyptians. Like Amélineau, Cheikh Anta Diop wonders why much emphasis has not been laid on Egyptian contribution to civilisation. Cheikh cites Amélineau: "I have discovered then, and clearly discovered, that the most famous Greek systems, notably those of Plato and Aristotle, had Egypt as cradle. I have equally discovered that whatever we may admire in Greeks, we should not despise or simply spurn in Egyptians. Nowadays, whenever two authors collaborate, credit of their common work goes unquestionably to the two collaborators: I do not understand why ancient Greece would be attributed the honour of ideas that were borrowed from Egypt" (Amélineau, '*Prolégomènes*', Introduction, pg. 8-9).

Amélineau shows that if some of the ideas of Plato have become obscure, it is because allusion is no longer made to their Egyptian source, for example, that is the case with the ideas of Plato on the creation of the world by the creator. On the other hand, we know that Pythagoras, Thales, Solon, Archimedes, Erastosthenes studied in Egypt itself, and the list does not stop there. Egypt was really the classical land where two-third of Greek scholars and philosophers studied. In reality, we could claim that during the Hellenistic period, Alexandria in Egypt was the intellectual centre of the world where all the Greek scholars much spoken about today gathered. We cannot overstress the fact that all these scholars received their training, outside Greece, that is, in Egypt.

Even Greek architecture has its roots in Egypt. Graeco-Roman monuments are merely replicas of Egyptian monuments: we know that Notre Dame of Paris with its towers would be an easy fit in the hypostyle hall of the Karnak temple, and more so in Greek pantheon.

The kind of fable, typically negro or koushite, which consists in depicting animals on stage was introduced in Greece by Egyptian Negro, Esope, the muse of the '*Fables de La Fon*taine'. Edgar POE, in 'Some words with a Mummy' (*Nouvelles histoires extraordinaires*) provides a key indication of the scope of scientific and technical knowledge from ancient Egypt. This also applies to the art of preparing mummies in Egypt. To ancient Egyptians, survival in the beyond could only be guaranteed on one condition: that the corpse of the defunct should preserve its anatomic cohesion (the review, '*Histoires et Civilisations*', No.37, April 2017, pg.28-40).

Herodotus, the father of history had already received information from the mouth of Egyptian priests, highlighting the mathematical essence of the Great Pyramid of Cheops. Several mathematicians and astronauts devoted books to the study of this pyramid, whose astonishing revelations as you would have thought sparked a wave of contentions, not reflected in the form of a consistent presentation. He equally quotes the view of Father Moreaux that, the great pyramid does not represent an onset of groping about for a culture that is at its peak and which, on the verge of disappearing, attempts, in an ultimate flash of pride to bequeath to future civilisations, a testimony of the zenith of its superiority. Cheikh Anta Diop,op.cit., pg. 359-400.

"Conversely, Greeks borrowed their gods from Egypt. Almost all names of gods in Greece originated from Egypt. It is obvious that they were derived from barbarians, Herodotus so believed, in his research (Barbarian means stranger, bereft of any prerogative nuance)". Thus, the Egyptian origin of civilisation and its extensive appropriation by Greece constitutes a historical evidence, we could join Amélineau in asking why, despite these facts, emphasis is on the role played by Greece and the role of Egypt ever more overlooked. Cheikh Anta Diop explains that logic of this attitude can only be grasped, by getting to the bottom of the matter: "Given that Egypt is a Negro country and the civilisation developed there attributed to Negroes, any thesis designed to proof the contrary cannot prosper. Thus, it is wiser and more advisable to purely and simply strip Egypt off all its creations, in favour of a people of white origin. Such false attribution of values of an Egypt, cast as white, to a Greece equally white, reveals a profound contradiction that provides little proof of the Negro origin of the Egyptian civilisation". As can be perceived, contrary to what André Siegfried posits, far from being able to develop skills, the coloured man, was even first to develop them as Negro at a time when all white races were still plunged in barbarism, barely capable of developing a civilisation.

By stating that these ancestors of Negroes, who now live mainly in Black Africa, were the first to invent mathematics, astronomy, the calendar, arts, religion, agriculture, social organisation, medicine, writing, techniques, architecture, they were the first to erect edifices with 6 000 000 tonnes of stones (great pyramid) as architects and engineers and not only as labourers, that they constructed the gigantic temple of Karnak, this cluster of pillars, with its famous hypostyle hall in which Notre-Dame of Paris and its towers could fit, that they sculpted the first colossal statues (Colossus of Memmon, etc.). By stating all this, we are just affirming no more than the modest and actual truth, which nobody can refute, nowadays with any valid arguments.

Henceforth, the Negro must be capable of wresting back control over continuity of his national past, drawing from it the moral benefit necessary to reconquer his place in modern world, without lapsing into the excesses of a Nazism from the wrong way, for the civilisation he claims to spring from could have been created by any other human race.

Inasmuch as one could talk of a race that had been placed in a favourable, as well unique cradle.

Indeed, Egyptian civilisation is amazing, fascinating owing to: its longevity of more than three thousand years, stability of its institutions, rationality of its social organisation, its ethics, its ideal justice, its philosophical systems, its scientific knowledge, its spirituality embodied in texts about pyramids and temples, architecture, art, mummification. These are fruits of a multimillenal human experience acquired in the course of an extensive evolution along the Nile starting from around the African Great Lakes, under an inter-tropical latitude, where man was born.[184] Thus, it is but normal that with all this, Africa should be the source of the first large-scale human civilisation.

It is this rich past that bred the fundamental values of the Mind, knowledge, culture, science, religious beliefs, state authority, etc., that must serve as a springboard for an African Renaissance. The latter should find in the African past true vectors of its development, to contradict those who wrongfully, or hastily concluded that Africa has no history. Whereas, Africa is the first experimental laboratory for perfect fundamental values: spirituality, intellectual, cultural, mystical life, rational organisation, the sense of ethics, justice, aesthetics, scientific and philosophic knowledge, artistic intelligence, security, etc. Unfortunately, colonisation derailed this very beautiful evolution. African Empires that took over from this declining Egyptian civilisation constitute another illustration of African vitality.

IV- Dynamism of the Great African Empires

The dynamism of the Great African Empires is political and social on the one hand, and economic on the other.

1- Dynamism of the Great African Empires at political and social level

Apart from ancient Egypt, Africa witnessed other brilliant civilisations from the 10th to the 15th century before the arrival of the Whites. This include the Empires of Ghana, Mali, Kanem Bornu, Songhai, Oyo, Yoruba, Kongo, Benin Kingdoms, etc.

---

[184]Ibid., pg. 216.

These Empires grew autonomously as organised and prosperous societies. Their political, administrative, religious and economic organisation revolved around a strong central authority, a king vested with divine powers, especially in West Africa, and was often incarnated by the Chief. Africa did not wait for the Western Christian to forge links with gods. Reverend Father Tempels demonstrates this fully in his book, '*la Philosophie bantoue*'. All cultures have always had such ties. Africa is no exception. Ghana was renowned for its gold resources and its wealth.

Mali was known for its great kings, notably Sundiata Keita "the lion of Mali" and Kankan Moussa, the latter reigned from 1312 to 1332 for 20 years, he undertook a pilgrimage to Mecca with the intention of imposing his power over Arab sovereigns. He was accompanied by close to 60 000 servants, carrying about two tonnes of gold. It goes without saying that, his appearance at Cairo in Egypt, dazzled the world, for he was perceived as the lord of Eldorado. He subsequently showered Cairo with streams of his generosity. Nobody was left out, as every officer of the court or holder of a Sultanian function received from him a sum of gold.[185]

He ordered the building at Timbuktu of the Great Mosque of Djingareyber. Kankan Moussa, also called Mansa Moussa, made Mali famous in the entire Arab world, from Andalusia to Khorasan, and European maps show a road crossing the desert to end at the kingdom of the king of goldmines[186]. In like manner, the Catalan Atlas drawn by Abraham Cresques for the King of France, Charles V the Wise, clearly bears the name of the capital "ciutat de Melli", and the author of Tarikh el-Fettach affirmed: "we have heard many of our contemporaries say that there are four sultans in the world, namely the Sultan of Bagdad, the Sultan of Cairo, the Sultan of Borno and the Sultan of Mali".[187] Kankan Moussa was the equal of world greats at that time, owing to his aura and that of his Empire that he led to the pinnacle of success. The Emperor of Mali used to deal with the sovereigns of Maghreb as equals within the frame of Umma (community of believers). In 1330, he sent

---

[185] Joseph Ki-Zerbo, Ibid.,pg.135.
[186]Ibid.,pg. 136.
[187] Ditto.

an ambassador to meet Morocan Sultan, Abul Hassan. He forged ties with King John II of Portugal.[188]

For more than one century, during the good times, Mali developed a political integration model whereby peoples as varied as the Tuareg, Wolof, Malinke, Bambara, Songhai, Fufulde, Toucouleur, Yalunka paid allegiance to the same sovereign. Men, goods and ideas circulated within this environment. There was maximum security. On the other hand, the king of Kongo, Mani-Kongo maintained privileged relationship with the king of Portugal.

Meanwhile, Benin, an ancient kingdom in the Gulf of Guinea, current Nigeria, founded in the 12th century, was a city far more advance in urban planning than most great European towns at the time.[189] Ife (Nigeria) Art and craft and Benin art have become renown in the world following the discovery of masterpieces in bronze (brass) or baked clay. This is a nature-inspired royal art that portrays the kingdom's magnificent celebrations. Benin art is a more powerful, symbolist and concise art.[190] Ife art is older. It produced masterpieces, most of which were ferried away by the British military expedition of 1897. Ife masterpieces are on the par with the best pieces of Greek statuary due to its plastic perfection.

Precolonial African societies were human communities organised on matrilineal or patrilineal lines. Several clans closely linked, in general, by the language community constituted an ethnic group. Respect for elders and parents was common practice. Youth were admitted into adulthood through social initiation and education. After going through a succession of tests and baptisms, members of an age group could then be admitted into the life of men and women, and be allowed to have a say in city matters. Land was collective property. It was farmed using highly sophisticated methods. Community work was one of the methods used to combat individual weakness. Religion and art were closely related. Negro art, particularly music and sculpture, was devoted to religious ends.

In a nutshell, precolonial black Africa, so long as it maintained contact with the rest of the world, rallied to perform a significant economic, cultural and artistic duty. Indeed, the fact that the Negro-

---

188 Ibid., pg. 142.
189 Ibid., pg.164.
190 Ditto.

African sector of this complex economic chain was planned on the spot by Africans show that black Africa had been mature as far back as that time to serve as prised interlocutor of any partner on the international scene.

Cheikh Anta Diop underscores that right up to the 15th century, Africa never lost its civilisation as is proven by this excerpt from Frobenius: '*Histoire de la civilisation africaine*', trad., Back et Ermont, Gallimard, Paris, 1938, 5e édition pg14-15) : "When they (the first European navigators of the end of the Middle Ages) arrived in the Gulf of Guinea and landed at Vaida, the captains were astonished to find streets well cared for, bordered for several leagues in length by two rows of trees".

Revelations made by navigators of the 15th to the 17th century provide ocular proof that Negro Africa extending south of the Sahara desert was in the midst of a bloom, espousing the full splendour of harmonious and well-planned civilisations. These European conquistadors crushed the said civilisation in their wake. This is because the Newfoundland, America, was in need of slaves and Africa could offer hundreds, thousands, loads of slaves. The idea of Barbarian Negro is a European invention that as result, held sway Europe right up to the beginning of this century.

These texts from Portuguese travellers of the 15th to the 18th century, cited by Frobenius, concur with those Arab authors of the 10th to the 15th century. The social organisation of Negro States referred to by Frobenius, the royal pomp reigning there is described by an Arab writer, Ibn Batouta, who visited the Empire of Mali at the time. This writer emphasise that Kankan Moussa, a predecessor of Soleiman Mança gave to Es-Saheli, who built him a mosque at Gao, 40 000 Mithkals, amounting to about 180kg of gold. This figure provides an inkling to the wealth of the country during the precolonial era.

Moreover, another passage of Ibn Batouta casts aside the legend that insecurity prevailed in black Africa prior to European colonisation and that Europeans brought peace, freedom, security. Perfect security reigned across the country, he affirms. People could live and travel there without fear of theft or plunder.

Delafosse considers that the Empire of Mali is one of the most important Empire that ever existed in the universe. The king of Mali dealt with the the king of Portugal as an equal at the peak of his reign

(Delafosse, *Les Noirs de l'Afrique*, Payot,1922, pg.62). It is obvious that, far from being mere kinglets, emperors of Black Africa dealt on an equal basis with their most powerful Western peers. On the basis of available documents, Cheikh Anta Diop believes that Neo-Sudanese Empires date back to several centuries, before the existence of similar Empires in Europe. The Empire of Ghana was founded, no later than, about 300 years B.C. and lasted up to 1240. Whereas, we know that Charlemagne, founder of the first Western Empire following the barbarian invasions, was crowned in 800. The magnificence of Ghana had already attained similar heights or was superior to that of the Empire of Mali. That was the status of African States at the time when they came in contact with the West in the modern era.

Cheikh Anta Diop observes that at this period when in the Western Middle Ages, only absolute monarchs were recognised, in Black Africa, monarchies were constitutional: the king was assisted by a council of people with members chosen by different social groups. Rather than a start, this spelled the crowning of a long evolution, whose early stages can only be discerned by referring to Nubia and Egypt: that is the only way of restoring continuity in this chain. Whatever the angle from which the history of Africa is studied, it boils down to Meroitic Sudan and Egypt. African culture was in full bloom during this period.

2- Cultural impetus of precolonial Africa

In this flattering overview of Africa's dynamism in this era, Timbuktu portrays a striking portrait. Timbuktu is a locality founded in 1100 after Jesus Christ. It grew up to be an important religious and intellectual centre, whose influence spread beyond Africa. Timbuktu formed part of the Empire of Mali, and then fell under the control of the Songhai Empire, which at its peak in the 15th century extended from Senegal to the Niger loop. Timbuktu stood out since the Middle Ages, owing to the culture of writing that flourished alongside oral tradition. It is related to the prosperity of this town, situated at the crest of "Black countries", Sudan and Maghreb. In 1506, African traveller and diplomat, Léon, testified to the splendour of this great cultural and commercial hub of the Songhaï Empire. The wealthy monarch of Timbuktu had in his possession a good number of golden plates and sceptres. This hub abounded with doctors, judges, priests and other well-read dignitaries. The fame of the Timbuktu manuscripts is thus closely tied to that of the town, the founding deed dates back to about two centuries. In 1324, the monarch of the Empire of Mali, Kankan Moussa, went on pilgrimage to Mecca. The magnificence of the expedition with 60 000 servants and slaves, silverware and gold in abundance (inference is made to 10 tonnes), such that price of the precious metal dropped in Cairo for several years, forms part of the myth surrounding the founder of Timbuktu, recorded in Tarik Es-Sudan, a chronicle of the great Empires of West Africa. It is on his return from this pilgrimage, three years later, that Kankan Moussa conquered the town and built the Mosque of Djinguereber, and that the first written documents were published there. In the 15th century, the Mosque of Sankore, which became a top level Islamic university centre, was built. The magnificence of Kankan Moussa seduced Egyptian scholars in particular, who followed him to his country. Knowledge-sharing between Cairo, Damas and the well-read of West Africa was made easy by the Muslim religion and a language (Arab) implanted since two centuries among elite of the religion. At Timbuktu, masters dispensed teachings at their homes, as well as in schools founded by the great families of traders. The teachings consisted in analysing theological and law books, this system of teaching as well as patronage of jurists and scholars, persisted. As from the 14th century, the Islamised society warranted reference legal texts, notably for marriages, successions, trade, real estate. Books were first conveyed by merchants from the North and East and copied on the spot. But, starting from the 16th century, a local production of comments, summaries and analyses of the Koran was put in place, which later developed into a common practice as from the 17th century. Jealously preserved within families from generation to generation, these manuscripts survived for centuries. To make up for losses due to conflicts, attacks by worms, sand and humidity, they have been regularly recopied up to date. All are written in Arab or in *Ajami*, transcribed into the Arabic alphabet of local languages. This involved 500-page books, Korans, grammar or collection of poems, as well as hand out material. What is priceless in learning the history of Timbuktu, are archives, texts specific to the town or religion, letters, contracts, inventories and fatwas that precise, in all fields, legal stances including jurisprudence were not clear. The number of manuscripts drawn from the town's collections is today estimated at 100 000. Little known, these texts hold an extraordinary key to understanding the history of the region. By deciphering and mostly questioning them, we may deepen the links between oral tradition and written legacy. Their interest, is that they prove that there existed, from the 16th century a cultural life and well-read societies in the religion, and that they included sub-Saharan Africa in the Muslim grandeur and grandeur in general.

Timbuktu is a magnificent city adorned with its mausoleum of saints, which strikes the mind in a city that has profound respect for the memory of men who live an exemplary life, to the point that Timbuktu was nicknamed "town of 333 saints" (*Hors-série: science et Avenir. Le fabuleux héritage des Empires disparus*, No.185 April/May 2016 pg70-72).

More so, political unity, cultural unity was already entrenched in Black Africa within the different Empires. Certain languages, raised to official languages for they were spoken by the emperor, served as administrative languages and started dominating the others that tended to become regional dialects like Breton, Basque, Occitan in France, through a similar process (Cheikh Anta Diop op.cit.,).

African art like the great sculptures created from baked clay, bronze and stone of the IFE culture in Nigeria had attained great heights in creativity, exuding a balance and serenity that challenges masterpieces of the ancient Greek era. The same applies to the ivory sculptures of Central Africa.

Thus, Cheikh Anta Diop affirms that, "what characterises Negro art as a whole, is the freedom exuded by artists in their plastic creation, artists are sure of their genius, confident of the authenticity of their inventions. Bold freedom, powerful rhythms, forever valuable plastic invention, this are the general features of Negro art. African art has always been at the service of a social cause and must remain so. African artists have always created beauty, aesthetics through the meaning" (Ibid).

Africa and Africans must draw from this dynamic and flattering past extolled by burkinabé historian, Joseph Ki-Zerbo and Senegalese scholar, Cheikh Anta Diop, to invent their future and their renaissance as advocated by certain cantors: Léopold Sédar Senghor, Kwame Krumah, Cheikh Anta Diop, Gamal Abder Nasser, Mouamar Kadhafi, and, most recently, Thabo Mbeki, Marcien Towa, Njoh Mouelle, Engelbert Mveng, Edem Kodjo and other renown Africans and Africanists.

3- Economic dynamism of precolonial Africa

Africa's economic life in that era was blooming. The reality of West Africa is well-known. One of the enabling conditions for trade was security along roads. It seemed to have been perfectly ensured by Ghana and Mali. Trans-Saharan arteries were the first links forged by West Africa with the outside world. These were mostly meridian roads whose popularity can be likened to the camel caravans, but equally care for the oases that furnish tens of water tanks for drinking by an average caravan. A camel may gulp down 100 litres of water on the spot and caravans usually comprised hundreds, or even thousands of them. The roads used were known by Arab travellers or geographers like Ibn Batouta and Léon, the African.[191]

Around the 8th to the 12th century, the road from Morocco leading to Sudan was extremely busy. This 90-day journey, according to Ibn Kaldoum led to two ports: Tamedelt in the North and Awdaghost in the South. With the decline of the Empire of Ghana, this road gradually gave way to the much more secure road of the West, that linked Sidjilmasa, South of Morocco to Walata and Timbuktu, passing through Teghaza. The importance of this road is the fact that it ferried towards Sudan common salt from Teghaza, sold there at the weight of gold. Indeed, Sudanese people had no mines and used as substitute, salt products derived from ashes of certain stems. The Teghaza road therefore became the great artery between Mali and the outside world. Pilgrims travelled on this road to Mecca, passing through Touat, including caravans from Morocco, like those which, in 1350, comprised the prodigious explorer of tracks, Ibn Batouta. Important trace centres like Djenne and Gao gained a lot from this road.

Other trans-Saharian roads also played an important role. That of central Sudan, known as Garamantes, between Fezzan and Gao; the Gadamès road to AIR and Niger; the Gadamés road to Fezzan through Ghat, which served as a caravanist hub with Agadès as the main centre; the Fezzan road to Chad, through Bilma and Kawar was no doubt the old Roman road used by Generals Septimus Flacus and Julius Maternus, in the 1st century of the Christian era in their expedition towards the South. It had the advantage of comprising a succession of prosperous oases, which made it a relatively easy road to travel. Bilma in particular, in the middle of the salt mines of Kawar remained a

[191]Ibid., pg. 165.

departure point for camels which, in their thousands every year, transported bars of salt from AIR to Gao. In the 15th century, according to Ibn Khaldoum, caravans passing through Hoggar often comprised right up to 12 000 camels. The most eastern trans-Saharian road was the famous DARB el-Arbain, or 40-day road linking Egypt to Darfour.[192]

At the end of these meridian tracks, there existed very busy transverse roads linking caravan ports, like that of Walata leading to Timbuktu, Gao, Darfour, and through Sennar and the Blue Nile, to the Red Sea ports (Souakim, Zeila), and then to Mecca and the Indian Ocean.

Ingredients hauled through the Northern roads remained almost the same. Gold, slaves, kola, rubber, pepper, ivory, skins were ferried from Black countries. Salt, iron bars or copper, fabrics, pearls, manuscripts were obtained from the Maghreb and the East. The importance of these trans-Saharan roads had been underscored extensively. For many centuries, they constituted the heartbeat of West Africa in terms of outlet to the outside world.

In fact, economic and political factors interacted. Political advancement was tied to economic prosperity to the point where kings quickly planned trade such that it benefitted them like in Ghana. But, trade itself was closely dependent on peace and political stability. That besides, kings always made attempts to have control over at least one, if not two of the caravan traffic poles, notably the salt mines in the North and the goldmines in the South. The fact that Mali attained this double objective no doubt contributed to its exceptional splendour.[193]

Bida, Kano, Djenne, Mopti were major metropols for international cosmopolitan trade. These were meeting points for miners, blacksmiths, brass and silver jewellers, builders, wood workers, wood sculptors, weavers, glassmakers, manufacturers of pearls, potters, all activities of this era. Large-scale economic and commercial activities were the order of the day. The Malinke, Bambara, Dioula, Soninkr, Haussa, to name a few, proved to be formidable traders and businessmen.

This review of Africa's glorious past is proof that Africa and Africans had the possibility of taking control at all levels: spiritual, intellectual, scientific, moral, ethical, aesthetical, economic, cultural,

---

[192]Ibid., pg. 168.
[193]Ibid., pg. 168-169.

and political. Cheikh Anta Diop's notion of African Renaissance refers to several aspects: African historical conscience, strengthened by in depth and autonomous knowledge of the entire African cultural past such as we have reviewed at length. He includes fruitful dialogue between Africans and their own cultural legacies: dances, musical, oral and written literature, artistic and aesthetic values, social values, African languages. Note that the new creativity of Africans in the world of today, where there is need not only to receive, but also to give, participate, build, act, influence, is a source of hope. To Cheikh Anta Diop, pan-Africanism amplifies this quest by black man for his past in view of his renaissance. Victory can only be achieved by embracing forgotten values.

Africa was truly the first laboratory for perfect values, for it succeeded in moulding a standard complete and perfect man at a given time in its history; a brilliant civilisation like that of ancient Egypt as well as the Great Empires. Founding axis of knowledge crucial to development was thus in place. It stemmed from Africa, cradle of humanity and the relay was taken by ancient Greece and Rome. It is normal for Africa to rediscover this axis, now that it has regained its independence.

Chapter III

Pan-Africanism and African Renaissance

I- Genesis of Pan-Africanism and Founding Fathers

Pan-Africanism played and is still playing a very important role in African Renaissance.

In an excellent book on Pan-Africanism (Pan-Africanism, the ideal and Movement, 1776-1991, Second Edition, Howard University Press 1994), P. Olisanwache Esedebe described the genesis of Pan-Africanism in connection with the American declaration of independence (1776). He stressed the contribution of the debate on the destiny of human races in ideological and theological formulations. The author draws inspiration from the studies of James Africanus Beale Horton, a Sierra-Leonian, who takes into account the work of early Christian writers of ancient Africa (Clement of Alexandria, Origen, Tertullian, Saint Augustine), on the theory of historical cycles. In his view, no condition is permanent or immutable on earth. There is a natural law of evolution and dissolution, civilisations spring up, grow and fall, and may then rise again after some time. He believes that a continent that had lived its moments of glory may rise again, as is the case of Africa that must absolutely rediscover its past glory and even do better. Distinguished French historian and internationalist, Jean Baptiste Duroselle, develops this idea of the cycle of decline of human societies in his excellent book: *Tout Empire périra*, a publication of the Sorbonne 1981. This revolutionary vision of a new Africa that rises from its ashes like a sphinx is equally our conviction. But we must progress even further than our ancestors and predecessors in this vision, such as to appropriate the perfect fundamental values that constitute a universal compass, an ideal and sure path towards advancement of human societies. As for Kwame Nkrumah, he developed the theme of African Renaissance, in his book, *Le Consciencisme,* in which he dwells at length on the second European renaissance, that of the 15th century, the first, according to him, being that which, as from Antiquity, was initiated by Greek philosopher, Aristotle. All this influences the author to stress on the importance of history in African renaissance project, just like Cheikh Anta Diop who insists on Africa's glorious past, which also constitutes the first birth of Africa. He believes that African Renaissance must insist on the manner by which its history is portrayed. African society must be considered as enjoying its own integrity. Its history must reflect the continent and contacts with Europeans must only feature therein as regards the experience of Africans. He is in favour of African unity as a single block, a struggle he advocated within the Organisation of African Unity (OAU).

In a speech delivered in September 1998, during the 29th anniversary of the Libyan revolution, Muamar Khadafi took this Pan-African struggle a step further. He expatiated on the extraordinary resources of Africa, in the same style as Cheikh Anta Diop in his book, *les fondements économiques et culturels d'un État fédéral d'Afrique noire*, Paris, Présence africaine. Khadafi advised those who do not identify with africanity to leave the continent. He condemned those who enjoy pleading for grants from Europe. He called on Africans to rise above linguistic, ethnic and tribal divisions. He expressed strong convictions that Africa is potentially richer than Europe and America, and that the day the continent rises up, those plundering African resources, Europe and North America, may plunge into an abyss. Khadafi pledged to convene special confabs designed to review the OAU Charter and give a fresh impetus to OAU. This pledge was concretised at Sirte in Libya, in 1999, and led to the birth of the African Union (AU).

Pan-Africanism calls for such birth in perfect fundamental values. Edem Kodjo also revealed that the idea of African Renaissance is born from the concept of Pan-Africanism per se. For the Founding Peers, this was designed to awaken a continent kept in darkness, enslaved and marginalised. This continent has enormous values that fertilised famous civilisations, and they must spread once more in the aftermath of the dark periods of slave trade and colonialism, gloomy centuries. Africa must spring up from its ashes. It must affirm its positivism and capitalise on its spiritual and material wealth. The continent must become the centre of the world and take part in world geopolitics and not remain a relic of history anymore, but become a key actor on the international scene.[194] Edem Kodjo stresses on the strategic and

[194] Edem Kodjo, *Panafricanisme et Renaissance africaine*, Éditions Graines de Pensées, Lomé, 2013, pg.125.

geostrategic dimension of Pan-Africanism, in the like of Pan-Hellenism or Pan-Germanism.

Pan-Hellenism is a movement developed in Greece in the era of Pericles during the second half of the 5th century before Jesus Christ, to unite Greek cities in their fight against Persian domination. Pan-Hellenism was the fruit of such resolution. Edem Kodjo points out that it is the first time in history that the prefix pan was used, borrowed from the Greek words 'pan', 'pantos' (all).[195] Increasingly and as years go by, this prefix 'pan' reflects the will to come together and achieve a superior goal. This justifies the strategic, geopolitical and geostrategic dimensions of Pan-Africanism. Pan-Africanism must not be confined to its emotional dimension, it should rather serve as an instrument to propel Africa forward. Edem Kodjo equally calls to mind Pan-Slavism concerned with grouping all Slavic-speaking peoples to form a political union based on this common language. He also referred to Pan-Americanism, known through the doctrine posited by US President Monroe (America for Americans) that tended to promote American isolationism, with a view to prevent European intrusions into the Latin-American zone.

Japanese geopoliticians themselves developed the Pan-Asian concept, the sphere of co-ownership of the Great Eastern Asia. Modern Pan-Africanism owes its main motivation to such ambition of history genesis. From the onset, the historical Pan-Africanism was a movement concerned with the advancement of black people, long sold as slaves, debased, despised, with no recognised rights. This Pan-Africanism has evolved in minds, to become an ideology meant to convince African States to unite and constitute a geopolitical and geostrategical force in the contemporary world.[196]

Pan-Africanism is a painstaking and careful reconstruction that takes time, but that must, above all, enable Africa to develop at a sustained pace. That is why Edem Kodjo talks of this angle in the sector-specific, regional approach to attain continental unity within the nearest future. He even suggests that regional communities should transcend their economic feature to dress a political attire and become federations of authentic federated States. This idea was developed in Lome at the Pax Africana Colloquium centred on the theme: "Federalism as an

[195]Ibid., pg. 15.
[196]Ibid., pg. 19 et s.

instrument to achieving African unity"[197] He also suggests a reinforcement of the legislative duties of the African Parliament set up in Johannesburg and that its members be elected through direct universal suffrage. In this way, this Parliament would become a real legislative power. The African Court on Human and People's Rights would progressively become a genuine judiciary power at continental level. He even proposes Decade Goals for Pan-Africanism, for the millennium or centenary seem far away.

Pan-Africanism therefore enjoins Africans to gather behind this commitment to take their destiny into their hands, in order to make of Africa, the new frontline of best opportunities for human development and advancement. Early advocates of Pan-Africanism emerged from the Caribbeans, in the like of Anténor Firmin, intellectual and politician, Firmor and Benito Sylvain of Haiti, Edward Wilmot Blyden of Jamaica and Henry Sylvester Williams of Trinidad.

Joseph Benito wrote a reference book: *De l'égalité des races humaines, anthropologie, positive,* designed to combat the theory of *L'essai sur l'inégalité des races humaines*, propounded by the Count of Gobineau (1955), ideological basis of the great racist theories. During the First Pan-African Conference, organised at the Westminster Hall of London, on 23rd, 24th and 25th July 1900, the issue of concern was the equality of races, the universal capacity of humans, including blacks, for self-development and self-advancement.[198] All races possess such capacity, it is not a monopoly of the white race alone. Slavery was at the backdrop, because the situation of Blacks in America, the Caribbeans or in Africa was a marginal condition. This mark of intelligence specific to every human being is pertinent as noted in the modern evolution of black man who excels in all fields of knowledge, thanks to the rational approach, specific to every human creature. To these Pan-Africanists, are added William Edward Burghardt Dubois and Marcus Garvey. Dubois was a sociologist, an editorialist and an Afro-American writer of Haitian origin, and a fervent advocate of the rights of Blacks in the United States of America. Garvey, of Jamaican origin, an autodidact, was an influential field activist, more popular, cantor and stubborn advocate of a return of the descendants of black slaves to Africa. He initiated and organised the Back to Africa

---

[197]Ibid., p. 131.
[198] Idem.

movement. As a businessman, he took bold initiatives for Negroes of the Diaspora to return to Africa. But quite rapidly, he came up with a much more continental concept of Pan-Africanism. He then spoke more of Africans and not only of blacks. In his conception, the entire continent was burning with the idea of Pan-Africanism.

Africans then increasingly joined the Pan-Africanist movement, especially Anglophones, Jomo Kenyatta, Hastings Kamuzu Banda, Obafemi Awolowo, Kwame Nkrumah, Julius Nyerere who later became Statemen in their respective countries. Note that among them featured Nkrumah who later became the strongest advocate of Pan-Africanism. Likewise Francophones, through negritude, made their contribution to the excitement about this ideology of African emergence: Léopold Sédar Senghor of Senegal, Aimé Césaire of the Martinique, Léon Gontran Damas of Guyana.

This positive evolution of Pan-Africanism and the struggle for African Renaissance naturally led to the birth of the Organisation of African Unity (OAU), created in May 1963, and to its renewal through the African Union, founded in 2002.

II- Role of the OAU-AU and African Renaissance

OAU sped up the evolution of African Renaissance towards its unity and identity, despite its mishaps. Of all regional organisations, the League of Arab States, created in 1947, the Organisation of American States, created in 1948, the Association of South-East Asian Nations, founded in 1967, the Organisation of African Unity, now the African Union, was the most prominent, active and effective organisation, according to the testimony of former Secretary General, Edem Kodjo. It obtained the most remarkable results. Edem Kodjo adds that, at political level, the OAU - AU obtained remarkable success, in which these organisations can only take pride. The OAU, and subsequently the AU made it such that all African States are independent today and can seat on the same table. No independent State has failed to consider gaining admission into the OAU as an expression of African and even universal assertion. To be able to attend an OAU summit and announce that their country is henceforth independent and to seat with other States is a ground breaking event and a legitimate pride for every Member State and its leaders. It is not easy to build such an instrument, he stated. He admits, however, that the OAU was designed on a certain understanding, sincere and committed Pan-Africanists on the one hand, in the likes of Kwame Nkrumah and the Casablanca group, concerned with taking African Unity further and very rapidly. On the other hand, those not particularly enthusiastic about Pan-Africanism, thought it was an institution, a kind of African UNO that made it possible every year, for certain issues to be tackled, concert and obtain a convergence of views about the outside world, and on all what is happening at the United Nations. Thus, countries attend summits, discuss problems, coordinate actions, prevent conflicts between States, and attempt to resolve emergent conflicts as is done within the UNO. This actually puts the organisation in the limelight with regard to other groups of organised States, even if the OAU and AU are still unable to clarify the rules they have set and that are fixed such as: the sovereignty of States, non-interference in the affairs of States, inviolability of frontiers derived from colonisation, all things that can only end in a status quo. Can anything better be done in the face of the fragility of African States?

The OAU, after all is said and done, has resolved problems related to freedom movements, it has mobilised African and international aid, played a significant role in setting the African continent free and even getting rid of the odious Apartheid system in South Africa. Everybody has recognised and commended the OAU-AU. The OAU has organised Africa into regional economic communities. The Economic Community of West African States (ECOWAS), the Economic Community of Central African States (ECCAS), North Africa, Southern African Development Community (SADC), Common Market for Eastern and Southern Africa (Comesa). And the African Diaspora is considered as a sixth region.

It is true, OAU failed to achieve African unity as all Pan-Africanists desired, but in terms of approaches towards such unity, a groundwork has been laid. At economic level, it adopted the Lagos Plan to evolve towards a common African market.[199] The results are far from the

[199] At the time when the World Bank imposed the Berg Plan on Africa, the name of American economist, Professor Eliot Berg used by this top financial institution dominated by Americans and Europeans and their highly liberal ideas, for free trade and open markets. One more plan that effectively failed to prosper. Regarding this Berg Plan and the Lagos Plan, Charlemagne Pascal Messanga Nyamding in his study, *Repenser le développement à partir de l'Afrique*, Afrédit l'Africaine d'édition, Paris, 2012, pg 81-124.

target, but the idea is conceived and initiated, the OAU adopted the Charter on Human and People's Rights, which was unthinkable a few years back. Edem Kodjo considered that these fundamental rights were the sole preserve of Europeans and Americans. These are fundamental rights advocated by the UN Charter, the Universal Charter of Human Rights, and subsequently appropriated by the OAU-AU Charter. The limitation or inability to perfectly integrate this culture of fundamental values poses a problem. This incapacity to enrich these values, prevents Africa, from obtaining effective results in terms of freedom, democracy and governance. This holds because these fundamentals if applied in all fields, will always produce the positive results expected, for it is their primary and ultimate vocation.

The Lagos Plan advocated an endogenous and self-centred development. African leaders in Lagos stated that Africa should stop producing what it does not consume and consuming what it does not produce. Whereas, this is precisely what the Berg Plan proposed. A plan organised around what is liberal, with completely open markets in its most extreme form. It enabled the economies of developed countries to continue running at the detriment of that of Africa. And as if by magic, the plan gave way to the structural adjustment programmes. Edem Kodjo stresses that the Berg Plan was an insult to Africa. He was astonished that everybody accepted it, but for Adebayo Adedeji, the then Executive Secretary of the UN Ecconomic Commission for Africa (ECA) himself.[200]

The evolution from OAU to AU is a positive stride towards African Renaissance through an ideology conditioned by time and circumstances. Edem Kodjo discloses that the AU is trying to define a sort of architecture of common shared values like: democracy, governance, acceptable and transparent elections, human rights, a social and harmonious economic development. It forges an architecture and also relies on NEPAD (New Partnership for Africa's Development) for the achievement of major inter-African projects. The normative infrastructure is under construction, having as vision to inculcate in Member States a number of concepts and ideals known as shared values. It is a major novelty at the level of the African Union, Edem Kodjo proclaimed. And it is but normal that Africa should target a positive normative evolution, for African officials and elites are

[200] Edem Kodjo,op.cit., pg 94-95.

progressively espousing the culture of fundamentals that are a mainstay as was the case in the West over many centuries, if not millenna.

The African Union has equally recorded real progress, thanks to its Peace and Security Council that meets whenever the need arises. It measures the intensity of conflicts, seeks to prevent them whenever possible, and prescribes directives to follow in order to put an end to prevailing conflicts.

Fifty years after its independence, Africa is starting to have a perception and an understanding of its future, it must make true its Renaissance, by becoming a real power in the world, in the likes of the European Union which it seems to emulate as model, the United States of America, Japan, China, Russia, India, Brazil. For that purpose, it must commit and ultimately embrace on a permanent basis the rationale of irrevocable fundamentals of optimal development that has proven successful to other human communities, by building on its human, spiritual, moral, intellectual, psychological, civic, scientific, technological, industrial potentials, unwavering drive towards economic, social and cultural development. This is a very solid and powerful spiritual, intellectual, moral frame that Africa must ultimately conquer. Because, like all developed continents, Africa must conquer and master the Mind, awakening of the Mind, or spiritual capacity. This is the vector of any genuine enriching human revolution. These are real absolutes that do not relate to the colour of the skin or the environment, it is the sole preserve of humans, whether white, yellow or black. So long as a people has not yet understood, accepted, sought ways of attaining it, the illuminating lights of eternal knowledge will not be accessible to them, and under-development would remain endemic. This, as a matter of fact, is the ultimate level in the renaissance of a people that paves the way to a lasting and eternally glorious future. It is this final, complete, irrevocable phase that grants access to the world of ideas. In a nutshell, it is a renaissance that leads to new birth in true knowledge, and the supreme stage of knowledge that leads to outright and comprehensive development of man and to general development. It is a phase of thought renewal that rises up to the level of the infinite and eternity. So we must have a clear grasp of the true rationale of things, so we may embark on constant development, because we can discern the real sense of all fundamentals. We can therefore effectively transform our environment to extract, not only all the material goods and services useful to human life, but also spiritual wellbeing and happiness.

All in all, the African Renaissance, and even those that existed before it, that is, Europe, the Meiji Era in Japan and South-East Asia, all lead to a new birth in the supreme universe of ideas or supreme ideas and perfect knowledge. We would have evolved from ignorance to knowledge, darkness of the Mind to illumination of the Mind, minority to majority according to Kant, the philosopher, I may even say from superiority to eternity, in reality, from the human dimension to the divine dimension. The Mind must be submerged to capture the realms of the sublime. The line of humans who dominate the world always draws its inspiration from the confines and original matrix of creation. The scholar, Cheikh Anta Diop, has amply demonstrated that. To lay the groundwork for its lasting development, Africa cannot avoid this return to the creative and fertile sources of humanity, though the continent happens to be the cradle not only of humanity, but equally of knowledge. Cheikh Anta Diop even wonders whether Judaism and Christianity do not stem from the ancient Egyptian civilisation. The human development chain has the same source, it is found in the Mind. Subsequently, all depends on the sensibility of each and every one, to generate certain differences corresponding to hot or cold environments. The human being is made of flesh and Mind. Why then would the mind of some be creative than others, once we understand that, the process of awakening this mind, its regeneration and its renewal to the eternal and marvellous sources of life would become obvious. And it has already been illustrated how Africa initiated the first movement of perfect knowledge, copied by others, ancient Greece and Rome.

As for Thabo Mbeki, at his swearing-in as President of South Africa, he proclaimed that the 21st century shall be African. This prophetic statement is symptomatic of the legitimisation discourse he developed around the idea of a renaissance of the African continent. This theme of Africa's Renaissance, according to President Thabo Mbeki, is developed in the book: *Thabo Mbeki. The man I Know.*

The speech on African Renaissance is, above all, a component of the policy to portray the image and power of the Pretoria regime, which stands out as a model of non-racialism, democratisation and advocacy for renaissance of the continent. In a more extensive definition, Thabo Mbeki is convinced that African Renaissance must be interpreted as a renewal of Africa in terms of democratisation, as well as economic and cultural development. In his view, African Renaissance aims to build a New African World characterised by democracy, peace and stability, sustainable development and better life for the people, equality among nations and a system of international governance that is fair and democratic. The high standard education parameter must be crucial in the quest for this Renaissance. We would like to add and repeat that African Renaissance and this high standard education must first produce a new man and creator capable of spurring a comprehensive development of Africa.

The theme of African Renaissance also expresses economic interest in terms of business and investment opportunities. This African Renaissance in its neo-liberal vision, sparked criticisms, but it has the courage of charting a course to be explored for an emergence of African economies, given that liberal economy is now a mainstay worldwide. It is now important for Africa to tackle it intelligently and systematically, and to integrate it in the structural and cultural scheme of Africa, centred on communitarianism, solidarity and freedom.

The New Partnership for Africa's Development (NEPAD) strives towards a more open economy for the economic development of Africa, in order to stimulate its renaissance and afford it a more concrete content.

III- NEPAD (African Union Development Agency), an African development strategy purely for Africa

NEPAD changed its appellation in January 2018 during the African Union Summit to become the African Union Development Agency.

Thus, NEPAD (New Partenership for Africa's Development or the New Partnership for the Development of Africa) has as intent to encourage a sustainable development on the continent, fight against poverty and social exclusion, promote the role of women in all activities, halt the marginalisation of Africa in the globalisation process. Five Heads of State were the driving force behind NEPAD: Olusegun Obasanjo (Nigeria), Thabo Mbeki (South Africa), Abdelaziz Bouteflika (Algeria), Abdoulaye Wade (Senegal), Hosni Moubarak (Egypt).

NEPAD, to a point, replaces the Lagos Plan for the development of Africa (1980-2000) and other spin-off African programmes. We could make mention of: Africa's Priority Programme for Economic Recovery (1986-1990) and 1995 Cairo Agenda that all ended in a failure.

The goals of NEPAD were as follows:

- Achieving and sustaining an average annual Gross Domestic Product (GDP) rate of more than 7%,
- Ensuring that the continent achieves the agreed International Development Goals (IDGs), notably:
  - ✓ Reducing by half the percentage of people living in abject and severe poverty, by the year 2015,
  - ✓ Ensuring education for all children of primary school age by the year 2015, that is the training and knowledge capacity,
  - ✓ Promoting gender equality and women's empowerment,
  - ✓ Reducing the rate of infant and post-infant mortality by the year 2000,
  - ✓ Reducing by three quarters the rate of maternal mortality by the year 2015,
  - ✓ Providing access to generic health for all those in need by the year 2015,
  - ✓ Implementing as from 2015 sustainable regional development strategies to compensate losses in ecological resources by the year 2015.

Implementing NEPAD warrants that a number of conditions- political, economic, geographical, be put together. The political conditions concern peace, security, governance, democracy and human rights. The economic conditions involve improving the quality of economic and public finance management, corporate governance and economic governance (creation of a healthy legal and judiciary environment). And finally, regarding geographical conditions, NEPAD retained the sub-region, region and continent as special environment for the implementation of projects.

NEPAD retained ten super priority areas whose projects must be rapidly executed and that would have a rippling effect on future actions in other priority areas. These areas are as follows: political governance, economic governance and private capital flows, infrastructure, education, health, new information and communication technologies (ICTs), agriculture, energy, access to developed markets, the environment.

Three organs are tasked with implementing NEPAD: the Implementation Committee composed from the onset of fifteen Heads of States and then twenty since the AU Summit of July 2002 at Durban in South Africa, notably the five founding Heads of State and fifteen others, at the proportion of three per region. Cameroon is part of the NEPAD Heads of State and Government Orientation Committee. For the promotion of Governance, the Heads of States and Government created the African Peer Review Mechanism (APRM) in 2002 at Maputo. Cameroon joined this mechanism in April 2003.

Nepad organised the Second African Rural Forum in Africa on the theme: "Transforming the rural sector through development tools, job creation and professional integration of young people" in Yaounde on 7th to 9th September 2016. Dr Ibrahim Hassane Mayaki, Executive Secretary of the NEPAD Planning and Coordination Agency declared that young people represented 60% of the continent's population and according to him, the rural sector is also a key to development. For that reason, the rural sector must be afforded infrastructures in the domains of energy and transport. Emphasis must also be placed on issues related to employment of young people in rural areas such as to render them attractive. The Yaounde deliberations led to adoption of the Plan for Development of the Rural Sector in Africa.

NEPAD estimates at 64 000 million dollars, the annual amount of resources necessary to achieving an annual growth rate of 7%, agreed in the International Development Goals, to reduce poverty in Africa by the year 2015. NEPAD intends to seek and find considerable additional resources to financing the projects retained.

It must however be pointed out that implementation of NEPAD is severely delayed by virtual indifference of the international private sector due to the political and economic insecurity prevailing in Africa, leadership conflict and its cumbrous organisational chart.

Despite all these, NEPAD has the advantage of being a continental development plan conceived by Africans for themselves, with a view to relief the continent of its misery and the precarious nature of its current condition. For the first time since colonial invasion, Africa has begun implementing its own development vision, its own strategy and methods for achieving it. Although in favour of a neo-liberal conception, NEPAD is an original plan, generally consistent, whose implementation is expected to be integral for Africa. It matches Africa's vision of African Renaissance. It is a blend of two plans: MAP and the Omega Plan. MAP (Millenium Partnership for Africa Recovery Programme) was initiated by Presidents Thabo Mbeki, Abdel Aziz

Bouteflika and Olusegun Obasanjo. This programme is inspired by the theme for African Renaissance, rekindled and broadened by Thabo Mbeki in his swearing-in address in 2002. The Omega Plan of Senegalese President, Abdoulaye Wade, made public in 2001, extends and magnifies the ideas developed in his book: *Un destin pour l'Afrique (Destiny for Africa),*Edition Michel Lafon, 2005. The Omega Plan seeks to propel Africa into the circle of the developed world, through investment in its physical capital (basic infrastructure, roads, bridges, airports), and then in human capital, via education, training and health, finally by way of investment in agriculture, livestock, fishery and forestry that occupies more than 2/3 of African populations. While MAP is marked more by investment of symbolic power and the political dimension of African Renaissance in Pan-African imagination, the Omega Plan is rather a practical case of development economics, which eased the blending of these two programmes at Lusaka in July 2001.

Edem Kodjo, former Secretary General of OAU, acknowledges the importance of NEPAD in the Pan-African development project. He strongly affirmed that: "NEPAD must be implemented because NEPAD somewhat sums up the hopes of Africa. Sectors like those of infrastructure and energy are given priority by NEPAD. It must not only be implemented, but while achieving it, Pan-Africanism should be advocated, for NEPAD is an instrument of Pan-Africanism". African unity will not be achieved only through the geographical approach, but also via the sector-specific approach. Whole sectors are aimed to be subject of NEPAD actions for a far-reaching inter-African cooperation. In the domain of energy, we will discover that Africa that possesses substantial resources in this domain, is nevertheless, the continent most in need of energy. And this is the continent with the greatest volume of unconsumed resources in the world. I do not believe that Africa consumes 20% of its power capacities. Reference is often made of the Great Inga Dam. This Great Inga Dam has the possibility of satisfying needs of the entire African continent. Once its final phase (phase 3) shall be executed and integrated to other mechanisms that NEPAD is putting in place, other hydroelectric capacities, roughly put, will afford the African continent a minimum of 60% energy for its total population. That 60% of total African population should, from the 2040s be provided with electricity, is a revolutionary prospect, a giant step. Edem Kodjo, *Panafricanisme et renaissance africaine*, op.cit., pg 123-124. Edem Kodjo places Pan-Africanism at the heart of African Renaissance.

Chapter IV

Charter of African Cultural Renaissance

The African Charter for Cultural Renaissance was adopted at Khartoum in Sudan on 24th January 2006. This instrument must guide and constitute a source of pride for Africa within the purview of its spiritual and cultural renaissance. Its preamble affirms that any human community is necessarily governed by rules and principles based on culture; and that culture should be regarded as the set of distinctive linguistic, spiritual, material, intellectual and emotional features of the society or a social group, and that it encompasses, in addition to art and literature, lifestyles, ways of living together, value systems, traditions and beliefs. That any African cultural policy should of necessity enable peoples to evolve for increased responsibility in its development. That despite cultural domination which, during the slave trade and the colonial era, led to the depersonalisation of part of the African peoples, falsified their history, systematically disparaged and combated African values, and tried to progressively and officially replace their languages with that of the colonial masters, the African peoples were able to find in African culture, the necessary strength for resistance and the liberation of the Continent. That the unity of Africa is founded first and foremost on its history.

That it is imperative to resolutely ensure the promotion of African languages, mainstay and media of tangible and intangible cultural heritage in its most authentic and essentially popular form and also as a factor of a development open to the world.

That culture constitutes for our peoples the surest means to chart Africa's own course towards technological development, and the most efficient response to the challenges of globalisation. That African cultural diversity requires universal mobilisation to promote dialogue between civilisations.

In this regard, the African Charter for Cultural Renaissance has as objectives: to assert the dignity of African men and women, promote freedom of expression and cultural democracy which is inseparable from social and political democracy, encourage cultural co-operation among Member States with a view to the strengthening of African unity through the use of African languages and the promotion of inter-cultural dialogue, promotion of science and technology, as well as traditional systems of know-how using the general History published by UNESCO as a valid base for teaching the History of Africa, innovate, protect and promote the freedom of artists, intellectuals and men and women of culture, creators, private developers from the private sector, local associations, strengthen ties with the African Diaspora worldwide in the areas of culture, education, science and technology, finance and economy.

It is on this solid and immortal platform that the creative Mind fosters the distinctive values transcending the eras that Africa would exclusively achieve its global, educational, economic, political, cultural and social development. This is the challenge facing Africa and Africans. Such development cannot be a spontaneous occurrence, for every human community must first be born carnally, and then spiritually in a gradual manner, to access the knowledge and grasp the fundamentals of life.

Africa could not emerge from several centuries of darkness and bondage and accede as if by magic to such knowledge, especially after it went through more than five centuries of slavery, colonialism, neo-colonialism, a voracious exploitation of its resources, after its glorious past related above. Europe had equally gone through long centuries of hibernation, alienation and serfdom.

Do not overburden Africans. Their chaotic evolution is a more or less normal process for human societies that do not always grasp at one go all the twists and turns of the knowledge expected to release them from the chains of ignorance. All peoples follow this precipitous and extremely difficult path. Africa is ready for this take-off, for the knowledge that paves the way for a better future is almost within grasp. Béchir Ben Yahmed, publisher of the famous journal, *Jeune Afrique*, admits that certain African countries are already entering the vicious circle that leads to development, for they now know how to achieve it.

All modern economic theories analysing African societies have often failed to take full account of this prior facts essential to global development. Whereas, these are developing painstakingly and with time. These economic and developmentalist theories dwell more on immediate economic factors with its vectors of profitability, growth rate and production, and not sufficiently on cultural factors which are needed the most by Africa to rebuild its mentality and its severely broken spirit.

Achille Mbembe, author of the book *de la post colonie* (2000) urges reflection on the policy of the possible and not only on that of fatality and failure. To him, Africa must once more become its own centre, its own strength. It must rise to the level of the world and create for itself and for the world something exceptionally new.[201] Africa must become a creator through the mastery of true knowledge. It is on this basis that one can gradually become a creator to generate all what is new, that one can innovate and invent.

Mamadou Diouf, Senegalese historian living in the USA goes one step further to state that conditions must be created for a true civic conscience-awakening, to afford Africa political and economic autonomy and participation in enriching human condition.[202] He even adds that gradually, Africa is regaining a wining position in a globalised world. It is no longer a continent that falters and that benefits from globalisation, but a continent witnessing a progressive inception of physical, financial, intellectual infrastructures and a profound desire to change the African situation. Moreover, Africa is endowed with a formidable asset, its young population left with no other choice but to open up to the world, to be ambitious.

All in all, Africa is on track and joining the domineering chain of humanity to become a key link that can pull the continent to the top. This is in order to afford the continent the extra mettle it still possesses in abundance, for a humanity which is seemingly running out of steam and suffocated by excessive materialism and is in dire need for that. Africa also has real need for globalisation, it belongs there.

This African Cultural Renaissance stands out in different literary publications of African researchers: in philosophy, Beninese Paulin Hountondji, *philosophie africaine,* 1997, Stanislas Spero Adotevi, *négritude et négrologue*, 1992, Cameroonians Fabien Eboussi Boulaga, *la crise du Muntu*, 1977, Marcien Towa, *Essai sur la problématique philosophique dans l'Afrique actuelle*, 1971 and *Identité et transcendance*, 2012, Ebénézer Njoh Mouelle, *de la médiocrité à l'excellence*, 1971, *l'idée de progrès dans la diversité de cultures*, 2012,

[201] Jeune Afrique Économie, No.2745 of 11 to 24 August 2013, pg. 135.
[202]Ibid.,pg. 128.

in collaboration with Thierry Michalon, Ghanian Kwasi Wiredi, Philosophy and African culture, 1980, Kenyan Henry Odera Oruka sage, philosophy indigenous Thinkers and modern debate on African philosophy 1990. Historians: Cameroonian Achille Mbembe, *de la post colonie*, 2000, Senegalese Mamadou Diouf, *Histoire du Sénégal*, 2001, *l'économiste malawite*, Tandika Mkandawire who advocates an endogenous development of Africa in his books, notably: African intellectuals and nationalism in the changing global context, 2001 and From maladjusted states to democratic development states in Africa.

African Cultural Renaissance encompasses the determination to revive the general history of Africa, which is an undertaking as much as political project. The founding fathers of the OAU had as early as 1964 hoped that it should be a subject with similar teaching across the continent. The project owner of such an achievement is the United Nations Organisation for Education, Science and Culture (UNESCO), mandated this time by the AU. At the end of October 2013, it organised in Accra, Ghana: the Regional Conference on Teaching of Africa's General History in African institutions of Higher Learning.

The choice of Ghana was not fortuitous. It is the country of Kwame Nkrumah, one of the founding fathers of Pan-Africanism who organised the first international conference for Pan-Africanists in 1962. He erected a memorial in Accra dedicated to one of the fathers of Pan-Africanism, American-born William Edward Burghardt du Bois, who died a Ghanian at Accra in 1963. There is also Trinidadian attorney, George Padmore, a friend of Nkrumah, Pan-Africanist militant whose gravestone is found in the courtyard of an Accra library bearing his name.

The Accra Conference had more than one objective. It had to examine the possibilities of intensifying the use of Africa's general history in teaching and harmonising such teaching in different regions of the continent for the purpose of integration. And then brainstorm on training for teachers tasked with teaching the courses in primary, secondary and high schools. Finally, find ways of making volumes of Africa's general history available and accessible to documentation centres, national and university libraries. This says much about the place of history in the awakening of African consciences, despite trials and tribulations of its development.

In 1964, African leaders, concerned with encouraging the collective acquisition of knowledge by their different peoples and departing from a vision of a continent inherited from the colonial era, opted to start over. This task, entrusted to UNESCO, was a long-drawn-out task whose first phase, that of fine-tuning and outlining the undertaking and its different volumes, took much of the decade of African independence and ended in 1999 with the publication of Volume 8.

In Africa, nowadays, only Ghana, Benin, Kenya, Uganda, Tanzania and South Africa have a general history of Africa in their national university libraries. UNESCO is no longer in possession of any reserve stock, since the remaining 6800 volumes were destroyed owing to the high cost of storage.[203]

With respect to African Cultural Renaissance, Cheikh Anta Diop again provides an excellent illustration in his book, *L'Antiquité africaine par l'image*, (*African Antiquity In Picture)*, Présence africaine, 1976, through his comments on conclusions of the report on the Cairo Conference convened at his behest from 28th January to 3rd February 1974, which had discussions on the settlement of ancient Egypt and deciphering of the Meroitic writing. He relates that "African historiography therefore wrote a memorable page at the Cairo Conference. New African classics must be inspired by hallmarks of the Egyptian-Nubia culture, just like Western classics draw from ancient Greek-Latin culture". It is not possible to develop a wealth of human science without referring systematically to Egypt in all aspects of culture: any African expert who wishes to undertake a scientific venture has no choice, he can only flirt with Egyptian cultural facts. Imagine a Western human science attempting a scientific venture while staying adrift of Greek-Latin culture, such a person would be a simpleton or a joker. All aspects of the cultural life of black Africa refer back to Egypt and only a lack of initiative can obscure the fact. Linguistic studies can only find their historical dimension in such return to the ancient ancestral hearth. New schools on literature, philosophy, civil or military architecture, music, sculpture, painting, etc., must follow suit. This involves rediscovering cultural roots and not a servile imitation.

Egyptian musical brand faithfully recovered, in relative manner, based on a study of well-preserved musical instruments, the harmonic symphony of strings. The orchestral music thus reproduced is obviously

---

203 Jeune Afrique du 1er au 7 décembre 2013, op.cit.,pg. 40-41.

similar to African music. We could even cite sport fighting techniques or the myths of our medieval history.

As a matter of fact, the Pharaoh rejuvenation ceremony throws stark light on regenerative rites that Sundiata of Mali had to perform, if not at outward physical level, at least in terms of ontology, for his full vital energy to be capable of reigning in a country, a region where persons with a disability, even wounded soldiers, were banned from the throne. Likewise, the ram god, spitting thunder, represented on frescoes at the Abomey palace, obviously reflect the Nile Valley, despite the fact that this art is recent. One way or the other, an age-old tradition was preserved and handed down from generation to generation.

There is a parallel between typical lines of modern Negro-African poetry and those of the Karnak "poetic stele" (temple of god Amon), some 800 years ago before Homer, relating the victories of Thutmosis III.

As part of the African reform programmes, teaching of Greek philosophy (Plato, Epicurus, Aristotle...) should be preceded by teaching of Egyptian philosophy to better highlight the filiation fibre that unite the former with the latter. Teaching of Egyptian law should prioritise a study of Roman law in law history curriculas. A scientific theory of African law must start with a study of Egyptian law.

Current monotheistic religions are offshoots of Egyptian religion: most particularly the figure of Christ is identical, point by point, to that of Osiris (god of ancient Egypt), even the word Christ originated in Egypt, evolved to Greece, and was later applied to Jesus in the 4th century. Osiris is admittedly a prototype of the god of the revealed religions: Judaism, Christianity, and Islam. His throne is the first image to date of the throne of God in human history.

It would be interesting to conduct research on an experimental aesthetics that should consist in a harmonic analysis of all the different styles of African sculpture. It would then be ascertained whether the extremely realist Nigerian art from Ife conforms to the golden section or not (this is the Egyptian notion of divine proportion) that inspired Greek canon in its architecture, for instance the Ionic, doric and Corinthian orders.

In this same vein, studies may be conducted on what we refer to as the "law of dissimilarity" between different African expressionist styles. In other words, it is the law expressed in the form of a digital report, whereby style intentionally and consistently varies from the golden section. This abstract mathematical ratio should always correspond to a plastic invention, a mode of expression in terms of how form is portrayed.

Indeed, the golden section of divine proportion, is merely an average value of the one that corresponds to the most perfect naturalism, at the pace of nature development, be it the growth of plants or the spacing rhythm and reduction of spirals of a shell. It therefore reflects proportions that from assumption are neither too colossal nor too spindly. But, it would be interesting to study the sculptural meaning of other shells framing that of the golden ratio and know how they are unconsciously used by different expressionist schools worldwide. The golden section is perceptible on a good number of Egyptian monuments, particularly on those of the Former Empire at Karnak and at Gizeh, etc.

Whatever the case, the revelation above calls for a review of universal history to afford Blacks the leading role they effectively played in building civilisation.

Here again, Jean Tabi Manga comes to our rescue on Renaissance of Africa to affirm that: "The first lesson learned is that the renaissance movement served as a great catalyst of progress everywhere in all domains, notably social, intellectual, cultural, economic and industrial progress. In a nutshell, Renaissance acts as a powerful catalyst of emergence. It has been found that this movement enables any given society, after reflection on its future, to break and fall back in the face of the challenges it encounters…"

The process of death and of renaissance may bear different forms depending on the civilizational spheres. Europe drew revitalising resources from its historical and cultural background that led to the continent's rebirth, that is, to build a triumphant intellectual, philosophical, economic and industrial modernism that constitutes the substance of current globalisation. Europe therefore reinvented the Indo-European cultural model that provided the key to organisation of Western society using its triple functionality such as described by G. Dumézil. This basic pattern was enriched by contribution from the protestant reform.

Asian itineraries follow a different pattern. Japanese, Chinese and Korean Renaissances are equally conceptual paradigms that accelerated the emergence of their society. The Asian approach to emergence is the active result of a fundamentally dialectical process. China, Japan and South Korea performed an admirable transplant of westernisation that revitalised Confucian cultural tradition. The first movement was to undertake a critical analysis of their traditional culture, keeping only elements capable of receiving Western transplant organ. Westernisation of the East, initiated under the Meiji Era in Japan, enabled it not to suffer from globalisation, but to rather become an influential actor. Hence the emergence of Asia.

The second lesson that can be drawn from the experiments, patterns of renaissance related above, is that emergence is the ultimate point of global renaissance movement. From a philosophical stance, emergence is a final terminal of renaissance.

As for that, cultural paradigm should be constructed conceptually such as to justify and institute emergence by shedding light on sector-specific policy approaches to instil consistency, cohesion therein. In the case of Chine, the concept of "market socialism" provided clarifications and direction to its approach. For that purpose, cognitive justification of this emergence approach must be defined[204].

However, the ground-breaking studies of Cheikh Anta Diop and Engelbert Mveng reveal that African Renaissance has its resounding cultural source that clarifies the cultural unity of Negro-African world. This illumination source is Ancient Pharaonic Egypt. In the African Renaissance process, Ancient Pharaonic Egypt functions intellectually and exactly as the Indo-European in the European trajectory of renaissance. Through what is known as trifunctional ideology, the Indo-European enabled the revelation of fundamental values that rendered European modernism possible (Jean Tabi Manga op.cit.,pg. 85).

In the case of Africa, Jean Tabi Manga recalls the original culture obtained from the Egyptian crossing (Negro-African, ethics, semitic) that sum up all cultural shades specific to Negro-Egypt, Ancient Negro-Egypt. Values conveyed by the Ancient Negro-Egyptian revolve around spiritual life and human freedom.

---

[204] Jean Tabi Manga, op.cit.,pg 62-64.

Such solidarity is part of community solidarity spirit proper to the African soul. It is cultivated by several African leaders: Kwame Nkrumah advocates political and economic communalism, Julius Nyerere African socialism, just like Léopold Sédar Senghor who adopted the African form of socialism as doctrine for his political party, an African socialism which, according to Léopold Sédar Senghor uses Marxist dialectic as method of analysis, planning as management tool, but rejects atheism in favour of the sacred, vital trait of spiritual life among Negro-Africans, Paul Biya, President of the Republic of Cameroon, developed his Cameroonian society project based on community solidarity as fundamental traditional value. That said, Léopold Sédar Senghor is credited with socialist type society, Paul Biya, a liberal type or communal liberalism.

Tabi Manga underlines however that African democracy should be similar at intellectual and political level to that of emerging Asian countries. That is the synthesis trajectory between Western liberalism and community solidarity values, as a development philosophy. Our view is that in order to achieve this, the advent of a new, perfect and creative African as solely capable of cultivating a mind at that realm should be encouraged.

Africa through Cultural Renaissance definitely got back to the true teaching that began during the age of Antiquity and brutally halted as from the 15th century by the slavery imposed by the West. This Renaissance enabled Africa to rediscover the founding axis of knowledge and creator of development. Africa must therefore work hard for the advent of the new African, who is perfect and creator of development (a Homo Deus), now that the path leading there is fully paved by those who performed this feat. This rigorous structuring of the Mind and the African Man would finally enable Africa to take off and embark on its development, by relying on a productive cultural model founded on a culture of the sacred and community solidarity specific to the African soul.

Chapter V

Advent of the new, perfect African and creator of development: architect and model of modern time Africa

We have striven, throughout this book, to demonstrate that practice of perfection is the supreme stage that leads humanity to true and authentic knowledge. This authentic knowledge offers multiple theoretical and concrete capacities that renovate the intelligence of man such as to afford him practical abilities. These abilities would then forge his mind and thoughts, transforming him into a new being in terms of intelligence, so that he can be perfect and a creator of development. This virtually confers him a divine status, a godlike man, a Homo Deus[205]. It must be underscored that, as a matter of fact, it is by lifting himself up to the level of God, or to put it simply, through an effort at transcendence that man can acquire such status. It is his prime purpose and he must achieve it.

In reality, it is this man who has become perfect and complete that can create, because he has gone through an initiating training for that purpose. This African model is a reference for development who, is as a point fact, the architect of modern time Africa, owing to his virtuous and operational life. Prof. Ebénézer Njoh Mouelle buttresses this point by emphasising that, "development should be concerned mostly with enabling the advent of a particular type of man: the creator" (*De la médiocrité à l'excellence. Essai sur la signification humaine du développement* : Éditions Clé, 1998, pg.8). In the quest for progress, essence must be to forge a perfect and complete man. This is the means by which such a man can attain fulfilment. In this regard, he cultivates profound and positive qualities that confer him the keys to effective action. Africa and African States must forge a model of man, characterised by strong spiritual, intellectual, moral, mental, civic, behavioural, scientific, aesthetic, technical and technological values. Each of these rational and rigorous postures must be served and sustained in all wheels of society: families, schools, religious, civil and

---

[205] Psalm 8 of the Bible: "You wanted it a little less than a god…"

political associations, public and government enterprises and institutions. Evaluation must be regular to ensure that the contents of theoretical and practical know-how corresponds to the type of society being built, and to the economic and production sectors. In this context of optimal development in forging man, all avenues to different skills must be explored. Focus should not only be on scientific and technological fundamentals and efforts must be made to ensure that moral, civic and ethical fundamentals are also well-assimilated, in order to forge a well-balanced man rather than a technical monster. Such practical orientation in the training of Africans must develop a solid culture, driven by perfection and excellence, to maintain very high standards in different socio-economic achievements. We have demonstrated with great insistence, all efforts made by developed and emerging countries to forge a type of man who is highly educated and trained, and who made development possible in these parts of the world. Recourse to all schools of thought is often necessary: - current and divine, mystical, philosophical, metaphysical, esoteric, cultural, scientific, technological, economic and political schools of thought. Development is a global process that requires a global approach.

The equation of forging the African man requires that his level of conceptual and operational capacity should, in terms of quality, reach a ratio of at least more than 60% of spiritual power and thought, where such conceptual power ratio must be even higher for the African elite, for we have explained at length that the Mind, in particular, constitutes the force that garners energies and not brain, education should therefore lay emphasis on spiritual training that teaches one to sustain and forge thought, for the generation of influential ideas and themes, to the point of developing a reference system for multifaceted values constantly employed to resolve all development problems. Development can only succeed through this global approach. Creativity is thus the preserve of man the architect, for he can find the keys that open the door to an optimal transformation of societies. The African creative man is only gradually emerging, his advent and generalisation are the challenges facing the educational and cultural systems of Africa in the 21st century as well as future centuries. Creativity is the man's supreme capacity for action, for it affords him the superior and divine nature. Investing in construction of roads, bridges, airports, agriculture, tourism and other activities would constitute signs of progress. But, without a well-trained man who must execute these projects, the added value of all these investments will remain forever low, and Africa shall continue to make extensive use of foreign expertise that induces high financial sacrifice. And finally, foreign aid will always be recycled by donors through their consultancy firms. Investing heavily in quality training for African human resources therefore constitutes a major challenge. We must proceed sector by sector, assess the expertise sought, and select those who must be trained, produce them, conscious that Africans may ultimately master and control these sectors. This is what can help revert the dependency trend, such that Africa should not continue to contract debts, with the money put to little use in our continent, to the point of remaining stuck in an infernal circle of aid, to re-colonisation as alluded to by the title of the now famous book written by Tibor Mende.

In this light, Cardinal Christian Tumi, developed the theme of the new man, mindful that God alone is capable of offering each Cameroonian, or even each African a new heart and mind. God alone can change our heart of stone and offer us a heart of flesh, a heart that loves and loves fellow man. God alone is capable of offering civic virtues: love for the country, love for work well done, solidarity among citizens (My Faith: a Cameroon to be Renewed, Cardinal Christian Tumi, Éditions Vérités, 2011, pg 11). He goes on to state as we have explained that if Europeans are leaders of the world, today, in the domains of science, technology and economics, it is thanks to the Christian religion they practiced at a given period of their history. He reiterates that the United States of America was founded by Christians from England, Pilgrim Fathers, and that the 13th century universities (Sorbonne, Oxford, Bologne) were created by the Church. He deplores the fact that European leaders refused to make mention of the Christian roots of the continent in the European Union treaty. He affirms that Statesmen must master the central truth of the universe whereby: God alone governs the world and is the soul of the world. He calls on God to give everyone a new heart. And we follow suit by stating that this new heart would enable man to love perfect knowledge, Sophia and to become a creator. Creativity depends on appropriation and practice of perfect knowledge, not otherwise. Creativity is not an act of the common natural man, but of man who is completely superior and renewed in terms of his intelligence. To become a creative being, requires a rigorous structuring of the mind around perfect values that confer concrete multiple skills and capacities. Once man is thus very well-trained, development, an in depth structural transformation of the society, becomes a concrete reality, for we know that of all things man is the measure according to Protagoras, a Greek philosopher. He is the first and last wealth, the alpha and omega in development. So long as this reality is not well understood by Africans in order to give priority only to the quest for funds for physical investments, added value shall remain forever low. Africans must have full mastery of science, techniques, technology, creativity and industry. But the whole process depends on the creative man. He is the catalyst of development. That is the central truth of this book. Once man reaches this very high level, he can become a creator of multiple wealth, one of the many targets of development.

To conclude this chapter in a convincing manner, we would paraphrase Descartes who once declared that, "I think, therefore I am", to equally state that, "I am perfect, therefore I am creator", for perfection opens the door to pure knowledge and creativity.

Conclusion

Africa, dream bearer and pacesetter or the African dream for an optimal development of the continent

Extensive discussion of perfection and perfect fundamental values in regard to Africa's development has made it crystal clear to me that this very high level can only be bequeathed by God, gods or superior men to man, for the purpose of transforming him into a creator of tangible and intangible wealth. That is the trajectory followed by all peoples and human societies that have achieved genuine development and not otherwise. I found no society that achieved development without securing this high spiritual transformation for man. Africa, like other continents before it, cannot do without this fundamental regeneration of its children, since it is the cradle of humanity and the first human civilisation in the age of Antiquity, with Ancient Negro Egypt as a worthy symbol. In a nutshell, a perfect, complete and regenerated man that can be creator of development. Perfect fundamental values are undoubtedly the gateway, for they constitute a science structured and proven by concrete development facts. That is, as a point of fact, the ultimate contribution of this book that proves why Africa must by all logical means, forge a complete man, who alone is capable of creating development. The common man will never succeed. For that purpose, education and training standards must be extremely high, with priority given to all aspects: spiritual, moral, intellectual, civic, behavioural, scientific, technical, technological, industrial, material and financial.

In reality, the conclusion of this book came to me, in August 2016, as I spent a restful weekend at our family home in Namba (Manjo), among my family-in-law. I love this tiny village set 2 kilometres from Manjo centre town, with a luxuriant and very beautiful evergreen foliage backdrop during the rainy season. Clear water running into the village with its source from a mountain concealed by vegetation. Greenery that is forever fresh, even during the dry season. This peaceful and friendly abode is ideal for meditation. An environment that could only strongly inspire my commitment to putting perfect fundamental values into practice, as Ariadne's thread to embark on development. Thus, in the course of this lengthy study I was emboldened to advocate for evolution, in an Africa that is still struggling to contend with many hurdles on the path to its development, but is at the same time striving relentlessly to appropriate perfect values essential for its progress. This study equally led me to methodically explain what is referred to as perfect fundamental values, where perfection is the epicentre, how perfection was conceived by God, the source and creator of all things on the one hand, and by different human cultures on the other. In this light, human societies have succeeded in cultivating a wealth of perfect fundamental values that constantly serve as springboard for development. These fundamental values are also a positive science in constant need. The United Nations is a forum par excellence that groups all world cultures and where some of these values are conceived and recycled. Africa shall in 2050 have a population of more than 2000 million inhabitants composed mostly of young people. By relying more and more on this human potential and a better training on perfect fundamental values, and on its abundant natural resources, the continent can be bearer of a dream for people and for humanity at the dawn of this 3rd millennium and for future millennia. A dream founded on the fact that the continent still offers the best opportunities for development in all sectors. This significant dream for a wonderful and marvellous life must not lead the continent to consider development only as promotion of materialism, whose destructive effects on human life are quite visible nowadays. The science, skills, technology developed with much success by the West have provided human beings and humanity with enormous welfare facilities in all sectors of social life, to the point where attempts have even been made to breed a Transhuman being that cannot die or whose lifespan will be extended by sophisticated devices. This spectacular evolution in science and technology has provoked many problems: drugs, homosexuality, excessive individualism, greater rivalry between nations, growing disparity between rich and poor countries, uneven distribution of wealth, national egoisms, hardening of the human heart, will of domination, extremism, exclusion, terrorism, etc. This, to a large extend, is what the frantic quest for enrichment and domination of fellow man has brought about, destroying the innermost humanist fibre that pushes man to altruism and to seek for the wellbeing of fellow man, in view of an active and virtuous human fraternity. In this way, the existing humanism at the beginning of human history, so well sustained in ancient Africa, ancient Greece, ancient Rome and Europe in the age of Renaissance is gradually dying out. It is on this shaky world platform, full of uncertainties that Africa, on the edge of the laborious path to development, is expected to feed its dream, and to give humanity a fresh development impetus, bearer of an ever better future. Africa's rich history and culture founded on values of perfection, solidarity, sharing, communitarianism, fraternity, altruism, overflowing soul and wisdom conditions the continent to a more humanist approach to development. Africa must know how to appropriate science, skills and technology for the purpose of aiding man to achieve fulfilment, which is the ultimate goal of his being (body and mind), giving priority to the Mind, which is the essence of man. It procures and upholds life.

Africa must better integrate its development plan in Mind dynamics, for the Mind is permanent and immortal, it is bearer of life and a fully successful life. It can lift man to a state of bliss, procuring him blessed happiness, for he would be fulfilled not only with material wealth, but above all with the spiritual wealth that affords him a constantly virtuous life.

Africa must offer humanity what founding fathers of the United States of America were able to give to what has today become the great American people that is an eternal spiritual dimension devoted to the American dream. This dream has helped successive generations to build a strong and prosperous country, where people live in freedom and perpetual happiness, at the same time, they hold life as a sacred value. Even if this beneficial reality of America's founding fathers has suffered a severe blow due to excessive materialism onslaughts, it remains the platform that keeps the American dream alive. President Barack Obama, an American Black repeated this assertion and fulfilment of this dream with disconcerting clarity (Barack Obama: *The American Promise*. His greatest speeches, 156 pg. February 2009, and *The Audacity of Hope: Thoughts on Reclaiming the American Dream,* 445 pg. March 2009, France).

The Formulation and practice of this dream therefore offers Africa its revenge to return to the front of the platform, millennia after being the pioneer brilliant human civilisation through ancient Egypt, and after being proclaimed as the cradle of humanity. This African dream for humanity should abound with freshness and spirituality. In reality, the Mind is sacred and reflects the divine. It is faithful and is a constant inspiriting source for all beneficial human actions. Given that the Mind is intangible, it regenerates ad infinitum in a fiery fire that burns the impurities and imperfections in the life of man, to bring forth a Man, new in perfection and sublimity. This ascendant and asymptotic line of a pure, holy, virtuous, perfect life, must be nourished by a stimulating and eternal vigour. It is this positive dream of a humanity that subjugated material to its wellbeing and at the same time is losing its grip on it, that Africa must seek and put in practice for its development. In this way, Africa would place humanism once more at the heart of development issues for a humanity, regenerated and reconciled with itself. Africa would thus enable humanity to fully live and relive the fundamental values of science, technology, industry, through production of material goods within a framework driven by the spiritual values of peace, truth, love, wisdom, the sacred, intelligence, solidarity, communitarianism, freedom and happiness innate in the Christianity, Islam and animism that spiced and structured African culture. Africa will, in this way, rediscover a solid and consistent cultural foundation that paves any ideal path to development, by laying emphasis on the community solidarity proper to the African soul according to the beautiful formula of Prof. Jean Tabi Manga already cited above. This is because any logical and rapid development must rely on a clear cultural foundation that awakens the Mind and is the Ariadne clew that leads to development. This African dream, expected to feed on the perfect fundamental values retraced in this book, would enable the African continent to play a crucial role in the future of humanity as was the case in the age of Antiquity, and to once more be a continent capable of setting the pace in world history. The West have done in the same way, from the 19th century right up to date, thanks to its Judaeo-Christian culture, bearer of progress, or as Buddhist Asia, India of Hindu culture and Indonesia of Muslim culture are gradually doing.

This means that a new African Man, who is perfect and creative, revitalised by knowledge and practice of perfect fundamental values shall be the architect of this powerful dream. This humanity, renewed and reconciled by the genius of spiritual power and not only by excessive materialism, afford in the ongoing globalisation, the opportunity to transform the human from his often conflictual diversity, to a human who, in reality, at divine level, man is one with himself and one with God, as explained by Christianity and certain philosophers like Plotinus the disciple of Plato.

Perfect fundamental values, especially those of spiritual, immaterial and immortal essence are the platform that would drive the dream of Africans from generation to generation for global prosperity of their continent and humanity. Africa and the black race may thus regain the leading position they held at the beginning of humanity, thanks to this positive dream of perfect fundamental values whose immortal foundation is the Mind and not the brain alone.

In reality, prospects of demographic evolution show that from the year 2050, Africa shall be the most populated continent in the world. In this light, Béchir Ben Yahmed of *Jeune Afrique*, demonstrated that high demography usually has as corollary development thrust. For this dream to come true, Africa must uphold its connection with the divine, the Eternal Spirit and a power that illuminates the world eternally. This connection of man and God has nothing to do with the secularism that posits separation of religions and the State, to best preserve the space of one another. The creator of all things is, on His part, above religious and human chasms and the diverse interpretations they make of His wonderful words. He remains a steady source of inspiration, as has been well understood by the great American people and expressed in their famous slogan, “In God we trust”. Though the secularism of this people is well entrenched.

Through perfect fundamental values, Africa can thus rebuild for itself a strong and founding cultural basis that it still seems to lack today, or that is not well assimilated or experimented and should allow the continent to turn to others with a more solid identity. Thanks to these significant perfect values, Africa can further enrich its cultural heritage founded on community solidarity. Through its dream, bearer of perfect values, Africa would thus be a reference for humanity that is increasingly suffering from lack benchmarks, for it is moving further away from the centre of the eternal realities incarnated by perfect fundamental values. Humiliated, broken, disintegrated by more than 4 centuries of slavery, colonisation and the most abject exploitation, Africa can find in perfect fundamental values, its reconstruction and its spiritual, intellectual, moral and cultural reconstitution, for a definite positive and successful take-off towards its true development. In contradiction thus of French agronomist, René Dumont, who in 1960 rightly said that Africa is on the wrong footing, we can affirm at this dawn of the 21st century, more than 50 years after the independence of African countries, that the continent is finally on a good footing, under the light of the implementation of perfect values that are more and more universal. Through an extensive and constant implementation of these perfect values, Africa has thus entered its phase of final spiritual healing. For it has attained its innermost soul and that is where true healing takes place. And only perfect fundamental values can lead to the perfection that offers such healing. These values are at the core of the Mind which is the depth of every human, for perfection of the being illuminates the heart and the mind with all positive lights that wipe off any acrimony and any self-withdrawal, since it bears love, altruism and sublime values. Thus, once we attain this supreme spiritual phase, even the most bitter past perishes, leaving only the beneficial light of love, peace and success to shine. At this phase, Africa can consider itself definitely healed of the trauma it has suffered for centuries. The continent can then reconcile with itself and with others in a win-win partnership, using the time-honoured expression. Africa may embark triumphantly on the path to its comprehensive development with spiritual and cultural weapons, given that culture is the basis of development as President Léopold Sédar Senghor was wont to say. With perfect fundamental values, Africa can offer its culture a very high level that structures the continent, renders it more consistent and further confirm its African and community identity. Africa can through this perfection regain the pantheon of the most brilliant cultures that bred humanity.

All in all, this new African creature must seek perfect development in all dimensions, for full satisfaction and fulfilment of Africans, to emerge once and for all from misery and poverty, other peoples have done so before. Christian, Muslim, animist religions and communitarianism blended with a scientific and technological approach in the African context should facilitate the emergence of a new man and a context best equipped to meet the challenges and stakes inherent to the contemporary world.

We can conclude with this testimony of young generations of former Israeli President Shimon Peres, who also admits to Africans that: "The new age is that of science supremacy. You cannot obtain science without war. Take the case of Mark Zuckerberg and his Facebook. He accomplished a revolution without an army, without violence and it is an absolute success. Science has no borders and you cannot stop it. It has no banner. Science is neutral. High Tech without morals or humanity may destroy the planet. Religions were created to set the pace for humanity." He goes on: "Children should be allowed to dream. They have the answer in them. History is optimistic. In 20 years' time (around 2040), the world will have 10 000 million inhabitants. Never have we attained such a lifestyle, better feeding, better health, better education, and better medicine. Everything is better than before. Dream more, dream bigger. Count the number of dreams. If the number of your dreams is greater than the number of your achievements, you are young": *Journal Le Point* N° 2300 of 6 October 2016. The African dream and development of this continent must enable an achievement of all these formidable opportunities in education, health, agriculture, livestock, tourism, food industry, sports, culture and industrialisation for the material wellbeing and happiness of Africans. This path is obvious and well traced. Implementation of perfect fundamental values, the highway widely open for that purpose.

The next book, on its part, will explore efforts by African States to achieve development by relying on the perfect values developed extensively in this book.

Postface

In contrast to the preface, often found at the beginning of a book, the post face you are about to read is more of a warning, extra information in the form an explanation, an illustrated commentary of my play *Ils ont mangé mon fils (They ate my son),* whose tragedy focuses more on questioning and exploring a complex society where modern values of civilisations clash with the irrational, and less on the madness of Jean, hero of the play. The brilliant preface of this publication is written by Amadou Lamine Sall. I intend to dwell on certain pertinent aspects that, albeit it's of little significance to the whole magisterial reflection of Essousse Erik.

The present postscript explicitly explores avenues for new research, identifies ground-breaking issues worth exploring, highlights more general concerns directly related to those excellently developed in *Perfect fundamental values and the development of Africa : from African Renaissance to Illumination.* An influential theme centred on Africa's development, a theme that breaks way from a pessimism often amplified in titles like: Black Africa on the wrong footing, and what if Africa was rejecting development.

Just as we are about to set down this important book, it must be reiterated, as a warning, that the intention of this author is not to oppose views on Africa's progress, such as subjectively described in *l'Aventure ambiguë* of Cheick Hamidou Kane between the Chief's sister, *la Grande Royale* and the people of Diallobé. His criticism is merely an attempt to illustrate how Africa must appropriate the founding and essential axis of true knowledge, revolving around the fundamental values of perfection and excellence.

And the expression that shines through right from the incipit is undoubtedly that of African illumination. In the Preface of my book, *Le Merveilleux temps des phonons et des photons, Essais sur les fondements scientifiques de la communication africaine*, Paul Wafo wrote that, "certain modes of communication remain a mystery, if not obscure… A good number of philosophers and writers have pitted occultism against science, perfection against imperfection, excellence against mediocrity, under-development against development." I too, have subjectively explored this matter in *Ils ont mangé mon fils* where Félix tells Andréas: "*We are neither fools nor the last, owing to our rejection of science and rationality*" (Fame Ndongo, 2007: 35).

Essousse Erik also reflects on African Renaissance. This cultural renovation is underway in literary, arts, scientific, economic and social fields. Renaissance Africans are resolutely committed to a revival of the erstwhile Africa's perfect fundamental values, a sharp and fresh awareness of the relationship art has with the present and the past, a perfect awareness of descending from a particular historical era, parting from a colonial past, but a direct beneficiary of the past. The mind of every Renaissance African is characterised by: a strong desire for interiority, a breakaway from his relations with obscure forms of power, a need to rediscover himself as a person worthy of interest. Progress is today at the centre of his concerns. The Renaissance African has a new relationship with Africa and the world, a new aspiration to live. Condemning an abstract and theoretical life, he tends to be increasingly analytical. The Renaissance African has opened a new era of inventiveness and innovation in all domains. Early Africans were authors of some extraordinary inventions listed in my book *Essai sur la sémiotique d'une civilisation en mutation. Le génie africain est de retour* (L'Harmattan, Paris, 2015, 268 pg.). As Polish Copernic (1473-1543) casts doubt on Aristotle's geocentric system, while positing a system whereby planets gravitate around the sun, on circular orbits, thereby setting the pace for Italian Galileo (1564-1642). The Church's authority and power in Africa became threatened by reconsiderations of its truth. Nowadays in Africa, religious denominations have lost ground to other beliefs or systems, capable of satisfying the need to believe and better meet the aspirations of time. Likewise, superstitions are prospering and men are increasingly putting their faith in traditional healers who invert modern medicine. New churches and the irrational are making fortune.

Many researchers are embracing African communication theories, dynamics of circular geometry and art considered as vector of progress. This conscience-awakenness has given birth to a new desire to be reacquainted with African skills as opposed to the most recent scientific discoveries. It's a return to African ideas and art, which is discerned.

Driven by a determination to reconstitute Africa's perfect fundamental values again and revisit its development reference systems, Essousse Erik's analysis espouses Africa's emancipation programme. How are Africans rising to the challenge of perfection and excellence? How can these two paradigms make progress possible in Africa? Essousse Erik's book has the audacity to pose these questions and many others. By accepting, for the sake of development, to put African societies to test of perfect and eternal knowledge, the challenges and stakes involved must be identified. Essousse Erik has resolutely set the tone. By associating development to knowledge, his analysis most effectively lifts another veil, knowledge of figurative culture in an art that for centuries, no longer excludes from its scope, instruments of scientific theories like those of physics, mathematics, biology and communication science. African crypto-communication best crystallises these exchanges. The goal being to portray norms that govern African cultural values, not from a metaphysical standpoint anymore, but as a genuine scientific explanation. There is need therefore to ascertain their contribution to the evolution of humanity. The Universe constitutes both truth and contingency, as African scholars believed. With an end to convictions and other deterministic logics in Cartesian discourse, science has become complex again. Rationality can no longer be universal, likewise science. A different course or culture is the law of diversity considered as an object of science. Whereas in Africa, the taste is widespread. Félix deplores: "That is why we are the last in the world. An example is we account for 2% of world trade. That is the rank of Africa" (Fame Ndongo, 2007: 35). This confirms how current Essousse Erik's book is on the issue of Africa's development, an issue of constant concern for the World as a whole. This book implicitly condemns the non-appropriation of perfect and eternal knowledge, mentalities, their inherent tendency to obstruct progress and development owing to the ignorance and lethargy that they posit.

From African Renaissance to Illumination, such is the last segment of the book. From his Latin lux ancestors, light is the illumination unit that expresses the sensation experienced in the face of a surface irradiated by a luminous source. In my book, *Le Merveilleux temps des phonons et des photons*, I focus on this force and its role in crypto-communication and demonstrates that an infusion of lights exists: visible and invisible. Our brain only grasps "visible light" wavelength contained between 0.4 and 0.8 micrometre: (10^{6} m) 145.

In *Ils ont mangé mon fils*, Andréas intimates in page 94 that "Jean shall be the light of our village!" A light emitted by the bright, brilliant, erudite African soul, master of the techniques and secrets of progress. Symbol of a new African, driven by aspirations for lasting development in the era of total emergence. In page 92, Yacob warns: "Let us refrain forever from obstructing the construction of bridges, roads, dispensaries, schools… through occult means…" Patrick Drout states that there are seven levels in the human conscience. Level 7 then levels 14, 21, 28, 35, 42, 49. Level 42, he claims, "…is the cosmic realm: lights that shine, the level of frequent intelligence, the light of creation. Scope of relativist energy." *Espace de lumières,* one of my collection of poems, is a prototype of such experience. This light is a vital force and energy transmitted by a genius who stirs wavelengths on a frequency that can be captured by recipients. These are luminescent bodies "a body of lights composed of photons (a particle representing a quantum of light or other electromagnetic radiation) emitted on a particular frequency. There is also need to reawaken this African cultural genius, while promoting good as a source of development and fulfilment of people." The Sociologist states that: Bridges, roads, block-built houses, vehicles, electricity, drinking water, etc., oppose initiation rites, incantations, sacred forces, cosmic energies and above all the mystical power of nocturnal spirits. Hence these social splits reflect, above all, conflicts of cultures, or even civilisations and hurdles to the level of will power (Fame Ndongo, 2007: pg 60).

More objectively, this book written by Essousse Erik constitutes a step into a more important reflection to be conducted on the development of Africa. A regional economic development (Pierre Samuel Nemb: 2017) that made the most of major assets of every region in the era of decentralisation. It is in this light that I also imagined a systematic inventory and a thorough examination of all African perfect fundamental and authentic values, bearing in mind that our agnostic relation in the Universe is essential to survival of humanity, confronted today to an economist world of destruction. The drama of the era that is ours and which is the source of all perils, owing to an obsolete positivism, whose most spectacular expression is the ephemeral materialism that now claims to rule Africa. Africans disregard the humanism and spiritualism that is the genuine soul of Africa. Ebénezer Njoh Mouelle dwells brilliantly on such human signification of development in his essay of 1970 titled, *De la médiocrité à l'excellence*.

Sustainable development or better still human development of the entire planet can only have its meaning in such perceptiveness.

Specifically, Essousse Erik's book is structured into an infinitely recurring sequence, owing to the presence of a foreword, an introduction, thematic titles, etc. Such a composition confers on this harmonious whole, a convoluted feature, maybe open, but also some sort of ambiguity, to the point where changes in perspectives bloom. The introduction does not portray the same image as that of the four parts of the fragments, this image becomes compact in an attempt at a synthesis, and it also intentionally takes a political turn. As a distant spectator, I have therefore tried to reconstruct its contribution to a more general reference framework where, just like in the West, it is understood that the concept of culture may stimulate development in Africa, for the two obtain as actions participating in the emancipation of peoples. We believe that its actions must be related to perfect and eternal knowledge (Essousse Erik), to excellence (Njoh Mouelle), or even to the invisible (Fame Ndongo), the great effect of the evil wizard is still steeped in obscure elements. Félix told Andréas: "your airplanes are invisible. You have never given a public explanation of how they are manufactured and how they are used" (Fame Ndongo, 2007: pg 36). Africa's development must not be guided by the goetia that teaches subjection to evil fetishes. Damaging effects of African negative fundamental values have constantly indicated that they cannot be sustained, despite the wizard's apparent nocturnal pleasure. Félix to Andréas: "it seems that at night, you live in castles. But we don't see them" (Fame Ndongo, 2007: pg37). Based on its humanist dimension, this contribution by Essousse Erik implicitly condemns ignorance. The researcher recommends a form of perfect and eternal knowledge. Ndongo states that: "Rejecting negative metamorphoses is that which renders us more human" (Mendo Ze, 1988). The book raises the awareness of all social stakeholders in view of endowing every African with perfect and eternal knowledge. Salvation of every society lies in a profound change in the mentality of its members. The African must transcend dark forces to attain the enlightening forces of know-how, stamp out all obscure trainings that obstruct development, peace, progress and remain incompatible with human rights and lights. Perfect and eternal knowledge offer an opportunity to Africa, their appropriation is now unavoidable to breed this new *homofaber*, *Homo Deus*, perfect and creator. Find the means capable of making education one of the pillars. Start with target political and cultural actions, promote forums for light and be architects of a newfound multi-purpose African genius. That is the new method for reviewing the issue of development in Africa!

Prof. Jacques Fame Ndongo

Bibliography

I-Books and reviews on religions, holiness, purety, perfection,

A- Holy books

1- *Louis-Second, la Sainte Bible*, Alliance biblique universelle. Alliance universelle, 1910, 1277 pg

2- *La Bible de Jérusalem*, Nouvelle édition revue et augmentée, éditions du CERF 2001. 1899 pg

3- *Le Nouveau Dictionnaire biblique* révisé et augmenté, Éditions Emmaüs, 2004, 1364 pg

4- *Le Saint Coran et la traduction en langue française*. Complexe de Roi Fahd, 604 pg

5- Christian Jacq, *Le message des constructeurs des cathédrales*, éditions du Rocher 1980. 215 pg.

6- R.P. Placide Tempels, *La philosophie bantoue*, Présence africaine, quatrième édition. 2013, 123 pg

7- Maurice Bucaille. *La Bible, le Coran et la science. Les Écritures saintes à la lumière des connaissances modernes*, Seghers, Paris 1976, 438 pg.

B- Reviews on religions and holiness

1- Le Point n° 2049-2050 des jeudi 22 et 29 décembre 2011. Questions et réponses sur l'existence de Dieu. Ce que disent les scientifiques 185-146.

2- Le point Historia. Hors-série, février–mars 2014. Tout ce qu'on ne vous a jamais dit sur la Bible 114 pg.

3- Le Point Références novembre décembre 2010. Christianisme, Judaïsme, Islam, Bouddhisme, Taoïsme. Sexe et religion, Les textes fondamentaux 130 pg.

4- Le Point Références mai–juin 2014, Protestantisme, Les textes fondamentaux.

5- Les dossiers de la recherche, Dieu et la science septembre-octobre 2010, n° 43.

6- Le Point Références, Mars – avril 2013. L'Islam, faits et mythes 130pg

7- Historia. Février 2011 n° 770, Abraham. L'itinéraire étonnant du père des trois religions P 19-48.

8- Le Point Références janvier–février 2012, Les grands mystiques (Catherine de Sienne, François d'Assise, Thérèse d'Avila, Maitre Eckart), Les textes fondamentaux 130 pg.

9- Le Point Hors-série n° 5, février–mars 2010, Bouddha, le libérateur, la vie, sa légende, ses concepts clés, le bouddhisme 114 pg.

10- Le monde des religions, Mahomet cet inconnu. La vie et le message du prophète de l'Islam, 2003, pg 18.32.

11- Le Nouvel observateur Hors-série, Nouvelle formule. L'origine du monde, les mythes d'hier et d'aujourd'hui : Égypte, Grèce, hindouisme, Bouddhisme, Aztèques, Aborigènes, Dogons. La science face à Dieu. Les nouveaux mystères de l'univers 99 p hors-série n° 48 avril 2012.

12- Le Point hors–série n° 12. Juin–juillet 2012. Confucius, le vrai maitre de la Chine. Son histoire 114pg.

13- Le Point Références, juillet août 2016. La Grèce et ses dieux, Les textes fondamentaux 148.

14- Le point références, Mars-Avril 2012, Du Veda à Gandhi. La sagesse de l'Inde, Les textes fondamentaux. 130 pg

15- Le Point n° 1997-1998, jeudi 23 et 30 décembre 2010, spécial Égypte. Du nouveau sur Toutankhamon. Les mœurs des sociétés des pharaons 65 pg.

16- Historama, histoire Magazine n° 56 octobre 1988, Les pharaons de l'Aube P32-53.

17- Le Point Références décembre 2016- janvier 2017, Le Bien et le Mal, Les textes fondamentaux. 122 pg.

18- Les cahiers Science et Vie, Histoire des civilisations. N° 164 octobre 2016, Les secrets des cathédrales 98pg.

II– Other books

1- Abraham Maslow, *Devenir le meilleur de soi-même. Besoins fondamentaux, motivation et personnalité*. Éditions, Nouveaux Horizons, 2011 383 pg.

2- Adamou Ndam Njoya, Njoya, *Réformateur du royaume Bamoun*, 1978, Belgique, 100 pg

3- Albert Munster, *Et si l'Afrique refusait de partir*, Seuil, Paris 6e, 1969, 455 pg.

4- Barack Obama, *L'audace d'espérer. Un nouveau rêve américain*, Presses de la cite, 2009, France 445 pg.

5- Barack Obama. *La promesse de l'Amérique. Ses plus grands discours*, 2009, 156 pg

6- Bernd Heine et Dérek Nurse, *Les langues africaines*, Karthala, 2004, 461 pg.

7- African Charter on Democracy, Elections and Governance Addis Abeba, 30 January 2007.

8- Cheik Anta Diop,*L'Antiquité africaine par l'image. African Antiquity in pictures*, Présence Africaine, 1976 159pg.

9- Cheikh Anta Diop, *Nations Nègre et cultures, De l'antiquité nègre égyptienne aux problèmes culturels de l'Afrique noire d'aujourd'hui*, 4e édition, Présence africaine, 1979, 564 pg.

10- Cheikh Mbacké Diop, *Cheick Anta Diop et l'œuvre*, Présence africaine, 2011, 409 pg.

11- Daniel Etounga Manguele, *Cent ans d'aliénation*, Stock 1985, 328 pg

12- *Dictionnaire Le Petit Larousse* illustré, 2002. 1776 pg

13- Ebénézer Njoh Mouellé, *De la médiocrité à l'excellence. Essai de signification humaine du développement,* 3e Éditions, Clé, Yaoundé, 1998, 174 pg.

14- Edem Kodjo, *Panafricanisme et Renaissance africaine, Graines de Pensées,* Togo, 2013, 155 pg.

15- Engelbert Mveng, *Spiritualité et Libération en Afrique,* L'Harmattan, 1987, 123 pg.

16- Erik Essousse, *La Liberté de la presse au Cameroun. Ombres et lumières*, L'Harmattan, 2008, 367 pg.

17- Eugène Nyambal, *Créer la prospérité en Afrique, dix clés pour sortir de la pauvreté*, L'Harmattan, 2006, 196 pg.

18- Hugues François Onana, *Pratique de la gouvernance au Cameroun. Entre désétatisation et démocratisation, L'Harmattan*, 2011, 243 pg.

19- Jean-Baptiste Duroselle, Tout Empire périra, Publications de la Sorbonne, 1981, 349 pg.

20- Jean Tabi Manga, *Des voix... à la voie du temps, Variations sur la Renaissance, L'émergence et la modernité africaines*, Sopecam 2014, 291 pg.

21- Joseph Ki–Zerbo, *Histoire de l'Afrique*, Hâtier. France 1978, 731 pg.

22- Mbog Bassong, *La Pensée africaine, Essai sur l'universisme philosophique*, Kiyikaat, 2012, 358 pg.

23- Cardinal Christian Tumi, A *Cameroon to be Renewed*, Veritas, 2011, 271 pg.

24- Mgr Victor Tonye Bakot, *Les proverbes Bassa, Pour une approche culturelle Mbene*, Du Schabel, Yaoundé, 2017. 199 pg.

25- Narcisse Mouelle Kombi, *La Démocratie dans la réalité camerounaise. Libertés, légitimité et modernité politique sous PAUL Biya,* 2014, 355 pg

26- Paul Biya, *Pour le Libéralisme communautaire*, Pierre Marcel Favre ABC, 1987, France, 158pg.

27- Pierre Lanares, *Qui dominera le monde ?,* Éditions SDT France, 1982, 574 pg.

28- Pierre Grimal, *L'Empire romain*, de Fallois, Paris 1993, 221 pg.

29- René Dumont, *L'Afrique est mal partie*, du Seuil, 2012, 280 pg.

30- Richard Laurent Omgba, *Culture et émergence d'une nation, pour une approche humaniste du développement au Cameroun*, l'Harmattan, 2016, 286 pg.

31- Tibor Mende, *De l'aide à la recolonisation*, du Seuil 1975, 276 pg.

32- Tabo Mbeki,*The man I know, Picador Africa,* Johannesburg, 2016, 539 pg

Reviews and journals

1- Revue science et avenir, Le fabuleux héritage des Empires disparus n° 185, avril-mai 2016. 82 pages, Paris.

2- Le Point Références avril-mai 2009. N° 22, La pensée noire : Malcom X, Aimé Césaire, Martin Luther, Frantz Fanon, Les textes fondamentaux 130 pg.

3- Le Point Références, septembre – octobres 2008, La pensée politique : Machiavel, Locke, Rousseau, Tocqueville, Marx. Les textes fondamentaux 114 pg.

4- Le Point Références, Mars-Avril 2012. Les Maîtres de la raison : Descartes, Locke, Leibnitz, Les textes fondamentaux, 114 pg.

5- Le Point Hors-série n° 23, juillet août 2009, Le bonheur : Épicure, Marc Aurèle, Rousseau, Boudha, Confucius. 130 pg

6- Le Point Références, Mars-Avril 2011, La Renaissance, Les textes fondamentaux, 130 pg

7- Le Point hors–série, avril 2010, La Pensée des Lumières, Voltaire, Rousseau, Diderot, Hume, Smith, Kant. Les textes fondamentaux 130 pg.

8- Le Point Références, juillet août 2011. La sagesse grecque, 296 pg.

9- Le Point Références novembre – décembre 2011, Comprendre le Moyen-âge, Les textes fondamentaux, 130 pg.

10- Le Point Références, Mars-Avril 2014, Les Maîtres du secret, L'ésotérisme occidental : Pythagore, Platon, Paraclèse, Nostradamus, guenon, Crowey, Les textes fondamentaux. 114 pg.

11- Le Point Références, septembre-octobre 2014, Ces voyages qui ont changé le monde : Christophe Colomb, Marco Palo, Alexandra David-Néel, Bougainville, Livingstone, Chariot. Les textes fondamentaux, 114 pg.

12- Le Point Références, Mars-Avril 2016, Comprendre l'économie, Smith, Ricardo, Marx, Keynes, Hayek, Coase, Friedman, Les textes fondamentaux, 122 pg.

13- Le Point Références, septembre – octobre 2010, La liberté. Sénèque, Saint Paul, Sade, Tocqueville, Sartre, Foucault, les textes fondamentaux. 130 pg

14- Le Point Références, novembre 2012, L'âme de l'Afrique, épopées, contes et légendes, 130 pg.

15- Dossier pour la science n° 94 Janvier-Mars2017, Évolution de la saga humanité, 112 pg.

16- Revue La recherche Hors-série N 17, Mars-Avril 2016, L'odyssée de l'homme. Scénario de nos origines, 98 pg.

17- Les atlas de l'histoire, août 2016, Atlas des Afriques, Les siècles d'or, Esclavage, colonisation et résistance, XXIe siècle : les défis d'un continent convoité, 98 pg.

18- Le Nouvel observateur. Hors-série n° 65 Mai-Juin 2007. Comprendre le capitalisme. Des théories fondatrices aux dérives de la mondialisation : avec Daniel Cohen, André Compte-Sponsville, Marcel Emche, Amartya, Sen. 82 pg.

19- Le Point Hors-série juin-juillet 2009, Numéro3, Marx. Ce qu'il a vraiment écrit, comment sa pensée a été détournée, 122 pg.

20- Revue sciences humaines, Mensuel n° 290, mars 2017, La mondialisation en question, 70 pg

21- Les collections de l'histoire, trimestriel octobre 2012, N° 57, La Chine 1912.2012, D'un Empire à l'autre 98pg.

22- 24 Les grands dossiers des Sciences humaines n° 45, Les grands penseurs de l'Éducation : Socrate, Locke, Montaigne, Rousseau, Piaget, etc. Janvier-Février 2017, 93pg.

23- Le Point n° 2347 du 31 août 2017. Extraits d'"Homo deus" et rencontre avec l'auteur Yuval Noah Harari, pg 44-53.

24- Le Point n° 2324 du 23 mars 2017, Comment on ressuscite un pays ? pg 18-37.

25- Le Point n° double 2364-2365 des jeudis 21 et 28 décembre 2017, La Perse, De Cyrus Le Grand à l'Iran d'aujourd'hui. Darius, Persépolis, Zarathoustra, chiisme, Ispahan, Le réveil d'une civilisation extraordinaire, 146 pg.

Table of contents

Structures éditoriales du groupe L'Harmattan

L'Harmattan Italie
Via degli Artisti, 15
10124 Torino
harmattan.italia@gmail.com

L'Harmattan Hongrie
Kossuth l. u. 14-16.
1053 Budapest
harmattan@harmattan.hu

L'Harmattan Sénégal
10 VDN en face Mermoz
BP 45034 Dakar-Fann
senharmattan@gmail.com

L'Harmattan Cameroun
TSINGA/FECAFOOT
BP 11486 Yaoundé
inkoukam@gmail.com

L'Harmattan Burkina Faso
Achille Somé – tengnule@hotmail.fr

L'Harmattan Guinée
Almamya, rue KA 028 OKB Agency
BP 3470 Conakry
harmattanguinee@yahoo.fr

L'Harmattan RDC
185, avenue Nyangwe
Commune de Lingwala – Kinshasa
matangilamusadila@yahoo.fr

L'Harmattan Congo
67, boulevard Denis-Sassou-N'Guesso
BP 2874 Brazzaville
harmattan.congo@yahoo.fr

L'Harmattan Mali
Sirakoro-Meguetana V31
Bamako
syllaka@yahoo.fr

L'Harmattan Togo
Djidjole – Lomé
Maison Amela
face EPP BATOME
ddamela@aol.com

L'Harmattan Côte d'Ivoire
Résidence Karl – Cité des Arts
Abidjan-Cocody
03 BP 1588 Abidjan
espace_harmattan.ci@hotmail.fr

L'Harmattan Algérie
22, rue Moulay-Mohamed
31000 Oran
info2@harmattan-algerie.com

L'Harmattan Maroc
5, rue Ferrane-Kouicha, Talaâ-Elkbira
Chrableyine, Fès-Médine
30000 Fès
harmattan.maroc@gmail.com

Nos librairies en France

Librairie internationale
16, rue des Écoles – 75005 Paris
librairie.internationale@harmattan.fr
01 40 46 79 11
www.librairieharmattan.com

Lib. sciences humaines & histoire
21, rue des Écoles – 75005 Paris
librairie.sh@harmattan.fr
01 46 34 13 71
www.librairieharmattansh.com

Librairie l'Espace Harmattan
21 bis, rue des Écoles – 75005 Paris
librairie.espace@harmattan.fr
01 43 29 49 42

Lib. Méditerranée & Moyen-Orient
7, rue des Carmes – 75005 Paris
librairie.mediterranee@harmattan.fr
01 43 29 71 15

Librairie Le Lucernaire
53, rue Notre-Dame-des-Champs – 75006 Paris
librairie@lucernaire.fr
01 42 22 67 13

www.ingramcontent.com/pod-product-compliance
Lightning Source LLC
LaVergne TN
LVHW021148061026
849535LV00002B/393
* 9 7 8 2 3 4 3 1 9 5 7 0 4 *